Expressive Japanese

Expressive Japanese

A Reference Guide to Sharing Emotion and Empathy

Senko K. Maynard

University of Hawai'i Press
HONOLULU

Senko K. Maynard was born and educated in Japan, graduating with a B.A. from Tokyo Gaikokugo Daigaku. She spent her senior year of high school as an American Field Service scholarship recipient and went on to further education in the United States as a graduate student. This culminated in a doctorate in linguistics from Northwestern University. She has taught Japanese language and linguistics at the University of Hawai'i, Connecticut College, Harvard University, and Princeton University, and is currently Professor II of Japanese language and linguistics at Rutgers University. Professor Maynard has published more than eighty articles and reviews in American, Japanese, and international journals, and is the author of some dozen books in English and Japanese, including *An Introduction to Japanese Grammar and Communication Strategies* (1990); *Japanese Communication: Language and Thought in Context* (1997); *Principles of Japanese Discourse: A Handbook* (1998); and *Linguistic Emotivity: Centrality of Place, the Topic-Comment Dynamic, and an Ideology of* Pathos *in Japanese Discourse* (2002).

Printed in the United States of America
05 06 07 08 09 10 6 5 4 3 2 1

Library of Congress Cataloging-in-Publication Data

Maynard, Senko K.
Expressive Japanese : a reference guide to sharing emotion and empathy / Senko K. Maynard.
p. cm.
Includes bibliographical references and indexes.
ISBN 0-8248-2844-5 (hardcover : alk. paper) —
ISBN 0-8248-2889-5 (pbk. : alk. paper)
1. Japanese language—Textbooks for foreign speakers—English. 2. Japanese language—Rhetoric. 3. Language and emotions—Japan. I. Title: Reference guide to sharing emotion and empathy. II. Title.
PL5395.5.E5M39 2005
495.6'82421—dc22

2004018502

University of Hawai'i Press books are printed on acid-free paper and meet the guidelines for permanence and durability of the Council on Library Resources.

Designed by inari information services
Printed by The Maple-Vail Book Manufacturing Group

Contents

Preface

When we communicate across languages, we sometimes face difficulties expressing our feelings. How should I show happiness and joy, or surprise and disbelief? How should I reveal my anger and fear? Or should I reveal those feelings at all? Should I yell, or should I keep silent? What emotion is my partner trying to convey through those curious expressions? Is it love or just teasing? These questions become increasingly relevant as one becomes more competent in the language being learned, and more aware of and sensitive to speech partners.

In addition to these basic questions, learners often wonder how or how not to express the desire for sharing emotional closeness, i.e., empathy. How should I express heartfelt feelings toward my friend? How should I reveal my inner self to reach my friend's heart? We also wonder how to convey the varying emotionally revealing personal and interpersonal responses toward events under discussion. For example, how do I share with my partner the feeling of loss and suffering resulting from an incident? In general, what kinds of strategies are available for sharing feelings and for encouraging warm empathy? Meeting these personal and interpersonal needs is an important part of daily communication.

Emotion and empathy as expressed in Japanese are the themes of this book. By "emotion" I mean a surge of various human feelings, including, for example, the sense of being deeply moved, as well as such basic emotions as happiness, loneliness, and anger. "Empathy" refers to the warm sharing of emotion, to familiarity, and to intimacy between speakers. Emotion and empathy are so pervasive in language that communication can hardly sustain emotional neutrality. It is true that in certain uses of language, for example, in written legal documents, the language is purposefully as emotion-free as possible. However, in daily life, emotion and empathy are expressed in every possible way in many different varieties and intensities. Language is not understood only for its informational content, but also felt for its emotion and empathy.

Although feelings play an enormous part in people's lives, in foreign language education, the expression of feelings is often neglected. In 77 entries, this book introduces, catalogues, and explains "expressive Japanese," namely, emotion words and expressive strategies frequently used in contemporary Japan.

To benefit from this book, the reader should have a firm grasp of the fundamentals of elementary Japanese, including basic vocabulary and grammar. Basic knowledge of hiragana, katakana, and kanji is also expected. In terms of the Japanese Language Proficiency Test (administered by the Japan Foundation Language Center), the reader is expected to possess at least Level 3 knowledge. More concretely, this book assumes knowledge of the basic materials covered in my 1990 book for elementary Japanese students, *An Introduction to Japanese Grammar and Communication Strategies*. To assure the background understanding associated with each entry, the reader is encouraged to consult books and dictionaries that explain basic elementary Japanese.

This book can be used as a reference for students studying Japanese language and culture at institutions or as a guide for students studying on their own. It can be read from beginning to end or episodically, with the reader going directly to the items of interest. It can also be used as a reference using either the English cues or the Japanese (key) expressions as listed in the indexes.

More specifically, this book can be used in the following ways; (1) to look up Japanese expressions when you want to express your emotion and empathy, (2) to find out what Japanese emotion words and expressive strategies mean and how they are used, (3) to familiarize yourself with a variety of contemporary Japanese expressions representing multiple genres, and particularly (4) to learn expressive Japanese that usually does not appear in language textbooks, including playful and creative uses.

Expressing one's feelings is both dangerous and rewarding. Emotion and empathy are so close to the heart that one can both hurt and be hurt by others, especially when expressions misfire in foreign languages. At the same time, to be able to touch someone's heart in another language is all the more rewarding.

This book contains explanations and examples based on how the Japanese language is typically used. But it does not mean that the reader should imitate everything. As we all know, language learning is a creative experience, requiring much more than simple imitation. Language is also filled with playfulness and creativity, and it always communicates one's sense of self and identity. The expressions contained in this book often illustrate these aspects of the Japanese language. Given many examples, the reader must remain critical of specific expressions, and make up his or her own mind in choosing whatever is appropriate. I hope that by learning and going beyond the examples given in this book, the reader will explore not only the emotional side of Japanese communication but also the many emotional voices reverberating in all of us.

For many years I have enjoyed teaching Japanese language and linguistics at American institutions (in chronological order, the University of Hawai'i, Connecticut College, Harvard University, and Princeton University), and especially at Rutgers University. I thank students and colleagues I have met at various places for their friendship, inspiration, and encouragement. This book is dedicated to past, present, and future students of the Japanese language at Rutgers University. It is also dedicated to students learning Japanese on their own or at many institutions worldwide. For those students who are interested in exploring expressive Japanese (as well as my related studies in Japanese linguistics and discourse analysis), some of my theoretical and pedagogical works are listed in the References.

My special thanks go to Patricia Crosby, executive editor at the University of Hawai'i Press, for her faith in me and her guidance throughout this project. I am grateful to Nancy Woodington for her thoughtful copyediting. Last but not least, thank you, Michael, for everything.

Fall 2003
"On the Banks of the Old Raritan"

Abbreviations

Grammatical terms

Adj	adjective
Adj basic (= dictionary form)	basic, dictionary form of the adjective
Adj-*i*	*i*-type adjective
Adj-*na*	*na*-type adjective
Adj pre-nominal	adjective form appearing before a nominal
Adj stem	stem of the adjective
Adj-*te*	*te* form of the adjective
N	noun
V	verb
V basic	basic form of the verb (i.e., dictionary form)
V formal	formal ending of the verb; *desu/masu* form
V informal	informal ending of the verb; *da* form
V pre-nominal	verb form appearing before a nominal
V stem	verb stem (*masu* form minus *masu*)
V-*te*	*te* form of the verb

Speech styles

≠	supra-polite style
≈	casual style
□	blunt style
v	vulgar (youth) style

Speaker identification

f	female
m	male

c child

t teenage

y young adult

a mature adult

s senior

Other

↑ rising tone

* ungrammatical/unused form to be avoided

< > speech balloons (in comics)

/ line change in speech (in comics)

、 short pause in conversation

、 reproduced *tooten* comma in the authentic text

notably long pause in conversation

extended pause in conversation

= speech takeover by the speech partner; no pause between speaking turns

(...) portion deleted from the original for convenience

lit. literal translation

... unfinished lingering utterance

I

Introduction

1
On Expressive Japanese

Expressive Japanese and Its Organization

When discussing emotion, some classical (Western) categories might come to mind. For example, Aristotle's list of emotions includes anger, mildness, love/friendship, enmity/hate, fear, lack of fear, shame, shamelessness, favor, goodwill, lack of goodwill, pity, indignation, envy, emulation, and contempt. The Cartesian list includes surprise, love, hate, desire, joy, and sadness. These words, however, are emotions (not emotion expressions), and they do not necessarily serve as organizational categories representative of Japanese emotive words or expressive strategies. Consequently, rather than starting with known emotion categories available in the West and looking for corresponding phrases, I started from the Japanese side and collected a pool of Japanese emotive words and expressive strategies useful for students of Japanese language and culture. I also chose these expressions on the basis of their functional importance and relative frequency in ordinary contemporary Japanese language.

Through my earlier studies in Japanese language and emotion (S. Maynard 1993, 1998b, 2000, 2001a, 2002), I had become aware that emotion and empathy involve far more than a mere listing of emotion words and phrases, as has been done in the past. For example, knowing the word *okoru* 'to get angry' is not that useful for expressing anger. Yes, it is possible to use it as a warning as in *Okoru yo, moo honto ni* 'I'm going to get mad, really'. But other strategies, such as the interjection *Nani?!* 'What?!' or the cursing word *Baka!* 'Fool!' are quite effective when expressing one's anger. Given a specific context, simply ignoring your partner and remaining silent may be more effective. As a result, expressions introduced in this book span different grammatical categories, from particles, phrases, and sentence structures to discourse and interactional strategies.

In my studies of language and emotion, I also realized that emotive expressions encompass more than the traditional concepts of emotion. This book contains such expressive strategies as self-mockery, regret, and disappointment, as well as a whole range of feelings, empathy, and attitudes that fall outside the scope of what is normally associated with the word "emotion."

Because of the wide range of grammatical categories and the extensive emotion and empathy expressions selected, it was necessary to establish a reasonable organization. I have organized these expressions into situationally and functionally cohesive entries, partly from the English and partly from the Japanese point of view. Approaching emotion and empathy from the English point of view is necessary to meet the expressive needs of English speakers. Approaching from the Japanese point of view is also necessary for bringing into the open the kind of expressive Japanese that English speakers may not *a priori* find important or necessary. All of the classical emotions usually recognized in the West are accounted for in the process (especially but not exclusively) in Chapter 5.

Presenting a body of information about language and culture across languages and cultures poses some fundamental problems. Language and culture show internal variations, and they themselves change, transform, merge, and contradict constantly. In a sense, to say "the Japanese language" is a misnomer, because it contains different genres, registers, and individual speaker variations. Language is filled with many different voices, and linguistic heterogeneity is the norm. As a result, explaining about "the Japanese language" becomes an inherently partial task, and it is impossible to touch on all social and individual variations. It is important, therefore, to realize that examples and explanations contained in this book represent only some of what constitutes the Japanese language.

Still, it is possible to observe similarities and differences in how one expresses (or does not express) emotion and empathy in a given context across English and Japanese. And there is a gap between what one language/culture may find reasonable and what the other language/culture may not, even in the selection of entries. This gap is manifest in the organization of the entries, as well as in how emotion and empathy are understood (or more accurately, felt). One of the missions of this project is to bridge this gap as much as possible. It is my hope that students who learn from *Expressive Japanese* will extend their knowledge far beyond what this book contains and will express emotion and empathy despite (and because of) the inevitable limitations of languages and cultures.

Emotion and empathy are explored in Parts II and III, respectively. Part II introduces various kinds of emotions, expressed in different intensities. It also addresses the issue of how to express emotion in certain personal relationships, for example, when in love, when love ends, when facing conflict, and so on. Part III discusses strategies for sharing empathy, including ways of self-revelation, and appeals to the sense of dependency on and concern for one's partner and the interaction itself. Part III also introduces expressions that promote shared feelings. These co-experienced feelings broaden the sphere of communication and touch on those cases where words do not fully describe one's desire for empathy.

It is important to note that although Parts II and III are divided into separate units for convenience, they are not mutually exclusive. Emotion and empathy overlap, and entries are categorized according to their primary functions. The chapters in Parts II and III bear broad situational and functional titles under which relevant entries are grouped together.

English cues appearing as entry titles lead the reader to some frequently used comparable Japanese key expressions. Following the explanation of key expressions, sample sentences and conversations I have created are discussed. Next, authentic examples taken from different genres of contemporary Japanese discourse are introduced. These examples guide the reader in an understanding of how these expressions are used for sharing emotion and empathy.

At the end of the volume, the reader will find the appendix, in which I provide information about authentic data sources. The reader unfamiliar with authentic sources is encouraged to read this section before proceeding to the entries. Two reference lists are also provided; one contains references for learning the Japanese language, and the other a list of works cited. The indexes include English cues and Japanese expressions. The English cues are English phrases leading the reader to comparable Japanese expressions and situations. The reader who wants to look up Japanese emotion words and expressive strategies should use the index of Japanese expressions. The indexes can be used almost as dictionaries.

Emotion Words and Expressive Strategies

As a student of the Japanese language, you will have learned vocabulary and grammar to convey straightforward information. But when it comes to sharing feelings, you may know only a limited number of words and sentence structures. Ultimately, true communication requires speakers to be able to share not only information but also feelings. Language learning void of shared emotion and empathy leaves us feeling empty. Interpreting how others feel while at the same time expressing one's own feelings in Japanese requires the knowledge of how Japanese is and is not used for expressive purposes.

Human emotions are complex, overlapping, and often subtle. These changing emotions are expressed through multiple, and even contradictory ways. Strategies expressing emotion include facial expression, tone of voice, discourse structure, topic selection, interactional style, gesture, laughter and cries, physical proximity, and so on. Language is only one way to show emotion; a book like this, which concentrates on certain linguistic signs, can account only for limited cases.

This book concentrates on emotion words and expressive strategies. Emotion words are phrases that refer to certain emotions, as in *kanashii* 'sad' and *atama ni kuru* 'to get angry'. Expressive strategies are non-referential words that do not so much describe emotion as realize emotion-expressive acts. For example, when a person says *Aitai yo* 'I really want to see you', the particle *yo* adds to the intensity of desire. Here *yo* itself does not refer to emotion or empathy. *Yo* expresses emotion and empathy because of how and where the speaker uses it in context.

Likewise, the question noun *nani* 'what' functions in a similar way, as in *Nani!* 'What!' uttered as an interjection in a conflict situation. Attitudinal adverbs such as *doose* in *Doose dame daro* 'It will be no good anyway' also express the speaker's emotion, although they do not refer to a specific meaning, as in, say, the case of adverbs of manner like *hayaku* 'fast' in *Hayaku hashitta* 'I ran fast'. A grammatical structure such as an exclamative sentence also enacts the speaker's emotional state, as in *Nanto ano hito ga kuru to wa!* 'Boy, what a surprise that he came!'. Sound change, such as *oishii-tt* instead of *oishii* 'delicious' ('great' in very casual speech) also expresses intensity of emotion. Again, emotions are expressed through these strategies not by the meaning of the phrase or by grammatical structure, but by usage.

Interactional strategies, for example, requesting permission to ask a personal question, as in *Kiite ii?* 'Is it O.K. to ask you (this question)?' work in a similar way. Seeking permission to ask a personal question communicates kindness and considerateness, which in turn encourages empathy. In another example, the tautological expression *Kachi wa kachi da* 'Victory is victory' doesn't really make sense literally. Rhetorical strategies like tautology communicate emotion although (or because) they do not literally mean what they say. Instead, they realize meaning by the fact of the speaker's using them in the appropriate context. Onomatopoeic and mimetic words are particularly frequent in expressive Japanese. The mimetic phrase *shimijimi* 'with deep fond feelings' strikes an emotional chord among Japanese speakers and adds to the feeling of empathy. In addition, sharing jokes and banter increases the sense of empathy. In reality, these emotion words and expressive strategies are mixed in overlapping, accumulating, and sometimes contradictory ways.

Constraints on Expressive Japanese

It is particularly important to understand that emotion words and expressive strategies are under constraints in terms of grammar and situation. First, in terms of grammar, emotion words and expressive strategies are primarily used by the speaker who directly experiences these emotions. Second, in terms of situation, many of the emotion words and expressive strategies reveal one's inner feelings rather directly, and as a consequence they should be used only within certain boundaries.

Grammatical Constraints

Emotion words and expressive strategies cannot, as a rule, be used in reference to persons other than the speaker. In cases where they do refer to persons other than the speaker, most must either be used in quotation or must go through grammatical manipulations that explicitly mark them.

This is particularly true in the case of adjectives of emotion, for example, *kanashii* 'sad'. Now, *Kanashii* 'I'm sad' is grammatically correct, but **Ano hito wa kanashii* 'He is sad' is not acceptable under ordinary circumstances. Instead, what is acceptable is *Ano hito wa kanashi soo da* 'He appears to be sad'. In Japanese it is necessary to mark the sentence if it is not about the speaker's but about someone else's emotion. The reason for this is that, although one can experience one's own emotions directly, someone else's emotions are not so accessibile.

The distinction in Japanese is not necessarily required in other languages. In English, for example, it is possible to say "I'm happy" and "I think so" as well as "Yamada is happy" and "Yamada thinks so." It is important to remember that in Japanese, the distinction is obligatory, and extra attention must be paid when referring to one's own or another's thoughts and feelings.

The following list provides frequently used means for marking someone else's emotions.

1. With expressions that indicate appearance:

悲しそう	*kanashi soo*	seems sad
悲しいみたい	*kanashii mitai*	appears sad
悲しいような顔	*kanashii yoona kao*	face that seems sad

2. With the suffix *-garu*:

悲しがる	*kanashi garu*	shows signs of sadness

3. With speculative modals:

悲しいんだろう	*kanashii n daroo*	perhaps sad
悲しいのかもしれない	*kanashii no kamo shirenai*	may be sad

4. In a question:

悲しいですか	*Kanashii desu ka.*	Are you sad?
悲しいんですか	*Kanashii n desu ka.*	Is it that you are sad?
悲しくない？	*Kanashiku-nai?*	Aren't you sad?

Non-adjectival expressions have a similarly restricted use. Examples include *tamaranai* 'cannot help but' and *shikata ga nai* 'cannot bear', which refer directly to the speaker's inner feelings. The same restriction applies to the utterance-final *to omou* 'I think', which signals the speaker's own speech.

When using these strategies, adjustments like the following are necessary.

1. 山田さんは、恋人に会いたくてたまらない**ようです**。

   Yamada-san wa, koibito ni aitakute tamaranai **yoo desu.**

   It seems that Yamada cannot help but really want to see her lover.

2. 山田さんは、さびしくてしがたがない**のでしょう**。

   Yamada-san wa, sabishikute shikata ga nai **no deshoo.**

   I think perhaps Yamada cannot bear the overwhelming feeling of loneliness.

3. (≈) 山田さんはそういうふうに思う**らしい**。

   Yamada-san wa soo yuu fuu ni omou **rashii.**

   Yamada seems to think that way.

Other expressive strategies, simply because they enact the speaker's speech acts, must appear in indirect discourse (as in quotation), as shown below.

4. その時彼は、「なに！」と言って近づいてきた。

   Sono toki kare wa, "Nani!" to itte chikazuite-kita.

   Then he said "What!" and approached me.

5. なんとあの人が来るとは！　心の中でそう叫んだ。

   Nanto ano hito ga kuru to wa! Kokoro no naka de soo sakenda.

   Wow, what a surprise that he came! I screamed in my heart.

6. その人は「聞いていい？」とたずねてから、質問した。

   Sono hito wa "Kiite ii?" to tazunete kara, shitsumon shita.

   After saying "May I ask you this?" the person asked me a question.

Situational Constraints

As for situational constraints regarding the use of emotion words and expressive strategies, it is best to avoid direct expression of emotion in formal contexts, where more objectified and consequently more polite expressions are preferred. Generally, descriptive expressions are more distant and formal than interjectional expressions. One strategy is to use an adverb (instead of an adjective) with the verb *omou,* as in *Kanashiku omou* '(lit., I think it to be sad) I feel it is sad', instead of *Kanashii* 'I'm sad'. Another is to refer to the situation itself instead of one's own feelings, as in *Kanashii koto desu* 'It is a sad thing'. In conversation one may add such prefaces as *yappari* 'after all', to make the utterance less direct.

7. うれしく**思っております**。

   Ureshiku **omotte-orimasu.**

   I find it pleasing.

8. 悲しい**ことです**。

   Kanashii **koto desu.**

   It is a sad situation.

9. **やっぱり**うれしいです。

   Yappari ureshii desu.

   Yes, indeed, I'm pleased.

Despite the situational constraints mentioned above, it is also important to realize that language provides a means for expressing one's emotion and empathy in personal ways. One such example is to use emotion words and expressive strategies in subordinate clauses that retain conversational features. In a conversation inserted into an utterance, the speaker is able to convey such empathy as familiarity, friendliness, and warmth and still maintain a certain level of politeness and formality. In other words, by framing direct expressive strategies in casual style within a subordinate clause (e.g., quotation and similar structures), the speaker maintains the ongoing formal style. Even though emotion words and expressive strategies are disguised in a subordinate clause, feelings are directly expressed. Note the informal form *katte-yaru* in (10), and the informal form *toku shita* followed by an interactional particle *ze* in (11), although both sentences as a whole maintain the formal style.

10. その時、絶対**勝ってやる**、って思ったんです。

    Sono toki, zettai **katte-yaru,** tte omotta n desu.

    Then I thought to myself "I'm going to win no matter what!"

11. きょうは一日あったかくて**得したぜ**、みたいな日でした。

Kyoo wa ichinichi attakakute **toku shita ze**, mitaina hi deshita.

It was warm all day today, and I felt like "I got lucky today!"

Historical Perspectives: Voices from the Heart

Before we begin the study of expressive Japanese, it may be useful to understand the academic context. This is particularly important because a focus on emotion and empathy has tended to be slighted in modern linguistics and pedagogy in the West. Japanese linguistics and Japanese language pedagogy also have largely concentrated on areas other than emotion and empathy.

More than two hundred years ago, Japanese language scholars of the Edo period (A.D. 1603–1868) approached language in a way radically different from that of modern Western linguists. Those scholars viewed language not as a tool for rational thinking but as an expressive means for sharing emotion and empathy. For example, Akira Suzuki (1764–1837), in his 1824 work *Gengyo shishuron,* identified the essence of the Japanese language by the phrase *kokoro no koe* 'voices from the heart'.

The Edo scholars were neither directly interested in constructing a theory of language nor in offering a systematic analysis of the Japanese language. Their concerns were more immediate, namely, how to compose and appreciate great *waka* (31-mora poems). Suzuki identified four parts of speech—today's nouns, adjectives, verbs, and particles. He grouped the first three and called them "three types of referential words." Particles, which he labeled as the *te-ni-o-ha* category, represent the fourth group. Significantly, for Suzuki, these *te-ni-o-ha* particles are most essential in the Japanese language, and they express feelings and attitude; they echo not thoughts in the mind, but "voices from the heart." It makes sense that Suzuki identified *te-ni-o-ha* particles as being qualitatively different from referential words. Particles do not really refer to objects and things in the way that nouns and verbs do. These seemingly empty words fulfill the important functions of connecting words, identifying the speaker, and expressing the speaker's heart.

More recently, another Japanese language scholar, Yoshio Yamada (1873–1958), immortalized the emotive aspect of the Japanese language by the term *kantai no ku* 'vocative-emotive phrase'. Yamada (1936) took the position that the study of grammar is a study of methods in which one not only presents thought, but also expresses emotion. He then studied Japanese emotive sentences in detail. For example, *Uruwashiki hana kana!* '(What) a beautiful flower!' expresses how much the speaker is moved by the flower's beauty. In contemporary Japanese, an adjective-noun combination such as *Kireina hana!*

'Beautiful flower!' is an example of *kantai no ku*. Although this phrasal expression contains no verb, it is not ungrammatical. Rather, it is a prime example of expressive Japanese. Among Japanese language scholars, including Suzuki and Yamada, there has been a clear tradition of understanding language as a source of emotion and sentiment.

Given the historical context, in which emotion and empathy have attracted less attention than they deserve, the prioritization of expressive aspects of language on which Japanese language scholars have insisted is significant. As I found in my earlier works (1993, 1998b, 2000, 2001a, 2002), if one approaches language from the perspective of emotion and empathy, many expressive aspects of Japanese grammar and interactional strategies reveal themselves. Although the Japanese language can be a tool for rational thinking, one can achieve a deeper understanding of it by focusing on expressive Japanese.

Language, Emotion, and Culture

When learning expressive Japanese, one cannot ignore the general issue of emotion, culture, and society. Is emotion the same across cultures, or is it culture-specific? This question is both old and new in academia. The universalist answers yes to the first question, the relativist to the second. Linguists and language educators have long debated how language and emotion are related to the concept of universality and relativity. In terms of language learning, one may ask, Are emotional experiences the result of nature or nurture?

The answer to the question lies somewhere between; neither an extreme universal nor a solely relative position is tenable. People share fundamental universal human emotions across languages, cultures, and societies. At the same time, emotions are nurtured in society and exist as a part of the cultural sentiment common to members of a particular society. Japanese emotions, therefore, are in many ways particular to Japanese language, culture, and society, although they sustain commonalities with other languages.

It is also true that language plays a key role in identifying, experiencing, and sharing feelings with others. Although human emotions are universal across languages and cultures, how those emotions are expressed, or not expressed, depends largely on how the language is structured and used. In the process of enacting these socioculturally restricting linguistic choices, emotions often become particularized and specialized. A person belonging to a social group does not experience emotion in total freedom; emotion is inevitably influenced by group membership. Even when an individual rebels against such common social emotion and attempts to break free from it, the very manner of rebellion will not be completely free of the community's emotion. Humans are nurtured by and socialized within a community (or communities) that inculcates commonly understood and internalized emotions. This is a reality from which there is no escape. On the level of actual communications, certain aspects of emotion, however universal, are relative and particular to language, culture, and society.

Think of the example of human experience called "romantic love." What are the elements of a great romantic love story? Is forbidden love a critical ingredient of romantic love, as in *Romeo and Juliet?* Can romantic love coexist with a practical, ordinary marriage? Is the ideal love relationship the same among some Japanese people as it is among some American Catholics? Think of another example, that of expressing kindness and concern toward others. Do you feel better when a person you hardly know approaches you in a friendly and frank manner? Or will you feel more comfortable if the person shows some reserve by using hesitant expressions? Although obviously there are individual differences among Japanese and among Americans, if you responded yes to the first, you are more strongly endorsing emotion as understood in American culture. If your answer to the second question is yes you are more closely following a traditional Japanese paradigm. Kindness and concern in anticipation of friendship are similar but not identical across cultures. Consequently, subtle differences are likely to emerge.

Does all this mean that foreign language students cannot understand feelings as native speakers do? No need to despair. The relativist position does not preclude the possibility of crossing emotional borders. On the contrary, learning a foreign language offers opportunities for expressing, experiencing, and sharing heretofore unknown or unclear emotions and empathy. By focusing on expressive Japanese, the reader may learn to appreciate different types and gradations of feelings that can be communicated more clearly through the Japanese language than in the reader's own native language. Part of learning a foreign language is discovering different feelings in our hearts. To experience different feelings is to discover different senses of self within ourselves.

I should also point out that the Internet has promoted the globalization of cultures at an ever-increasing speed, and as a result, the universalist position seems to have gained ascendancy. But despite the ongoing homogenization of cultures, cultures sustain local particularities (glocalization) and show tendencies toward heterogenization. M. Maynard (2003), through a study of Japanese advertising, shows how a global product is glocalized to accommodate to Japan. Globalization and glocalization occur simultaneously, and the opposing tendencies of cultural universalism and relativism not only coexist, but interact and influence each other. Learning foreign languages has become globalized through easy access to foreign language Web sites filled with linguistic and cultural icons. At the same time, the Japanese language sustains itself, although it is spoken by diverse groups of people inside and outside of Japan. The reader is encouraged to explore ongoing cultural globalization and glocalization phenomena in the process of learning the Japanese language.

A few words about "emotion" in the context of "the Japanese" are perhaps in order. It is sometimes suggested that Japanese speakers are not emotional, or at least that they do not show emotion. This view is often presented by outside observers, adding to the perception that Japanese speakers are different from or even in polar opposition to them. Among Japanese speakers, however, there is an understanding that they are emotional and that they have a rich experience of deep and subtle emotions. The outside observer's judgment may be impaired by the absence of verbal expressions and strategies that are either comparable or quickly translatable to those found in the observer's world. Or perhaps the unfamiliar observer has access only to formal occasions, where Japanese speakers are most likely to be reserved. Under this circumstance, it is easy to misinterpret the situation and conclude that Japanese speakers generally do not express emotion.

Another point raised about emotion with regard to the Japanese is that its expression is influenced by social factors. Japanese speakers express emotion in different ways to an intimate than they do to someone to whom one must show politeness. This is true as well in other cultures, but the social constraints seem relatively strong, and therefore obvious, for Japanese speakers. According to Kudo and Matsumoto (1996), Japanese people are happiest when things are going smoothly and they are having a good social relationship with the people close to them, while Americans are more likely to find happiness and joy in personal achievements and in closer friendships with others. The authors also noted that while Westerners find the deepest sadness in death and separation, the Japanese grieve most when faced with relationship problems, especially problems with close and intimate others. Japanese people also feel anxiety more acutely when human relationships are going poorly, whereas strangers trigger Americans' strongest fear. In general an American's anger is strongly associated with social injustice, while a Japanese person's anger is targeted toward unacceptably poor behavior on the part of strangers, and not so much toward the poor behavior of the people close to them.

These differences seem to reinforce the relative importance social relationships play in how Japanese speakers feel and the constraints Japanese culture and society exert on how Japanese speakers express or do not express their feelings. These social constraints provide a sense of social and psychological cohesiveness among Japanese speakers. By following—or sometimes violating—these constraints, Japanese speakers communicate feelings in many ways.

This said, I should also emphasize the internal variability and fluidity of the Japanese language and culture. As I pointed out earlier, although the tendency is to discuss "Japanese" language and culture together for convenience, neither is homogeneous. Every label is inherently limiting, because the act of labeling paints the picture with one sweeping stroke. In real life, as many entries introduced in this book illustrate, the Japanese language is used in a variety of personal and creative ways. Constant reminders that generalized differences do not account for all speakers of the Japanese language, and that individual variations abound, are indispensable.

Learning Expressive Japanese Critically and Creatively

As the reader must be aware, language learning demands courage. It is not enough to repeat and imitate what the textbook offers or what the teacher says. The student of a foreign language must be able to gain insight into how the language is structured, how it is actually used, and how language itself constitutes a part of the interaction. By observing multiple cases, the student must be able to identify patterns of strategies frequently used in certain circumstances. By learning from textbooks, workbooks, reference books, and how-to books, the student of Japanese must not only accumulate knowledge, but also organize it so that it makes sense. Ultimately, with only limited resources, the student must create a world wherein he or she shares in the Japanese language.

Learning expressive Japanese, however, requires a special awareness. Expressing emotion and empathy is so closely related to our essence of self that it becomes personal in a way that a traditional knowledge of grammar does not. When people express emotion in certain ways, the kind of emotion and the way it is expressed reveal their character. For example, one may be viewed as strong, forthcoming, pushy, timid, giving, warm, understanding, and so on. Using certain conventionalized (and sometimes ritualized) expressive Japanese may make you feel you are forced to reveal too much or too little of the wrong kinds of emotions. Using not-so-straightforward expressions in Japanese may make you feel unnecessarily weak and may threaten your sense of pride.

In my personal view, it is not worthwhile to jeopardize one's personality or integrity when learning a foreign language. At the same time, it is important to be tolerant of the social and cultural conventions of the target society. In the balance between these two forces, a student of the Japanese language must reconcile and find a comfort zone. Language, whether native or foreign, inevitably conveys a person's sense of self.

Another sensitive situation is gender-related speech style. A female student of the Japanese language is expected in many ways to behave like a native Japanese woman. This may be uncomfortable, because expressing emotion in the "feminine" speech and "being like a Japanese woman" can lead to feelings of powerlessness. A female student may find that she has only limited access to certain expressions, although she may have more varieties to choose from in certain circumstances. Male students may find it uncomfortable to speak bluntly, especially toward women, and may feel they do not have access to certain forms of expressive Japanese when they wish they did.

Some native speakers also find it uncomfortable to follow some of the (traditional) values, and they find their voices in their own ways. As I discuss in Chapter 2, speech styles stereotypically associated with "masculine" or "feminine" speech are used by both genders for expressive purposes. Certain Japanese values may not be very appealing; the reader may feel uncomfortable and may be critical of any number of the features of expressive Japanese. We should be reminded, however, that it is through this critical stance that we may be able truly to understand both how Japanese speakers feel and how we feel ourselves.

A student of Japanese must also keep in mind that the Japanese language is heterogeneous, varied, and constantly in a state of change. In my earlier studies (1997a, 1997b) I presented the variability of the Japanese language and the need for critical pedagogy. To understand these variations and changes, a critical perspective on learning is necessary. Students and teachers must always be sensitive to what is really happening in the use of the Japanese language.

Students must also be critical of what is presented as pertinent information on learning Japanese, because messages come in varied and not always consistent ways. For example, one how-to book on business encounters suggests that the speaker should reveal emotion straightforwardly (*jibun no kanjoo o sutoreeto ni dasu*). Accordingly, one should say *Watashi wa kore ga ii to omou* 'I think this is good', specifying clearly that "I" think so and so, instead of *Kore wa ii* 'This is good' (Moriya 1999, 172). Moriya in general recommends a direct and sometimes unexpectedly self-revealing manner of communication for business interaction. As a student of Japanese, you should be both open to and critical of suggestions from this or any other source. Amid all the advice, you want to find your personal voice.

To find this voice, you must be willing to go beyond the stereotypical hegemonic force and maintain a critical and creative attitude. The enormous project of learning a foreign language, especially its expressive language, may test you in ways that other experiences have not. What this book can do is to assist you in the endeavor by providing explanations and examples of frequently observed phenomena in Japanese communication. I hope you will explore the emotional side of Japanese communication well beyond what this book reveals, and share emotion and empathy in and through the Japanese language.

2

Expressive Japanese and the Characteristics of Japanese Discourse

Expressive Japanese, Politeness, and Style

Politeness is a term that covers multiple aspects of Japanese communication and involves both verbal and nonverbal strategies. This section discusses strategies focusing on verb forms and speech styles. In addition, we study how emotion and empathy are expressed through the mixture of styles.

Politeness Levels

Emotion words and expressive strategies, like all speech in Japanese, associate a certain level of politeness with different verb forms. Respectful and humble verb forms are primarily associated with the relative statuses of the persons involved (including speaker, partner, and third parties). The use of style is partly influenced by the relationship between speaker and partner and the particular situation. In this book, the following politeness levels are identified.

supra-polite	use of respectful and humble forms, [V/Adj formal] forms, prefixes *go-* and *o-*, and other very polite strategies
polite	use of [V/Adj formal] forms, and other moderately polite strategies

Expressions not enacting politeness are not necessarily impolite, however. They become impolite only when used in situations where polite expressions are expected. In this book, supra-polite speech is marked by the symbol (≠).

Adjusting Distance and Intimacy

Use of polite forms becomes problematic when social convention recommends polite forms, but the speaker wishes to use less polite forms to show intimacy. Because polite forms largely convey social distance, they are the opposite of the desire to express intimacy. In this regard, Fukao's (1998) report is useful. Fukao investigated how college students in Japan feel about choosing politeness levels, namely, how the feeling of *shitashisa* 'familiarity, closeness, intimacy' is expressed when politeness is socially expected, as when juniors address seniors. Juniors begin to feel uncomfortable using polite expressions as intimacy increases, and they gradually use less polite expressions, mixing moderately polite forms with less polite and casual forms. Seniors also allow and/or encourage less polite forms from juniors to whom they feel close.

It is also known that in social encounters outside college as well, when a person of a socially higher rank starts using a friendly casual style, the lower-ranking partner also begins to mix in less formal expressions. Although the lower-ranking partner maintains the overall politeness level, such strategies as the sentence-final '[V/Adj-*te*] form and the particle *ne* are incorporated into discourse to express intimacy. For example, by adding *mitai,* a [V-*te*] form, and *ne,* as in *Sono koto ga shokku datta mitai deshite ne* 'Apparently it was a shock', the speaker communicates a desire for intimacy.

When intimacy is sought, to insist on a politeness level that expresses distance is "impolite." In such cases, a polite response communicates a rejection of overtures to intimacy and is likely to be considered unfriendly and unkind. The speaker's wishes to share feelings are expressed by a variety of emotive words and expressive strategies aimed at closing the psychological distance. Speakers constantly adjust politeness levels, searching for a compromise between distance-maintaining politeness and politeness expressed through intimacy-seeking friendly expressions.

Styles

The following styles in Japanese are identified in this book.

formal	use of [V/Adj formal] forms, limited use of particles, formal vocabulary
casual	use of [V/Adj informal] forms, frequent use of particles, casual vocabulary, interjections
blunt	use of [V/Adj informal] forms, assertive and forceful expressions, in many cases stereotypically associated with "masculine" speech
vulgar	use of vulgar style, often associated with youth speech

Formal style is used unless there are reasons to do otherwise. It is the style of choice in public and official situations and on all occasions where the speaker interacts with the partner(s) whom he or she wants to be polite to or maintain distance from. Using formal style is an important part of realizing politeness. Casual style is normally chosen in private situations, though also in public situations if interpersonal familiarity and intimacy are already established. It is preferred when the situation does not require formal style and when the speaker senses that the familiar and casual attitude is either tolerated or appreciated.

Blunt style is chosen when the speaker pays little attention to how he or she should speak. The reason for such a choice is often emotional. Blunt style communicates strong assertion and is often accompanied by a raw emotion like anger or rejection. Because blunt style is straightforward and closes the psychological distance between speakers, in certain circumstances it can also convey intimacy and closeness. Certain blunt expressions are slangy. Such a style is identified as vulgar style, and its use is limited to very casual and often youth-associated speakers and partners. In this book, formal style appears without a mark. Casual style is marked with (≈), blunt style with (□), and vulgar (youth) style with (v). For Japanese key expressions, a style designation is given only when the expression appears in a sentence, or when the expression's stylistic feature is particularly important. No style markers are assigned in authentic examples.

For the entries in this book, examples created for explanatory purposes mostly appear in the [V/Adj informal] style. Where stylistic differences are at issue, [V/Adj formal] examples are also presented. For convenience, only informal or formal forms are modeled in many cases. Additional formal and informal forms are also available for use where appropriate, unless noted otherwise.

Depending on the methods of communication, three different styles are recognized in Japanese: (1) spoken, (2) written, and (3) speechlike written. Spoken style includes official speech, speech exchanged in formal meetings, business conversations, and casual personal and intimate conversations, among others. Written style is used in letters, documents, novels, print media such as newspapers and magazines, and so on.

The speechlike written style is a recent development and requires some explanation. In the early 1980s, Makoto Shiina explored a style that distinctly carries with it straightforward and unconventional spoken language characteristics (e.g., *Ka* in 1984). This style was named *Shoowa keihakutai* 'Shoowa light-touch style', but Shiina's writing style has mellowed in recent years, and *Shoowa keihakutai* has become largely obsolete.

More recently, another speechlike style has been recognized. This style, called *Shin genbun itchitai* (Satake 1995), is primarily used by youth in communication through the Internet, in magazines targeted to youth, and in many of the romance novels for girls. Although the Japanese is written, it is written as if talking to a friend. It frequently uses interjections, particles (such as *ne*, *sa*, and *yo*), sound changes (e.g., *suggoku* 'extremely' instead of *sugoku*, *naantonaku* 'somehow' instead of *nantonaku*) and short contracted forms (e.g., *tabechau* 'to end up eating' instead of *tabete-shimau*, *konaida* 'the other day' instead of *kono aida*). Because of its spontaneity, speechlike written style tends to be simple, sporadic, and emotion-filled. In this book some authentic examples are drawn from the speechlike written style as it appears in romance novels for girls and on Internet bulletin boards. Characteristics of *Shin genbun itchitai* are also incorporated into many essays written by writers much older than the generation Satake identifies.

Style Mixture

Although we recognize the four styles in spoken Japanese and the three styles of communication method introduced above, these styles are not always used independently. Styles are often mixed, even in a spoken or written discourse segment produced by a single person and addressed to the same partner. See Entries 33 and 76 for additional information.

In a series of studies (S. Maynard 1991a, 1991b, 1993), I focused on the formal and casual styles in terms of verb forms and characterized their use as follows. Casual style is used when (1) the speaker is emotionally excited, (2) the speaker is involved in the event almost as if being right there and then, (3) the speaker expresses internal feelings in an almost self-addressed utterance, (4) the speaker creates utterances together with the partner, (5) semantically subordinate information is presented, and (6) the speaker expresses social familiarity and closeness. On the other hand, the formal style is used when (1) the speaker expresses thoughts addressed to the partner and (2) when the speaker communicates primary information directly addressed to the partner.

When casual style appears in predominantly formal style discourse, it marks surprise, abrupt remembrance, or sudden emotional surge. In the narrative text, the writer is in the narrative world there and then, taking a perspective internal to the narrative world. Casual style embedded in formal style achieves immediacy and directness in expression and a narrative-internal perspective.

Conversely, when formal style appears in predominantly casual discourse, it marks the speaker/writer's awareness of speech levels. For example, when a writer is more conscious of the reader, and thus more socially aware, the writer organizes words and thoughts as social convention requires, and formal style is chosen if appropriate. In narrative text, formal style is used to express a narrative-external voice, a voice that allows the narrator to direct commentary toward the reader. Formal style adds to the impression that the writer is making a conscientious effort to address the reader.

In more recent studies on style shifts (S. Maynard 2001a, 2001b, 2002), I discussed how emotion plays a part in the selection of speech styles. For example, when a speaker feels vulnerable and hesitant, the speech shifts to a softer, gentler, often more polite style. The casual style used by lovers allows direct and forceful expression of emotion, and this behavior is predicated on mutual intimacy. Analysis of dramatic discourse has revealed that stylistic shifts also occur according to emotional development over time, as enacted in a television drama series. (This is explained in Entry 33.)

Above all, in a series of studies (S. Maynard 1991a, 1991b, 1993, 1997a, 1997b, 1999, 2001a, 2001b, 2002), I have emphasized that stylistic choices are motivated not only by social factors and constraints but also by personal emotions and desires. In fact, stylistic choice and style mixture result from a compromise between two forces, social norms and individual expressivity. The same person may mix styles when addressing the same partner depending on situation, emotion, and desire.

A representative example of style mixture appears in a conversation segment taken from *Long Vacation* (episode 6).

南：　瀬名君、ずっと友達でいようね。
瀬名：　気持ちわるい。
南：　たとえ恋人できたとしても、結婚したとしても、あ瀬名君結婚できないかもしれないか。そしたら老人ホームに訪ねていってあげるよ。
瀬名：　いいです。
南：　そしたら縁側で、お茶しよう**ぜ**。
瀬名：　「しよう、**ぜ**」？
南：　**ぜ**！#

Minami: Sena-kun, zutto tomodachi de iyoo ne.
Sena: Kimochi warui.
Minami: Tatoe koibito dekita to shitemo, kekkon shita to shitemo, a Sena-kun kekkon deki-nai kamoshirenai ka. Soshitara roojin hoomu ni tazunete-itte-ageru yo.
Sena: Ii desu.
Minami: Soshitara engawa de, ocha shiyoo **ze**.
Sena: "Shiyoo, **ze**"?
Minami: **Ze!**

Minami: Sena, let's be friends forever, right?
Sena: Sounds awful.
Minami: Even when you have a lover, and even when you get married, ah,

Sena, you may not be able to marry. Then I will visit you at the nursing home.
Sena: No, thank you.
Minami: Then, let's have tea together ("*ze*") on the veranda.
Sena: You mean "*ze*"?
Minami: Yes, "*ze*."

In this example, Minami uses the particle "*ze*," which is associated with blunt style. Sena is surprised to hear *ze*, but then Minami assertively repeats it. Although in general Minami's speech is casual and sometimes blunt, because of its extreme forcefulness and bluntness, the use of *ze* catches attention. By using *ze*, Minami conveys a strong assertive attitude. At the same time, the blunt style is often stereotypically associated with the "masculine" voice, and accordingly, Minami presents such a voice. Mixing into conversation the extremely blunt *ze* also shows creative playfulness on Minami's part.

Although this is one example, mixing styles occurs frequently in ordinary speech as well as in written discourse, although less so in the latter. Fluidity and variability of style are the norm. The choice of style is partly socially motivated, but it is also motivated by other factors that are primarily under the speaker's control. Stylistic choice, style shift, and style mixture function as strategies for expressing emotion and empathy, and as expressive strategies for presenting the speaker's character(s). Style mixture is also used for creative purposes as well, for example, for parody and playful role-playing.

Style is not necessarily directly linked to demographic and social factors. Rather, it may serve as a tool used by speakers to redefine the situational context in which their verbal interaction takes place. For example, using a few casual verb endings in predominantly formal style adds a sense of intimacy to the situation. A friendly context is created anew, to the extent that it is interpersonally acceptable. In this sense situational context is not totally given, nor is it predetermined. The context is something that speakers manipulate as a part of expressive communication.

Being Expressive and Variations in the Language

A student of Japanese should be aware of different varieties and variations of the Japanese language. Choosing the wrong form at the wrong time can cause problems. Youth language addressed to an audience of seniors, for example, would be not only rude, but silly, and is considered characteristic of *jooshiki shirazu* 'a person who lacks social grace'.

There are at least three major factors associated with linguistic variation:

the traditional concept of gender, the speaker's age and generation, and the speaker's regional background. How society understands gender plays a role in language variation, and I touch on the more assertive "masculine" style and the less assertive "feminine" style, emphasizing their ongoing changes. Linguistic variation is also related to one's generation. Youth language in particular is often discussed as something extraordinary. Given that many of the readers of this book are young (and young at heart) and are likely to have opportunities to be exposed to youth language, I present its characteristics briefly, and I touch on how a student of the Japanese language may deal with the ever-changing nature of language. In addition, different geographical regions are associated with different dialects. In this book some Kansai dialect examples are introduced.

With the technological advancements that change the way Japanese people communicate on a daily basis and with media saturation, differences among varieties of the Japanese language are decreasing. But social and psychological motivations exist for sustaining linguistic variability. Think of the language variety shared by closely connected members of a group, for example, a regional dialect used in Tokyo or a style shared by members of a high school clique. Because it differs from other varieties, a specific style functions as an emotional bond, enhancing a sense of belongingness.

More Assertive "Masculine" and Less Assertive "Feminine" Styles

With respect to the styles discussed earlier, it is possible to recognize more or less assertive (or blunt, strong, or forceful) styles. More assertive and blunt style is stereotypically associated with the traditional "masculine" voice, and less assertive and blunt, with the "feminine" voice.

Traditionally, some Japanese speakers have made a clear distinction between masculine speech (or men's language) and feminine speech (or women's language). Although the clear distinction between these varieties has largely faded, and speakers use both styles for expressive purposes, it is necessary to understand their characteristics. Older speakers tend to retain the distinction, so using gender-associated varieties without understanding their effects and consequences is not recommended.

The primary differences between traditional "masculine" and "feminine" speech include:

Traditional Masculine Speech

1. The speaker completes sentences with the [V/Adj informal] form immediately followed by interactional particles *ne(e)* and *yo*, as in *Ii nee* 'That's nice', *Aitsu yoku benkyoo shita yo* 'He studied hard', and *Rippana tatemono da ne* 'This is a fine building, isn't it?'

2. The speaker ends sentences with *n da*, as in *Kinoo itta n da* 'So I went yesterday'.
3. *Daro(o)* is frequently preferred to *desho(o)*, as in *Ashita wa ame daro(o)* 'Tomorrow will be rainy' and *Sonna koto nai daro(o)?* 'That can't be, can it?'.
4. The use of the abrupt negative command is available, as in *Suru-na* 'Don't do that'.
5. The abrupt volitional form is used, as in *Jaa, ikoo* 'Let's go'.
6. The abrupt question form is used, as in *Dare to iku n dai?* 'With whom are you going?'.
7. Certain expressions are limited to masculine speech, for example, the particles *zo, ze*, and *na*, the exclamative *iyaa* 'wow', certain slang and cursing words, and so on.
8. The prefixes *o-* and *go-* are used, but not so extensively as in feminine speech.
9. Certain phrases are considered masculine, such as *meshi* and *kuu*, as in *Meshi kui ni ikoo* 'Let's go out to eat'. (In traditional feminine speech, it is likely to be: *Gohan tabe ni ika-nai?*)
10. The vowel combination *ai* sometimes changes to *ee*, as in *dasee* 'not cool' instead of *dasai*, and *ika-nee* 'I'm not going' instead of *ika-nai*. Also note the use of *sugee* instead of *sugoi*, and *osee* instead of *osoi*.

Nowadays, items 1, 2, and 5 are widely used by female speakers as well. As for item 8, it has been reported that female speakers do not use these prefixes any more frequently than men. Items 3, 4, 6, 7, 9, and 10 largely remain associated with the "masculine" voice. When choosing these expressions, female speakers should be aware of the consequence (sounding more assertive by echoing the "masculine" voice).

Traditional Feminine Speech

1. Instead of using the [V/Adj informal] form plus *ne* and *yo*, the speaker prefers *wa ne(e)* and *wa yo*, as in *Ii wa nee* 'That's nice' and *Ano hito yoku benkyoo shita wa yo* 'He studied hard'. *Da* immediately before *ne(e)* and *yo* is deleted, as in *Rippana tatemono ne* 'This is a fine building, isn't it?'.
2. The speaker ends sentences with *n da* less frequently; instead, *no* appears, as in *Kinoo itta no* 'So I went yesterday'.
3. *Desho(o)* is frequently preferred to *Daro(o)*, as in *Ashita wa ame desho(o)* 'Tomorrow will be rainy' and *Sonna koto nai desho(o)?* 'That cannot be, can it?'.
4. The abrupt negative command is avoided; instead, *Shi-naide(-kudasai)* '(Please) don't do that' is preferred.
5. The use of the abrupt volitional form is restricted; rather than *Jaa ikoo* 'Let's go', for example, *Jaa ikimashoo* is often used.

6. The use of abrupt questions is usually avoided. Questions ending with *no* and *no ne* are used instead.
7. Certain expressions are limited to feminine speech, for example, the interjection *ara maa* 'wow', sentence-final *wa* [pronounced in a higher tone] and *kashira* 'I wonder', the personal pronouns *atashi* and *atakushi* 'I', and so on.
8. The prefixes *o-* and *go-* are more extensively used.
9. Certain phrases are considered feminine, such as *suteki* 'nice' and *kawaii* 'cute'.
10. In general, older women tend to speak politely, sometimes extremely politely.

Note that usage of items 1, 2, and 5 is declining and the forms associated with the traditional "masculine" counterpart expressions are frequently used. Male speakers using the expressions listed above should be aware of the consequence (sounding less assertive by echoing the "feminine" voice). Items 1 and 7 especially are strongly associated with the "feminine" voice. Male speakers should avoid these expressions unless they are intended.

In general, "feminine" speech projects gentleness, and "masculine" speech projects forcefulness. Because of these traditional associations, gendered voices are often heard in speech styles. It is important to keep in mind that in reality, female speakers may choose a forceful style, and male speakers a gentle one, because the concept of gendered voices interacts with other variables, including (1) psychological factors like identity; (2) social and ideological factors, for example, the power associated with the more assertive "masculine" style; and (3) such situational factors as speaking in public. The choice between "feminine" and "masculine" styles is motivated by multiple, sometimes contradictory factors, and a person is likely to speak differently as the occasion warrants, fluctuating between more assertive "masculine" and less assertive "feminine" styles. "Masculine" and "feminine" styles are not mutually exclusive, and "feminine" and "masculine" voices should be viewed as matters of degree, not as opposites.

Within the "feminine" style, there are strongly feminine and moderately feminine varieties. The same can be said about the "masculine" style. Overall impressions of gentleness and bluntness can be achieved by a number of linguistic and other expressive strategies. Again, it is important to keep in mind that "masculine" and "feminine" varieties are not necessarily connected with the speaker's gender.

Speech styles associated with gender differences may be used for expressive purposes, for example, to emphasize one's gender in intimate relationships. A man may highlight "masculine" style and speak bluntly when he wants to foreground his masculine identity (e.g., to his girlfriend). The same speaker is likely to avoid blunt style toward another woman. Likewise, a woman may choose a highly "feminine" style to express femininity toward a specific person (e.g., a boyfriend), or under certain other circumstances, as when femininity is favorably evaluated. The same speaker may avoid the less assertive "feminine" style when her professional authority is at stake.

Gender-Associated Styles in Transition

Traditionally, "feminine" speech was considered the kind of language women should use. Numerous books are available to tell women how to talk (e.g., Sakai 1996). However, such discourse itself reflects an ideology that discriminates against women. Instead of blindly accepting a special "ladylike" language variety (different from ordinary Japanese language) that woman must adhere to, it makes more sense to understand "feminine" speech style as an option available for all speakers' expressive purposes.

Japanese speakers are free to use different styles under different circumstances. Even so, certain emotive words and expressive strategies are more restricted to either the more assertive "masculine" or the less assertive "feminine" style. When someone says something insulting to a woman, in response she is not likely to yell out *Kuso! Bakayaroo!* 'Shit! Idiot!'. If she does, she is likely to be criticized for being out of line and not behaving properly.

At the same time, it is often said that Japanese women's speech is becoming more like men's speech and that gender differences in language use, particularly among youth, are becoming something of a myth. Women are viewed as being more aggressive than once thought, particularly in private and casual situations. The language used by young women and for young women in the media can also take on features traditionally considered restrictively "masculine." For both informal and casual speech, gender differences in the Japanese language are becoming less clear.

Some studies support this claim. Traditionally, for example, use of the interactional particle *yo* immediately following [V/Adj informal] is restricted in "feminine" speech. Instead of saying *Koko ni kaite aru yo* 'It's written here', "feminine" speech prefers *Koko ni kaite aru wa yo*. Likewise, instead of *Nihonjin da yo* 'He is Japanese', *Nihonjin yo* is preferred. However, according to Endoo (1998), among women residing in Tokyo in the late 1990s, the preferred form is the [V/Adj informal] and [N] immediately followed by *yo*. Combinations such as *da wa yo* and *da wa ne* are rarely used. It is not difficult to find texts where a female character speaks in a style traditionally considered "masculine." For example, in the novel *Kitchin* by Banana Yoshimoto, Mikage, a young woman says *Dakara, shoojiki ni itte ii yo* 'So it's OK to tell the truth' (Yoshimoto 1991, 45). In this book, I have given many examples where female speakers frequently use the style traditionally associated with "masculine" speech.

The traditional view advocates that women use polite expressions more frequently than men, particularly the supra-polite style with its respectful and humble forms. However, Endoo (1998) observed that women do not frequently use humble forms with the exception of [V-*te* + *itadaku*]. But she noted that the [V-*te* + *itadaku*] form is frequently used by both female and male speakers.

Takasaki (2002) also points out a blurring of the differences between male speakers' and female speakers' speech. Question sentences ending in *ka ne*, *ka na*, and *da yo ne* (thought to be restricted to "masculine" speech) and question sentences ending in *no* and *no ne* (thought to be restricted to "feminine" speech) are both used across genders. In general, female speakers do not delete *da*, although deletion is traditionally expected. And male speakers do sometimes delete *da*. Likewise, *atakushi* 'I', which used to be associated with "feminine" speech, is rarely used, and female speakers primarily use *watashi* instead. As a vocative, female speakers, like male speakers, frequently use only the last name without -*san*.

The increasing similarity between so-called men's language and women's language has also been noted in the mass media. A newspaper article (*Joomoo shinbun*, 2000), quoting Orie Endoo, reports that in the television drama *Beautiful Life* (2000, Fuji Television), from which many examples in this book are taken, women are more aggressive than men in speech and in interaction. Female characters in the drama use phrases traditionally considered "masculine" (e.g., *un* 'yes', and *oi* 'say') as frequently as male characters. The only difference was the use of *ore* 'I' which remained limited to the male characters. Interestingly, Kyooko, the heroine of the drama, uses almost the same speech style with her lover, her elder brother, and her female best friend. The traditional image of women speaking in a special language with a heightened sensitivity to others is simply not evident in this drama, and increasingly so in ordinary lives.

Youth Language

Among generational variations in the Japanese language, youth language is often noted for its newness, creativity, and peculiarity. Youth language is the language spoken by teens and those in their early twenties. Some features of the so-called youth language, however, span the generations, with some youth expressions taking root in the speech style of people in their thirties and even in their forties and fifties. And older people who want to be close to or identify with youth may purposely select youth language.

As a matter of course, it is expected that people speak differently and use different vocabulary as they age. For example, in childhood a young male speaker may always refer to himself as *boku*, but later in life he is expected to use *boku, ore, watashi*, or *jibun*, depending on the speech situation. The command expression *nasai* reflects the speaker's dominance and is often used by parents toward their own children; therefore, young people use them less frequently (Ozaki 2001). The [V/Adj formal] form followed by the particle *naa* as in *Samui desu naa* 'It is cold, isn't it?' is considered *ojisan-kotoba* 'middle-aged male speech' and is not used when the speaker is young. Using age-sensitive variations conveys different feelings associated with different identities. In this sense, generational variations represent another aspect of expressive Japanese.

A more prominent phenomenon is the language of the young that shows significant differences from the language of older generation. Young people tend to use youth language among themselves more frequently (to maintain a sense of camaraderie) than they do with people of other generations. In formal situations, young people are expected to use the dominant adult speech varieties. Under such circumstances, speaking youth language reflects a lack of education, humbleness, and grace.

Here are some characteristics of youth language in Japan in the late 1990s (information attributed to Yonekawa [1999]). Similar characteristics appear in some examples contained in this book taken from sources as recent as 2003.

Vocabulary

1. Invention and use of *ru-kotoba* (new verbs created by adding *ru* to nouns)

マクる	*makuru*	to go to McDonald's
コクる	*kokuru*	to confess (comes from *kokuhaku suru*)
ラーメる	*raameru*	to eat *raamen* noodles

2. Invention and use of the suffix *-raa* (*-raa* is added in reference to people who do things to excess)

シャネラー	*shaneraa*	a person who is crazy about the Chanel brand
マヨラー	*mayoraa*	a person who loves and overuses mayonnaise

Grammatical and rhetorical characteristics

1. Use of self-alienating expressions. For example, the speaker uses alienating expressions in reference to her own behavior, as if talking about someone else's behavior.

   a. (Two young female friends talk about drinking.) Both *kekkoo* and *nome tari shite* add to the sense of distancing her behavior (see Entry 25 for *kekkoo*; Entry 63 for *tari shite*).

   (≈ft1): お酒あんまり飲めないって言ってなかった？
   (≈ft2): うん。でもホントは、**結構飲めたりして**……

   (≈ft1): Osake anmari nome-nai tte itte-nakatta?
   (≈ft2): Un. Demo honto wa, **kekkoo nometari shite.**

(≈ft1): Didn't you say that you can't drink (alcoholic drinks) much?
(≈ft2): Yes. But, in truth, maybe I can drink a lot.

2. Use of objectified expressions. The speaker describes her behavior as if observed by someone else. Note that *mitaina* is used to describe the speaker's own feelings, although originally its use was restricted to the description of someone else's situation. (See Entry 64 for further discussion.)

   b. (≈) 今朝、起きたら頭も痛いし、メッチャ、ブルー入ってる**みたいな**……

   Kesa, okitara atama mo itai shi, metcha, buruu haitteru **mitaina**……

   This morning when I got up, I had a headache and felt really depressed, like…

3. Use of excessively self-conscious expressions. The speaker uses phrases that reflect a judgment of someone else when describing herself or himself.

   c. あたしって**意外と**シャイなんです。

   Atashi tte **igai to** shai na n desu.

   (You may not think so, but) surprisingly, I am shy.

   d. (A man asks a young man about his job.) Note the adverb *ichioo* 'to some extent', which reflects a judgment that could come from someone else. The utterance carries a sense of degrading (and humbling) attitude on the speaker's part.

   (ma1): ご職業は？
   (my1): **一応**、銀行員です。

   (ma1): Goshokugyoo wa?
   (my1): **Ichioo**, ginkooin desu.

   (ma1): Your occupation?
   (my1): Uh, a banker, a sort of, I guess (although you may not necessarily expect that).

4. Use of vague expressions. The speaker uses *toka* as a topic marker, giving the impression that the topic is unspecific. A half-question-like rising intonation (marked by ↑) also offers a useful strategy when making a point. Because it expresses self-doubt, the point is made less assertively.

   e. (≈) 学校**とか**眠くなるんじゃない？

   Gakkoo **toka** nemuku naru n ja-nai?

   Isn't (something like) school a place that makes you sleepy?

f. (≈) あたしはね、佐川先生のお気に入り↑らしいんだよ。

Atashi wa ne, Sagawa-sensei no okiniiri ↑rashii n da yo.

You know, I seem to be a favorite student (?) of Professor Sagawa.

These manipulations give the impression that the speaker is being solicitous of and considerate to the partner. In other words, by using youth language, speakers "soften" their statements. The motivation for adding this softening effect, however, is not limited to accommodating others' feelings. As Satake (1997) notes, *sofutoka* 'softening' is a rather aggressive strategy that the speaker, vulnerable and fearful of the partner's possible criticism, uses to silence potential disagreement.

Generational Variations and Language Change

Through time, mature Japanese speakers have lamented on how difficult it is to understand youth language. Let me cite one example from the sources discussed in this book, the television drama *Long Love Letter Hyooryuu Kyooshitsu*, episode 5. Hatsuko Kawa, a female high school student hurt in a huge school explosion, is in the hospital. Asked by reporters what happened, Hatsuko answers.

だから何回も言ってるんだろうが。#ていうかあん時、マジすげー揺れて、まじスゲー風吹いて、私的にびっくりみたく思ってたら、マジ何が何だかわかんねえことんなって、超ガーンとかいって、地面落ちて、腰うって、ヘッドうって、超イテーとか思ってたら、ここにいたんだっつうの。

Dakara nankai mo itteru n daroo ga. Te yuu ka an toki, maji sugee yurete, maji sugee kaze fuite, watashiteki ni bikkuri mitaku omottetara, maji nani ga nan da ka wakan-nee koto n natte, choo gaan to ka itte, jimen ochite, koshi utte, heddo utte, choo itee to ka omottetara, koko ni ita n da ttsuu no.

I'm telling you many times. I mean, at that time, seriously it shook a lot, and it got really windy, and I was thinking, like, this is quite a surprise to me, and then I couldn't tell what's what; then all of a sudden with a big shock, I fell on to the ground, hit my back, and hit my head; I was feeling that this is extremely painful, and when I realized [came to], I was here, that's what I'm telling you.

The two middle-aged reporters, completely perplexed, turn around, face the camera, and confess that they didn't understand a word of what she was saying (*Nani o itteru n da. Sukoshimo wakara-nai.* 'What is she saying? I don't understand it at all'). This speech contains many features of youth language: *te yuu ka* 'to tell the truth', *maji* 'seriously', *watashiteki ni* 'to me personally', *choo* 'super', *heddo* 'head', *choo itee* 'super painful' and *ttsuu no* 'I'm telling you'. Youth language is likely to be received with amazement by the mature population.

Note also that although this is an utterance made by a female student, her speech bears features stereotypically associated with more assertive "masculine" style. She is portrayed as a bad student and her speech style helps characterize her as a bad, boylike, wild youth.

As has always been the case, today's youth language is likely to become tomorrow's dead one. But some elements will stay and be accepted more or less as ordinary speech. Many expressions introduced in this book represent these cases. They include *mukatsuku* (Entry 10), *choo* (Entry 24), *te yuu ka* (Entry 44), *ja-nai desu ka* (Entry 47), *mitaina* (Entry 64), *maji* (Entry 67), and *ttsuu no* (Entry 73). To a student of the Japanese language, these expressions are as important as traditional expressions, because they have become integrated into standard casual speech. But although stylistic judgments vary among Japanese speakers, some of the youth-associated expressions in this book are often considered more vulgar than others. These expressions are marked with (v).

I should add two well-known changes to the Japanese language that are currently underway, namely, *ra*-deletion and *sa*-insertion. *Ra*-deletion is a phenomenon observed among relatively young speakers, who delete *ra* from the verb potential form. Instead of *taberareru* 'can eat', for example, *tabereru* is used. Although some people see merit in this shift, pointing out that it helps distinguish the potential meaning from the passive and respectful meanings that are associated with the *rareru* form, there is still significant resistance to its legitimacy.

Another phenomenon is *sa*-insertion, in which *sa* is inserted in the causative form (unless already present). For example, instead of *kaeraseru* 'to let someone return', *kaerasaseru* is used. This form is largely used in causative-plus-*itadaku* expressions, as in *Dewa kaerasasete-itadakimasu* 'Well then, I will be leaving now'. Or a person may say very politely *Yomasasete-itadakimasu* 'I will read it with your permission' instead of *Yomasete-itadakimasu*.

It is thought that *sa*-insertion and the use of the *sa*-inserted expression add to politeness, and this style was initially used in the service industry. For example, when the person in charge calls out customers' names, he or she may say *Dewa onamae o yobasasete-itadakimasu* 'Then, let me call your names now' instead of using *oyobi shimasu*. There is a tendency to believe that the longer the expression, the more polite it becomes. Accordingly, adding *sa* in the causative plus *te-itadaku* expression conveys politeness, although again this expression is disapproved by some of the more mature population.

Language is continually in flux, and a book like this one can capture only a certain moment in time. Consequently, it is important for the student of the language to remain attuned to what is current. In Japan, publications that comment on the latest popular expressions (including youth language) are easily available (for example, Shuueisha's *Imidas* and Asahi Shinbunsha's *Asahi gendai yoogo jiten chiezoo*, both published annually). It is not difficult to find Internet sites where youth language (*wakamono kotoba*) is discussed by professional linguists as well as by the general public.

Regional Variations

Although there are many regional dialects in Japan, the major, important dialect divisions are between the Ryuukyuan dialects (of Okinawa) and the mainland dialects. Mainland dialects are customarily divided into three large groups: eastern Japan, western Japan, and Kyuushuu. There are, however, major differences between the eastern group on the one hand and the western and Kyuushuu group on the other.

Students who travel to the Kansai area (which includes Kyoto, Osaka, and Kobe) will find significant differences in the use of the Japanese language from those who go to the Kantoo area (Tokyo and its vicinities). The language of the Kansai area is called the "Kansai dialect" (*Kansai-ben*), and, more restrictedly, the "dialect of Osaka" (*Oosaka-ben*). It shows some contrast with the dialect of the Kantoo area, or Tokyo speech.

The principal differences are in some vocabulary, in certain word formations (for example, in verb conjugations), and in the tone system. For example, the verb form *Moo haratta* 'I already paid' in Tokyo speech is *Moo haroota* in Kansai dialect. Adverbs also differ: *Takaku natta* 'It became expensive' in Tokyo speech is *Takoo natta* in Kansai dialect. For the negative *nai* in Tokyo speech, the Kansai dialect uses *n* or *hen*, as in *Kyoo wa ika-nai* 'I won't go today' versus *Kyoo wa ika-n* or *Kyoo wa ikahen*. The tone system difference between the two varieties is also quite noticeable. For example, *ko-ko-ro* 'heart' is pronounced in Tokyo with low-high-low tone, and with high-low-low tone in Osaka. Likewise, *a-ta-ma* 'head' is pronounced in Tokyo with low-high-high tone, and with high-high-low tone in Osaka. A survey of the major differences between eastern, western, and Kyuushuu varieties appears in Table 1.

Although regional dialects thrive in contemporary Japan, most people are able to switch to the so-called Tokyo speech, the dialect given prestige as the speech variety common among all speakers. Most of the media follow Tokyo speech, except in certain entertainment industries, where the Kansai dialect may be used. (Refer to Table 2 for a list of representative Kansai dialect expressions.) Among Japanese speakers, the ideal speech is thought to be the kind that NHK (Nihon Hoosoo Kyookai, the public broadcasting service in Japan) announcers use in reading the daily news. It is a good idea to listen to their Japanese as a model for the most acceptable accent, speed, and tone of the Japanese language.

Table 1

		Eastern	Western	Kyuushuu
Be-verb	雨だ	ame da	ame ja, ame ya	ame ja, ame da
Past tense	払った	haratta	haroota	haraata
Negative	書かない	kaka-nai	kaka-n, kakahen	kakan
	書かなかった	kaka-nakatta	kaka-nanda, kaka-nkatta	kakanjatta, kakankatta
Progressive	している	shiteiru	shiteoru, shitoru, shichoru	shiteoru, shitoru, shichoru, shiyoru
Causative	行かせる	ikaseru	ikaseru	ikasuru
	来させる	kosaseru	kosaseru	kosasuru
Command	起きろ	okiro	okiyo, okii	okiyo, okire, okiro
	しろ	shiro	seyo, see	sero, seyo, see
Volitional	来よう	koyoo	koo	koo, kuu
Adverb	寒く	samuku	samuu	samuu

Table 2

Entry	Kansai dialect	Tokyo speech
10 (d)	カッコええ	カッコいい
16 (a)	あかん	だめだ
16 (a)	まちごうた	まちがった
16 (a)	失敗や	失敗だ
16 (a)	感じじゃないねん	感じじゃないのよ
16 (f)	タイプやから	タイプだから
16 (f)	タイプやんか、あいつは	タイプだろう、あいつは
32 (d)	なんぼでも	いくらでも
66 (c)	勝ってしまうんやろな	勝ってしまうんだろうな
68 (c)	宣伝やってるやんか	宣伝やってるじゃない、宣伝やってるだろ
70 (g)	つないでもらうねん	つないでもらうのよ
73 (c)	言ってるやんか	言ってるじゃないか、言ってるだろ
74 (h)	女やわ	女だな
74 (h)	女やでえ	女でなあ、女でねえ
77 (d)	そうや	そうだよ
77 (d)	ええ	いい
77 (d)	乗っとった	乗っていた

The Kansai dialect (the Osaka dialect in particular) has been associated with comical variety shows in the media. As Kinsui (2003) notes, historically the Osaka dialect has been linked with a talkative, joking, flighty, yet practical and materialistic person. As a result, the Osaka dialect may communicate a certain stereotypical character as well.

A conversation segment taken from a television variety show, *Doomoto Tsuyoshi no shoojiki shindoi*, hosted by Tsuyoshi Doomoto (male, b. 1979) presents an example of variability in the Japanese language. He is a talent/singer (a member of the singer/dancer duo KinKi Kids) born in Nara and speaks the Kansai dialect as one of his routine speech varieties. In this show, Tsuyoshi invites a guest, Sakura Uehara (female, b. 1977 in Tokyo, with whom he had worked six years before) as a guest, and they visit a beauty salon. There they give each other a shampoo, and when Doomoto pretends to be a hairstylist, the following exchange takes place.

上原：　ほんとになんか不安なんだけど。
堂本：　だいじょうぶ、だいじょうぶ。えと、とりあえずひざに。
上原：　ちょっとちょっと待って。こうでしょう？基本が**なってないです**。
堂本：　雑誌いろいろ**ございますけど**。
上原：　あなんか、もうちょっと若い子が見るような。
堂本：　（ある雑誌を渡しながら）お願いします。
上原：　ちょっと**強制かよ**。
堂本：　（上原の髪を見て）長いなあ。**長いで**。

Uehara: Honto ni nanka fuan na n da kedo.
Doomoto: Daijoobu, daijoobu. Eto, toriaezu hiza ni.
Uehara: Chotto chotto matte. Koo deshoo? Kihon ga **natte-nai desu.**
Doomoto: Zasshi iroiro **gozaimasu kedo.**
Uehara: A nanka, moo chotto wakai ko ga miru yoona.
Doomoto: (*aru zasshi o watashi nagara*) Onegai shimasu.
Uehara: Chotto **kyoosei ka yo.**
Doomoto: (*Uehara no kami o mite*) Nagai naa. **Nagai de.**

Uehara: Really, I'm worried.
Doomoto: It's fine, it's all right. Uh, first, (putting this) on your lap.
Uehara: Wait, wait a minute. Isn't it this way? You don't know the basics at all.
Doomoto: There are several magazines here, Madam.
Uehara: Ah, do you have magazines for younger people?
Doomoto: (*handing her a magazine*) Please.

Uehara: Wait, are you forcing this on me?
Doomoto: (*looking at Uehara's long hair*) It's long. It's long, really.

In this conversation, both Doomoto and Uehara use casual style for the most part, but there are some notable mixtures of politeness levels and styles. Regarding the variations Doomoto uses, note (1) the supra-polite expression, *gozaimasu kedo*, and (2) the Kansai dialect *nagai de*, which would be *nagai ne*, or *nagai yo* in Tokyo speech. Doomoto is role-playing a hairstylist, so he chooses the supra-polite style, as if he were addressing a customer. A hair salon is a public space, and often requires formal speech. He also uses *nagai de*, which shows a contrast with the immediately preceding expression *nagai naa*. When Doomoto inserts the Kansai dialect, the viewer is reminded of his regional identity and his self-revealing attitude.

Uehara uses the variations (1) *natte-nai desu* and (2) *kyoosei ka yo*. *Natte-nai desu* goes against the ongoing casual style. This formal style is chosen in association with enacting a stylist-client role relationship at a hair salon. The style chosen in *kyoosei ka yo* is a challenge to what Doomoto is doing; for that purpose, the very blunt style stereotypically associated with more assertive "masculine" speech is useful. Conversational interaction is filled with many speech variations and varieties. Through the combination of all these, speakers express their emotion and their desire for empathy.

The Rhetoric of *Pathos*

The characteristics of the Japanese language discussed so far in Chapters 1 and 2 and other expressive features to be introduced in this book do not exist as a result of coincidence. Language usage is cohesive; it reflects certain underlying preferences and tendencies of the culture of which it is a part. In a series of earlier works (S. Maynard 1998b, 2000, 2001a, 2002), I have characterized these preferences in the Japanese language by the term "Rhetoric of *Pathos*." *Pathos*, along with its two other complementary elements, *logos* and *ethos*, are terms from Aristotelian rhetoric. In the classical sense, *logos* refers to rational arguments, and *ethos*, to the presentation of the speaker's character and personality, especially the person's reliability. *Pathos* refers to an appeal to the feelings of the audience. In Japanese, the importance of rhetoric is often placed on *pathos* and on the play of emotion in the partner's feelings.

I have made this point based on a variety of characteristics observed in the Japanese language and its use. For one, unlike the English language, which prefers to describe events in terms of an [agent-does] structure, the Japanese language prefers to express events in terms of a [topic-comment] relationship. The [agent-does] structure captures the event as action, that is, someone does something to someone. In the [topic-comment] structure, the speaker's personal emotion and attitude become relatively more prominent. In English, the [agent-does] structure is so strong that even the possession of something is expressed by it, as in "Tanaka has two children." In Japanese, an existential sentence is used instead, as in (*Tanaka-san ni wa*) *kodomo ga futari iru* '(As for Tanaka) there are two children'. In the Japanese version, the topic 'Tanaka' is introduced first, and the state related to Tanaka is offered as a (personal) comment.

The Rhetoric of *Pathos* also prefers, as Y. Ikegami (1981, 1991) points out, to describe events in terms of [something-becomes], rather than in terms of [agent-does]. An expression such as *Rokugatsu ni kekkon suru koto ni narimashita* 'It has become that we will be getting married in June' is a case in point. Instead of describing events as "an individual does something," in some situations, the Japanese language prefers to describe the event as "a state becomes." According to Jinnai (1998: 124), the *ni narimasu* expression is preferred by the general public as being soft, polite, and generally pleasing. Also, as is represented by the use of *kekkon suru koto*, there is a preference in Japanese toward nominalization of the event. The nominalized event readily provides a topic that, in turn, encourages personal commentary to follow. In this way Japanese expressions tend to avoid the rigid [agent-does] structure. Instead, sentences are often constructed with relatively fluid and shifting points of view, which ultimately foreground shared emotion and empathy.

Discourse organization follows the topic-comment order on paragraph as well as textual levels. An essay-like rhetorical movement, *ki-shoo-ten-ketsu*, also encourages shared feelings (see S. Maynard 1998a). Above all, discourse itself aims to create empathy on the basis of speaker's and partner's shared experience.

The Rhetoric of *Pathos* also reveals the fundamental force that pulls the Japanese language toward a certain point of view. In Japanese, there is a marked tendency to mistrust the persuasive potential of words. Language itself is not enough for communication; instead, shared feelings are assumed. In the Rhetoric of *Pathos*, the way to persuade others is not to argue outright, but to share a topic thrown into the discourse as a target of emotion. Speaker and partner, by sharing the emotional target from the same perspective, co-experience the feelings.

The language emerging here is a language of feelings, one that does not necessarily praise the persuasive argument. Unlike communication in which arguments are exchanged in a dialogue, Japanese rhetoric sometimes emerges as a confession of feelings not unlike a monologue. Certain utterances are not made to declare a position in opposition to a partner's. Rather, the Japanese speaker's sense of self is anchored privately, as if in a monologic world, but still the speaker reaches the partner through emotion and empathy. Once that monologic world has been shared, its interpretation is heavily dependent on the partner and the place of communication.

When a speaker of the Japanese language expresses thoughts and feelings in social interaction, it becomes important that he or she give regard to the partner so that the partner will co-experience emotion and empathy. Through dialogue the speaker and partner hope to draw closer and share the moment in empathy. For Japanese speakers, language serves to facilitate this co-experience of the world. This is so even when speaker and partner are in conflict. Solutions are often sought not so much through constructive criticism and persuasive argument in a dialogic process, as through emotional reconciliation.

Not to mislead the reader, I must emphasize that the Japanese language is perfectly capable of describing events as [agent-does], and in fact this structure occurs frequently. It predominates in such genres as legal documents, procedural manuals, news reports, research papers, and so on. The Japanese language is certainly capable of using logical and cohesive arguments to carry on a debate, for example. Occasionally Japanese is wrongly criticized for being "illogical." It is important to avoid the misunderstanding that the Japanese language lacks the capacity for logical discourse.

I must also emphasize that the Rhetoric of *Pathos* is not something that is available only in Japanese. Every language possesses emotion words, expressive strategies, and its Rhetoric of *Pathos*. Emotion and empathy are important ingredients of every human communication and social interaction.

Still, it is abundantly apparent that in ordinary Japanese discourse, the Rhetoric of *Pathos* is at work in significant ways. The Japanese language encourages certain forms of the Rhetoric of *Pathos*, and discourse as a whole makes it possible for speakers to share the kind of emotion and empathy encouraged by their community. When one looks at language from the perspective of *pathos*, often-ignored features stand out. The Rhetoric of *Pathos*, when applied to Japanese discourse, offers a constructive approach that enables students to focus on expressive Japanese and guides them to learn characteristics of the Japanese language that they have not fully explored before.

3
On Entries

Organization of Each Entry

Each entry is titled with an English cue. The cues are: (1) descriptions of feelings for which comparable Japanese expressions are presented; (2) specific communication functions associated with certain situations for which Japanese strategies are given; or (3) grammatical and interactional categories associated with different expressive strategies. Each English cue is followed by a list of Japanese key expressions, or occasionally a term related to the entry. These key expressions in Japanese are equivalent to or match, to various degrees, what is presented in the English cue. Primary and frequently used key expressions are presented for each entry. There is some overlap among cues, key expressions, and examples. (The reader is encouraged to refer to the indexes.) Some cross-references to other related entries accompany the examples for reference and review.

The main body of each entry consists of explanation and examples. In most cases, explanation is supplemented by two kinds of examples, my own and those taken from authentic sources. Almost all entries come with one or more of the 179 examples I have created; authentic examples, which total 479, appear in all entries. The authentic examples are helpful for understanding how the key expressions are used in context. All examples appear with situational information. Some are in dialogue form, while others are non-conversational written passages.

For those examples I have created, I give the following demographic information. Female speakers are identified as f1 and f2, and male speakers as m1 and m2. Each speaker is identified as c (child, 5–12 years old), t (teenage, 13–19 years old), y (young adult, 20–35 years old), a (mature adult, 36–65 years old) and s (senior, more than 65 years old). The speaker (my1), for example, is a young, adult male and the first speaker with that designation. The marking (my1a) is such a speaker's first speech in the conversation. The final letter indicates a speaker's turn and is used only when multiple turns are taken by the same speaker.

For each authentic example, the source is identified, and situational context is provided with specific speaker names. Authentic examples illustrate the context in which the expression is actually used, validating the explanation provided. Some entries come with a note or an additional information section containing information pertinent to the emotion words and expressive strategies under discussion. Supplemental examples also appear in these sections.

Japanese expressions are presented in the normal script, combining hiragana, katakana, and kanji. Sometimes the same phrase may appear in different scripts; this variation is conventionalized in the Japanese print media, and accordingly, I have used varied scripts. When the original text is accompanied by hiragana readings (*furigana* or *yomigana*), they are reproduced as they appear. Each sentence is followed by a *roomaji* transliteration. Romanization follows the Hepburn style, but has these slight variations: (1) long vowels are represented by double vowels; (2) the glottal stop is represented by *t* instead of a double consonant (*itchi* instead of *icchi*); and (3) syllabic *n,* when followed by a vowel, is presented as *n'* (*ren'ai*). The utterance-final glottal stop transcribed as a small *tsu* in Japanese is spelled out as *tt.* Japanese words in English follow the Romanization unless the words are conventionalized; accordingly, *Tookyo* appears in the Romanization but Tokyo in the English translation. In the transliteration, phrases are divided for convenience only. Each sentence is followed by an English translation. English translations are all mine, unless otherwise noted. When translating into English, I followed the original Japanese as closely as possible, but I do not intend my translation to be the only acceptable version. Other translations are certainly possible, and my translations are provided primarily to help clarify the meaning.

Sources of Authentic Examples

This book contains many examples taken from various genres. I have collected these examples with the purpose of conscientiously assembling a broad sample of what is available in contemporary Japanese discourse. Language becomes meaningful in a given situation. Without that specificity, explanation becomes vague and abstract. This is particularly true in the case of expressive Japanese. Because expressive Japanese communicates emotion and empathy, it is less effective if explained in abstract descriptive terms alone. Authentic examples show how expressive Japanese is used by specific speakers in particular situations.

By observing and interpreting expressive Japanese in multiple situations depicted in different genres, it is possible to gain insight into the patterns and characteristics of its use. The authentic examples contain the kinds of expressions with which the emotion words and expressive strategies under discussion frequently occur. Learning these expressions along with the specific expressive Japanese is important, because this is how the language is actually used. Through the repeated observation of similar situations, it is possible to increase one's understanding of how emotion words and expressive strategies help define the feelings that emerge in Japanese discourse.

Familiarizing yourself with authentic examples is also helpful for appreciating how the Japanese language is creatively (and sometimes playfully) used in real-life communication. In general the examples created by textbook writers are purposefully controlled, so they often lack variability, surprise, creativity, and boldness. To remedy that problem, for this volume I deliberately sought out real-life examples taken from authentic situations. The reader will find in many authentic examples lively voices of emotion that echo Japanese speakers' feelings.

I have chosen authentic examples from different genres available in the media. First, I draw examples from several television dramas. Twenty or so new dramas are aired four times a year, depicting various aspects of Japanese lives, among them romance, family, business, crime, and school situations. The social significance of these dramas is evident. They are reported in various media events that include press releases well in advance and photo events introducing starring actors/actresses. Their ratings are carefully followed and reported in media-related magazines and on Internet Web sites.

Obviously language spoken in drama is not the kind that naturally occurs. But the language used in popular television dramas is a part of the speech culture, a speech created for mass consumption, and is indeed shared among the masses. Mizuhara (1999) mentions that among all forms of drama, television dramas most resemble ordinary speech (compared to plays and movies), although with the caveat that differences between ordinary speech and dramatic discourse always exist. Kumagai (2003) also recognizes the advantages of using television dramas for the study of Japanese language and comments on the usefulness of the contemporary television dramas I analyzed in S. Maynard (2001a). Koyano (1996) points out that the relationship between natural speech and speech used in Japanese contemporary television drama is bidirectional, with one influencing the other.

The actual speech appearing in a drama results from decisions made by multiple players—playwright, director, producer, and actors. Their decisions are often based on how the naturalness and easiness of the speech will be readily understood by the general audience. Language in a televised drama is thus both influenced by and sensitive to ordinary speech. Because of the close association between the language of television dramas and ordinary language, many of the examples taken from dramas in this book offer a rich source for expressive Japanese.

I have also chosen four popular teleision variety shows. First is *SMAP x SMAP,* a variety show featuring the five-man singer/dancer group SMAP. The two shows I have chosen were aired live with minimum editing, and the men in the group were in their mid- to late twenties at the time. Some of the speech samples are representative of speech variations typically used by young men, as members of SMAP address other members of the group, guests, the studio audience of two-hundred female fans, and the general television audience. Second, from the television reality-variety show *Ainori* I have selected two specific episodes. *Ainori* documents how people in their mid- to late twenties interact (particularly in love relationships) during their around-the-world tour in a van. Their casual talk is a good linguistic sampling of young adults' speech. Third are two episodes from a celebrity-and-guest variety show, *Doomoto Tsuyoshi no shoojiki shindoi.* In this program, Tsuyoshi Doomoto (age 24) invites guests from the entertainment industry and interacts with them. He mixes the Kansai dialect in his speech, and his language represents that of young adults. The last television program, *Santaku,* was chosen from the television talk show genre. *Santaku* is a program in which two celebrities, Sanma Akashiya (age 48) and Takuya Kimura (age 30), chat, play, and otherwise publicly act out their friendship.

From the entertainment-oriented print media come different kinds of comics. Comics are known to contain emotionally tense moments. Although the language in comics differs from naturally occurring language, it has its advantages. Select visual signs accompanying verbal expressions provide useful contextual information for understanding expressive Japanese. I also cite different kinds of novels—romance novels, mystery novels, and general novels. In these genres, emotion words and expressive strategies tend to appear less frequently. When the narrator tells the story, and when direct quotations appear, useful examples can be found. For very advanced students, *Kanjoo hyoogen jiten* by Akira Nakamura (1979) offers a Japanese dictionary of emotion words collected from modern Japanese novels.

Among published dialogues, I have chosen *taidan* interviews (printed in a magazine). The *taidan* is an up-close and personal interview in which revelations into the character of the person being interviewed are expected. Because it is a written and published record, it does not directly reflect naturally occurring conversation. Those interviewed, however, include people of different generations with varied backgrounds, and their speech styles provide a useful resource.

I have also made use of essays, nonfiction, and newspaper articles. First I collected short essays written by several contemporary writers from magazines. Many of these essays are written in a speechlike style, and it is not difficult to find expressive strategies in them. Then I selected a collection of essays by a novelist/essayist, in which the author emphasizes the importance of human emotions. I also quote from nonfiction in which the writer reports on his (dangerous) trip abroad and shares his thoughts and feelings about various scenes and events.

As for newspaper articles, I have taken articles available on-line, reporting the collision of two vessels that occurred in early 2001. Because of the tragedy involved, emotions play an important part in these news reports. In addition, I collected some examples from the bulletin boards of Internet Web sites, where emotional messages are abundant.

Because examples from a single novel or a movie, or a single speaker or a writer, for that matter, would probably show only a limited use of the Japanese language, I was at pains to collect examples from a variety of sources. It is impossible to observe every possible use, however, so I have made a conscientious effort to collect representative samples that should be useful for pedagogical purposes from contemporary ordinary Japanese language.

In each entry, authentic examples are presented in the same order as key expressions. When many examples are associated with the same key expression, they are presented in the order in which the sources have been enumerated above. The one exception is that examples from Internet bulletin boards are placed before all others.

Some of the works have published English translations, which I used whenever available. For television dramas, comics, and novels, summary plots with main characters are provided in the Appendix. Also included in the Appendix is a brief description of each data source, along with detailed information regarding media sources and publishers. Throughout this book, authentic sources are specified by title (for television dramas, television variety shows, novels, nonfiction), by dialogue number (for interview dialogues), or by writer's last name (for essays).

All sources from which I draw examples are well known in the Japanese media and publishing industry. It is not difficult to obtain additional information on these sources through published books, comic books, videotapes, DVDs, and Internet Web sites. Television stations' Web sites lead you to drama series and variety shows, and comic books host their own Web sites. Novels, comics, and related materials are widely available at bookstores and dot-com bookstore sites. Videotapes and DVDs of television dramas are available for purchase at video outlets and dot-com stores. Emotion words and expressive strategies contained in this book appear frequently in other related (and unrelated) works of similar genres as well. Students interested in finding other examples or students prepared to study other samples of discourse should explore the many works available in the Japanese media.

Terms Related to Intimacy, Social Territory, and Self-Revelation

When discussing expressive Japanese, it is perhaps useful to consider three interlocking aspects, namely, the sense of intimacy, the concept of social territory, and ways of revealing oneself in relation to the partner. These aspects intermingle with how emotion and empathy are expressed and shared, and it is always a good idea to gauge these elements of human relationships when revealing feelings and attitude.

First, the sense of intimacy is often experienced in Japanese as *amae* 'sweet dependency', which refers to a psychological and emotional sense of dependency. *Amae* is etymologically related to *amai* 'sweet' and refers to sweet, tender, and all-forgiving (parental, particularly mother's) love. *Amae* is the warm, all-accepting, dependent relationship Japanese people enjoy with intimates. It is felt not only in childhood, but, more important, throughout a person's lifetime.

Amae above all involves the desire to be (passively) cared for by another. At least two persons must be involved; one to seek dependence, and the other to accept it. Once the *amae* relationship has been established, one can be selfish and dependent, yet still be accepted and forgiven. *Amae* can be seen as a kind of social contract that allows emotions to be freely expressed with approval and tolerance. When such a relationship is recognized by both parties, their interaction changes. For example, interactional particles are frequently used, familiar and friendly vocatives appear, and a somewhat selfish way of demanding is likely to be accepted. *Amae* promotes certain emotion words and expressive strategies, and *amae*-seeking expressions further reinforce and nurture the intimate relationship.

While the desire for intimacy is a common human experience, most people also want to maintain a certain distance. Dependency on others conflicts with the desire for independence. The sense of *amae* nurtured among Japanese speakers comes in various varieties and intensities. Although not everyone finds comfort in being dependent to the same degree, the *amae* relationship is common enough to be useful for understanding expressive Japanese.

The concept of social territory is also important in expressive Japanese. The style and manner in which one expresses emotion and empathy often depend on awareness of social territory. Traditionally, two territories are recognized, *uchi* and *soto*.

Uchi 'in, inside, internal, private, hidden' and *soto* 'out, outside, external, public, exposed' refer to social and psychological spaces identified among Japanese speakers. Speakers belonging to an identical group usually consider themselves *uchi* members. In fact, Japanese speakers refer to their work affiliation as *uchi no kaisha* 'our company', for example. Also, as a self-referencing term, *uchira* 'we, the members of a group' is used, implying the significance of group unity. *Uchi* members share a sense of intimacy and are likely to use expressive Japanese more freely among themselves.

Speakers outside the *uchi* group are *soto* persons. Japanese speakers tend to use more formal and distant expressions toward *soto* persons. For example, when a person meets someone new who represents an unfamiliar company, this someone is a *soto* person, and is spoken to formally.

All cultures offer methods (linguistic and other) for distinguishing between those who are familiar and those who are not. But for Japanese speakers, whether or not the partner is an *uchi* member is important. Choice of style largely depends on the *uchi/soto* distinction. Many features of expressive Japanese are more frequently and extensively used among *uchi* members. And using emotive words and expressive strategies enhances the sense of belonging to the same social territory. As a result, expressive Japanese can be a tool for increasing intimacy and for enhancing the sense of *uchi* membership.

The *uchi* and *soto* worlds are by no means fixed. For example, at a party held for graduates of the same university, everyone considers himself or herself an *uchi* member. But among these, those who used to belong to the same association (say, a skiing club) during the same year consider themselves *uchi* members and the others *soto* members. The style and the manner in which one communicates depend on multiple *uchi* and *soto* spaces that fluctuate depending on the immediate context of the situation.

In human interaction, emotion may override established social conventions, so that some emotion words and expressive strategies can sometimes be used toward strangers. The relationship between social territory and use of expressive Japanese is not necessarily predetermined. It fluctuates and is manipulated as well.

As for self-revelation, the Japanese speaker who both feels intimate with the partner and locates himself or herself in the same social territory is most likely to express true feelings. Where the relationship is one of trust, people naturally reveal more of their inner selves than otherwise.

Japanese speakers are known to distinguish between *tatemae* 'principles, public face' and *honne* '(private) true thought and feelings'. *Tatemae* is something that a person should follow based on conventionalized principles and social expectations. *Honne*, however, is what lies deep in one's heart. It refers in particular to a person's inside and to what a person truly thinks and feels. For speakers of the Japanese language, it is important to maintain *tatemae* in many public situations, but it is equally important to express *honne* to people who share intimacy and social territory.

Expressive Japanese often reveals *honne*, the emotion usually closely guarded in one's heart. Of course, a speaker may use emotion words and expressive strategies as a manipulative tool implying different levels of *tatemae* and *honne*. People may, for example, pretend to be drunk and reveal emotion straightforwardly even when that kind of act is inappropriate and not easily tolerated by the recipient. It is also true that people lie by insisting that they are revealing *honne*. Nonetheless, the distinction between *tatemae* and *honne* is sensitively associated with how one goes about sharing emotion and empathy.

II

Emotion

4

When Deeply Moved

1. Being Emotional and Being Moved

Key Expressions

感情	*kanjoo*	feelings, emotion
感情的	*kanjooteki*	emotional
情が深い	*joo ga fukai*	having deep feelings of compassion and love, caring deeply
(≈) 感動した	*Kandoo shita.*	I was moved.
感動的	*kandooteki*	moving
感激！	*Kangeki!*	Deeply touched/moved!
ジーンとする	*jiin to suru*	to experience deep surging emotion
しみじみ	*shimijimi*	with deep fond feelings

Explanation

Kanjoo 'feelings, emotion' is one of the most frequently used descriptive terms when referring to human emotions. *Kanjooteki* 'emotional' is usually used in the negative sense of being "too emotional." *Joo ga fukai* describes a person who is emotionally sensitive and who has a deep sense of compassion and love.

When deeply moved, one may specify one's feelings by commenting, for example, on how beautiful the scenery was or how sad the story turned out to be. However, when the speaker wants to convey the overall feeling of being moved or touched, the phrases *kandoo* 'being moved' (as in *kandoo suru* 'to be deeply moved' and *kandooteki* 'emotionally moving') and *kangeki* 'being deeply moved' are useful. These phrases describe an overall feeling that something is moving and poignant. The speaker may use *Kangeki!* as an interjection to reveal directly how moved he or she is.

Onomatopoeic and mimetic adverbs, including *jiin to* and *shimijimi*, are also used to describe how deeply one is moved. *Jiin to* 'with deep, surging emotion' is an adverbial phrase that describes the deep, moving emotion that pierces and resounds through one's heart. *Shimijimi* 'with deep fond feelings' is related to the verb *shimiru* 'to soak, to seep into', and it refers to emotion that soaks and fills one's heart deeply and quietly. It is often associated with longing for something that no longer exists.

Examples

a. (Two friends talking about a common acquaintance)

(fa1): あの人はすぐ**感情的**になるんです。
(ma1): 困りましたねえ。問題が解決できなくて。

(fa1): Ano hito wa sugu **kanjooteki** ni naru n desu. (see E. 72 for *n desu*)
(ma1): Komarimashita nee. Mondai ga kaiketsu deki-naku te. (see E. 18 for *komarimashita*; E. 63 about sentence-final [V/Adj-*te*])

(fa1): He gets emotional right away.
(ma1): That is a problem. We can't find a solution to the problem.

b. (≈) あいつは頭がいいだけでなく、**情が深くて**いいやつだよ。

Aitsu wa atama ga ii dake de naku, **joo ga fukakute** ii yatsu da yo. (see E. 30 for *aitsu* and *yatsu*)

He is not only brilliant, but also very compassionate; he's a really nice guy.

c. (Two young friends talking about a movie they saw)

(≈fy1a): 結局ふたりは別れてしまったのね。
(≈fy2a): かわいそうだったわね。
(≈fy1b): ええ。
(≈fy2b): あの別れのシーンのふたりの姿には**ジーンときちゃった**。
(≈fy1c): **感動的**だったねえ、ほんとに。
(≈fy2c): 愛と別れについて**しみじみ**考えさせられる映画だったわねえ。

(≈fy1a): Kekkyoku futari wa wakarete-shimatta no ne. (see E. 17 for *wakarete-shimatta*)
(≈fy2a): Kawaisoo datta wa ne. (see E. 61 for *kawaisoo*)
(≈fy1b): Ee.
(≈fy2b): Ano wakare no shiin no futari no sugata ni wa **jiin to kichatta.** (see E. 28 for *futari*)

(≈fy1c): **Kandooteki** datta nee, honto ni. (see E. 48 about inverted word order)
(≈fy2c): Ai to wakare ni tsuite **shimijimi** kangaesaserareru eiga datta wa nee.

(≈fy1a): So, after all, the two went separate ways.
(≈fy2a): Poor things.
(≈fy1b): Indeed.
(≈fy2b): I was emotionally overwhelmed when I saw them in that parting scene.
(≈fy1c): It was really moving (and poignant), wasn't it?
(≈fy2c): It was a movie that made you think deeply about love and separation.

Authentic Examples

a. (Taken from BBS for *Beautiful Life*)

すっごい**感動しました**。

Suggoi **kandoo shimashita**. (see E. 24 about *suggoi*)

I was extremely moved.

ほんとに**感動的でした**。

Honto ni **kandooteki deshita**.

It was indeed moving.

最高の**感動**！

Saikoo no **kandoo**! (see E. 23 for *saikoo*)

Utmost sense of being moved!

感動と切なさで何と言ったらいいのかわかりませんが。

Kandoo to setsunasa de nan to ittara ii no ka wakarimasen ga. (see E. 31 for *setsunasa*; E. 53 about the difficulty of expressing one's feelings in words)

Deeply moved and making the heart ache—I'm not quite sure how to put it into words.

ジーンときました。

Jiin to kimashita.

I was profoundly moved.

b. (Taken from *Taiga no itteki*, 144)

しかし、ぼくは、**感情**というのはものすごく大事なことだと思うのです。**感情**のない人間といったら、これはロボットですから。人間は**感情**が豊かなほうがいいと思う。喜び、悲しみ、怒り、さびしがり、そして笑い、そういうふうな**感情**ができるだけ幅ひろく、いきいきと豊かにある人のほうが人間らしい、という気持ちをもっています。

Shikashi, boku wa, **kanjoo** to yuu no wa monosugoku daijina koto da to omou no desu. **Kanjoo** no nai ningen to ittara, kore wa robotto desu kara. Ningen wa **kanjoo** ga yutakana hoo ga ii to omou. Yorokobi, kanashimi, ikari, sabishigari, soshite warai, soo yuu fuuna **kanjoo** ga dekirudake haba hiroku, ikiiki to yutaka ni aru hito no hoo ga ningen rashii, to yuu kimochi o motteimasu. (see E. 24 for *sugoku*; E. 47 for *to ittara*, E. 5 for *yorokobi*; E. 7 for *kanashimi*)

But I think emotion is something that is very important. A person without emotion is a robot. To me, human beings are better off having rich emotions. I have a feeling that a person is more humane who has as wide a range of emotions as possible—joy, sadness, anger, loneliness, and laughter—and who has rich and vivid emotions.

c. (Taken from *Himawari nikki*, 197) Konomi's boyfriend, Satoo, tells Konomi how much he was moved when he found out about the group of students in charge of growing flowers.

「ああ、あの子達は、この花のために、土まみれになってがんばってたんだ……。そう思ったら、なんか、すげー**カンドーして**…。(…)」

"Aa, ano kotachi wa, kono hana no tami ni, tsuchimamire ni natte ganbatteta n da…… Soo omottara, nanka, sugee **kandoo shite**… (…)" (see E. 62 for *nanka*; E. 24 and Chapter 2 for *sugee*)

"Wow, those students were working hard getting themselves dirty, all for these flowers. When I thought so, I was really moved. (…)"

d. (Taken from interview #82, with Masashi Sada, musician) Sada mentions that he was moved by a message delivered to him from a popular female singer.

さだ：　コンサートを終えてホテルへ戻ったら百恵ちゃんからメッセージが届いてた。「やっと、この歌をさださんがつくってくださった気持ちがわかる日がきました。本当にありがとうございました。山口百恵」って。**感動した**。

林：　まあ、いいお話。

Sada: Konsaato o oete hoteru e modottara Momoe-chan kara messeeji ga todoiteta. "Yatto, kono uta o Sada-san ga tsukutte-kudasatta kimochi ga wakaru hi ga kimashita. Hontoo ni arigatoo gozaimashita. Yamaguchi Momoe" tte. **Kandoo shita.**

Hayashi: Maa, ii ohanashi.

Sada: When I returned to the hotel after my concert, there was a message from Momoe. It said, "Finally the day has arrived when I understand how you felt when you composed this song for me. Thank you so much." I was deeply moved.

Hayashi: Wow! What a wonderful story!

e. (Taken from *Taiga no itteki,* 173)

最近、ある医師のかたから、とても**感動的な**、そして不思議な話をききました。

Saikin, aru ishi no kata kara, totemo **kandootekina,** soshite fushigina hanashi o kikimashita.

Recently I heard, from a medical doctor, a very strange and moving story.

f. (Taken from *Kitchin*, 50 [English translation, 32]) As she meets someone she knew before, the narrator realizes that much time has passed.

彼も年を取ったなあ。と私は**しみじみ**思う。これじゃあおばあちゃんも死ぬはずだわ。

Kare mo toshi o totta naa. To watashi wa **shimijimi** omou. Kore jaa obaachan mo shinu hazu da wa. (see E. 56 for *mo*)

I felt very keenly how old he had become. (There is no translation for the third sentence in *Kitchen,* which I render as "No wonder my grandmother has died.")

Additional Information

The following list provides additional vocabulary associated with *joo* 'feelings, emotion'.

情	*joo*	feelings, emotion
情が移る	*joo ga utsuru*	(lit. infected feelings) to become emotionally attached to, often due to familiarity
情に厚い	*joo ni atsui*	(lit. thick feelings) very empathetic
情にもろい	*joo ni moroi*	(lit. emotionally fragile) to have a tender heart, sentimental
情け深い	*nasakebukai*	sympathetic, merciful

愛情	*aijoo*	love, affection
同情	*doojoo*	sympathy, compassion
人情	*ninjoo*	warm human feelings
友情	*yuujoo*	friendship

2. Moved to Tears

Key Expressions

涙	*namida*	tears
(≈) 泣いた	*Naita.*	I cried.
ポロポロ（と）	*poroporo (to)*	with teardrops
(≈) ウルウル	*uruuru*	with eyes filled with tears
(≈) 目頭が熱くなった	*Megashira ga atsuku natta*	Warm tears welled up in my eyes.

Explanation

Feelings associated with tears are multiple and sometimes contradictory. They extend from sadness to anger, joy, and compassion. Phrases associated with crying and tears are used to describe a state of being overwhelmingly touched and moved. Mimetic and onomatopoeic words associated with *namida* 'tears' are often used to describe the specifics of the condition.

Expressions such as *poroporo* (*to*) 'with teardrops' and *uruuru* 'with eyes filled with tears' are the representative ones. *Poroporo* is a mimetic word describing small pieces or drops falling down one after another. If there is only one tear drop involved, the phrase *poro-tt* or *porori* is used. *Uruuru* is also a mimetic word that describes eyes filled with tears. Originally used in comics, it now appears in ordinary language as well.

When tears begin to well up in one's eyes, or when one is moved to tears, the experience is described as *megashira ga atsuku naru* (lit., eyelids [close to one's nose] become hot). *Megashira ga atsuku naru* is an idiomatic expression that the speaker uses to express the deep emotion which brings him or her to tears, as in *Sono hanashi o kiite megashira ga atsuku natta* 'That story brought tears to my eyes'.

Examples

a. (Two girls discussing their friend Emi)

(≈ft1a): 恵美ちゃんね、偉い先生にすごくほめられてね。それで、感激して泣き出しちゃったんだって。

(≈ft2a): そうなんだ。
(≈ft1b): **涙ポロポロ**流して。
(≈ft2b): へえ。そんなに感動したの。

(≈ft1a): Emi-chan ne, erai sensei ni sugoku homerarete ne. Sorede, kangeki shite **nakidashichatta** n datte. (see E. 1 for *kangeki shite*)
(≈ft2a): Soo na n da. (see E. 46 for *Soo na n da*)
(≈ft1b): **Namida poroporo** nagashite.
(≈ft2b): Hee. Sonna ni kandoo shita no. (see E. 21 for *Hee*; E. 16 for *sonna ni*; E. 1 for *kandoo shita*)

(≈ft1a): Emi was praised a lot by a well-respected teacher. And, she was so moved, she began to cry, I heard.
(≈ft2a): I see.
(≈ft1b): She was in tears.
(≈ft2b): Wow. She was that much moved, I see.

b. (≈) 親子が再会するシーンを見ていたら、目頭が熱くなった。

Oyako ga saikai suru shiin o miteitara, **megashira ga atsuku natta.**

When I was watching the scene where the parents and the child were reunited, warm tears began to well up in my eyes.

Authentic Examples

a. (Taken from BBS for *Beautiful Life*) These "crying" and "with tears" phrases express how much viewers were moved.

泣けちゃった。

Nakechatta.

I cried.

大泣きしました。

Oonaki shimashita.

I cried a big cry.

マジ**泣きました。**

Maji **nakimashita.** (see E. 67 for *maji*)

Seriously, I cried.

思いっきり**泣きました。**

Omoikkiri **nakimashita.**

I cried to my heart's content.

ポロポロと涙が出てきちゃった。

Poroporo to namida ga dete-kichatta.

Tears came out drop after drop.

感動**ウルウル**。(see E. 1 for *kandoo*)

Kandoo **uruuru.**

Moved with tears.

目が**ウルウル**しています。

Me ga **uruuru** shiteimasu.

My eyes are filled with tears.

涙、涙、涙。

Namida, namida, namida.

Tears, tears, tears.

b. (Taken from *Ren'ai hakusho*, 14: 53) Kaho's boyfriend doesn't understand her, and Kaho describes how sadness is surging in her heart. Kaho narrates the story in a casual spoken style, as if she were directly talking to the reader.

こみあげてきた感情が**涙**に変わって、瞳から、どっと溢れてくる。
ひどい。
ひどいよ。

Komiagete-kita kanjoo ga **namida** ni kawatte, hitomi kara, dotto afurete-kuru. (see E. 1 for *kanjoo*)
Hidoi. (see E. 7 for *hidoi*)
Hidoi yo. (see E. 24 about repetition; E. 55 about the use and non-use of *yo*)

The emotion surging in my heart transformed into tears, and they are pouring out of my eyes.
Awful.
It's really awful.

c. (Taken from *Kitchin*, 11 [English translation, 7]) The narrator describes a boy named Yuuichi Tanabe.

焼香しながら彼は、**泣きはらした**瞳をとじて手をふるわせ、祖母の遺影を見ると、また**ぽろぽろと涙をこぼした。**

Shookoo shinagara kare wa, **nakiharashita** hitomi o tojite te o furuwase, sobo no iei o miru to, mata **poroporo to namida o koboshita.**

His hands trembled as he lit the incense; his eyes were swollen from crying. When he saw my grandmother's picture on the altar, again his tears fell like rain.

d. (Taken from *Ren'ai hakusho*, 14: 56) Kaho wants her boyfriend to understand her.

でも、あたしには、とっても大切なことだって。
翼くんに、わかってほしかったから。
そう思ったら。
なんだか、**目頭がじわっと熱くなる。**

Demo, atashi ni wa, tottemo taisetsuna koto da tte.
Tubasa-kun ni, wakatte-hoshikatta kara.
Soo omottara.
Nandaka, **megashira ga jiwa tto atsuku naru.**

But, for me, it is a very important thing.
I wanted Tsubasa to understand that.
I thought so, and then.
I feel warm tears welling up in my eyes.

e. (Taken from *Jisshuusen chinbotsu*, Feb. 17, 2001) The father of one of the students who was lost at sea expresses his anger toward the submarine's captain.

怒りがおさまらぬといった表情で話し始めた亮介さんだったが、祐介君が世界各地の紛争に悲しむような「心のやさしい子だった」と話すうちに、声を詰まらせて**涙**をぬぐった。

Ikari ga osamara-nu to itta hyoojoo de hanashi hajimeta Ryoosuke-san datta ga, Yuusuke-kun ga sekai kakuchi no funsoo ni kanashimu yoona "kokoro no yasashii ko datta" to hanasu uchi ni, koe o tsumarasete **namida** o nugutta. (see E. 7 for *kanashimu*; E. 6 for *yasashii*)

Ryoosuke began to speak with an expression on his face showing unstoppable anger, but as he went on to say that Yuusuke was a "tenderhearted son" who was saddened by world conflicts, he choked up and wiped off his tears.

3. Heartfelt Emotion

Key Expressions

(v) 胸キュン	mune kyun	heart-aching
(≈) 胸が一杯になった	*Mune ga ippai ni natta.*	I was filled with emotion.
胸がときめく	mune ga tokimeku	to be thrilled, to feel one's heart throb with joy and anticipation

心あたたまる	kokoro atatamaru	heartwarming
心がふるえる	kokoro ga furueru	heart-trembling (with deep emotion)
心に残る	kokoro ni nokoru	to stay/remain (for a long time) in one's heart

Explanation

Mune '(lit.) chest' and *kokoro* 'heart' (in the emotional and spiritual sense) are two words closely associated with emotion. Unlike *hara* 'belly', which is often associated with anger, *mune* and *kokoro* connote overwhelming feelings of being touched and moved.

Mune kyun is a phrase that comes from *mune ga kyun to naru/suru* '(lit.) the chest is aching'. *Kyun* points to a sharp pang in the heart that has a connotation of sadness and heartache. *Mune kyun* means a sharp, aching feeling and is used primarily by young people in casual speech, although *Mune ga kyun to naru* 'My heart is aching' is more widely used. *Mune ga ippai ni naru* '(lit.) one's chest is filled to the rim' expresses a feeling of having one's heart overfilled with emotion. *Mune ga tokimeku* (also *kokoro ga tokimeku*) refers to an emotion (often associated with romance) so thrilling that one can almost feel the heart palpitate or throb with anticipation and excitement.

Kokoro refers to many things, including mind, heart, soul, and spirit, and it is used in many ways for describing emotion. Among the phrases associated with *kokoro*, *kokoro (ga) atatamaru* is frequently used for describing a general heartwarming sense of goodness. When a person is deeply moved and touched, *kokoro ga furueru* is used to communicate the heart that trembles with emotion, and *kokoro ni nokoru* is used to express an emotion etched deep in one's heart.

Examples

a. (Two girls talking about the movie they just saw)

(vft1): あの映画の別れのシーン、**胸キュン**だったね。
(≈ft2): そうだね、愛し合ってたのにね。**心に残る**シーンよね。

(vft1): Ano eiga no wakare no shiin, **mune kyun** datta ne. (see E. 35 for *wakare*)
(≈ft2): Soo da ne, aishiatteta noni ne. **Kokoro ni nokoru** shiin yo ne. (see E. 32 for *aishiau*)

(vft1): The parting scene of that movie, that made my heart ache, did it yours?
(≈ft2): Sure did. They were in love, you know. That scene certainly will stay in my heart.

b. (≈) 結婚式でうれしそうな親友の姿を見ていたら、幸せで**胸が一杯になった。**

Kekkonshiki de ureshisoona shin'yuu no sugata o miteitara, shiawase de **mune ga ippai ni natta.** (see E. 5 for *shiawase*)

When I was watching my best friend being delightedly happy at the wedding, I was filled with an overwhelming sense of happiness.

c. (≈) あしたはいよいよ恋人が帰ってくると思うと、**胸がときめく。**

Ashita wa iyoiyo koibito ga kaette-kuru to omou to, **mune ga tokimeku.** (see E. 31 for *koibito*)

When I think that tomorrow my boyfriend is coming home, I can feel my heart throbbing with joy and anticipation.

d. (Two female friends commenting on the talk they heard at a meeting)

(fa1a): **心あたたまる**お話でしたね。
(fa2a): ほんとに。感動的でした。
(fa1b): ええ。
(fa2b): 特に最後が感動的で、**胸が一杯になってしまって。**

(fa1a): **Kokoro atatamaru** ohanashi deshita ne.
(fa2a): Honto ni. Kandooteki deshita. (see E. 1 for *kandooteki*)
(fa1b): Ee.
(fa2b): Toku ni saigo ga kandooteki de, **mune ga ippai ni natte-shimatte.** (see E. 17 for *natte-shimatte*)

(fa1a): It was a heartwarming story, wasn't it?
(fa2a): Indeed. It was very moving.
(fa1b): Yes.
(fa2b): Especially the last part was moving, and I was simply filled with emotion.

Authentic Examples

a. (Taken from BBS for *Beautiful Life*)

胸がきゅーっとなった。

Mune ga kyuu tto natta.

I felt my aching heart (lit., chest).

胸がしめつけられるぐらいステキでした。

Mune ga shimetsukerareru gurai suteki deshita. (see E. 13 for *suteki*)

It was so wonderfully moving that I felt my chest squeezed (with emotion).

胸がつまる想いで見ていました。

Mune ga tsumaru omoi de miteimashita.

I was watching (the drama) with the feeling of my whole chest filled with emotion.

胸が苦しかった。

Mune ga kurushikatta.

I felt choked up with emotion.

心に残る最後でした。

Kokoro ni nokoru saigo deshita.

The ending (of the drama) was so moving that it will stay in my heart.

心が洗われる話でした。

Kokoro ga arawareru hanashi deshita.

It was a story purifying my heart. (*Arawareru* literally means 'to be washed'.)

心のふるえを感じました。

Kokoro no furue o kanjimashita.

I felt my heart tremble.

b. (Taken from interview #82, with Masashi Sada, musician) The following appears as a comment Hayashi makes after the interview.

私の年代ですと、あの歌、あのメロディー、すべて青春とオーバーラップしてご本人とお会いして**胸がキュンとなる**のであります。

Watashi no nendai desu to, ano uta, ano merodii, subete seishun to oobaarappu shite gohonnin to oaishite **mune ga kyun to naru** no dearimasu.

Commenting from the perspective of my generation, I must say that each song and melody of his reminds me of my youth, and when I see the very musician who created it, my heart aches with nostalgia (I feel a pang in my heart with nostalgia).

c. (Taken from *Ren'ai hakusho*, 14: 12) Kaho describes her feelings at the time of the junior high school graduation ceremony.

『蛍の光』を聴いてたら、なんだか、**胸がぐっときちゃった。**

"Hotaru no hikari" o kiitetara, nandaka, **mune ga gutto kichatta.** (see E. 17 for *kichatta*)

When I was listening to "Auld Lang Syne," I was overwhelmed with a strong emotion grabbing my chest.

d. (Taken from *Himawari nikki*, 217) Konomi narrates the following as if talking directly to the reader. Note the use of *kokoro no ito no hibiki* and *kokoro o furuwaseru*, both of which refer to *kokoro* for describing feelings of being moved.

それでも、がんばって、目をふさいでしまわないで。
あなたの**心の糸の響き**を、聞いて。
あなたの**心を、震わせて**くれるものを探して。
きっと、どこかにあるから——。

Soredemo, ganbatte, me o fusaide-shimawa-naide.
Anata no **kokoro no ito no hibiki** o, kiite.
Anata no **kokoro o, furuwasete**-kureru mono o sagashite.
Kitto, dokoka ni aru kara—.

Even then, please do your best and don't close your eyes to the hardship.
Listen for the sound of the strings in your heart.
Look for something that makes your heart tremble.
Surely, you will find that something somewhere (in your reach).

e. (Taken from Shooji 2003b, 56) In an essay titled *Moriawase no shisoo to wa* (The thought of combination platter), the writer comments on how much he likes the combination platter by the phrase *kokoro ga tokimeku.*

「盛り合わせ」は**心がときめく。**
居酒屋に入って、「エート、何にしようか」と、アゴに手を当ててメニューを見ていく。

"Moriawase" wa **kokoro ga tokimeku.**
Izakaya ni haitte, "Eeto, nan ni shiyoo ka" to, ago ni te o atete menyuu o mite-iku.

"Combination platter" makes my heart throb.
I go into a pub, and I look at the menu with my hand placed under the chin, thinking, "Let me see, what should I order?"

f. (Taken from *Taiga no itteki*, 21) The author explains how a ray of hope becomes increasingly meaningful when one is in despair.

＜旱天の慈雨＞という言葉があるが、からからにひび割れ、乾ききった大地だからこそ降りそそぐ一滴の雨水が甘露と感じられるのだ。暗黒のなかだからこそ、一点の遠い灯に**心がふるえる**のである。

"Kanten no jiu" to yuu kotoba ga aru ga, karakara ni hibiware, kawakikitta daichi da kara koso furisosogu itteki no amamizu ga kanro to kanjirareru no da. Ankoku no naka da kara koso, itten no tooi hi ni **kokoro ga furueru** no dearu. (see E. 72 about the *no da* expression)

There is an expression, "Mercy rains down at the time of drought." A drop of rain becomes a sweet dewdrop because the land is cracked, dry, and completely arid. Because it is in total darkness that a single distant light makes one's heart tremble.

Additional Information

The following list provides additional vocabulary associated with *mune* 'chest' and *kokoro* 'heart'.

胸が熱くなる	*mune ga atsuku naru*	to feel one's chest heated with emotion, to be moved
胸が痛む	*mune ga itamu*	to feel the heart ache, to feel pain
胸が裂ける	*mune ga sakeru*	to feel the heart torn, to feel the heart split in half (with sadness)
胸が騒ぐ	*mune ga sawagu*	to feel uneasy (with a feeling that something bad may happen)
胸をふくらませる	*mune o fukuramaseru*	to feel one's chest filled with hope and anticipation
胸を焦がす	*mune o kogasu*	to burn one's chest with yearning and longing
心が洗われる	*kokoro ga arawareru*	to feel one's heart washed, to feel purified
心が軽い	*kokoro ga karui*	the heart is bouncing; to feel positive, optimistic, and happy

心が通う	*kokoro ga kayou*	to communicate heart to heart
心が乱れる	*kokoro ga midareru*	to feel one's heart in turmoil, to be filled with a thousand thoughts and feelings
心が沈む	*kokoro ga shizumu*	to have a sinking heart
心を開く	*kokoro o hiraku*	to open one's heart
心を奪われる	*kokoro o ubawareru*	to have one's heart stolen
心を動かす	*kokoro o ugokasu*	to move someone, to touch someone's heart
心を打たれる	*kokoro o utareru*	to feel the heart tapped, to be touched, to be deeply moved
心を許す	*kokoro o yurusu*	to open and share one's heart with someone else

4. Moved with Exclamatives

Key Expressions

なんとあの人が来るとは！	*Nanto ano hito ga kuru to wa!*	Boy, what a surprise that he came!
(≈) なんて素晴らしいんだろう	*Nante subarashii n daroo!*	How wonderful it is!
(≈) その子の親はどんなに心配だろう	*Sono ko no oya wa donna ni shinpai daroo.*	How worried that child's parents must be!
(≈) 立派になったものだ	*Rippa ni natta mono da.*	(He) sure has become great, indeed!
みんな元気でありがたいことです	*Minna genki de arigatai koto desu.*	It sure is fortunate that everyone is in good health.
よく食べること！	*Yoku taberu koto!*	Does he ever eat!

Explanation

The interjection *nanto* 'surprise! unbelievably! believe it or not! guess what!' is an emotive phrase added as a preface to a surprising exclamatory expression.

The speaker uses *nanto* when he or she, in amazement, breaks unexpected and extraordinary news. When *nanto* is used, the partner anticipates a surprising item to follow. By using *nanto,* the speaker successfully communicates amazement while inviting the partner's curiosity. This *nanto* appears both in the structure [*nanto* + V/Adj informal *to wa*] or followed by a full sentence.

Exclamative sentences in Japanese are formed by using the question word *nanto* 'what/how', and more frequently its colloquial version, *nante. Nanto* exclamatives start with [*nanto/nante* + Adj (+ N)] or [*nanto/nante* + Adj + *koto*] may be followed by *da* or *daroo* after a nominal. The *koto da*(*roo*) exclamative is more frequently used in writing. It should be noted that exclamative sentences carry with them a confessional and directly self-revealing tone. Because of this, when the speaker directly addresses the partner, it is often used in a quotation marked with *to omou* 'I think that', which makes the statement more suitable to the situation.

Another structure that functions like an exclamative sentence is the sentence with *dorehodo,* or the more casual *donna ni,* in the structure [*dorehodo/donna ni* + V/Adj informal + *daroo*] or [*dorehodo/donna ni* + V/Adj pre-nominal + *koto ka*]. This exclamative structure is used primarily in written text. It describes the speaker's exclamation but is not closely associated with surprise, as is the *nanto/nante* exclamative sentence.

The nominalizer *mono* literally means 'things, objects' and is frequently used in the *mon*(*o*) *da* structure. Certain uses of the *mon*(*o*) *da* structure, such as [V/Adj pre-nominal + *mon*(*o*) + *da*], express deep emotion combined with a sense of surprise, especially in the sense that the speaker is moved by how things are or how things have changed. It also expresses the speaker's surprise, particularly when the *mono da* structure is accompanied by *yoku* 'well'. When *mon*(*o*) *da* accompanies the expression of desire (*tai, hoshii*), the speaker expresses a deeply felt desire, as in *Rainen koso ii toshi ni shitai mono desu* 'I really hope to make the next year a really good year'.

Similarly, the nominalizer *koto* 'things, objects, facts' becomes useful when the speaker is moved to exclamation. The *koto da* structure, [V/Adj pre-nominal + *koto* + *da*] is used with certain emotive adjectives (for example, *arigatai* 'grateful', *urayamashii* 'envious', *itamashii* 'pitiful', *kekkoona* 'wonderful', *ureshii* 'pleasing', and *osoroshii* 'dreadful').

In both *mono da* and *koto da* structures, the implication is that, contrary to the normal course of events or the expected turn of events, something unexpected has resulted, and the speaker is moved by it. The emotion expressed is experienced not suddenly but usually after being nurtured in one's mind for a while and is surprising and exclamatory.

It is also possible to express an exclamatory attitude in other ways than by using the structures mentioned above. When a sentence is made into a nominal phrase with [V/Adj informal + *koto!*], it becomes exclamative, as in *Yoku taberu koto!* 'Does he (ever) eat a lot!' The *koto* nominal exclamative is stereotypically associated with the "feminine" style.

Examples

a. (≈) あの事件からずっと、**どれほど苦しんだことか**。こんな気持ちは、誰にも分からないだろうが。

Ano jiken kara zutto, **dorehodo kurushinda koto ka.** Konna kimochi wa, dare ni mo wakara-nai daroo ga. (see E. 16 for *konna*; E. 63 for *ga*)

Since that incident, how much have I suffered! These feelings are something that nobody would understand, though.

b. (Two mature men reminiscing about the past)

(ma1a): 久し振りに来てみましたが、この建物も古くなった**ものです**ねえ。
(ma2): それはそうです。もうあれから15年もたっているんですから。
(ma1b): そんなになりますか。

(ma1a): Hisashiburi ni kite-mimashita ga, kono tatemono mo furuku natta **mono desu** nee. (see E. 56 for *mo*)
(ma2): Sore wa soo desu. Moo are kara juugonen mo tatteiru n desu kara. (see E. 72 for *n desu*)
(ma1b): Sonna ni narimasu ka. (see E. 16 for *sonna ni*)

(ma1a): I came here after a long absence; this building has certainly become old, indeed.
(ma2): It is natural to be so. It's been fifteen years since then.
(ma1b): So many years have passed, I see.

Authentic Examples

a. (Taken from *Muko-dono*, episode 4) An announcer introduces Yuuichiroo on a live radio talk show.

なんと、すばらしいビッグゲストの方に来ていただいています。イエイ。

Nanto, subarashii biggu gesuto no kata ni kite-itadaiteimasu. Iyei.

What a surprise! A wonderful guest is here with us. Yeah!

b. (Taken from *SMAP x SMAP*, New Year's special) An announcement is made with *nanto*, encouraging the audience's anticipation.

木村：	ま、今日は、今日は、1、2、3、4人で、お届けしましたが、**なんと**！
剛：	**なんと**！来週1月14日の、スマスマから、
中居：	稲垣が、
中居と木村一緒に：	戻ってきます！
Kimura:	Ma, kyoo wa, kyoo wa, ichi, ni, san, yonin de, otodoke shimashita ga, **nanto!**
Tsuyoshi:	**Nanto**! Raishuu ichigatsu juuyokka no, suma-suma kara,
Nakai:	Inagaki ga,
Nakai to Kimura issho ni:	Modotte-kimasu! (see E. 51 about the joint creation of an utterance)
Kimura:	Well, today, one, two, three, four of us were here for the program, but, believe it or not!
Tsuyoshi:	Unbelievably! From the next SMAP x SMAP show on January 14,
Nakai:	Inagaki,
Nakai and Kimura together:	Will be back!

c. (Taken from *Kitchin*, 7 [English translation, 4])

先日、**なんと**祖母が死んでしまった。びっくりした。

Senjitsu, **nanto** sobo ga shinde-shimatta. Bikkuri shita. (see E. 17 for *shinde-shimatta*; E. 21 for *bikkuri shita*)

When my grandmother died the other day, I was taken by surprise.

d. (Taken from *Dokkin paradaisu*, 3: 94) Ai criticizes herself in an exclamative sentence.

亜衣は、**なんてドンカンなんだろう**。
"パラダイスKIDS"最後の日になって、やっと暁兄のそんな気持ちに気づくなんて……。

Ai wa, **nante donkanna n daroo**. (see E. 42 about the use of a personal name as a strategy for self-reference)
"Paradaisu Kids" saigo no hi ni natte, yatto Akira-nii no sonna kimochi ni kizuku nante...... (see E. 16 for *sonna*; E. 15 for *nante*)

How insensitive I (Ai) am!
To notice my brother Akira's similar feelings on the last day of the Paradise Kids' performance...

e. (Taken from interview #75, with Tadanori Yokoo, artist) Yokoo explains how much he liked the Takarazuka revue by using an exclamative sentence in a quotation.

横尾： 3 年前に（…）見て、うわー、宝塚って**なんて僕にぴったりなんだろう**と思って、それ以来、毎回見てます。

Yokoo: Sannen mae ni (…) mite, uwaa, Takarazuka tte **nante boku ni pittari na n daroo** to omotte, sore irai, maikai mitemasu. (see E. 47 for *tte*)

Yokoo: Three years ago I saw (…), and then I thought "Wow! What a perfect match, Takarazuka and me!" and since that time I go to see every show.

f. (Taken from *Himawari nikki*, 154) Konomi describes her feelings. In this expression although the verb does not appear, the adjective and noun that follow *nante* function as an exclamative expression.

それは、感動。
抑えきれない感動。
なんてきれいなシーン。
こんなきれいなシーンを、今までわたしは見たコトなかった。

Sore wa, kandoo. (see E. 1 for *kandoo*)
Osaekire-nai kandoo. (see E. 24 about repetition)
Nante kireina shiin.
Konna kireina shiin o, ima made watashi wa mita koto nakatta. (see E. 16 for *konna*)

That is the feeling of being moved.
The feeling of being moved that cannot be subdued.
What a beautiful scene it is!
I have never seen such a beautiful scene.

g. (Taken from *Tsubasa o kudasai*, 104) Tsubasa tells Kyooka why he is thankful to her. The exclamative sentence is self-quoted with *tte*.

「(…) 笑って俺の手を引いて、近くの病院まで連れていってくれたんだ」
「…………」
「**なんて優しいんだろう**って、感動したね。(…)」

"(…) Waratte ore no te o hiite, chikaku no byooin made tsurete-itte-kureta n da." "…………" (see E. 75 about silence)
"**Nante yasashii n daroo** tte, kandoo shita ne. (…)" (see E. 6 for *yasashii*; E. 1 for *kandoo shita*)

"(…) She smiled and took my hand, and walked me to the hospital nearby."
"…………"
"I was moved, thinking how kind she was. (…)"

h. (Taken from *Kitchin*, 66 [English translation, 42])

いやなことはくさるほどあり、道は目をそむけたいくらいけわしい …. と思う日の**何と多いことでしょう**。

Iyana koto wa kusaru hodo ari, michi wa me o somuketai kurai kewashii….to omou hi no **nanto ooi koto deshoo**. (see E. 9 for *iyana*)

There are many days when all the awful things that happen make you sick at heart, when the path before you is so steep you can't bear to look.

i. (Taken from *Taiga no itteki*, 188) The author comments that one should choose life in the way that it is true to oneself. Again, the exclamative sentence appears within a quotation.

(…) 自分自身がこれでいいのだ、自分はこういう生きかたを選んだのだ、このことで悔いはないのだ、ああ、**なんと自分は幸せな人間だろう、と思える**のだったら、むしろそのほうがいいのではないか、と考えたりすることもあります。

(…) Jibun jishin ga kore de ii no da, jibun wa koo yuu ikikata o eranda no da, kono koto de kui wa nai no da, aa, **nanto jibun wa shiawasena ningen daroo, to omoeru** no dattara, mushiro sono hoo ga ii no de wa nai ka, to kangaetari suru koto mo arimasu. (see E. 72 for *no da*; E. 42 for *jibun*; E. 5 for *shiawasena*)

(…) If one can think that this is right, I chose this way of life, there is no regret for choosing this, and what a happy human being I am, then that is perhaps better than other ways. Sometimes I think this way.

j. (Taken from *Dokkin paradaisu*, 3: 55) In this scene, Ai's friend Kaoru shows up as a man, although he was dressed as a woman before. In Akira's and Kaoru's speech, *mon(o) da* is used to add to the exclamative effect.

「それにしても、変われば変わる**モンだ**よな。兄貴たちが今の薫 … さんを見たら、腰抜かすぜ」
(…) 暁兄が、出された紅茶を飲みながらつぶやいた。
「そうだね。あの頃の僕は、女として暁くんにホレてた**ものだ**けどさ」
なんて。
イタズらっぽく言って、亜衣に寄り添う薫さん。

"Sore ni shitemo, kawareba kawaru **mon da** yo na. Anikitachi ga ima no Kaoru-san o mitara, koshi nukasu ze."
(…) Akira-nii ga, dasareta koocha o nominagara tsubuyaita.

"Soo da ne. Ano koro no boku wa, onna to shite Akira-kun ni horeteta **mono da** kedo sa"
Nan te.
Itazurappoku itte, Ai ni yorisou Kaoru-san. (see E. 42 about the use of personal name as a strategy for self-reference)

"But seriously, has he completely changed! If my brothers see Kaoru as he is today, they will be totally shocked."
(…) Akira mumbled so, while drinking the tea served.
"That's probably true. At that time, I was indeed in love with Akira as a man would love a woman."
Such a thing (Kaoru says).
Saying so half-jokingly, Kaoru stands right next to me (Ai).

k. (Taken from *Himawari nikki*, 17) Konomi is surprised by how talkative her best friend Oseki is and expresses her feelings through the *koto* nominal exclamative.

まー、お関の**しゃべること、しゃべること**！

Maa, Oseki no **shaberu koto, shaberu koto**!

Wow, how talkative Oseki is! Really talkative!

l. (Taken from Uchidate 2003b, 58) In this essay titled *Nee moratte yo* (Please, please accept this), the writer laments how readily people purchase home exercising equipment and then soon give up using it.

私の友人たちは三日坊主が多く、効果が出る前にトレーニングをやめる。そのため「ねえ、もらってよ」という電話の**多いこと多いこと**。

Watashi no yuujintachi wa mikkaboozu ga ooku, kooka ga deru mae ni toreeningu o yameru. Sono tame "Nee, moratte yo" to yuu denwa no **ooi koto ooi koto**. (see E. 59 for *Nee*)

Many of my friends are the type who give things up in a few days, so they stop before the training produces results. Because of this, do I ever get so many phone calls that say, "Please, please accept this"!

5

Experiencing Emotion

5. Joy and Happiness

Key Expressions

(≈) うれしい！	*Ureshii!*	Wow, I'm pleased! I'm delighted! I'm glad.
幸せ	*shiawase*	happy
満足	*manzoku*	satisfied, contented
(v) ラッキー！	*Rakkii!*	Lucky!
(≈) やった！	*Yatta!*	Success! I did it!
(≈) バンザイ！	*Banzai!*	Great! Congratulations! Cheers!

Explanation

There are many ways to express happy feelings. Using terms like *ureshii* 'pleased, delighted, glad', *shiawase* 'happy', and *manzoku* 'satisfied, contented' is one. When used as interjections, these adjectives function as exclamatives. They have a distinctly colloquial tone.

Using other interjections such as *rakkii* 'lucky', *yatta* 'success, I did it' and *banzai* 'cheers' is another. *Rakkii!* and *Yatta!* used as interjections are restricted to casual situations, and the first is more common among young speakers. *Rakkii* used as a descriptive term as in *Rakkii desu* 'I feel lucky' is more widely used than it is as an interjection. *Yatta* is also used when the speaker recognizes the partner's effort and enjoys the partner's success with him or her. In a formal situation *Yarimashita ne* can be used. However, avoid this expression toward a person to whom it is proper to show respect, because *yarimashita* has a slight patronizing tone, implying approval of someone else's achievement. *Banzai* is used as an interjection to add to the congratutory mood. (When yelling out *banzai*, speakers often raise both arms. Unlike other phrases introduced in this entry, *banzai* is also used to praise the imperial family.)

The choice of expression depends on the person the speaker is addressing. In formal situations, especially when talking with someone to whom you should maintain some distance from or be polite toward, interjections and the interjectional use of adjectives should be avoided. Instead, adjectives should be used for descriptive purposes. It is important to keep in mind that, as explained in Chapter 1, use of emotion words and emotive strategies that directly express your own feelings is restricted. When reporting how you felt, use quoted interjections, as in "*Shiawase!*" *tte omotta* 'I thought "How happy!"' Even when they appear in quotation, such interjections give vividness to the discourse. At the same time, by integrating the phrases into indirect discourse, the style and the tone appropriate to the situation remain in place.

Other descriptive terms referring to joy and happiness include:

幸福	*koofuku*	happiness
幸運	*kooun*	good fortune
楽しい	*tanoshii*	having fun, enjoyable
楽しさ	*tanoshisa*	fun
喜び	*yorokobi*	pleasure, delight, joy

Examples

a. (A person making a formal speech at a ceremony) The speaker uses a descriptive expression by using the emotion word as an adverb in *ureshiku omotte-orimasu*.

(≠) 本日は、身に余る賞をいただき、大変ありがたく、**うれしく思っております**。

Honjitsu wa, mi ni amaru shoo o itadaki, taihen arigataku, **ureshiku omotte-orimasu**.

Today it is an honor to receive this wonderful (of which I am undeserving) award, which I accept with gratitude, and I am very pleased.

b. (Two women talking after lunch)

(≈fy1a): 今日のランチおいしかったー.
(≈fy2): **満足？**
(≈fy1b): **満足、満足！**

(≈fy1a): Kyoo no ranchi oishikattaa.
(≈fy2): **Manzoku?**
(≈fy1b): **Manzoku, manzoku!** (see E. 24 about repetition)

(≈fy1a): Today's lunch was delicious.
(≈fy2): Satisfied?
(≈fy1b): Very satisfied!

c. (Two teens sharing happiness)

(≈ft1a): 彼が映画にさそってくれたんだ。
(≈ft2a): ほんと？
(vft1b): **ラッキー！**
(≈ft2b): **やったね。バンザイ！**

(≈ft1a): Kare ga eiga ni sasotte-kureta n da.
(≈ft2a): Honto?
(vft1b): **Rakkii!**
(≈ft2b): **Yatta** ne. **Banzai!**

(≈ft1a): He asked me out to a movie.
(≈ft2a): Really?
(vft1b): Lucky me!
(≈ft2b): You did it. Wow, great!

Authentic Examples

a. (Taken from *Beautiful Life*, episode 7) Satsuki, Shuuji's former lover, praises Shuuji's work.

さつき： でもすごいよ。#仕事大変なの？
柊二： ちょっと。#でも、#すごいって言われると、素直に**うれしい**よ。

Satsuki: Demo sugoi yo. Shigoto taihen na no? (see E. 13 for *sugoi*)
Shuuji: Chotto. Demo, sugoi tte iwareru to, sunao ni **ureshii** yo. (see E. 25 for *chotto*)

Satsuki: But you're great. Is your work demanding?
Shuuji: A bit. But when you say I'm great, I am genuinely pleased.

b. (Taken from *Majo no jooken*, episode 1) Masaru tells Michi how happy he is.

大： 俺さ、すっげえ**幸せ**だ。

Masaru: Ore sa, suggee **shiawase** da. (see E. 24 and Chapter 2 about *suggee*)

Masaru: Me, I'm really happy.

c. (Taken from interview #83, with Rei Asami, actress) Note that Asami adds *to omoimasu* to make the emotion word less direct. In this way she maintains a somewhat formal tone during the interview.

林：　それでもなおかつ、そういう妻を愛し、舞台を見て「よくやったね」と言ってくださるご主人なんでしょ。
麻美：　それはとても**幸せだと思います**ね。

Hayashi: Sore demo naokatsu, soo yuu tsuma o aishi, butai o mite "Yoku yatta ne" to itte-kudasaru goshujin na n desho. (see E. 32 for *aishi*)
Asami: Sore wa totemo **shiawase da to omoimasu** ne. (see E. 24 for *totemo*)

Hayashi: Even so, he loves his wife, and after seeing your performance he kindly says, "You did it well." He is that kind of husband, right?
Asami: I do think that is very fortunate (and I'm happy).

d. (Taken from *Ren'ai hakusho*, 14: 14) Kaho expresses her happiness with the term *manzoku.*

あたしが植えたチューリップが、花壇で、いっせいに咲いている。
われながら、**満足**。

Atashi ga ueta chuurippu ga, kadan de, issei ni saiteiru.
Ware nagara, **manzoku.**

The tulips I planted are in bloom altogether in the flower bed.
To me, a great satisfaction.

e. (Taken from *Muko-dono*, episode 5) Kaede asks Yuuichiroo a favor. Finding out that Yuuichiroo is willing, she is elated.

かえで：　Tシャツにサインして。
祐一郎：　あ、はい、いいですよ。
かえで：　**ラッキー**！

Kaede: T-shatsu ni sain shite.
Yuuichiroo: A, hai, ii desu yo. (see E. 13 for the use of *ii desu yo*)
Kaede: **Rakkii!**

Kaede: Can I have your autograph on the T-shirt?
Yuuichiroo: Sure, no problem.
Kaede: How lucky!

f. (Taken from *Chibi Maruko-chan*, 14: 134) Tamae suggests that Maruko ask her father a favor.

たまえ：　＜頼むだけ／頼んで／みれば？＞＜もし／連れてって／もらえたら／**ラッキー**じゃん＞

Tamae: Tanomu dake tanonde-mireba? Moshi tsuretette-moraetara **rakkii** jan.

Tamae: Why don't you ask him anyway? If he takes you there, you are lucky.

g. (Taken from *Himawari nikki*, 212) Konomi and Satoo are elated as they find out that their friend Shidoo has also passed the entrance examination to the high school he wanted to attend.

それを聞いたとたん、
「**やったー！**」
わたしと佐藤くん、受話器に向かって叫んじゃったー！

Sore o kiita totan,
"**Yattaa!**"
Watashi to Satoo-kun, juwaki ni mukatte sakenjattaa!

As soon as we heard that,
"We did it!"
Satoo and I screamed into the phone.

h. (Taken from Iijima 2003a, 132) In this essay titled "Yokan" (Premonition), the writer comments on how disappointing it was finally to get to New York City only to find that so many of her friends were out of town.

どうしても、ニューヨークに一泊したくて、ここまでたどりつくのに大変な思いをした。ようやくついて、**ヤッター**遊ぼう！と張り切ったのに。

Doo shitemo, Nyuuyooku ni ippaku shitakute, koko made tadoritsuku no ni taihenna omoi o shita. Yooyaku tsuite, **yattaa** asoboo! to harikitta noni.

No matter what, I wanted to stay overnight in New York City, and I had to go through a lot to get here. Finally I got here, and I was like, I did it, I'm going to have fun! but.

i. (Taken from interview #78, with Naoki Ishikawa, adventurer)

林：　おおー。東京でふつうの学生生活やっていて、デートしたり合コンしたりする生活なんかとは、比べものにならないくらい**幸せ**なのかしら。
石川：　そういう生活も好きですけど、今、俺、すげえところを歩いてるな、と思うことがすごく**楽しい**というか、**うれしい**というか。(...)
林：　ともかく無事に帰ってこられて、よかったですよね。
石川：　ほんとに**ラッキー**ですね。

Hayashi: Oooo. Tookyoo de futsuu no gakusei seikatsu yatteite, deeto shitari gookon shitari suru seikatsu nanka to wa, kurabemono ni nara-nai kurai **shiawase** na no kashira. (see E. 29 for *deeto suru*; E. 15 for *nanka*)

Ishikawa: Soo yuu seikatsu mo suki desu kedo, ima, ore, sugee tokoro o aruiteru na, to omou koto ga sugoku **tanoshii** to yuu ka, **ureshii**

	to yuu ka. (...) (see E. 13 and Chapter 2 for *sugee*; E. 63 for *to yuu ka*)
Hayashi:	Tomokaku buji ni kaette-korarete, yokatta desu ne. (see E. 22 for *yokatta*)
Ishikawa:	Honto ni **rakkii** desu ne.
Hayashi:	Oh. I wonder if you are much happier (to the extent that it is beyond comparison) that way than you are in Tokyo, leading an ordinary life doing such things as having dates and participating in co-ed parties.
Ishikawa:	I like that kind of life (in Tokyo) also, but should I say it is fun, or perhaps I should say delightful, when I realize, "Wow, right now I am walking through some awesome places."
Hayashi:	At any rate, it was good that you came back safely.
Ishikawa:	Yes, I've been really lucky.

j. (Taken from interview #79, with Nobuyuki Matsuhisa, owner and chef of Nobu Tokyo) When Matsuhisa expresses his excitement, he uses *Yatta!* in a self-quotation. By adding *to omoimashita ne*, he makes the expression indirect and more appropriate for the interview. At the same time his excitement is realistically presented, as if he were at the scene.

松久：	一口食べ、二口食べ、最終的に全部食べ終わったとき、僕**「やった！」とおもいましたね。**
Matsuhisa:	Hitokuchi tabe, futakuchi tabe, saishuuteki ni zenbu tabe-owatta toki, boku **"Yatta!" to omoimashita ne.**
Matsuhisa:	When they ate (my dish) with the first bite, second bite, and at the end they ate everything, I thought "Wow, I did it!".

6. Tenderness and Warmth

Key Expressions

やさしさ	*yasashisa*	tenderness, kindness
やさしいヤツ	*yasashii yatsu*	a tenderhearted, caring, and kind fellow, a loving person
あたたかい	*atatakai*	heartwarming

Explanation

Tenderness and warmth are described by adjectives like *yasashii* and *atatakai*. *Yasashii* (not in the sense 'easy') is used to describe a tender, warm, caring, and giving personality. *Yasashii* may be used in the form *yasashiku suru* meaning to be supportive, tender, and kind to someone else. For example, one may say *Ano hito wa watashi ni yasashiku shite-kureta* 'He was tender and considerate to me'.

Atatakai (not in the sense of temperature) and its casual version *attakai* refer to a heartwarming, concerned, and giving personality.

Examples

a. (A woman and her male friend chatting about a mutual friend)

(≈fy1): 彼ね、すぐにお見舞いに来てくれたんだ。
(≈my1): あいつはほんとに**優しい**ヤツなんだよ。

(≈fy1): Kare ne, sugu ni omimai ni kite-kureta n da.
(≈my1): Aitsu wa honto ni **yasashii** yatsu na n da yo. (see E. 30 for *aitsu* and *yatsu*)

(≈fy1): He came to see me (because I was sick) right away.
(≈my1): He is a real tenderhearted, kind guy.

b. **あたたかい**愛情に包まれて幸せな日々をすごした。

Atatakai aijoo ni tsutsumarete shiawasena hibi o sugoshita. (see E. 31 for *aijoo*; E. 5 for *shiawasena*)

Surrounded by warm love, I spent many happy days.

Authentic Examples

a. (Taken from *Beautiful Life*, episode 5) Shuuji and Kyooko, after an awkward date, get upset at each other.

柊二： 特別だと思ってんじゃないの？自分のこと。
杏子： そんな言い方しなくたって。もうちょっと、**やさしく**してくれてもいいんじゃないかな。
柊二： 充分**やさしい**んじゃないの。
杏子： **やさしい**かな。
柊二： だって、これ見よがしに**やさしく**されるのいやなんでしょ。

Shuuji: Tokubetsu da to omotte n ja-nai no? Jibun no koto. (see E. 42 for *jibun*; E. 30 for *no koto*)
Kyooko: Sonna iikata shi-nakutatte. Moo chotto, **yasashiku** shite-kuretemo ii n ja-nai ka na. (see E. 16 for *sonna*)
Shuuji: Juubun **yasashii** n ja-nai no.
Kyooko: **Yasashii** ka na.
Shuuji: Datte, koremiyogashi ni **yasashiku** sareru no iyana n desho. (see E. 9 for *iyana*)

Shuuji: Aren't you thinking that you are special? About yourself?
Kyooko: You don't need to put it in such a way. Wouldn't it be nicer if you were a bit more tender and loving?
Shuuji: Aren't I (already) tender and loving enough?
Kyooko: I wonder if you are.
Shuuji: But you don't like me to publicly display my tenderness and concern, right?

b. (Taken from interview #83, with Rei Asami, actress)

麻美： 主人の芸能好きは義父譲りですから、その意味ではとってもラッキーですよね。
林： 最高ですよね。理解ある**優しい**ご主人がいて。経済的にも非常に恵まれていらっしゃって。

Asami: Shujin no geinoo zuki wa gifu yuzuri desu kara, sono imi de wa tottemo rakkii desu yo ne. (see E. 24 for *tottemo*; E. 5 for *rakkii*)
Hayashi: Saikoo desu yo ne. Rikai aru **yasashii** goshujin ga ite. Keizaiteki ni mo hijoo ni megumareteirasshatte. (see E. 23 for *saikoo*)

Asami: My husband's keen interest in the entertainment business comes from my father-in-law, so in that sense, I am very lucky.
Hayashi: It's the best, isn't it. You have a tenderhearted, loving husband who understands you. And you are financially very secure, too.

c. (Taken from *Kitchin*, 29 [English translation, 19])

「(...) ...... **やさしい**子にしたくてね、そこだけは必死に育てたの。あの子は**やさしい**子なのよ。」
「ええ、わかります。」
「あなたも**やさしい**子ね。」

"(...)......**Yasashii** ko ni shitakute ne, soko dake wa hisshi ni sodateta no. Ano ko wa **yasashii** ko na no yo."
"Ee, wakarimasu." (see E. 66 for *wakarimasu*)
"Anata mo **yasashii** ko ne."

"(...) ...But I wanted above all to make a good kid out of him, and I focused everything on raising him that way. And you know, he is. A good kid."
"I know."
"You're a good kid, too." She beamed.

d. (Taken from *Dokkin paradaisu*, 34) Ai confesses her happiness, describing the tender love she receives from her brothers.

おにいちゃんたちの**やさしさ**に包まれて、亜衣はすごく幸せだよ！

Oniichantachi no **yasashisa** ni tsutsumarete, Ai wa sugoku shiawase da yo! (see E. 42 about the use of a personal name as a strategy for self-reference; E. 24 for *sugoku*; E. 5 for *shiawase*)

Surrounded by my brothers' tender care, Ai is (I am) very happy!

e. (Taken from *Muko-dono*, episode 1)

さくら：　世界で一番**あったかい**家をつくるの、ふたりで。

Sakura: Sekai de ichiban **attakai** uchi o tsukuru no, futari de. (see E. 23 for *ichiban*; E. 28 for *futari*; E. 48 about inverted word order)

Sakura: We'll make the warmest home in the world, the two of us.

Note

Certain *i*-type adjectives ([Adj-*i*]) take both *-mi* and *-sa* in their noun forms. For example, *atatakami/atatakasa* 'warmth', *kanashimi/kanashisa* 'sadness', *kurushimi/kurushisa* 'hardship', and *tanoshimi/tanoshisa* 'fun'. Only a limited number of adjectives have both the *-mi* and the *-sa* suffixes. When *-mi* is used, it emphasizes an emotive aspect associated with a particular case, whereas *-sa* is more objective and neutral. As a result, a speaker's personal joy leads to the use of *tanoshimi,* as in *Tanoshimi ni shiteimasu* 'I look forward to it'.

7. Sadness, Pain, and Difficulties

Key Expressions

悲しい	*kanashii*	(I'm) sad
悲しむ	*kanashimu*	to be sad
悲しそう	*kanashisoo*	appearing sad
つらい	*tsurai*	(unbearably) painful and difficult
心が痛む	*kokoro ga itamu*	to feel pain in the heart
痛み	*itami*	pain
ひどい	*hidoi*	nasty, hurtful, awful, destructive, devastating

Explanation

Expressing sadness is often an important step in being emotionally close to your partner. The adjectives *kanashii* 'sad' and *tsurai* '(unbearably) painful and difficult' are most frequently chosen when expressing sadness. *Kanashii* refers to sadness of various kinds, and related words, among them *kanashimi* 'feeling sadness', *kanashisa* 'sadness', and *kanashimu* 'to be sad, to grieve', also occur. *Tsurai* communicates a speaker's feeling of almost unbearable pain when he or she is faced with difficulties associated with sad events, misfortune, hardships, and life's vicissitudes in general. *Tsurai* covers a broad range of emotional difficulties, including sadness, loneliness, and hardship.

Kokoro ga itamu literally means that one's heart feels pain. Someone who comprehends others' emotional pain is considered a person who understands (*kokoro no*) *itami*. *Kokoro ga itamu* and *kokoro no itami* are more likely to be used in formal or written styles than in casual speech.

Hidoi communicates the speaker's evaluation of things, states, and people by pointing out how devastatingly awful and nasty they are. For example, one might say, *Hidoi hanashi desu yo ne* 'That's a terrible story, isn't it?' and *Hidoi hito da ne, kare tte* 'He's a nasty person'. *Hidoi* is frequently used as an interjection to communicate anger, hurt, and complaint, as in *Hidoi!* 'How awful!' *Hidoi* is also used to describe things that are excessively unpleasant, such as *hidoi ame* 'awful rain' or *hidoku inu ga hoeru* 'the dog barks uncontrollably'.

Examples

a. (Two girls talking about a friend who is moving away)

(≈ft1a): 何、**悲しそうな**顔してるの？
(≈ft2): 友達が東京へ行っちゃうんだ。
(≈ft1b): そう。別れるのは**つらい**よね。

(≈ft1a): Nani, **kanashisoona** kao shiteru no?
(≈ft2): Tomodachi ga Tookyoo e itchau n da. (see E. 17 for *itchau*)
(≈ft1b): Soo. Wakareru no wa **tsurai** yo ne. (see E. 35 for *wakareru*)

(≈ft1a): You look sad. What happened?
(≈ft2): My friend will be moving away to Tokyo.
(≈ft1b): I see. Parting is painful, isn't it?

b. (A friend is upset about her friend's unfortunate date)

(≈fy1a): あら、もう帰ってきたの？
(≈fy2): 今日のデート、大失敗。二時間も待たされてそのあげくコンサートに行ったら、彼チケット忘れてきて。
(≈fy1b): **ひどい**！**ひどすぎる**よ。

(≈fy1a): Ara, moo kaette-kita no?
(≈fy2): Kyoo no deeto, daishippai. Nijikan mo matasarete sono ageku konsaato ni ittara, kare chiketto wasurete-kite. (see E. 29 for *deeto*; E. 18 for *daishippai*)
(≈fy1b): **Hidoi! Hidosugiru** yo. (see E. 24 about repetition)

(≈fy1a): Are you back already?
(≈fy2): Today's date was a big failure. I had to wait for him for two hours, and then we went to the concert. But he forgot to bring the tickets.
(≈fy1b): Awful. That is simply too awful.

Authentic Examples

a. (Taken from *Kitchin*, 50 [English translation, 32])

断じて認めたくないので言うが、ダッシュしたのは私ではない。絶対ちがう。だって私はそのすべてが心から**悲しい**もの。

Danjite mitometaku-nai node yuu ga, dasshu shita no wa watashi dewa-nai. Zettai chigau. Datte watashi wa sono subete ga kokoro kara **kanashii** mono.

But it was not I who was doing the shifting—on the contrary. For me everything had been agony.

b. (Taken from Ebisu 2003, 118) In this essay about movies, the writer recalls how he felt when his wife passed away.

この翌日、女房はトイレで倒れて、そのまま意識が戻らず、あの世へ行っちゃった。**悲しかった**ですね。

Kono yokujitsu, nyooboo wa toire de taorete, sono mama ishiki ga modorazu, ano yo e itchatta. **Kanashikatta** desu ne. (see E. 17 for *itchatta*)

The next day, my wife fell down in the bathroom, and she never regained consciousness, and left this world. It was sad, indeed.

c. (Taken from *Taiga no itteki*, 201) The author explains the importance of experiencing sadness.

喜ぶのと同じように、本当に**悲しむ**ことが大事なのです。本当に**悲しむ**というのはどういうことか。自分のために**悲しむ**だけでなく、他人のために**悲しみ**、涙を流すことでもあります。

Yorokobu no to onaji yoo ni, hontoo ni **kanashimu** koto ga daijina no desu. Hontoo ni **kanashimu** to yuu no wa doo yuu koto ka. Jibun no tame ni **kanashimu** dake de-naku, tanin no tame ni **kanashimi**, namida o nagasu koto de mo arimasu. (see E. 42 for *jibun*; E. 2 for *namida o nagasu*)

Just like being joyous, it is important to experience true sadness. What does it mean to be truly sad? It means not only being sad for your own sake, but also being sad and shedding tears for others' sake.

d. (Taken from *Dokkin paradaisu*, 3: 95) Ai expresses how painful it is for her to have found out that Akira didn't really care for her, at least not in the way she did for him.

ズキン … ズキン
胸が痛い。
だけどこれは、銃で撃たれたせいじゃない。
暁兄の言葉が、亜衣の胸に、ポッカリ大きな穴を開けた。
(…)
暁兄、
胸が …… 痛いよ。

Zukin…zukin.
Mune ga itai.
Dakedo kore wa, juu de utareta sei ja-nai.
Akira-nii no kotoba ga, Ai no mune ni, pokkari ookina ana o aketa.
(…)
Akira-nii.
Mune ga……itai yo. (see E. 55 about the use and non-use of *yo*)

Pounding, pounding.
My heart aches.
But this is not because I was shot by a gun.
Akira's words made a huge hole in my heart.
(…)
Dear Akira.
My heart…aches.

e. (Taken from *Taiga no itteki*, 62) The author expresses how painful it is not to be able to understand today's youth.

私たちは政治や経済の世界が実際にはどのように動いていたかを最近あらためて赤裸々(せきらら)に見せつけられた。(…) 学校や教育の現場の無力さを、しみじみと感じさせられ、少年や少女たちの考えや行動を理解できない**痛み**をあじわった。

Watashitachi wa seiji ya keizai no sekai ga jissai ni wa dono yoo ni ugoiteita ka o saikin aratamete sekirara ni misetsukerareta. (…) Gakkoo ya kyooiku no genba no muryokusa o, shimijimi to kanjisaserare, shoonen ya shoojotachi no kangae ya koodoo o rikai deki-nai **itami** o ajiwatta. (see E. 1 for s*himijimi to*)

We were recently shown, clearly and in a renewed way, before our (own) eyes, how the worlds of politics and business have been operating. (...) We were forced to feel deeply the powerlessness of the schools and of the daily practice of education, and we felt the pain of not being able to understand the ways boys and girls think and behave.

f. (Taken from *Long Love Letter Hyooryuu Kyooshitsu*, episode 1) Fujisawa, one of Yuka's former students who dropped out from high school, talks on the phone.

藤沢： 俺働いてんだ。#すし屋で。#何か、スゲー**つらくて**さ。学校みたいにゆるくなくて。超**つれえ**けど、でもやっと、やっと、ひとりでやらせてもらえるようになったよ。

Fujisawa: Ore hataraite n da. Sushiya de. Nanka, sugee **tsurakute** sa. Gakkoo mitai ni yuruku-nakute. Choo **tsuree** kedo, demo yatto, yatto, hitori de yarasete-moraeru yoo ni natta yo. (see E. 24 and Chapter 2 for *sugee*; E. 24 for *choo*; Chapter 2 for *tsuree* instead of *tsurai*)

Fujisawa: I'm working now. At a sushi shop. It is very hard. It's not so flexible as school. It is really hard, but finally, finally I am permitted to make *sushi* by myself.

g. (Taken from *SMAP x SMAP,* New Year's special) Kimura makes a comment about Tsuyoshi's difficulty. Tsuyoshi cannot get ready in time for his trick on the live show, and undergoes a moment of panic.

木村： ていうかおまえの焦ってる顔が、すごいこう、アップ行くとちょっとなんか、すごく、こ、見てる方が**つらい**。

Kimura: Te yuu ka omae no asetteru kao ga, sugoi koo, appu iku to chotto nanka, sugoku, ko, miteru hoo ga **tsurai**. (see E. 44 for *te yuu ka*; E. 30 for *omae*; E. 62 for *nanka*; E. 24 for *sugoi* and *sugoku*)

Kimura: Frankly, when your panicking face appears on the screen in a close-up shot, uh, when I see it, it is painful to me.

h. (Taken from *Chibi Maruko-chan*, 14: 34) Maruko's mother and Maruko complain how nasty and hurtful the father is.

母： ＜ちょっと／おとうさん／**ひどい**わよ／せっかくまる子が／食べられるように／がんばってるのに＞

まる子： ＜そうだよ／**ひどい**よ＞

haha: Chotto otoosan **hidoi** wa yo. Sekkaku Maruko ga taberareru yoo ni ganbatteru noni. (see E. 14 for *sekkaku*)

Maruko: Soo da yo. **Hidoi** yo.

mother: Say, dear. That's nasty. You know, Maruko is making an effort to be able to eat it.
Maruko: That's right. That's nasty.

i. (Taken from *Ren'ai hakusho*, 14: 126) Kaho misunderstood Sumire's feelings, and Sumire is upset.

「果歩。**ひどい！**」
すみれちゃんが怒鳴った。

"Kaho. **Hidoi!**"
Sumire-chan ge donatta.

"Kaho. You are nasty and awful!"
Sumire yelled out.

Additional Information

Other descriptive words and phrases for sadness and suffering are listed below.

悲哀を感じる	*hiai o kanjiru*	to feel sorrow, to be sorrowful
気がめいる	*ki ga meiru*	to be depressed
苦悩	*kunoo*	anguish, agony
苦しむ	*kurushimu*	to suffer, to go through torment
苦痛	*kutsuu*	torment, painful feeling
もの悲しい	*monoganashii*	somehow generally sad, gloomy, melancholic
むなしい	*munashii*	with an empty feeling, feeling a sense of being in vain
悩む	*nayamu*	to be troubled by, to be tormented by
絶望	*zetsuboo*	desperation

8. Loneliness

Key Expressions

淋しい, 寂しい	*sabishii*	lonely
さみしい	*samishii*	lonesome
ひとりぼっち	*hitoribotchi*	feeling totally alone
孤独感	*kodokukan*	sense of solitude
わびしい	*wabishii*	lonesome, desolate, forlorn

Explanation

People speak of their loneliness by using words such as *sabishii*, *samishii*, and *hitoribotchi*. *Sabishii* and *samishii* both express lonely and lonesome feelings. It is also possible to use *sabishii* and *samishii* for describing a certain state of things, such as a deserted place, as in *hito ga dare mo i-nai samishii tokoro* 'a deserted place with nobody around'. But when used as an emotion word, it refers to loneliness, a sense of missing someone or something. *Hitoribotchi* '(lit.) only one person' is used when one feels alone and isolated, apart from other people. For example, you feel *hitoribotchi* when you realize that everyone else is in a group or at least a couple, but you are alone.

Kodokukan refers to a sense of solitude. *Wabishii* refers to quiet, lonesome, forlorn (with a touch of sorrow) feelings, when one is away from the bustling crowd. *Wabishii* is most frequently used in reference to a place, as in *wabishii tatazumai* 'lonely dwelling', conjuring up the image of a simple, rustic, and forlorn place. It can also be used in reference to a lifestyle, as in *wabishii jinsei* 'lonely life', with a sense of loss and sorrow.

Examples

a. (≈) 秋ってなんか**寂しい**ね。

Aki tte nanka **sabishii** ne. (see E. 47 for *tte*; E. 62 for *nanka*)

Fall is somehow lonely, isn't it?

b. (≈) こんな**孤独感**は今まで味わったことがなかった。

Konna **kodokukan** wa ima made ajiwatta koto ga nakatta. (see E. 16 for *konna*)

This kind of solitude, I have never felt before.

c. (Two men talking about a neighborhood)

(≈ma1): このあたり、けっこう**寂しい**ところなんだな。
(≈ma2): 借りてる家もなんか**わびしい**感じなんだ。ひとり住まいのせいもあるけどさ。

(≈ma1): Kono atari, kekkoo **sabishii** tokoro na n da na. (see E. 25 for *kekkoo*)
(≈ma2): Kariteru uchi mo nanka **wabishii** kanji na n da. Hitori zumai no sei mo aru kedo sa. (E. 62 for *nanka*; E. 63 for *kedo*)

(≈ma1): This neighborhood is kind of deserted, isn't it?
(≈ma2): The house I'm renting is a bit lonesome. It's probably because I live alone.

Authentic Examples

a. (Taken from BBS for *Beautiful Life*)

ちょっと**淋しい**です。

Chotto **sabishii desu.**

I feel a bit lonely.

なんだか**さびしいです**ね。

Nandaka **sabishii desu** ne.

I feel somehow lonesome.

これから日曜日が**淋しく**なります。

Kore kara nichiyoobi ga **sabishiku** narimasu.

From now on, Sundays will be lonesome.

さみしいよー。

Samishii yoo.

I feel lonesome.

さみしかったです。

Samishikatta desu.

I felt lonely.

b. (Taken from *Antiiku, seiyoo kottoo yoogashiten*, episode 3) Eiji listens to Tamami, who explains that she had some painful experiences in the past.

珠美： お昼とかも、いつもひとりで、誰もいないところで食べてた。 #**さみしかった**けど。でも、#でも …

エイジ： もういいって。##もういいじゃん。#な。

Tamami: Ohiru toka mo, itsumo hitori de, dare mo i-nai tokoro de tabeteta. **Samishikatta** kedo. Demo, demo…

Eiji: Moo ii tte. Moo ii jan. Na. (see E. 13 for *ii*; E. 73 about utterance-final *tte*)

Tamami: I always had lunch alone, where there was no one else. I felt lonely, but, but…

Eiji: That's over. That's over now, isn't it? Right?

c. (Taken from *Long Love Letter Hyooryuu Kyooshitsu*, episode 3) Yuka consoles Asami. Note the use of *sabishii* as a description of Asami's facial expression, as well as an expression of her feelings.

結花：　だから、これあなたのせいじゃないし。それにさ、なんか、そんな風に**寂しい**顔されちゃうと、私も**寂しい**し。

Yuka: Dakara, kore anata no sei ja-nai shi. Soreni sa, nanka, sonna fuu ni **sabishii** kao sarechau to, watashi mo **sabishii** shi. (see E. 62 for *nanka*; E. 16 for *sonna*; E. 63 for *shi*)

Yuka: So, as I'm saying, this is not because of you. Besides, somehow, when your face shows such loneliness, I feel lonely, too.

d. (Taken from interview #80, with Ukon Ichikawa, kabuki actor) In this interview, Hayashi wonders if Ichikawa spent some lonely time in his junior high school days. Showing such a concern communicates the speaker's desire for empathy.

林：　中学生から親御さんと離れて一人暮しでしょ。**寂しくなかった**ですか。

市川：　**寂しかった**ですよ。

Hayashi: Chuugakusei kara oyago-san to hanarete hitori gurashi desho. **Sabishiku-nakatta** desu ka.

Ichikawa: **Sabishikatta** desu yo.

Hayashi: You have lived alone, apart from your parents, since your junior high school days. Didn't you feel lonely?

Ichikawa: Yes, I did.

e. (Taken from *Dokkin paradaisu*, 3: 97) Ai expresses her feelings of loneliness in the narrative.

窓の外は冷たい木枯らし。
暗くて、**淋しくて**、ひどく長く感じた一日。

Mado no soto wa tsumetai kogarashi.
Kurakute, **sabishikute**, hidoku nagaku kanjita ichinich.

Outside the window, a cold winter wind is blowing.
The dark and lonely day that I felt to be horribly long.

f. (Taken from *Taiga no itteki*, 262) The author explains how the thirteenth-century high priest Shinran commented on loneliness.

おまえもきっといつか本当の**さびしさ**を感じるときがくるであろう。そのときにはその**さびしさ**から逃げるな。その**さびしさ**をごまかすな。適当にやりすごすな。きちんとその**さびしさ**と正面から向きあって、その**さびしさ**をしっかりと見つめるがよい。その**さびしさ**こそは運命がおまえを育てようとしているのだから、というふうに親鸞は答えるのですが(...)。

Omae mo kitto itsuka hontoo no **sabishisa** o kanjiru toki ga kuru dearoo. Sono toki ni wa sono **sabishisa** kara nigeru-na. Sono **sabishisa** o gomakasu-na. Tekitoo ni yarisugosu-na. Kichin to sono **sabishisa** to shoomen kara mukiatte, sono **sabishisa** o shikkari to mitsumeru ga yoi. Sono **sabishisa** koso wa unmei ga omae o sodateyoo to shiteiru no da kara, to yuu fuu ni Shinran wa kotaeru no desu ga (...).

There will come a time that you will feel truly lonely. Then, do not escape from that loneliness. Do not slight that loneliness. Do not deal with it lightly. Face that loneliness straight, and firmly cast your eyes on that loneliness. That loneliness is a testimony that your destiny is attempting to make you mature (through it). Thus said Shinran (...).

g. (Taken from *Long Love Letter Hyooryuu Kyooshitsu*, episode 3) A female student, Nishi, confesses her feelings.

西：　みんな私を見て笑うし、私だけ女の子のグループに入れないで、いつも**ひとりぼっち**。だから、こんなふうに、誰もいない世界に行ってしまいたいって思ってた。

Nishi: Minna watashi o mite warau shi, watashi dake onna no ko no guruupu ni haire-nai de, itsumo **hitoribotchi**. Dakara, konna fuu ni, dare mo i-nai sekai ni itte-shimaitai tte omotteta. (see E. 16 for *konna*)

Nishi: Everyone laughs at me and I alone cannot join the girls' groups. Always I'm totally alone. So I was thinking that it would be nice to go to a world like this, where no one else lives.

h. (Taken from *Majo no jooken*, episode 7) Michi asks Hikaru to swear that he will never leave her totally alone.

未知：　約束して。#私を**ひとりぼっち**にしないって。#絶対しないって。

光：　約束する。#絶対**ひとりぼっち**になんかしない。

Michi: Yakusoku shite. Watashi o **hitoribotchi** ni shi-nai tte. Zettai shi-nai tte.

Hikaru: Yakusoku suru. Zettai **hitoribotchi** ni nanka shi-nai. (see E. 15 for *nanka*)

Michi: Promise me. That you will never leave me totally alone. That you will never do that.

Hikaru: I promise. I will never make you feel alone, never.

9. Dislike and Hatred

Key Expressions

嫌い	*kirai*	dislike
大嫌い！	*Daikirai!*	I really hate it!, That's simply disgusting!
いやな	*iyana*	disagreeable, offensive, nasty
(≈) いやだ	*Iya da.*	I don't like it. I hate it. That's just offensive.
にくらしい	*nikurashii*	hateful, detestable
にくたらしい	*nikutarashii*	dreadfully hateful
憎しみ	*nikushimi*	hatred

Explanation

Dislike is conveyed by such adjectives as *kirai* 'dislike', *daikirai* 'abhorrent, disgusting', *iyana* 'disagreeable, offensive, nasty' and *iya da*. *Iyana* is a *na*-type adjective that describes something disagreeable and offensive—things and events that the speaker would rather avoid if at all possible. It is also used as an interjection for multiple purposes (as explained in the additional information). *Iya da* (and its colloquial version, *ya da*) are used for refusing something as well when responding to a request.

Hatred is communicated by *nikurashii* 'hateful, detestable' and *nikutarashii* 'dreadfully hateful', as well as by *nikushimi* 'hatred'. *Nikurashii*, with its more emphatic version, *nikutarashii*, expresses a feeling of hatred and detestation. *Nikurashii* and *nikutarashii* are usually used in reference to persons (and pets) only.

Examples

a. (Two schoolgirls chatting)

(≈ft1a): あたしあの先生**大嫌い**。
(≈ft2a): なんで？
(≈ft1b): 宿題たくさん出すから。
(≈ft2b): そんな。

(≈ft1a): Atashi ano sensei **daikirai.**
(≈ft2a): Nande?
(≈ft1b): Shukudai takusan dasu kara.
(≈ft2b): Sonna. (see E. 16 for *sonna*)

(≈ft1a): I really hate that teacher.
(≈ft2a): Why?
(≈ft1b): She assigns a lot of homework.
(≈ft2b): Such a thing (you shouldn't say).

b. (A mother and a daughter chatting) The daughter is upset with her elder sister.

(≈fc1a): お姉ちゃんたら、**にくたらしい**！
(≈fa1a): そんなこと言っちゃだめでしょ。
(≈fc1b): だって、いじわるばっかりするんだもん。
(≈fa1b): サキちゃんもお姉ちゃんが**いやな**ことするからじゃないの？
(≈fc1c): ああ、あんな人がお姉ちゃんだなんて、**やだ、やだ**。

(≈fc1a): Oneechan tara, **nikutarashii**!
(≈fa1a): Sonna koto itcha dame desho. (see E. 16 for *sonna*)
(≈fc1b): Datte, ijiwaru bakkari suru n da mon. (see E. 59 for *datte*)
(≈fa1b): Saki-chan mo oneechan ga **iyana** koto suru kara ja-nai no?
(≈fc1c): Aa, anna hito ga oneechan da nante, **ya da, ya da**. (see E. 16 for *anna*; E. 15 for *nante*)

(≈fc1a): I hate my sister.
(≈fa1a): You shouldn't say such a thing.
(≈fc1b): But, she bullies me around all the time.
(≈fa1b): Isn't that because, Saki, you do nasty things?
(≈fc1c): Ah, I hate it, to have such a person as my sister.

Authentic Examples

a. (Taken from *Long Love Letter Hyooryuu Kyooshitsu*, episode 4) Asami has just told Yuka that he loves her, but cannot get involved with her because of his responsibility of being a teacher. Asked by students, Yuka explains what happened. (In this conversation, Andoo says "*Rakkii*," because she herself is in love with her teacher, Asami.)

安藤： 何話してたの？
結花： 告白された。
大友： うそ。
結花： だけどフラれた。
金沢： まじで？
安藤： ラッキー。
大友： ちょっと待って。告白されたけどフラれたってどういうこと？
安藤： 男ってひとりよがりってことっしょ。そういう人好き。
結花： 私は**嫌い**。

Andoo: Nani hanashiteta no?
Yuka: Kokuhaku sareta. (see E. 32 for *kokuhaku suru*)
Ootomo: Uso. (see E. 21 for *uso*)
Yuka: Dakedo furareta. (see E. 35 for *furareta*)
Kanazawa: Maji de? (see E. 67 for *maji de*)
Andoo: Rakkii. (see E. 5 for *rakkii*)
Ootomo: Chotto matte. Kokuhaku sareta kedo furareta tte doo yuu koto? (see E. 47 for *tte*)
Andoo: Otoko tte hitori yogari tte koto ssho. Soo yuu hito suki. (see E. 32 for *suki*)
Yuka: Watashi wa **kirai**.

Andoo: What were you talking about?
Yuka: He told me that he loves me.
Ootomo: No kidding.
Yuka: But he dumped me.
Kanazawa: Seriously?
Andoo: How lucky!
Ootomo: Wait a second. What do you mean by being told you were loved and then being dumped?
Andoo: It just means that man is selfish. I like that kind of man.
Yuka: I dislike such a man.

b. (Taken from *Long Love Letter Hyooryuu Kyooshitsu*, episode 10) Students are too afraid to jump over the crevice caused by a huge earthquake. A female student, Fukasawa, screams.

深沢： **いや**。絶対**いや**。怖い、怖いよ。
Fukasawa: **Iya**. Zettai **iya**. Kowai, kowai yo. (see E. 11 for *kowai*; see E. 55 about the use and non-use of *yo*)

Fukasawa: No way. Absolutely no way. Scared, I'm really scared.

c. (Taken from *Chibi Maruko-chan*, 13: 43) Maruko's classmate, Maeda, tries to force other classmates to clean the classroom. Because Maruko is also in charge of cleaning the classroom, she becomes a target of nasty criticism. Maruko laments how much she hates the situation.

まる子： ＜あーあ / **やだ**な ....../ 気が重いよ＞
たまえ： ＜まるちゃん / かわいそう /......＞ ＜前田さんが / 提案したこと / なのに＞

Maruko: Aaa **ya da** na...... Ki ga omoi yo.
Tamae: Maru-chan kawaisoo...... Maeda-san ga teian shita koto na noni. (see E. 61 for *kawaisoo*)

Maruko: Ah, I hate it... I feel discouraged.
Tamae: Poor Maruko... Only because Maeda has made such a proposal.

d. (Taken from *Chibi Maruko-chan*, 13: 151) Maruko and her classmates are looking for fireflies. Maruko insists that they will find some. Maruko responds defiantly to Nagasawa's remark by characterizing Nagasawa's words as *nikutarashii koto*.

永沢： ＜今時　ホタル / なんて / いるもんか＞
(...)

まる子： ＜なにさっ / **にくたらしい事を** / 言う人達だねっ / 私達は ホタルを / 絶対　見つける / からねっ＞

Nagasawa: Imadoki hotaru nante iru mon ka. (see E. 15 for *nante*; E. 40 about rhetorical questions)
(...)
Maruko: Nani sa-tt. **Nikutarashii** koto o yuu hitotachi da ne-tt. Watashitachi wa hotaru o zettai mitsukeru kara ne-tt. (see E. 37 for *Nani sa-tt*)

Nagasawa: How can it be that there are fireflies in this day and age!
(...)
Maruko: What! Boy, you guys say such a dreadfully hateful thing! We will find fireflies no matter what!

Additional Information

Iya is used as an interjection in a variety of ways, as listed below.

1. In a negative answer meaning no. For example when responding to *Ja, kaiketsu desu ne* 'Well then, the problem is solved', one may say *Iya, zannen nagara mada mondai ga nokottemasu* 'No, unfortunately there are still some problems'.
2. When a person shows surprise to news supplied by the partner. For example, in response to *Yuushoo shita n desu yo* 'They won!' one may comment *Iya odorokimashita ne* 'Well well, that's a surprise'.
3. When the speaker wants to indicate an unexpected turn of events, as in *Ya da, kawaii. Kare tte, hazukashisoo ni shiteru kao mo kawaii* 'Wow, so cute. He is so cute even when he is shy'. This is primarily used in speech stereotypically associated with the "feminine" style.
4. As a refusal, as in *Iya da* (or *Ya da*) 'No way'.

10. Anger and Frustration

Key Expressions

腹が立つ	*hara ga tatsu*	to get angry, to be furious
頭に来る	*atama ni kuru*	to get mad, to lose your cool
(≈) ムカつく	*mukatsuku*	to get disgustedly mad
フン	*fun*	humph
怒る	*okoru*	to be angry

Explanation

A person who is angry communicates that feeling by phrases such as *hara ga tatsu*, *atama ni kuru*, and *mukatsuku*. Anger is metaphorically expressed as brewing in the belly, then getting to one's head. *Hara ga tatsu* '(lit.) the belly is standing up' is an idiom that points to deep anger and outrage. *Atama ni kuru* is also idiomatic and is frequently used to refer to anger that reaches to one's head and causes a loss of control.

Mukatsuku '(lit.) to feel sick to one's stomach' was originally used in the Kansai dialect to refer to the severe anger and disgust that make a person physically sick. This expression has become part of the general vocabulary, although its use is primarily limited to conversation.

Anger is also shown by interjections such as *Fun* 'Humph'. In addition, as explained in Entry 37, using *nani* 'what' as an interjection provides another means for expressing anger. Many curses are used in anger as well (see Entry 38).

It is also possible to describe a state of anger by the descriptive verb *okoru*. Although *hara ga tatsu, atama ni kuru*, and *mukatsuku* are used by a speaker to express his or her angry feelings, *okoru* describes a situation in which a person becomes angry. It can be used as a warning as in *Okoru yo, honto ni* 'I'm going to get mad, really.'

Examples

a. (Two teens talking about a common acquaintance)

(≈ft1a): たか子の態度、**ムカつく**。
(≈ft2): ほんと。**頭に来る**！
(≈ft1b): 夕べさ、たか子のこと考えてたら、**腹が立って**眠れなかったんだよ。

(≈ft1a): Takako no taido, **mukatsuku.**
(≈ft2): Honto. **Atama ni kuru!**
(≈ft1b): Yuube sa, Takako no koto kangaetetara, **hara ga tatte** nemure-nakatta n da yo. (see E. 72 for *n da*)

(≈ft1a): I'm really upset about the way Takako behaves.
(≈ft2): Really. She makes me mad.
(≈ft1b): Last night, I was thinking about Takako, and I got so angry, I couldn't sleep.

b. (≈) すぐやめないと**怒る**よ。

Sugu yame-nai to **okoru** yo.

Unless you stop it right away, I'm going to get mad.

Authentic Examples

a. (Taken from *Doomoto Tsuyoshi no shoojiki shindoi*, with Sakura Uehara as the guest) Uehara is upset about her hair, which Doomoto says is quite nice.

上原： そんな満足げな顔して見ないでよ。（堂本、笑う）**腹立つ**なあ。
堂本： いやいやいや全然。

Uehara: Sonna manzokugena kao shite mi-nai de yo. (*Doomoto, warau*) **Hara tatsu** naa.
Doomoto: Iya iya iya zenzen. (see E. 24 about repetition)

Uehara: Don't look so satisfied. (*Doomoto laughs*) It's upsetting.
Doomoto: No, no, no, not at all.

b. (Taken from interview #88, with Shunji Iwai, music video producer and movie director) Iwai reveals his feelings about awards.

林： (…) いっぱい賞をもらうといいですね。
岩井： でも、賞とかあんまり好きじゃなくて。もらってもあんまりうれしくない反面、落ちるとメチャ**腹が立つ**んです。

Hayashi: (…) Ippai shoo o morau to ii desu ne.
Iwai: Demo, shoo toka anmari sukija-nakute. Morattemo anmari ureshiku-nai hanmen, ochiru to mecha **hara ga tatsu** n desu. (see E. 24 for *mecha*)

Hayashi: (…) It will be nice to receive many awards, won't it?
Iwai: Well, I don't really like awards. I am not so overwhelmingly pleased, but if I fail to receive an award, I get desperately upset.

c. (Taken from *Long Love Letter Hyooryuu Kyooshitsu*, episode 1) Yuka explains to her colleagues how she got involved in the students' fight.

結花：　私が全員なぐったんです。**頭来ちゃった**んですよ。＃約束破ったから。

Yuka: Watashi ga zen'in nagutta n desu. **Atama kichatta** n desu yo. Yakusoku yabutta kara. (see E. 72 for *n desu*)

Yuka: I'm the one who beat him. I got really angry. Because he didn't keep his promise.

d. (Taken from *Santaku*) Sanma and Kimura are throwing darts. Sanma makes funny wisecracks as Kimura pauses dramatically before he makes his throw.

さんま：　おおカッコええカッコええ。（木村、笑う）心理作戦。心理作戦。
木村：　**あったま来んな**。
さんま：　ヘッよく言われる、**あったま来るって**。

Sanma: Oo kakko ee kakko ee. (see E. 13 for *kakko ii*; E. 24 about repetition) (*Kimura, warau)* Shinri sakusen. Shinri sakusen.
Kimura: **Attama kun na.** (see E. 27 for *attama* instead of *atama*)
Sanma: He-tt yoku iwareru, **attama kuru** tte. (see E. 48 about inverted word order)

Sanma: Wow, you look cool, really cool. (*Kimura laughs*) Psychological strategy. It's a psychological strategy, you know
Kimura: You really make me mad.
Sanma: Yeah, I'm often told so, I mean, I make them real mad.

e. (Taken from *Chibi Maruko-chan*, 14: 106) Maruko's father is furious as he reads in the newspaper that the price of cigarettes is being raised.

父：　＜くそ——っ / タバコが値上がり / するだとォ＞
＜**頭にくるなァ** / もうタバコ / やめるぞっ＞

chichi: Kusooo-tt. Tabako ga neagari suru da too. (see E. 38 for *kuso*; E. 27 for *kusooo-tt* instead of *kuso*)
Atama ni kuru naa. Moo tabako yameru zo-tt.

father: Shit. The price of cigarettes is going up?
It makes me really mad. I'm going to quit smoking, for sure.

f. (Taken from *Antiiku, seiyoo kottoo yoogashiten*, episode 8) Eiji, a former professional boxer, finds a newspaper article reporting scandalous things about him.

エイジ： 何だよこれ。**ムカつく**なあ。＃誰だよ、こんなの書いたのは。

Eiji: Nan da yo kore. **Mukatsuku** naa. Dare da yo, konna no kaita no wa. (see E. 16 for *konna*; E. 48 about the inverted word order)

Eiji: What's this? It makes me feel disgusted. Who is it, who wrote this?

g. (Taken from *Tsubasa o kudasai*, 33) Kyooka describes her impression of Tsubasa.

無邪気な顔。
思わずひねりつぶしたくなる。
(…… **ムカつく**)

Mujakina kao.
Omowazu hineri tsubushitaku naru.
(……**Mukatsuku**)

Innocent face.
Irresistibly, I want to twist and crush it.
(……Disgusting.)

h. (Taken from *Taiyoo wa shizuma-nai*, episode 6) Nao's father is upset that Ami visited the shop without the approval of her mother. Ami apologizes, but Nao explains that the father isn't really angry.

亜美： ごめんなさい。
直： ＃**怒ってんじゃない**から。＃父さん**怒ってない**よ。
亜美： でも。
直： お茶を出したから。

Ami: Gomennasai.
Nao: **Okotte n ja-nai** kara. Toosan **okotte nai** yo.
Ami: Demo.
Nao: Ocha o dashita kara.

Ami: I'm sorry.
Nao: It's not that my father is upset. He isn't angry.
Ami: But…
Nao: Because he served tea (for you).

i. (Taken from *Santaku*) Kimura takes Sanma surfing in December. By the time Kimura returns to the beach, Sanma, having been intimidated by the cold water, has already given up and is now relaxing and chatting with a group of local people. There he is enjoying seafood served to him. Sanma encourages Kimura to try some of the grilled fish.

さんま：　大丈夫？＃あ、これ、頭から。あつあつ。（木村、いわしの炭焼きを口に入れてもらう）すまんな、いろいろ迷惑かけて今日は。＃なあ。
木村：　**怒るよ**、本当に。
さんま：　さむいだろ。（さんま、笑う）
木村：　マジで。

Sanma: Daijoobu? A, kore, atama kara. Atsuatsu. (see E. 60 for *daijoobu*) (*Kimura, iwashi no sumiyaki o kuchi ni irete-morau*) Suman na, iroiro meiwaku kakete kyoo wa. Naa.
Kimura: **Okoru yo**, honto ni.
Sanma: Samui daro. (*Sanma, warau*)
Kimura: Maji de. (see E. 67 for *maji*)

Sanma: Are you OK? Here, this one, eat from the head. It's hot. (Kimura opens his mouth to receive the grilled fish from Sanma.) Sorry, I gave you a lot of trouble today. You know.
Kimura: I'm going to get mad, really.
Sanma: You must be cold. (*Sanma laughs*)
Kimura: Seriously (I'm going to get mad).

j. (Taken from *Tsubasa o kudasai*, 155) Kyooka visits Hatano's sister. Hatano committed suicide because he was bullied. Kyooka wonders why the sister does not accuse her for not helping Hatano.

「**怒らない**んですか？私のこと」
「言ったでしょう？責める気はないって。第一あなたは反省しているし……そんな人に**怒る**ことはできない。それに……**怒った**としても、あの子は帰ってこないもの」

"**Okora-nai** n desu ka? Watashi no koto." (see E. 30 for *watashi no koto*)
"Itta deshoo? Semeru ki wa nai tte. Daiichi anata wa hansei shiteiru shi……Sonna hito ni **okoru** koto wa deki-nai. Sore ni……**okotta** to shitemo, ano ko wa kaette ko-nai mono."

"Don't you get angry? About me?"
"Didn't I say already that I won't accuse you of anything? Besides, you are already remorseful about the incident. I cannot get angry toward such a person. And even if I get angry, my brother will not come back."

Additional Information

Other phrases and idiomatic expressions associated with anger include:

Phrases

激怒する	*gekido suru*	to be extremely infuriated
カッカする	*kakka suru*	to become flaringly angry
カンカンだ	*kankan da*	to become outraged
かんかんになって怒る	*kankan ni natte okoru*	to hit the ceiling, to fly into a rage
カッとする	*katto suru*	to become suddenly angry, to flare up (with anger)
キレる	*kireru*	(lit., to snap) to lose control over anger
プンプン怒る	*punpun okoru*	to be furious
八つ当たりする	*yatsuatari suru*	to vent one's anger on everything around

Idiomatic expressions

腹わたが煮えくり返る	*harawata ga niekuri-kaeru*	(lit., the guts boil) to boil with rage
堪忍袋の緒が切れる	*kanninbukuro no o ga kireru*	(lit., the cord on the patience bag breaks) to lose one's temper, to be furious beyond control

11. Worry and Fear

Key Expressions

不安なんです	*Fuan na n desu.*	I'm anxious (and concerned).
(≈) 心配だ	*Shinpai da.*	I'm worried.
怖い	*kowai*	scary, frightening
恐ろしい	*osoroshii*	threatening, fearful, dreadful, scary
恐怖	*kyoofu*	fear
(v) パニクる	*panikuru*	to be in a state of panic, to lose control
(≈) ビビる	*bibiru*	to be scared out of one's wits, to be (intimidatedly) scared

Explanation

When a person is anxious and concerned, *fuan* 'anxiety' and *fuanna* 'anxious' describe the feeling. A person may be worried about something, which is expressed by *Shinpai da* 'I'm worried'. *Shinpai* is also used as a noun as in *shinpai no tane* 'cause for worry'. *Shinpai suru-na* 'Don't worry' and its polite version, *Shinpai shinai-de*, are used as a general advice.

Kowai 'scary' and *osoroshii* 'threatening' are two emotion words typically used to convey fear. *Kowai* is used in reference both to the speaker's sense of fear and to the fear's source. Both *Aa, kowai* 'I'm scared' and *Asoko e iku no ga kowai* 'I'm scared of going there' are acceptable. *Kowai* is most often used when a speaker anticipates something harmful and wishes to avoid it. *Osoroshii* is used when the speaker is afraid of something that is likely to harm him or her. *Osoroshii* is used in a sentence that in some way indicates the source of fear, as in *Sensoo wa osoroshii* 'War is dreadful'.

Kyoofu is a descriptive term referring to fear. *Osoroshisa* may be used for descriptive purposes as well, with a slightly more spoken effect.

When describing behavior related to fear, *panikuru* describes being in a state of panic. Originating from the English word *panic*, *panikuru* is slanglike and its use is primarily limited to youth and young adults. *Bibiru* refers to a feeling arising from fear and/or shyness, and it often implies the speaker's hesitation and lack of courage. In an emotional context, a speaker uses *bibiru* when intimidated. Like the English expression "butterflies in the stomach," it expresses uneasiness, embarrassment, and fear at an impending stressful moment. *Bibiru* is usually used in casual spoken Japanese. One may also use *bibiru* as an interjection as in *Aa bibitta!* 'I got scared'.

Examples

a. (Two women talking about a family member traveling abroad)

(fa1a): 何だか**不安なんです**。家族が海外に行っていると。
(fs1): **心配しすぎ**ですよ、それは。
(fa1b): でも、何か**恐ろしい**事故にあうんじゃないかって**心配で**。

(fa1a): Nan da ka **fuan na n desu**. Kazoku ga kaigai ni itteiru to.
(fs1): **Shinpai shisugi** desu yo, sore wa. (see E. 48 about inverted word order)
(fa1b): Demo, nanika **osoroshii** jiko ni au n ja-nai ka tte **shinpai de**.

(fa1a): For some reason, I'm anxious and concerned. I mean, when my family members are abroad.
(fs1): You worry too much about that.
(fa1b): But, I'm worried that maybe they'll get involved in some terrible accident.

b. (A woman recounting a frightening experience to her friend)

(fa1): その細道、両側が崖なんですよ。すごく**怖くて**。
(fa2): そんな所だったんですか。観光地なのにけっこう**恐ろしい**ところなんですね。

(fa1): Sono hosomichi, ryoogawa ga gake na n desu yo. Sugoku **kowakute**.
(fa2): Sonna tokoro datta n desu ka. Kankoochi na noni kekkoo **osoroshii** tokoro na n desu ne. (see E. 16 for *sonna*; E. 25 for *kekkoo*)

(fa1): Both sides of that narrow path were cliffs. I was really scared.
(fa2): Such a place, I see. That is a sightseeing spot, but it sure sounds like a scary place.

Authentic Examples

a. (Taken from *Chibi Maruko-chan*, 14: 49) Maruko's mother reprimands Maruko, who is worried about the well-being of her best friend, Tamae.

まる子： ＜たまちゃん/どうしてるかな/ちょっと電話/してみよう＞
母： ＜ばかっ/よしなさい/こんな時に＞＜かえって/迷惑よ＞
まる子： ＜電話したいーっ/親友として/**心配だ**よォ＞

Maruko: Tama-chan doo shiteru ka na. Chotto denwa shite-miyoo. (see E. 25 for *chotto*)
haha: Baka-tt. Yoshinasai, konna toki ni. Kaette meiwaku yo. (see E. 38 for *Baka-tt*; E. 16 for *konna*)
Maruko: Denwa shitaii-tt. Shin'yuu to shite **shinpai da** yoo. (see E. 27 for *shitaii-tt* instead of *shitai*)

Maruko: I wonder how Tamae is doing. I guess I'll call her.
mother: That's foolish, dear. Stop that, at a time like this. It will bother her.
Maruko: I want to call her. I'm worried about her as her best friend.

b. (Taken from *Long Love Letter Hyooryuu Kyooshitsu*, episode 1) Teachers are talking about an incident where a student and a teacher got into a fight.

浅海： 乱闘事件？えっ、生徒同士のですか。
若原： いえ。生徒と女性教師の乱闘です。
関谷： ま、**怖い**わー。

Asami: Rantoo jiken? E-tt, seito dooshi no desu ka. (see E. 21 for *E-tt*)
Wakahara: Ie. Seito to josei kyooshi no rantoo desu.
Sekiya: Ma, **kowai** waa.

Asami: A fighting incident? What? Among students?

Wakahara: No. A fight between a student and a female teacher.

Sekiya: Oh my, that's frightening.

c. (Taken from *Chibi Maruko-chan*, 14: 38) Note the use of *kowai* and its nominal counterpart, *kowasa*.

山田： ＜山根君は / 台風が**怖い** / のかい？ / アハハー＞

山根： ＜そりゃ**怖い**よ / だって / 風や雨が / ものすごいん / だから＞

まる子： ＜そうだよ / 台風は / **怖い**んだよ / アンタ＞

山田： ＜オレは / おばけの方が / **怖い**もんねー＞

山根： ＜**怖さ**が / 違うだろ＞

Yamada: Yamane-kun wa taifuu ga **kowai** no kai? Aha haa.

Yamane: Sorya **kowai** yo. Datte kaze ya ame ga monosugoi n da kara.

Maruko: Soo da yo. Taifuu wa **kowai** n da yo, anta. (see E. 30 for *anta*)

Yamada: Ore wa obake no hoo ga **kowai** mon nee.

Yamane: **Kowasa** ga chigau daro.

Yamada: Yamane, are you afraid of typhoons? Ha-ha.

Yamane: Of course I'm afraid. They bring fierce wind and rain.

Maruko: That's right. Typhoons are scary, don't you know?

Yamada: To me, ghosts are scarier.

Yamane: You're talking about different kinds of fear.

d. (Taken from interview #89, with Baku Yumemakura, writer)

夢枕： アイデアはいっぱいあるんですけど、書きたい気持ちがすり減っちゃうことのほうが**怖い**んですね。アイデアがなくなる**恐怖**はないんです。

Yumemakura: Aidea wa ippai aru n desu kedo, kakitai kimochi ga suri-hetchau koto no hoo ga **kowai** n desu ne. Aidea ga naku-naru **kyoofu** wa nai n desu. (see E. 72 for *n desu*)

Yumemakura: I have many ideas, but I'm afraid that my will to write will gradually be consumed and decrease. I have no fear of running out of ideas.

e. (Taken from *Beautiful Life*, episode 6) Shuuji confesses that he was scared by using *bibiru*.

柊二： ふ。何だろうね。さっき**ビビった**からほっとしたのかな。

杏子： さっきって？

柊二： あ？やさっきさあ (...) 顔色真っ青だしさ、このまま体どうにかなっちゃうのかと思ってさあ。**ビビった**。

杏子： ごめんね。驚かせてごめんね。

Shuuji: Fu. Nan daroo ne. Sakki **bibitta** kara hotto shita no ka na. (see E. 22 for *hotto shita*)
Kyooko: Sakki tte? (see E. 70 about echo questions)
Shuuji: A? Ya sakki saa (...) kaoiro massao da shi sa, kono mama karada doonika natchau no ka to omotte saa. **Bibitta.**
Kyooko: Gomen ne. Odorokasete gomen ne. (see E. 21 for *odoroku*)

Shuuji: Whew. What is this? Maybe I'm relieved after getting scared earlier.
Kyooko: What do you mean by earlier?
Shuuji: What? Well, a while ago (...), you were totally pale, and I wondered if something serious might happen to you physically. I got scared.
Kyooko: Sorry. I'm sorry to surprise you like that.

f. (Taken from *Long Love Letter Hyooryuu Kyooshitsu*, episode 2) After an earthquake, Takamatsu comments on how scared he was.

大友： 終わった？
高松： 超**ビビった**。

Ootomo: Owatta?
Takamatsu: Choo **bibitta.** (see E. 24 for *choo*)

Ootomo: Is it over?
Takamatsu: Boy, was I scared!

g. (Taken from *Kitchin*, 19 [English translation, 12]) It is interesting to see that *bibitta* here is translated into "a little bit intimidated."

「みかげさん、家の母親に**ビビった**？」
彼は言った。
「うん、だってあんまりきれいなんだもの」

"Mikage-san, uchi no hahaoya ni **bibitta**?"
Kare wa itta.
"Un, datte anmari kireina n da mono." (see E. 59 for *datte*)

"Mikage," he said, "were you a little bit intimidated by my mother?"
"Yes," I told him frankly. "I've never seen a woman that beautiful."

12. Jealousy

Key Expressions

うらやましい	*urayamashii*	envious
嫉妬する	*shitto suru*	to be jealous
(焼きもちを)やく	*(yakimochi o) yaku*	to be jealous, to envy

Explanation

Urayamashii 'envious' is an adjective used to express, most often in a benign way, one's near-jealous admiration. It is not necessarily negative, but it does border on being grudgingly envious or jealous. *Shitto suru* 'to be jealous' is almost always negative and one should avoid saying it, if possible.

Yakimochi o yaku (lit., to roast a roasted rice cake) is an idiom often used to express envy and jealousy, especially toward people who are in love. The most common situation is where, seeing someone else involved in an intimate relationship, the speaker becomes envious. For example, you may find that a person you love behaves intimately with someone else, and you feel jealous. In this situation, your friends may advise you, *Yakimochi yaku-na yo* 'Don't be jealous'.

Example

a. (A young woman is a bit jealous of her elder sister getting ready to go out with a boyfriend)

(≈fy1a): **うらやましい**なあ。やっぱり私は邪魔かな。
(≈fy2a): 何が？
(≈fy1b): だって、ふたりだけで行きたいんでしょ、ハイキング。
(≈fy2b): なに、**焼きもちやいたりして**。
(≈fy1c): だって …

(≈fy1a): **Urayamashii** naa. Yappari watashi wa jama ka na. (see E. 57 for *yappari*)
(≈fy2a): Nani ga?
(≈fy1b): Datte, futari dake de ikitai n desho, haikingu. (see E. 48 about the inverted word order)
(≈fy2b): Nani, **yakimochi yaitari shite.** (see E. 63 for *tari shite*)
(≈fy1c): Datte… (see E. 59 for *datte*)

(≈fy1a): I'm envious. I'm afraid I am a bother, after all.
(≈fy2a): How so?
(≈fy1b): You want to go on hiking together, just the two of you, right?
(≈fy2b): What! You are jealous?
(≈fy1c): Well, but…

Authentic Examples

a. (Taken from *Chibi Maruko-chan*, 14: 130) Maruko's classmates are talking about Yamane, a boy who often suffers from stomach pain.

永沢：　＜胃腸の弱い人は／太らなくて／いいよ　キミ／モデルになれる／かもよ＞
山根：　＜えっ＞
小杉：　＜そんな山根君が／ちょっぴり／**うらやましい**なあ＞

Nagasawa: Ichoo no yowai hito wa futora-nakute ii yo. Kimi moderu ni nareru kamo yo.
Yamane: E-tt. (see E. 21 for *E-tt*)
Kosugi: Sonna Yamane-kun ga choppiri **urayamashii** naa. (see E. 16 for *sonna*)

Nagasawa: People with sensitive stomachs luckily don't get fat. You may be able to become a model.
Yamane: What!
Kosugi: I feel a bit envious of Yamane.

b. (Taken from *Kitchin*, 53 [English translation, 34])

私は思った。おばあさんの言葉があまりにやさしげで、笑ったその子があんまり急にかわいく思えて、私は**うらやましかった**。私には二度とない……。

Watashi wa omotta. Obaasan no kotoba ga amari ni yasashige de, waratta sono ko ga anmari kyuu ni kawaiku omoete, watashi wa **urayamashikatta**. Watashi ni wa nido to nai...... (see E. 6 for *yasashii*; E. 31 for *kawaii*)

Isn't that nice, I thought. Hearing the grandmother's gentle words and seeing the child's face suddenly turn adorable when she smiled, I became envious. I'd never see my own grandmother again.

c. (Taken from interview #83, with Rei Asami, actress) The following sentence appears in the comment Hayashi makes about the interview with Asami. Because *Aa urayamashii* is a direct exposure of emotion, it is enclosed within a quotation in a descriptive text.

こんな方が奥さまだったら、そりゃあご主人は大切にしますよね。ご自慢ですよね。**ああ羨ましい**と女性編集者と焼き肉を食べて帰った私です。

Konna kata ga okusama dattara, soryaa goshujin wa taisetsu ni shimasu yo ne. Gojiman desu yo ne. **Aa urayamashii** to josei henshyuusha to yakiniku o tabete kaetta watashi desu.

Well, if a person like her is his wife, the husband would surely treasure her. He must be proud of her. How envious [I am]! Saying so, I went home after going out to eat a grilled meat dish with a female editor.

d. (Taken from *Chibi Maruko-chan*, 13: 62)

永沢： ＜藤木君キミ / ボクと山根君のこと / **嫉妬してる**だろ？＞
藤木： ＜**嫉妬** !! ＞ ＜そんな / ... ボクはただ / ...... ＞

Nagasawa: Fujiki-kun kimi boku to Yamane-kun no koto **shitto shiteru** daro?
Fujiki: **Shitto**!! Sonna. ...Boku wa tada...... (see E. 16 for *sonna*)

Nagawawa: Fujiki, you are jealous of the relationship between me and Yamane, aren't you?
Fujiki: Jealous!! No, I only...

e. (Taken from *Majo no jooken*, episode 9) Kiriko confesses that she was in love with Masaru, who is in love with Michi.

桐子： まだわかんないんだ。あたしは、大さんのことが好きだった。っていうより、あんたに**嫉妬してた**。
未知： えっ？
桐子： いつも周りにチヤホヤされて、それを当然と思ってるみたいなあんたがすっごく頭に来た。

Kiriko: Mada wakan-nai n da. Atashi wa, Masaru-san no koto ga suki-datta. Tte yuu yori, anta ni **shitto shiteta**. (see E. 66 for *wakan-nai*; E. 30 for *Masaru-san no koto*; E. 32 for *suki*; E. 30 for *anta*)
Michi: E-tt?
Kiriko: Itsumo mawari ni chiyahoya sarete, sore o toozen to omotteru mitaina anta ga suggoku atama ni kita. (see E. 24 and E. 27 for *suggoku*; E. 10 for *atama ni kita*)

Kiriko: You still don't get it. I loved Masaru. More than that, I was jealous of you.
Michi: What?
Kiriko: You are always praised (and pampered) by people around you, and you accept it as if it were a natural course of events. I was very angry about you.

f. (Taken from *Long Love Letter Hyooryuu Kyooshitsu*, episode 2) Yuka and Asami are talking about intimate relationships.

結花： 私はねあなたじゃあるまいし生徒と恋愛関係なんてありえません。もしかして**やいてる**？

浅海：	うーん。まあ、認める。何つうの、#こう、男としてっつうか、教師としても、あんまそういうのないからさ。わりと**うらやましい**（...）。
Yuka:	Watashi wa ne anata ja aru-mai shi seito to ren'ai kankei nante ariemasen. Moshika shite **yaiteru**? (see E. 31 for *ren'ai*; E. 15 for *nante*)
Asami:	Uun. Maa, mitomeru. Nan tsuu no, koo, otoko to shite ttsuu ka, kyooshi to shite mo, anma soo yuu no nai kara sa. Warito **urayamashii** (...). (see E. 63 for *ttsuu ka*; E. 25 for *warito*)
Yuka:	As for myself, I'm not like you, you know. It is impossible to have a love affair with my student. Can it be that you are jealous?
Asami:	Well. I admit to that. How can I put it into words? As a man, and as a teacher, I don't have that kind of experience. So, I'm sort of jealous (...).

g. (Taken from *Long Vacation*, episode 5) Minami elaborates on her new boyfriend, but Sena shows little interest. He wants to end the conversation by saying, *Hai, wakarimashita*, to which Minami responds.

瀬名：	はい、分かりました。
南：	あっ、**焼きもち**。うー。
瀬名：	誰が。どこでどうやったら**焼きもちやける**んですか。
Sena:	Hai, wakarimashita. (see E. 66 for *wakarimashita*)
Minami:	A-tt, **yakimochi**. Uu.
Sena:	Dare ga? Doko de doo yattara **yakimochi yakeru** n desu ka? (see E. 40 about rhetorical questions)
Sena:	I got it.
Minami:	Oh, you are jealous. See.
Sena:	Who is jealous? How in the world can I get jealous over you?

h. (Taken from *Santaku*) Sanma comments on how cool Kimura was at the SMAP concert, which he went to see for the first time.

さんま：	ね、だから、#プロとしては正解だから。余りにもカッコええから、あのう要するに男として**焼きもち焼く**わけよ。
Sanma:	Ne, dakara, puro toshite wa seikai da kara. Amarinimo kakko ee kara, anoo yoosuru ni otoko to shite **yakimochi yaku** wake yo. (see E. 13 for *kakko ii*)
Sanma:	See, so, as a professional person, it's the right thing to do. You are so cool that, in fact, as a man, I get jealous of you.

6
Emotionally Evaluating

13. Nice, Cool! and Not So Cool!

Key Expressions

(≈) いいねえ	*Ii nee.*	That's nice, isn't it?
(≈) ステキ！	*Suteki!*	How wonderful!
(≈) すごい！	*Sugoi!*	Extraordinary! Awesome!
(≈) カッコいい	*kakko ii*	great, sharp, neat, nice-looking, stylish
(v) クール	*kuuru*	cool
(≈) イケてる	*iketeru*	excellent, great
(≈) いい感じ	*Ii kanji.*	Great (feeling).
(≈) カッコ悪い	*kakko warui*	unattractive, not stylish, awkward, embarrassing
(≈) ダサい	*dasai*	not cool, out of style, country-bumpkin-like, cheesy, anachoronistic

Explanation

Positive evaluation is expressed by a number of adjectives, including *ii* 'good', *sutekina* 'wonderful', and *sugoi* 'extraordinary, deserving (surprising) admiration'. *Ii* is used in a variety of ways (as discussed in the additional information), but the basic meaning is one of being good, right, and proper. *Suteki!* and *Sugoi!* are often used as interjections to express admiration of something as being wonderful and extraordinary. *Suteki* is primarily used in speech associated with the "feminine" style.

When admiring someone or something in casual speech, *kakko ii* and *kuuru* are used. *Kakko ii* refers to someone's attractiveness, particularly to a fashionable or sharp appearance. But the use of *kakko ii* is not limited to appearance. For example, beyond an expression like *kakko ii booshi* 'nice-looking hat', one like *kakko ii ikikata* refers to an attractive way of life that the speaker admires. *Kuuru* is similar in meaning to *kakko ii*, but because it is an English loanword, it is used with a sense of foreign appeal. *Kuuru* also implies someone who manages life in organized, purposeful, and controlled ways, calmly avoiding confusion, chaos, and panic. *Kuuru* is less common than *kakko ii* among mature adults. Although *kakko ii* is widely used, *kuuru* is generally restricted to youth.

Another expression is *iketeru,* which is associated with *ikeru* 'skillful, excellent'. *Iketeru* refers to general attractiveness arising from excellence. It has less to do with appearance than *kakko ii,* referring instead to an overall attractive quality of being excellent and deserving special admiration. *Ii kanji* (lit., good feeling) is used as a general evaluative phrase when admiring something.

When a speaker is not impressed or is downright disappointed, *kakko warui* and another adjective, *dasai,* are used. *Kakko warui* is used for something or someone shamefully unattractive. *Dasai* implies that something is out of touch, out of style, country-bumpkin-like, cheesy, anachronistic, or embarrassingly unattractive or unworthy. *Dasai* is primarily used by young people in casual speech.

Examples

a. (Two young women talking about a sweater)

(≈fy1a): まあ、**すてきな**セーター。
(≈fy2a): **いい**でしょ、これ。なかなかね。
(≈fy1b): 高かったでしょ？
(≈fy2b): ううん、バーゲンで買ったんだ。
(≈fy1c): **すごーい**。

(≈fy1a): Maa, **sutekina** seetaa.
(≈fy2a): **Ii** desho, kore. Nakanaka ne. (E. 48 about inverted word order)
(≈fy1b): Takakatta desho?
(≈fy2b): Uun, baagen de katta n da.
(≈fy1c): **Sugooi**! (see E. 27 for *sugooi* instead of *sugoi*)

(≈fy1a): Wow, what a nice sweater!
(≈fy2a): Isn't this nice? Pretty nice, isn't it?
(≈fy1b): Must have been expensive, right?
(≈fy2b): No. I bought it at a bargain sale.
(≈fy1c): Wow, awesome!

b. (Two young men commenting on a colleague)

(≈my1): 佐藤さんさ、今日もまた変わったファッションだね。
(my2): **ダサい**っすよ。あのジャケット。

(≈my1): Satoo-san sa, kyoo mo mata kawatta fasshon da ne.
(my2): **Dasai** ssu yo. Ano jaketto.

(≈my1): Mr. Satoo is wearing some strange clothing again today.
(my2): Cheesy, really. I mean, that jacket!

Authentic Examples

a. (Taken from *Himawari nikki*, 28) Konomi reveals her anticipation for the new academic year.

大騒ぎではじまった、中学三年最初の日。

でも、もしかしたら、最初の予感の通り、この一年は、何か**ステキな**コトがおこるかもしれない。

Oosawagi de hajimatta, chuugaku sannen no saisho no hi.

Demo, moshika shitara, saisho no yokan no toori, kono ichinen wa, nanika **sutekina** koto ga okoru kamo shirenai.

The first day of the third year at the middle school, the day that started with much fuss.

But, maybe, as I felt at the beginning, something nice may happen during this year.

b. (Taken from *Antiiku, seiyoo kottoo yoogashiten*, episode 4) Eiji and Momoko are riding the bus together. Note that Eiji uses *kakko ii* about Momoko's way of thinking.

桃子： 今の仕事ちょっと不本意っていうか、やりたいこととは違うんだよね。
エイジ： そうなんだ。
桃子： うん。(…) それにまあ、贅沢な悩みなのかもしれないけどさ。
エイジ： ふーん。
桃子： でも、#でも自分の力で上を目指したいと思ってるんだ。
エイジ： #上を目指すか。**カッコいい**なあ。頑張ってよ。

Momoko: Ima no shigoto chotto fuhon'i tte yuu ka, yaritai koto to wa chigau n da yo ne. (see E. 63 for *te yuu ka*)
Eiji: Soo na n da. (see E. 46 for *Soo na n da*)
Momoko: Un. (…) Sore ni maa, zeitakuna nayami na no kamo shirenai kedo sa. (see E. 63 for *kedo*)
Eiji: Fuun. (see E. 21 for *Fuun*)

Momoko: Demo, demo jibun no chikara de ue o mezashitai to omotteru n da. (see E. 42 for *jibun*; E. 72 for *n da*)
Eiji: Ue o mezasu ka. **Kakko ii** naa. Ganbatte yo. (see E. 70 about echo responses)

Momoko: My current job, I'm reluctant about it, or more truthfully, it's different from what I want to do.
Eiji: I see. I understand.
Momoko: Yeah. You know, it is perhaps a luxury to worry about it, though.
Eiji: I see.
Momoko: But, but I do want to make an effort and aim high.
Eiji: To aim high. That's cool. Good luck.

c. (Taken from *Chibi Maruko-chan*, 14: 103) Maruko chats with Tamae about Maruko's father.

まる子： ＜うちのおとうさんは／ハイライトなんだ／男は黙って／ハイライト／なんだって＞
たまえ： ＜へー／なんだか／**カッコイイ**ね＞
まる子： ＜**カッコイイ**／ってほどじゃ／ないけどね＞

Maruko: Uchi no otoosan wa hairaito na n da. Otoko wa damatte hairaito na n da tte.
Tamae: Hee, nandaka **kakko** ii ne. (see E. 21 for *Hee*)
Maruko: **Kakko ii** tte hodo ja-nai kedo ne. (see E. 63 for *kedo*)

Maruko: My father smokes Hi-Lite. He says, "Men just silently smoke Hi-Lite."
Tamae: I see, he's neat, isn't he?
Maruko: He isn't so neat, but...

d. (Taken from *Kitchin*, 10 [English translation, 6])

しかし彼の態度はとても"**クール**"だったので、私は信じることができた。

Shikashi kare no taido wa totemo "**kuuru**" datta node, watashi wa shinjiru koto ga dekita.

His attitude was so totally "cool," though, I felt I could trust him.

e. (Taken from *Muko-dono*, episode 3) Sisters comment on Sakura's cooking skill. *Ude o ageru* is an idiomatic expression meaning 'to improve one's skill'.

かえで： **イケてる、イケてる**。また腕あげたね。
あずさ： ほんと、おいしい。

Kaede: **Iketeru, iketeru**. Mata ude ageta ne.
Azusa: Honto, oishii.

Kaede: Great. Really great. You're getting better again.
Azusa: Really delicious.

f. (Taken from interview #87, with Muneaki Masuda, company president)

林： 増田さん、新しい歌手が出たりしたときに、これ**イケる**！みたいなことはわかります？
増田： すっごいわかる。(...)「これはダメ」「これは**イケる**」ってパッパパッパと言える。

Hayashi: Masuda-san, atarashii kashu ga detari shita toki ni, kore **ikeru!** mitaina koto wa wakarimasu?
Masuda: Suggoi wakaru. (...) "Kore wa dame" "Kore wa **ikeru**" tte pappapappa to ieru. (see E. 24 for *suggoi*)

Hayashi: Mr. Masuda, when a new singer makes his or her debut, can you tell if this singer will make it or not?
Masuda: Absolutely. (...) This one isn't good, this one is going to make it. I can tell right away.

g. (Taken from *Long Vacation*, episode 6) Sugisaki and Minami talk about Minami's job interview, which she failed.

杉崎： でもさ、あの、うそを、つかないで。
南： うそ？
杉崎： 面接。
南： ああ、知ってたんすか。やあ、あのほんとごめんなさい。つい**カッコ悪くて**。
杉崎： でも、**カッコ悪くても**、南ちゃんは南ちゃんでしょ。

Sugisaki: Demo sa, ano, uso o, tsuka-nai de.
Minami: Uso? (see E. 70 about echo questions)
Sugisaki: Mensetsu.
Minami: Aa, shitteta n su ka. Yaa, ano honto gomennasai. Tsui **kakko warukute.**
Sugisaki: Demo, **kakko warukutemo**, Minami-chan wa Minami-chan desho. (see E. 74 about tautology)

Sugisaki: But, uh, please don't tell a lie.
Minami: A lie?
Sugisaki: The interview.
Minami: Did you know about it? Uh, I'm really sorry. I felt that wasn't neat, and so...
Sugisaki: But, even if it isn't neat, Minami, for me you are the same you.

h. (Taken from *Muko-dono*, episode 1) Ryoo's friend comments on Yuuichiroo, who is a singer and songwriter. Note the use of *dasai* and its negative, *dasaku-nai*.

友達：	桜庭祐一郎のコンサートのチケットとってもらえないかなと思って。(...)
亮：	桜庭？#**ダセー**。
友達：	**ダサくない**よ。**クール**で、**カッコいい**じゃん。
亮：	**ダサい**んだよ。

tomodachi:	Sakuraba Yuuichiroo no konsaato no chiketto totte-moraenai ka na to omotte. (...)
Ryoo:	Sakuraba? **Dasee**. (see Chapter 2 about *dasee* instead of *dasai*)
tomodachi:	**Dasaku-nai** yo. **Kuuru** de, **kakko ii** jan.
Ryoo:	**Dasai** n da yo. (see E. 72 for *n da*)

friend:	I was thinking...is it possible to get me a ticket for the Yuuichiroo Sakuraba's concert?
Ryoo:	Sakuraba? So out of style.
friend:	He's not out of style. He's totally cool and good-looking.
Ryoo:	He is embarrassingly cheesy.

Additional Information

The adjective *ii* is versatile and frequently used in conversation. Some of its uses are:

1. In answer to a request. For example, responding to *Motte-kite-kureru?* 'Will you bring it to me?' a speaker may answer *Ii desu yo* 'Certainly'.
2. When soliciting or confirming agreement or approval, as in *Benkyoo suru koto. Ii?* 'To study hard. All right?'
3. To make a special request when the speaker begs for approval, as in *Ii desho? Onegai!* 'O.K.? Please!'
4. To mean that something is sufficient or enough, as when refusing an offer. For example, when a person asks *Ocha demo nomu?* 'Want to have some tea?' the answer may be *Ii* 'No (thanks)'. Or, when telling someone not to worry any more, a speaker might say *Moo ii yo. Shinpai suru na* 'That's enough. Don't worry'.
5. Idiomatically, as in *ii hito* 'lover' and *ii naka* 'in love (relationship)'
6. To mean something ugly and unappealing (with words that have a negative connotation), as in *ii haji sarasu* 'to show an embarrassing shame' and *ii meiwaku* 'unpleasant nuisance'.
7. In the form *Yokatta* to express relief (see E. 22).

14. Characterizing Events with Emotion

Key Expressions

せめて	*semete*	at best, at least
せっかく	*sekkaku*	especially, purposely
まさか	*masaka*	absolutely not, impossible

Explanation

A number of attitudinal adverbs express a speaker's emotional attitude. These adverbs differ from ordinary adverbs of manner that describe a verb, as in *hayaku hashiru* 'to run fast'. Instead, they reveal how the speaker feels.

Semete expresses the attitude that although the ideal result cannot be achieved, at least some attempt is made to realize it or some results are expectedly obtainable. For example, one may say *Semete nichiyoobi wa nonbiri shitai* 'At least on Sunday I want to relax' with the sense that on other days it is impossible to relax anyway.

Sekkaku is used to express the speaker's attitude that something is especially or purposely done, but that the intention is thwarted. For example, when a wife who has prepared dinner for her husband has realized that he ate elsewhere, she may say *Sekkaku junbi shita noni* 'I prepared it (especially for you), but...'.

Masaka implies a strong negative response to an event, with the speaker saying emphatically that something would never happen. A person of good character, for example, would never do the evil thing mentioned. The speaker expresses this by saying *Masaka ano hito ga sonna koto suru hazu nai* '(There is) absolutely no way that he would do such a thing!'

Authentic Examples

a. (Taken from *Chibi Maruko-chan*, 14: 158) The grandfather uses *semete* to express the feeling "at least."

祖父：　＜そうじゃ / 佐々木さんにも / おみやげにやろう＞

まる子：　＜そーだよねっ / 佐々木の / じいさんの / 苗木植えを / 断わっちゃったん / だからねえ＞

祖父：　＜**せめて** / おみやげに貝 / ぐらいはのう ...＞

sofu: Soo ja. Sasaki-san ni mo omiyage ni yaroo. (see E. 76 about the use of *soo ja*)

Maruko: Soo da yo ne-tt. Sasaki no jiisan no ueki ue o kotowatchatta n da kara nee. (see E. 17 for *kotowatchatta*)

sofu: **Semete** omiyage ni kai gurai wa noo...

grandfather: That's it. We'll give some to Sasaki as a souvenir.
Maruko: That's right. You said "no" to help Sasaki's grandfather plant seedlings, so.
grandfather: At least I should give some clams as a souvenir…

b. (Taken from *Furuete nemure, sanshimai*, 15: 38) Kunitomo, Yuriko's boyfriend, talks to Yuriko.

「僕も署へ戻らないと」
「じゃあ …… **せめて**玄関まで一緒に」

"Boku mo sho e modoranai to."
"Jaa……**semete** genkan made issho ni."

"I must return to the (police) station."
"Well, then, let me walk with you (to see you off) at least to the entrance."

c. (Taken from interview #83, with Rei Asami, actress) Asami expresses her hesitant feeling of "at least" by *semete*.

林： そのとき思ったんですけど、首筋の美しさが息をのむような感じでした。
麻美： そうですか。よかったです。**せめて**一つぐらいきれいなところがないと。（笑）
林： もちろん全体的にきれいでいらっしゃいます。

Hayashi: Sono toki omotta n desu kedo, kubisuji no utsukushisa ga iki o nomu yoona kanji deshita.
Asami: Soo desu ka. Yokatta desu. **Semete** hitotsu gurai kireina tokoro ga nai to. (*warai*) (see E. 22 for *yokatta*)
Hayashi: Mochiron zentaiteki ni kirei deirasshaimasu.

Hayashi: I thought then that the line of your neck was so stunningly beautiful.
Asami: Is that so? I'm relieved. At least one point of beauty, I hope I have. (*laugh*)
Hayashi: Of course, you are beautiful all over.

d. (Taken from Uchidate 2003b, 59) In this essay entitled "Nee, moratte yo" (Please, please accept this), the writer comments on how she feels about home exercising equipment that she doesn't use any more.

むろん、新品同様の物を捨てるのもイヤだが、何よりも**せめて**友人知人のところで役に立って、余生を有意義に送って欲しいのである。

Muron, shinpin dooyoo no mono o suteru no mo iya da ga, nani yori mo **semete** yuujin chijin no tokoro de yaku ni tatte, yosei o yuuigi ni okutte hoshii no dearu. (see E. 9 for *iya*; E. 72 for *no da*)

Of course, I don't like to throw away the equipment which is almost brand-new; but I at least want it to spend its useful days for the rest of its life in the homes of my acquaintances and friends.

e. (Taken from *Chibi Maruko-chan*, 14: 16) Maruko's father drives Maruko, her sister, and their grandfather to a restaurant located in Yokohama's Chinatown. Maruko expresses that they came to Chinatown deliberately by *sekkaku*.

まる子： ＜おとうさん／勝手に注文／しないでよ＞＜**せっかく**中華の／本場に来たんだから／ラーメンじゃなくて／他の食べたいよ＞
父： ＜うるさいっ／金のかかること／言うなっ＞

Maruko: Otoosan katte ni chuumon shi-naide yo. **Sekkaku** chuuka no honba ni kita n da kara raamen ja-nakute hoka no tabetai yo.
chichi: Urusai-tt. Kane no kakaru koto yuu-na-tt. (see E. 39 for *urusai*; E. 27 for *urusai-tt* and *yuu-na-tt*)

Maruko: Dad, don't make orders without asking us. We came all the way to the spot famous for Chinese food, so I want to eat something other than *raamen* noodles.
father: Be quiet. Don't say things that will cost me money.

f. (Taken from *Ren'ai hakusho*, 14: 97) Miho's boyfriend, Kaito, comes to visit Miho's home while she is away.

「おはよ」
目をこすりながら、海人さんが、笑う。
「**せっかく**、沖縄から会いに来たのに、誰もいないんだもんな」

"Ohayo"
Me o kosuri nagara, Kaito-san ga, warau.
"**Sekkaku**, Okinawa kara ai ni kita noni, daremo i-nai n da mon na."

"Morning"
Rubbing his eyes, Kaito smiles.
"I came all the way from Okinawa to see you, but nobody is home."

g. (Taken from *Long Love Letter Hyooryuu Kyooshitsu*, episode 1) Asami uses *masaka,* which is repeated by Yuka. The same attitude is shared.

結花： 昔さあ、#私が中学ん時、こういう迷信があってさ。新年の一番最初にしゃべる男の人とはその一年間縁があるみたいな↑
浅海： あー。
結花： しゃべっちゃった。
浅海： **まさか**、#まだその迷信信じてるとか。
結花： **まさか**。

Yuka: Mukashi saa, watashi ga chuugaku n toki, koo yuu meishin ga atte sa. Shinnen no ichiban saisho ni shaberu otoko no hito to wa sono ichinenkan en ga aru mitaina↑ (see E. 23 for *ichiban*; E. 64 for *mitaina*; E. 65 about the rising tone)
Asami: Aa.
Yuka: Shabetchatta. (see E. 17 for *shabetchatta*)
Asami: **Masaka**, mada sono meishin shinjiteru toka.
Yuka: **Masaka.**

Yuka: A long time ago, when I was in junior high school, there was this superstition. Like, you'll have some relationship with the man you first exchange words with in the new year.
Asami: I see.
Yuka: Whoops, I did speak with you.
Asami: It can't be that you still believe in that superstition, right?
Yuka: No way, (absolutely not).

h. (Taken from *Muko-dono*, episode 10) Satsuki comments that it is ironical that her family would find out about her brother's whereabouts in such an unexpected manner.

さつき： でも皮肉だよね。**まさか**、こんな形で兄貴の消息を知るなんてさ。

Satsuki: Demo hiniku da yo ne. **Masaka**, konna katachi de aniki no shoosoku o shiru nante sa. (see E. 15 for *nante*)

Satsuki: But it is ironic, isn't it? So unexpectedly to find out the whereabouts of our brother in this way.

i. (Taken from *Dokkin paradaisu*, 68) Ai asks a question, to which Akira replies with a strong denial. *Masaka* is used as an interjection.

「パパやママたち、もしかしてこの慶吾さんて人と知り合いだったかな？」
「**まさか**！同じ東大生っていったって、全学部合わせたら何千人もいるんだぜ。」

"Papa ya mamatachi, moshika shite kono Keigo-san te hito to shiriai datta ka na?"
"**Masaka!** Onaji toodaisei tte ittatte, zengakubu awasetara nanzennin mo iru n da ze."

"I wonder if Mom and Dad knew this person, Keigo."
"No way! Although they were students at the University of Tokyo at the same time, there are several thousand students enrolled in all of the departments."

15. Evaluating with *Nante* and *Nanka*

Key Expressions

(≈) 若いのに社長なんてすごい	*Wakai noni shachoo nante sugoi.*	Although he is so young, it is amazing that he is a company president.
(≈) そんな話なんて誰も信じない	*Sonna hanashi nante dare mo shinji-nai.*	Nobody believes in such a story.
また忘れるなんて！	*Mata wasureru nante!*	Boy, to forget it again!
(≈) あの人なんか大嫌い	*Ano hito nanka dai-kirai.*	That person, I really dislike.
(≈) 私なんかでいいの？	*Watashi nanka de ii no?*	A person like me, are you sure I'm suitable?

Explanation

Nante 'such (as)' is an emotive topic marker primarily used in casual speech (see Entry 47 for other topic-introducing strategies). *Nante* presents items the speaker views as extreme, beyond what is ordinarily expected. What precedes *nante* is presented as the content of the speaker's surprising exclamation; what follows is likely to be an evaluative expression.

Nante functions as an exclamative particle when appearing at phrase- and sentence-final positions. (Note that this *nante* differs from the *nan te* introduced in Entry 45.) *Nante* can be used both in positive and negative contexts, although negative use is more frequent. The *nante* used in negative contexts is interchangeable with *nanka*. *Nank*a is a colloquial version of *nado*, and it appears as a topic as well as elsewhere. Although it can occur in both positive and negative contexts, I focus on negative ones here. *Nanka* in non-negative contexts is briefly discussed in the note.

Nanka, following nouns and particles in negative contexts, adds a sense of denial and humility. First, *nanka* accompanies items the speaker does not like and those items that the speaker finds valueless or so nearly worthless as to evoke scorn. Those items marked by *nanka* are the emotional targets of the speaker's disdain, dislike, or surprise. For example, *Obasan no uchi e nanka ikitaku-nai* 'I don't want to go to (such a horrible place as) my aunt's home', showing the intensity of dislike or disapproval.

I must warn here that the "negative" quality associated with *nanka* should be broadly interpreted. Although the sentence may not contain *-nai*, the context may call for a negative interpretation. For example, if the speaker asks *Mada kakegoto nanka yatteru no?* 'Is he still doing such a thing as gambling?', strong dislike or disapproval of gambling is indicated.

Second, *nanka* marks the speaker's humility. *Watashi nanka* 'a person such as myself', used in the context of praise from other people, for example, communicates the speaker's humble attitude. To be humble about one's ability and talent goes a long way in Japanese communication. Furthermore, when a speaker uses *nanka* in self-reference, given a certain context, it signals the speaker's self-deprecatory attitude. When the speaker insists *Watashi nanka dame yo* 'I am not good at all', the speaker shows an attitude bordering on self-disparagement. The use of *nanka* for humbling purposes might sound degrading at times, but in general one should err on the side of humility.

Examples

a. (Two young women talking about a boy)

(≈fy1): バラの花束のプレゼント**なんて**、彼ってすてきね。
(≈fy2): まあね。

(≈fy1): Bara no hanataba no purezento **nante**, kare tte suteki ne. (see E. 47 for *tte*; E. 13 for *suteki*)
(≈fy2): Maa ne.

(≈fy1): Oh, a bouquet of roses for a present! How wonderful he is!
(≈fy2): I guess.

b. (Two teenagers talking about a boy) *Nanka* expresses the speaker's dislike toward the person more emotionally than, for example, *wa*.

(≈ft1): あたし、あの人**なんか**大嫌い。
(≈ft2): また、そんな、心にもないこと言って。

(≈ft1): Atashi, ano hito **nanka** daikirai. (see E. 9 for *daikirai*)
(≈ft2): Mata, sonna, kokoro ni mo nai koto itte. (see E. 16 for *sonna*)

(≈ft1): I really hate that guy.
(≈ft2): Again, you are saying something that isn't really in your true heart.

c. (Suzuki is asked to represent the group) Suzuki humbly denies her ability to serve as the group's representative.

(≈fy1a): じゃ、鈴木さん、私達の代表になってくれない？
(≈fy2a): 私**なんか**、だめよ。
(≈fy1b): そんなこと言わないで。
(≈fy2b): だめだってば、私**なんか**。

(≈fy1a): Ja, Suzuki-san, watashitachi no daihyoo ni natte-kure-nai?
(≈fy2a): Watashi **nanka**, dame yo.
(≈fy1b): Sonna koto iwa-nai de.
(≈fy2b): Dame da tte ba, watashi **nanka.** (see E. 73 for *tte ba*)

(≈fy1a): Then, Ms. Suzuki, please become our representative.
(≈fy2a): Me? I can't do that.
(≈fy1b): Don't say that.
(≈fy2b): No way, I'm not good enough, really.

Authentic Examples

a. (Taken from *Dokkin paradaisu*, 3: 127) Ai emotionally reveals her determination.

このまま、この家で暮らす**なんて**できないよ。

Kono mama, kono uchi de kurasu **nante** deki-nai yo.

As I used to, to live in this house, that is something I can't do.

b. (Taken from *Muko-dono*, episode 6) Yuuichiroo comforts Kaede as he expresses surprise. It turns out that Kaede's former boyfriend had already married.

祐一郎： すみませんでした。まさか結婚してた**なんて**。
Yuuichiroo: Sumimasen deshita. Masaka kekkon shiteta **nante.** (see E. 14 for *masaka*)

Yuuichiroo: I am sorry. Never did I think that he was married!

c. (Taken from *Dokkin paradaisu*, 3: 20) Ai's friend exclaims over how lucky Ai was.

「それにしてもラッキーねえ。あの、"パラダイス KIDS" を生で見られちゃう**なんて**。」

"Sore ni shitemo rakkii nee. Ano, 'Paradaisu Kids' o nama de mirarechau **nante.**" (see E. 5 for *rakkii*; E. 17 for *mirarechau*)

"But, by all means, how lucky you are! To be able to see a live show of *Paradise Kids.*"

d. (Taken from *Buchoo Shima Koosaku*, 5: 123) Instead of using *wa* in the expression *itami wa zenzen kanji-nai*, Yatsuhashi uses *nanka* for emphatic effect.

島： ＜体調はいかがですか / 苦しくないですか＞
八ツ橋： ＜大丈夫よ / 気が張ってるから / 痛み**なんか** / 全然感じない＞

Shima: Taichoo wa ikaga desu ka. Kurushiku-nai desu ka.
Yatsuhashi: Daijoobu yo. Ki ga hatteru kara itami **nanka** zenzen kanji-nai.

Shima: How do you feel? Aren't you sick and feeling pain?
Yatsuhashi: I'm fine. Because I am excited and concentrating, I don't feel pain at all.

e. (Taken from *Taiga no itteki*, 244) The author reports that a well-known writer confided the following.

(…) もしも生まれ変わったとしたら、おれはもう金輪際、二度と人間**なんか**に生まれ変わってきたくない、と、吐き捨てるように言われた (…)。

(…) Moshimo umare kawatta to shitara, ore wa moo konrinzai, nido to ningen **nanka** ni umare kawatte-kitaku-nai, to, hakisuteru yoo ni iwareta (…).

(…) He said, disgustedly, "If I were to be reborn, I would never want to be born as (such a thing as) a human being (…)."

f. (Taken from *Beautiful Life*, episode 1) Kyooko wonders if she is good enough to be a hairstyle model and expresses doubt and humility to Shuuji. Kyooko uses *watashi nanka de* instead of *watashi de*.

杏子： あの、ほんとに、私**なんか**でいいのかな。

Kyooko: Ano, honto ni, watashi **nanka** de ii no ka na.

Kyooko: Uh, really, am I really good enough?

g. (Taken from *Shiretoko Rausudake satsujin bojoo*, 44) Miyako praises Shimon for remembering many things, and Shimon makes a challenging remark.

「見下げる面もあるということだな」
「そう。山に入ると、わたしのこと**なんか**すっかり忘れて、十日も半月も電話もくれない点」
彼女は、ふたたび山頂を現わした羅臼岳を仰いだ。

"Misageru men mo aru to yuu koto da na."
"Soo. Yama ni hairu to, watashi no koto **nanka** sukkari wasurete, tooka mo hantsuki mo denwa mo kure-nai ten." (see E. 30 for *watashi no koto*)
Kanojo wa, futatabi sanchoo o arawashita Rausudake o aoida.

"You mean you despise some things about me, then."
"Yes, that's right. Your habit of not calling me for ten days or even half the month once you go into the mountains."
Saying so, she looked up toward the summit of Rausudake that was appearing again.

Note

Nanka as a topic marker may appear in non-negative contexts as well. First, *nanka* is used when the speaker gives an example, as in *Ano hito nanka ii desu ne* 'Someone like him would be nice, wouldn't it?'. It is also used when making a suggestion, as in *Kantanna supootsu nara, jogingu nanka doo desu ka?* 'If you are interested in simple sports, how about jogging?'.

Nanka also appears as a topic marker when presenting a topic with a sense of surprise in a non-negative context. The following authentic example offers a case where *nanka* is used in a non-negative way (*Kaho no otoosan nanka*) as well as with a derogatory and humble effect (*uchi no otoosan nanka*).

1. (Taken from *Ren'ai hakusho*, 14: 179–180)

 「だって、不潔じゃない。みじめじゃない。果保のお父さん**なんか**、大学教授でしょ …… それに比べて …… うちって ……」(...)
 「うちのお父さん**なんか**、ただのオヤジだし、カッコ悪いし」

 "Datte, fuketsu ja-nai. Mijime ja-nai. Kaho no otoosan **nanka**, daigaku kyooju desho. ...... Sore ni kurabete......uchi tte......" (...) (see E. 18 for *mijime*; E. 47 for *tte*)
 "Uchi no otoosan **nanka**, tada no oyaji da shi, kakko warui shi" (see E. 13 for *kakko warui*; E. 63 about the use of *shi*)

 "But, it is filthy, isn't it? Miserable, isn't it? Kaho's father is a university professor, right? In comparison, my situation is..." (...)
 "My father, he is just an old man, and he is not nice-looking at all."

Given a certain context, *nanka* may even express a boasting attitude instead of humility. When a speaker says *Boku nanka mada wakai kara nan demo yatte-yaroo to omotchau n desu yo* 'I am still young, so I have a tendency to think that I'll simply do anything', the psychology involved is subtle. The obvious attitude is self-deprecating, but the speaker conveys self-confidence as well. As seen in this case, the evaluative attitude the speaker conveys through *nante* and *nanka* can be complex, and the context in which the phrase occurs is required for appropriate interpretation.

16. Expressing "*Konna*" Feelings

Key Expressions

こんな	*konna*	this, such
そんな	*sonna*	that, such
あんな	*anna*	that, such
(≈) えっ、そんな	*E-tt, sonna.*	What? (You say) such a thing, but...

Explanation

In addition to the familiar demonstratives *kore, sore, are, kono, sono*, and *ano*, a second series of demonstratives—*konna, sonna*, and *anna*—is used with an increased intensity of feelings. *Konna* 'such', *sonna*, and *anna* are synonymous with *koo yuu* 'this kind of', *soo yuu*, and *aa yuu*, but the *konna* group expresses an evaluative (often but not necessarily negative, surprising, and excessive) attitude, while the *koo yuu* group generally does not.

When the *konna* group is used instead of the *koo yuu* group, the speaker reveals his or her evaluative attitude in an emphatic way, for example, *Sonna hanashi kiita koto ga nai* 'I've never heard such a story' in contrast with *Ma soo yuu hanashi desu kara yoroshiku* 'It's that kind of story, so please take care of it'. Partly because *konna* implies general unexpectedness and a sense of things in excess, it communicates surprise, extraordinariness, admiration, disdain, derogation, and so on. The specific meaning depends on what these phrases occur with and on context. *Konna, sonna*, and *anna* are used in the forms *konna ni, sonna ni*, and *anna ni* as adverbs.

Sonna is used as an interjection in response to the partner's unreasonable utterance. For example, in response to *Akiramero!* 'Give it up!' one may simply utter *E-tt, sonna* 'What! (You say) such a thing, but…'.

Examples

a. (≈) 私に**こんな**ことをやらせるなんて、余りにひどい。

Watashi ni **konna** koto o yaraseru nante, amari ni hidoi. (see E. 15 for *nante*; E. 7 for *hidoi*)

To make me do such a thing, that is simply too awful.

b. 新鮮な野菜って、**こんなに**おいしいんですね。

Shinsenna yasai tte, **konna ni** oishii n desu ne. (see E. 47 for *tte*)

Fresh vegetables are really delicious, aren't they?

c. (A teen confessing that she has to break up a romantic relationship)

(≈ft1a): **こんなに**愛してるのに、別れなければならないなんて。
(≈ft2): **そんなに**好きなの、**あんな**男が。いっそのこと別れちゃえば？
(≈ft1b): **そんな**！

(≈ft1a) **Konna ni** aishiteru noni, wakarenakereba naranai nante. (see E. 32 for *aishiteru*; E. 35 for *wakareru*; E. 15 for *nante*)
(≈ft2): **Sonna ni** suki na no, **anna** otoko ga. Isso no koto wakarechaeba? (see E. 32 for *suki*)
(≈ft1b): **Sonna!**

(≈ft1a): I love him so much, but we have to break up.
(≈ft2): You love him that much, that kind of a man? Why don't you break up with him once and for all?
(≈ft1b): Such a thing, you say!

Authentic Examples

a. (Taken from *Santaku*) At the start of the show, in the television station studio, Sanma comments how the entire studio arrangement differs from what he had in mind. Sanma thinks the studio set is too official and elaborate. Taking the opportunity, Kimura wryly hints that Sanma's attire is also out of place.

さんま： あかん俺まちごうた、これ。失敗や。あのこの番組は、##**こんな**感じじゃないねん。**こんな**はずじゃないねん。
木村： （さんまのジャケットに触れながら）や、あの#**こんな**はずでもないんですよ。

Sanma: Akan ore machigoota, kore. Shippai ya. Ano kono bangumi wa, **konna** kanji ja-nai nen. **Konna** hazu ja-nai nen. (see E. 18 for *shippai*)
Kimura: (*Sanma no jaketto ni furenagara*) Ya, ano **konna** hazu demo nai n desu yo.

Sanma: This is no good, I made a mistake about this. It's a failure. Uh, this program shouldn't be like this. It isn't supposed to be like this.
Kimura: (*touching Sanma's jacket*) No, this shouldn't be like this, either.

b. (Taken from *Chibi Maruko-chan*, 14: 125) *Konna Kosugi* 'this kind of guy, Kosugi' adds to the derogatory attitude.

まる子： ＜ちょっとアンタっ/いくら**こんな**小杉に/対してでも/失礼だよっ＞
山根： ＜おいさくら/"**こんな**小杉"/って言い方も/失礼だよ …＞

Maruko: Chotto anta-tt ikura **konna** Kosugi ni taishite demo shitsurei da yo-tt. (see E. 27 for *anta-tt* and *yo-tt*)
Yamane: Oi Sakura "**konna** Kosugi" tte iikata mo shitsurei da yo.

Maruko: Hey, you, that is rude even to this kind of guy, Kosugi.
Yamane: Wait a minute, Sakura. You saying "This kind of guy, Kosugi" is rude, too.

c. (Taken from interview #88, with Shunji Iwai, music video producer and movie director) Hayashi and Iwai discuss school systems in Japan.

林：　私、(...) やっぱり公立は荒れてるのかな、**こんな**女の先生たまらんな、とか思っちゃった。(...)
岩井：　ほんと、**こんな**やつが担任になったらPTAの人とかやきもきしそう。

Hayashi: Watashi, (...) yappari kooritsu wa areteru no ka na, **konna** onna no sensei tamaran na, to ka omotchatta. (...) (see E. 57 for *yappari*; E. 26 for *tamaran*; E. 17 for *omotchatta*)
Iwai: Honto, **konna** yatsu ga tannin ni nattara PTA no hito toka yakimoki shisoo. (see E. 30 for *yatsu*; E. 62 for *toka*)

Hayashi: I thought, "After all, public school students are undisciplined, and such a female teacher is unbearable."
Iwai: Really, if such a person becomes your child's teacher, the PTA members are likely to fret over that a lot.

d. (Taken from *Taiga no itteki*, 135)

戦争中のことを考え、そして戦後のことを考え、よくも**あんな**きわどいなかで自分が生きながらえてきたな、**あんな**悲劇は二度とくり返したくないなと思いつつ (...)。

Sensoochuu no koto o kangae, soshite sengo no koto o kangae, yokumo **anna** kiwadoi naka de jibun ga ikinagaraete-kita na, **anna** higeki wa nido to kurikaeshitaku-nai na to omoi tsutsu (...). (see E. 42 for *jibun*)

I think about the time during the war, the time after the war, and I think, "I did survive in such a dangerous time, and I hope that kind of tragedy will never be repeated (...)."

e. (Taken from *Strawberry on the Shortcake*, episode 6) Saeki asks a favor from Manato, who refuses it emotionally.

佐伯：　僕のかわりに言ってくれたまえ。
まなと：　#や、困りますよ、**そんな**の。唯のことだから、どっちみちあなたに確かめに来ますよ。
佐伯：　や、まあ、そうかもしれないけど。ワンクッションあるじゃない、僕から直接聞くより。
まなと：　**そんな**。

Saeki: Boku no kawari ni itte-kure tamae.
Manato: Ya, komarimasu yo, **sonna** no. Yui no koto da kara, dotchimichi anata ni tashikame ni kimasu yo. (see E. 18 for *komarimasu*; E. 48 about inverted word order)

Saeki: Ya, maa, soo kamo shirenai kedo. Wan kusshon aru ja-nai, boku kara chokusetsu kiku yori. (see E. 48 about inverted word order)
Manato: **Sonna.**

Saeki: Please talk to her on my behalf.
Manato: No, I can't (I'll be in trouble if I do such a thing). Besides, given her personality, Yui will come see you to confirm with you what I tell her.
Saeki: Well, it may be so. But it will be indirect, rather than hearing it directly from me.
Manato: Such a thing you say, but...

f. (Taken from *Ainori*) In this show, entitled "Saigo no machi de gyooten koodoo onna (Surprising female member's action at the final destination) Hisamoto, one of the program hosts, talks about how bad the love situation is turning out to be for Dobo, one of the male tour members. Imada, another host, agrees. Both Hisamoto and Imada speak in the Osaka dialect.

久本： ヤバい。タイミングが悪いなあ。
(...)
久本： えー**そんな**。なんなの。
今田： なんでやねん。こじれてるというか。
久本： なんでやねん。ドボくんがどっちか言ったらシャイなタイプやから、あんなの見たら、どちらか言ったら、燃えるというより引いてくタイプやんかあいつは。

Hisamoto: Yabai. Taimingu ga warui naa. (see E. 18 for *yabai*)
(...)
Hisamoto: Ee **sonna**. Nan na no.
Imada: Nande ya nen. Kojireteru to yuu ka.
Hisamoto: Nande ya nen. Dobo-kun ga dotchi ka ittara shaina taipu ya kara, anna no mitara, dochira ka ittara, moeru to yuu yori hiiteku taipu yan ka aitsu wa. (see E. 48 about inverted word order)

Hisamoto: No good. It's bad timing.
(...)
Hisamoto: Oh, no, that is too bad. What is this, really!
Imada: Why is it? It seems that things are mixed up.
Hisamoto: Why is it? Dobo is, if you ask me, shy, so witnessing that (incident), he is likely to withdraw rather than being madly in love.

17. Afterthoughts about Events

Key Expressions

(≈) 食べちゃった	*Tabechatta.*	I ended up eating all of it.
(≈) 忘れてしまいたい	*Wasurete-shimaitai.*	I want to forget it completely.
(≈) 宝くじにあたっちゃった	*Takarakuji ni atatchatta.*	(Surprisingly) I won the lottery.

Explanation

People not infrequently regret what they just did. That sense of regret, associated with the completion of an action, is expressed by [V-*te-shimau*] and its colloquial version *chau*.

Fundamentally, *te-shimau* emphasizes two meanings. First, the action referred to is captured as a whole (not as a combination of different processes or stages) and it has been completed. Because the event is captured as a whole, *te-shimau* often emphasizes the sense of completion and thus finality. Second, because the speaker emphasizes completion, the sense that what has been done cannot be undone comes to the fore. In addition to the senses 'end up doing' and 'finish doing completely', particularly when the speaker thinks the event is something he or she wishes were otherwise, *te-shimau* conveys a sense of regret.

Te-shimau may also be used for emphasizing completion only, without regret. It may, for example, be used as praise for a task successfully completed or something realized through good fortune. This interpretation appears when the speaker thinks such an event is unlikely to happen, although the speaker wishes that it would, as in *Takarakuji ni atatchatta* '(Surprisingly) I won the lottery'. In this case, the speaker expresses a kind of surprise (and sometimes embarrassment or humility) that an unexpected, uncontrolled, and perhaps undeserved fortunate event has occurred.

Under certain circumstances, an expression like *Katchaoo!* 'I'm going to buy it (anyway)' may convey both completion and regret even before the event has occurred. By saying *Katchaoo!* the speaker makes it clear that she or he is doubtful about purchasing the item in question, but will complete the act anyway. In this situation, there may be a sense of guilt for doing something not perfectly acceptable, but that sense coincides with a feeling of courage and daring for going ahead and doing it.

The *te-shimau* expression is combined with the causative and passive expressions to emphasize finality. Examples of this are *Kare ni shokujidai o harawasete-shimatta* 'I ended up making him pay for the meal' and *Tomodachi ni saki ni gookaku sarete-shimatta* 'My friend passed the exam before me (and I felt bad that I can't undo it)'.

Examples

a. (A mother asking her son about homework)

(≈fa1a): 宿題終わったの？
(≈mc1a): もちろん。もう**やっちゃった**よ。
(≈fa1b): ほんと？
(≈mc1b): 今日の宿題、簡単だったから、すぐ**終わっちゃった**。

(≈fa1a): Shukudai owatta no?
(≈mc1a): Mochiron. Moo **yatchatta** yo.
(≈fa1b): Honto?
(≈mc1b): Kyoo no shukudai, kantan datta kara, sugu **owatchatta**.

(≈fa1a): Are you through with your homework?
(≈mc1a): Of course. I've done it.
(≈fa1b): Really?
(≈mc1b): Today's assignment was very easy, so it was over right away.

b. (Two men talking about memories of a common friend)

(≈ma1): 俺また**思い出しちゃった**よ、あいつのこと。
(≈ma2): つらいことは**忘れてしまいたい**ものだけどね。

(≈ma1): Ore mata **omoidashichatta** yo, aitsu no koto. (see E. 30 for *aitsu no koto*; E. 48 about inverted word order)
(≈ma2): Tsurai koto wa **wasurete-shimaitai** mono da kedo ne. (see E. 7 for *tsurai*)

(≈ma1): I (regretfully) ended up thinking about him again.
(≈ma2): We do want to forget about painful memories, but, you know…

c. (≈) あの人のこと、好きに**なっちゃった**。

Ano hito no koto, suki ni **natchatta.** (see E. 30 for *ano hito no koto*; E. 32 for *suki*)

(Although I shouldn't,) I've grown to like him.

Authentic Examples

a. (Taken from *Strawberry on the Shortcake*, episode 4) *Karakatchau* and *okorasechau* both express the speaker's sense of regret and helplessness (although he shouldn't do it, he ends up doing it).

佐伯： 君の彼女にあやまっといてくれない？
まなと： 彼女？
佐伯： こう、つい**からかっちゃう**っていうか余計なひとことをポロッと言って**怒らせちゃう**んだよ。(…)
まなと： 沢村のことですか。
佐伯： うん。
まなと： 別に彼女じゃありませんよ。

Saeki: Kimi no kanojo ni ayamattoite-kure-nai? (see E. 30 for *kanojo*)
Manato: Kanojo?
Saeki: Koo, tsui **karakatchau** tte yuu ka yokeina hitokoto o poro tto itte **okorasechau** n da yo. (…) (see E. 63 for *te yuu ka*)
Manato: Sawamura no koto desu ka?
Saeki: Un.
Manato: Betsu ni kanojo jaarimasen yo.

Saeki: Will you apologize to your girlfriend for me?
Manato: Girlfriend?
Saeki: I somehow end up teasing her, or more truthfully, I end up making her angry by inadvertently saying something unnecessary. (…)
Manato: Are you talking about Sawamura?
Saeki: Yes.
Manato: She is not my girlfriend.

b. (Taken from interview #75, with Tadanori Yokoo, artist) Yokoo expresses surprise by *shichau.*

横尾： (…) 今の人たちは瞬時にして作品を受容**しちゃう**んですよ。

Yokoo: (…) Ima no hitotachi wa shunji ni shite sakuhin o juyoo **shichau** n desu yo.

Yokoo: (…) Young people today take in the work completely, in an instant.

c. (Taken from *Taiga no itteki*, 127) The author expresses regret by *taitoku shite-shimtta.*

ひょっとしたら、世の中はますます悪くなってあたりまえ、というあきらめを人間は**体得してしまった**のでしょうか。

Hyotto shitara, yo no naka wa masumasu waruku natte atarimae, to yuu akirame o ningen wa **taitoku shite-shimatta** no deshoo ka. (see E. 20 for *akirame*)

I wonder if human beings have ended up learning this feeling of resignation, that is, it is the natural course of events that the world increasingly worsens.

Additional Information

The *te-shimau* expression is used idiomatically, as in *yatchatta* 'I did it'. *Yatchatta* is used both in reference to oneself and to the partner when a failure occurs. For example, as given in the example, it is used when one recognizes that a mistake was made

1. (Taken from *Santaku*) During the program, Sanma and Kimura are throwing darts, with the idea that the loser pays for the expenses when they go out. Kimura can't hit the target and acknowledges that he's in trouble.

木村：　うわー**やっちゃった**。
さんま：　あ、**やっちゃった**ね。
木村：　**やっちゃった**。（もう一本投げて、はずれたのを見て）**やっちゃった**。
さんま：　**やっちゃった**。もう、もう＝
木村：　＝もう無理だ。

Kimura: Uwaa **yatchatta**.
Sanma: A, **yatchatta** ne.
Kimura: **Yatchatta**. (*Moo ippon nagete, hazureta no o mite*) **Yatchatta**.
Sanma: **Yatchatta**. Moo, moo=
Kimura: =Moo muri da.

Kimura: Oh no, I did it.
Sanma: Yeah, you did it, didn't you?
Kimura: I did it. (*He throws one more dart and reacts to his miss*) I did it.
Sanma: You did it. Not any more=
Kimura: =It's impossible now.

7

Responding to Circumstances Emotionally

18. When Facing Trouble, Failure, and Misery

Key Expressions

(≈) ダメだ	*Dame da.*	It's no good.
(≈) ヤバい	*Yabai.*	It's risky. A big trouble.
(≈) 弱ったな	*Yowatta na.*	I'm in jeopardy. That's a problem.
(≈) まいった	*Maitta.*	I'm in deep trouble. I've been had.
(≈) 困ったな	*Komatta na.*	I'm in trouble. I've got a problem.
(≈) しまった！	*Shimatta!*	Oops! Shoot! (I made a mistake.)
失敗	*shippai*	mistake, failure, goof
情け無い	*nasakenai*	regrettable, lamentable
みじめな	*mijimena*	miserable
ヘコむ	*hekomu*	to be beaten, discouraged, hopeless and depressed

Explanation

Damena, which is a *na*-type adjective, refers to conditions that are useless, hopeless, and, in general, simply not good. When a person has lost hope, *Moo dame da!* 'It's no good, completely hopeless!' is often used. *Dame da* is also used as a refusal to a request.

Yabai 'risky' is often used as an interjection when the speaker is in trouble. *Yabai* implies that the speaker is in danger or in trouble possibly because of something wrong or illegal. *Yabai* is restricted to casual situations, where blunt expressions are expected.

Other expressions to be used when one is in trouble include self-revealing phrases such as *Yowatta* 'I'm in jeopardy' and *Maitta* 'I'm in deep trouble'. *Yowatta* refers to the trouble associated with confusion, while *maitta* connotes defeat or being at a loss. Although these phrases are in the past-tense form, they do not describe events in the past; instead they indicate the speaker's current feelings. These expressions may be used by the speaker only about him- or herself. **Tomodachi ga yowatta* is not used.

The verb *komaru* refers to trouble in numerous ways, for example, (1) to point out that the speaker is in trouble, as in *Chotto komatteru n da* 'I'm having a problem'; (2) to describe other people's troubles, as in *Kimi ga kaeru to minna ga komaru yo* 'If you leave, everyone will be in trouble'; (3) to describe the source of trouble, as in *Chikoku suru no wa komarimasu yo* 'To be late is not permissible'; and (4) to refuse requests, with the implication that the speaker would get into trouble by granting them.

An English speaker who realizes that he or she has made a mistake may inadvertently say "Shoot!" or "Oops!" (at least). In Japanese, *Shimatta* is used for the same purpose. *Shippai* 'failure' and *daishippai* 'big failure' occur when a speaker realizes that something is a failure or a mistake. They may also be used as interjections.

Nasakenai 'regrettable, lamentable' is used when unhappy feelings result from a recognizable failure, while *mijimena* expresses a general miserable feeling. *Hekomu* is a verb used when one is feeling psychologically beaten and crushed.

Examples

a. (≈) これじゃ、**だめだ**。全然できてないよ。

Kore ja, **dame** da. Zenzen dekite-nai yo.

This is no good. Nothing is done right.

b. (≈) 弱ったな、また間違っちゃった。

Yowatta na, mata machigatchatta. (see E. 17 for *machigatchatta*)

I'm in jeopardy, I made a mistake again.

c. (A worker asking his coworker for permission to leave early) *Komatta* is used to refuse a request, and *yowatta* is used to express the consequent trouble.

(my1a): あの。
(≈my2a): え？
(≈my1b): 今日ちょっと早退したいんだけど。
(≈my2b): **困ったなあ**。俺ひとりになっちゃうよ。
(≈my1c): **だめか**。**弱ったなあ**。

(my1a): Ano.
(≈my2a): E?
(≈my1b): Kyoo chotto sootai shitai n da kedo. (see E. 25 for *chotto*; E. 63 for *kedo*)
(≈my2b): **Komatta naa.** Ore hitori ni natchau yo. (see E. 17 for *natchau*)
(≈my1c): **Dame** ka. **Yowatta naa.**

(my1a): Uh, excuse me.
(≈my2a): What is it?
(≈my1b): I want to leave early today.
(≈my2b): That's a problem, I'm afraid. I'll be the only one here.
(≈my1c): I can't? Shoot!

d. (Two young people standing in front of a concert hall)

(≈fy1a): ちょっと入場券見せて。
(≈my1a): あれ？**しまった**！忘れた。机の上に置いたままだ。
(≈fy1b): やだぁ。どうする？
(≈my1b): **失敗したなあ**。

(≈fy1a): Chotto nyuujooken misete. (see E. 25 for *chotto*)
(≈my1a): Are? **Shimatta!** Wasureta. Tsukue no ue ni oita mama da.
(≈fy1b): Ya daa. Doo suru? (see E. 9 for *ya da*)
(≈my1b): **Shippai shita** naa.

(≈fy1a): Can I see the tickets?
(≈my1a): Oh, no! Shoot! I forgot. I left them on the desk.
(≈fy1b): What a disaster! What are we going to do?
(≈my1b): Boy, did I make a mistake!

e. (A woman reminding her coworker of an appointment)

(fy1): もう五時過ぎてますよ。
(≈my1): えっ？重要な会議なのに、これじゃ遅れるな。**失敗**。**失敗**。

(fy1): Moo goji sugitemasu yo.
(≈my1): E-tt? Juuyoona kaigi na noni, kore ja okureru na. **Shippai. Shippai.** (see E. 21 for *E-tt?*; E. 24 about repetition)

(fy1): It's already past five o'clock, you know.
(≈my1): Really? It's an important meeting, and I'm going to be late. Oh no. What a goof!

f. (A man confesses that he made a mistake at work)

(≈ma1a): また**失敗**しちゃってさ。**情け無い**よ。
(≈ma2): 残念だったね。
(≈ma1b): **みじめな**気分さ、全く。

(≈ma1a): Mata **shippai** shichatte sa. **Nasake nai** yo.
(≈ma2): Zannen datta ne. (see E. 61 for *zannen datta*)
(≈ma1b): **Mijimena** kibun sa, mattaku.

(≈ma1a): I failed again. It's regrettable, you know.
(≈ma2): That's too bad.
(≈ma1b): I feel miserable, completely.

Authentic Examples

a. (Taken from *Chibi Maruko-chan,* 14: 13) Maruko's father, an inexperienced driver, takes his family for a ride.

まる子： <おとうさん / 気をつけてよ / ホントに / 死ぬかと思ったよ>
父： <ああ / **やばかった**な / あの車 / ベンツだったし / な ...... >

Maruko: Otoosan ki o tsukete yo. Honto ni shinu ka to omotta yo.
chichi: Aa **yabakatta** na. Ano kuruma Bentsu datta shi na......

Maruko: Dad, please be careful. I really thought I was going to die.
father: Yeah. It was pretty dangerous. Besides, that car was a Mercedes.

b. (Taken from *Strawberry on the Shortcake*, episode 2) Yui realizes that she has lost her key to the house and mumbles to herself.

唯： **ヤバい**よいきなり家の鍵。

Yui: **Yabai** yo ikinari uchi no kagi.

Yui: Oh no, big trouble, to lose the key to the house right away.

c. (Taken from *Muko-dono*, episode 1) During a conversation with Satsuki, Endoo, her coworker, realizes that he is late for a meeting. *Yabee* (instead of *yabai*) is used in blunt "masculine" style.

さつき： あ#あの#プロデューサー会議の時間じゃないですか。
遠藤： うそ、まじ？あ、**やべー**。じゃ俺、行くわ。
助手： じゃあ、私もそろそろ。

Satsuki: A ano purodyuusaa kaigi no jikan ja-nai desu ka.
Endoo: Uso, maji? A, **yabee**. Ja ore, iku wa. (see E. 21 for *uso*; E. 67 for *maji*)
joshu: Jaa, watashi mo sorosoro.

Satsuki: Uh, isn't it the time for the producers' meeting?
Endoo: You kidding? Serious? Oh, no, big trouble! I better go now.
assistant: I should be going too.

d. (Taken from *Buchoo Shima Koosaku* 5, 27–28) Shima finds out that a scandal is revealed in the newspaper. *Yarareta* '(lit.) I was beaten' is an interjection used when a speaker acknowledges defeat.

島：　＜やられた！！＞
社長：　＜うーん / **まいったな** /....../ どう対処したら / いいんだ＞

Shima: Yarareta!
shachoo: Uun **maitta na**....... Doo taisho shitara ii n da.

Shima: They got us!
president: Ahh. We've been had (they got us). How should we deal with this?

e. (Taken from *Antiiku, seiyoo kotto yoogashiten*, episode 7) Hideko asks her father, who is divorced, if she can stay with him. *Komaru* is used as a refusal to a request, and the father explains why he cannot grant the request.

ヒデコ：　ねえ、いいでしょ。#ね、いいよね。私パパといたい。パパと暮らしたい！#パパ。
父：　##それは**困る**な。
ヒデコ：　えっ？
父：　**困る**なそれは。#パパにはもうちゃんと、好きな人がいて、新しい暮らしをしてるんだ。#だからデコちゃんにそんなこと言われても**困る**んだよ。

Hideko: Nee, ii desho. Ne, ii yo ne. Watashi papa to itai. Papa to kurashitai! Papa. (see E. 59 for *ii desho*)
chichi: Sore wa **komaru** na.
Hideko: E-tt?
chichi: **Komaru** na sore wa. Papa ni wa moo chanto, sukina hito ga ite, atarashii kurashi o shiteru n da. Dakara Deko-chan ni sonna koto iwaretemo **komaru** n da yo. (see E. 48 about inverted word order; E. 32 for *sukina*; E. 16 for *sonna*)

Hideko: Please, it's O.K., isn't it? It's O.K., right? I want to be with you, Papa. I want to live with you, Papa.
father: That's a problem.
Hideko: What?
father: That's a problem. I have someone whom I love, and I have a new life now. So, Deko, your telling me such a thing puts me in a difficult spot.

f. (Taken from *Muko-dono*, episode 3) Yuuichiroo realizes that he forgot about the promise he made to Tsutomu. Yuuichiroo was supposed to teach Tsutomu how to ride a bicycle that day.

祐一郎： **しまった**！今日約束してたんだ。自転車教えてやるって。

Yuuichiroo: **Shimatta!** Kyoo yakusoku shiteta n da. Jitensha oshiete-yaru tte. (see E. 48 about inverted word order)

Yuuichiroo: Shoot! I fogot the promise I made for today. To teach him how to ride a bike.

g. (Taken from *Kitchin*, 61 [English translation, 38]) As explained in Chapter 1, *shimatta* appears in quotation so that the direct expressive strategy is integrated into the indirect discourse.

「おっと、あんまり大声でうたうと、となりで寝てるおばあちゃんがおきちゃう」
言ってから、**しまった**と思った。

"Otto, anmari oogoe de utau to, tonari de neteru obaachan ga okichau."
Itte kara, **shimatta** to omotta. (see E. 17 for *okichau*)

"Wait, *stop*. [If we sing too loud] We're going to wake my grandmother sleeping in the next room" Now I've done it, I thought.

h. (Taken from *Ainori*) In this show, "Saigo no machi de gyooten koodoo onna" (Surprising female member's action at the final destination), Miyaken, a male member of the tour, consoles Saki, a female member who is disappointed about a negative remark from Dobo, a male member of the tour whom she is in love with.

サキ： 分からな過ぎてなんか、**ヘコんだ**ね。
宮ケン： **ヘコんでも**全然いいし。そういう部分をみんなに見せてもいいと思うしね。
サキ： ありがとう。

Saki: Wakara-nasugite nanka, **hekonda** ne. (see E. 62 for *nanka*)
Miyaken: **Hekondemo** zenzen ii shi. Soo yuu bubun o minna ni misetemo ii to omou shi ne.
Saki: Arigatoo.

Saki: I simply couldn't understand (him) at all, and I was disappointed.
Miyaken: It's O.K. to be disappointed, you know. I think it's O.K. to show your feelings like that to other members.
Saki: Thank you.

19. Regrets and Self-Mockery

Key Expressions

くやしい	*kuyashii*	to feel painfully regretful, to feel helpless and angry, to feel frustratingly helpless
するべきだった	*suru beki datta*	should have done
すればよかった	*sureba yokatta*	would have been nice if I did
後悔する	*kookai suru*	to regret
(≈) 私が励まされてどうすんのよ	*Watashi ga hagemasarete doo sun no yo.*	What good is it that I'm the one being encouraged?

Explanation

The adjective for one's sense of regret is *kuyashii*. *Kuyashii* applies to multiple feelings (such as frustration, anger, and sadness) caused by injustice or conditions that cannot be resolved or overcome. When the speaker says *kuyashii*, he or she is frustrated from a sense of desperation and helplessness. *Kuyashii* conjures up the feeling that nothing one does is any good; the problem cannot be resolved to one's liking. The word may be used as an interjection to express frustration, as in *Kuyashii!* 'Ah, how frustrating!' It is particularly appropriate for the feeling that all your efforts will end in vain and that you will end up facing failure.

When describing feelings of regret, *beki* and the *ba*-conditional are used. Both are descriptive and are usually used in the past tense when expressing regret. *Beki datta*, in the structure of [V basic + *beki datta*], is used when the speaker recognizes that some obligation was not met. *Sureba yokatta*, in the structure [V-*ba* conditional + *yokatta*], shows general regret. The verb *kookai suru* 'to regret' also describes a general sense of regret.

When one catches oneself behaving in a silly way, a self-mocking expression may sometimes be appropriate. In such a case, *te doo suru,* in the structure of [V-*te* + *doo suru*], is used. This rhetorical question, literally meaning 'what do you do with it?', communicates (mockingly) a critical attitude. It is frequently used when talking to oneself, although it can criticize the partner as well.

Examples

a. すみません、もっと**注意するべきでした。**

Sumimasen, motto **chuui suru beki deshita.**

Sorry, I should have been more careful.

b. (Two college students talking about a common friend) The use of *beki datta* expresses the sense of obligation, although *agereba yokatta* does not.

(≈fy1a): 田中君ね、クラブやめたんだって。
(≈fy2a): ほんと？残念ねえ。
(≈fy1b): もっとやさしく**してあげればよかった。**
(≈fy2b): そうだね。この間のカラオケ、**誘ってあげるべきだった**かも。

(≈fy1a): Tanaka-kun ne, kurabu yameta n datte.
(≈fy2a): Honto? Zannen nee. (see E. 54 for *zannen*)
(≈fy1b): Motto yasashiku **shite-agereba yokatta**. (see E. 6 for *yasashii*)
(≈fy2b): Soo da ne. Kono aida no karaoke, **sasotte-ageru beki datta** kamo.

(≈fy1a): I hear Tanaka quit the student organization.
(≈fy2a): Really? That is too bad.
(≈fy1b): I should have been kinder to him.
(≈fy2b): I guess. Perhaps we should have invited him to the karaoke party we had the other day.

Authentic Examples

a. (Taken from *Muko-dono*, episode 9) Kaede asks Yuuichiroo to console their father. Kaede expresses her frustration by *kuyashii*, because she cannot quite do what she wishes to do herself.

かえで：お父さんのそばにいてあげてくんない？＃**くやしい**んだけど＃娘より息子の方が心地いい時ってあるよね。
さくら：＃＃おねえちゃん。

Kaede: Otoosan no soba ni ite-agete-kun-nai? **Kuyashii** n da kedo musume yori musuko no hoo ga kokochi ii toki tte aru yo ne. (see E. 47 for *tte*)
Sakura: Oneechan.

Kaede: Would you please be by (our) father's side? I hate to admit it, but there are some moments when he feels more comfortable with a son than with a daughter.
Sakura: Oh, my sis.

b. (Taken from *SMAP x SMAP*, special live show) Kimura tells how he felt during the time Goroo was unable to participate in the group activities.

木村： やっぱり５人じゃないとスマップじゃないという、言葉が、＃やっぱり、僕らに届いてきた時に、＃なんかこう、＃何てのすごいおもしろい感情なんだけど、うれしいの、うれしい、気持ちと、なに？っていう気持ちが両方、おきて、うん、言葉を聞いた瞬間**くやしかった**けどね、**くやしかった**けど、でも、そういうふうに、言ってくれる人達っていうのは、＃あのー、＃自分らにとってもすごく大きな存在だなと思ったし。

Kimura: Yappari gonin ja-nai to Sumappu ja-nai to yuu, kotoba ga, yappari, bokura ni todoite-kita toki ni, nanka koo, nan te no sugoi omoshiroi kanjoo na n da kedo, ureshii no, ureshii, kimochi to, nani? tte yuu kimochi ga ryoohoo, okite, un, kotoba o kiita shunkan **kuyashikatta** kedo ne, **kuyashikatta** kedo, demo soo yuu fuu ni, itte-kureru hitotachi tte yuu no wa, anoo, jibunra ni totte mo sugoku ookina sonzai da na to omotta shi. (see E. 57 for *yappari*; E. 62 for *nanka*; E. 24 for *sugoi*; E. 5 for *ureshii*; E. 37 for *nani?*; E. 42 for *jibunra*; E. 63 about the use of *shi*)

Kimura: When we heard that unless there were five members, the group would no longer be SMAP, somehow, what should I say, it was a strange feeling that I had. It was a mixture of being pleased and being outraged (something like I wanted to say "What the heck are you saying?"). The moment I heard that, I felt helpless and angry. I felt pain and the feeling of regret, but I thought those people who kindly say so are indeed very important for us.

c. (Taken from *Chibi Maruko-chan,* 14: 24) Maruko reports to Tamae, her best friend, how frustrated and upset she was when her father said nasty things to her.

まる子： ＜…まったく／頭にきちゃうよ／うちのおとうさん／にはっ＞
たまえ： ＜うん…／ちょっと／言いすぎ／かもね…＞
まる子： ＜でしょっ！？／わたしゃ／もう／**くやしくて**／**くやしくて**／朝っぱらから／燃えちゃったよ＞

Maruko: …Mattaku atama ni kichau yo, uchi no otoosan ni wa-tt. (see E. 10 for *atama ni kuru*; E. 17 for *kichau*; E. 48 about inverted word order)
Tamae: Un…chotto ii sugi kamo ne…
Maruko: Desho-tt!? Watasha moo **kuyashikute kuyashikute** asappara kara moechatta yo. (see E. 24 about repetition; E. 17 for *moechatta*)

Maruko: I get so angry with my father.
Tamae: Yeah, he says things that are a bit too nasty.
Maruko: Right, you think so, don't you? I was frustrated and angry and I got fired up since morning.

d. (Taken from *Chibi Maruko-chan,* 14: 35) Maruko is angry at her classmates saying unkind things about her. The onomatopoeic interjection *kiii-tt* communicates Maruko's stressed-out fury.

まる子： ＜キ――ッ/あんなこと/きこえよがしに/わざと…＞＜**くやし――っ**＞
たまえ： ＜まるちゃん/ここで怒っちゃ/またムダに/なるよ…＞

Maruko: Kiii-tt. Anna koto kikoeyogashi ni waza to... **Kuyashiii-tt.** (see E. 27 about *kyuashiii-tt*)
Tamae: Maru-chan koko de okotcha mata muda ni naru yo...
Maruko: Gee whiz, he's saying such a thing so that I can hear it....How frustrating and upsetting!
Tamae: Maruko, you shouldn't get angry now, it will be totally wasted.

e. (Taken from *Ren'ai hakusho*, 14: 10) Kaho finds out that a female classmate, Sumire, is wearing the scarf she (Kaho) knitted for her boyfriend. Kaho is hurt, angry, sad, and in shock, among other feelings.

びっくりして、
くやしくて。
腹立たしくって。
で、
そのあと、ちょっとみじめで。
そして、寂しくなって。
その全部の気持ちが、心の中でミックスシェークされて。
ぐるぐるしてた。

Bikkuri shite, (see E. 21 for *bikkuri suru*)
Kuyashikute.
Haradatashikutte. (see E. 10 about similar expressions of anger)
De,
Sono ato, chotto mijime de. (see E. 25 for *chotto*; E. 18 for *mijime*)
Soshite, sabishiku natte. (see E. 8 for *sabishii*)
Sono zenbu no kimochi ga, kokoro no naka de mikkusu sheeku sarete.
Guruguru shiteta.

Surprised,
Angrily frustrated.
Upset.

And,
After that, a bit miserable.
And, I got lonely.
All these feelings got mixed and shaken up inside my heart.
They were going around and around.

f. (Taken from *Long Love Letter Hyooryuu Kyooshitsu*, episode 1) Yuka explains how she left her teaching job.

結花：　で、やめさせられたってわけ。もともと向いてなかったのかも。あたしが生徒を救えるなんてあの頃思ってて。**悔しくて**さ。＃今もちょっと**後悔してる**けど。＃ちょっとじゃないか。すごく**後悔**。

Yuka: De, yamesaserareta tte wake. Motomoto muite-nakatta no kamo. Atashi ga seito o sukueru nan te ano koro omottete. **Kuyashikute** sa. Ima mo chotto **kookai shiteru** kedo. Chotto ja-nai ka. Sugoku **kookai**. (see E. 42 for *atashi*; E. 25 for *chotto*; E. 24 for *sugoku*)

Yuka: So, I was forced to leave my job. Maybe I wasn't suited for that job anyway. In those days I thought I could save my students. I was frustrated. I regret that a bit even now. No, not a bit. I regret that a lot.

g. (Taken from *Antiiku, seiyoo kottoo yoogashiten*, episode 4) Eiji and Momoko are on the bus. Eiji is impressed by Momoko and encourages her. Momoko, realizing that she is the one who should encourage Eiji, mutters to herself in self-mockery.

エイジ：　上を目指すか。カッコいいなあ。頑張ってよ。
桃子：　うん、ありがと。
(…)
桃子：　（ひとりごとを言う）私が**励まされてどうすんのよ**。

Eiji: Ue o mezasu ka. Kakko ii naa. Ganbatte yo. (see E. 13 for *kakko ii*)
Momoko: Un, arigato.
(…)
Momoko: (*hitorigoto o yuu*) Watashi ga **hagemasarete doo sun no yo.**

Eiji: To aim high. That's cool. Good luck.
Momoko: Yeah, thanks.
(…)
Momoko: (*talking to herself*) What good does it do that I'm the one being encouraged by him?

h. (Taken from *Long Love Letter Hyooryuu Kyooshitsu*, episode 1) Visiting Yuka, whose father runs a flower shop, at her home, Asami is given a tulip as a gift. Realizing that a man should give flowers to a woman, Asami is a bit confused. He mumbles self-mockingly to himself.

浅海： 俺が**もらってどうすんだよ**。

Asami: Ore ga **moratte doo su n da yo.**

Asami: What good does it do that I receive this?

i. (Taken from *Kookaku kidootai*, 81 [English translation, 83]) In this case *doo sun no* is used to criticize the partner.

トグサ： ＜なぜ / ジャマ / するん / です !? ＞
草薙： ＜頭狙って / **どうすんの** !/ 足よ　足 ! ＞

Togusa: Naze jama suru n desu!?
Kusanagi: Atama neratte **doo sun no**! Ashi yo. Ashi! (see E. 55 about the use and non-use of *yo*)

Togusa: <Out of/ my way/ major!!>
Kusanagi: <Don't/ aim for/ the head,/ Togusa!/ The legs,/ you/ fool!>

20. Giving Up

Key Expressions

しょうがない	*shooganai*	no way (to solve the problem), no use
しかた (が) ない	*shikata (ga) nai*	there is no solution
(≈) あきらめよう	*Akirameyoo.*	Let's give it up.

Explanation

When facing such insurmountable difficulties that one is ready to give up, *Shooganai* 'It's no use' is appropriate, as is the more formal *shikata* (*ga*) *nai*, which literally means that there is no way to solve the problem. *Shooganai* and *shikata* (*ga*) *nai* reveal the speaker's resignation: because the effort is futile, it should be abandoned. *Shooganai* and *shikata* (*ga*) *nai* are also used in combination with verbs, in the forms [V-*te mo shooganai*] and [V-*te mo shikata* (*ga*) *nai*].

The verb *akirameru* 'to give up' is used to describe one's intention of giving up. For example, realizing that there is no solution to a problem, you may say *Akirameyoo yo* 'Let's give it up'.

Examples

a. (≈) もう時間がない。**しょうがない**な。この仕事は明日にしよう。

Moo jikan ga nai. **Shooganai** na. Kono shigoto wa ashita ni shiyoo.

There is no time left. There is no way to do this. I'll finish this work tomorrow.

b. (Two people are giving up on a friend who hasn't shown up)

(≈fa1a): 山中君、三時間も待ったのに、来ないなんてね。
(≈ma1): もう、**あきらめよう**。もともと来るつもりなかったんじゃないか。
(≈fa1b): そうね。**しかたがない**わね。

(≈fa1a): Yamanaka-kun, sanjikan mo matta noni, ko-nai nante ne. (see E. 15 for *nante*)
(≈ma1): Moo, **akirameyoo**. Motomoto kuru tsumori nakatta n ja-nai ka.
(≈fa1b): Soo ne. **Shikata ga nai** wa ne.

(≈fa1a): We've waited for Yamanaka for three hours, but he hasn't shown up.
(≈ma1): Let's give it up. He probably didn't mean to come at all.
(≈fa1b): I guess so. There is no other way but to give up.

Authentic Examples

a. (Taken from interview #87, with Muneaki Masuda, company president)

増田： かっこよく言えば、妥協せずに自分の生き方を貫き通した結果敗れたんだし、**しょうがない**と割り切ることができました。

Masuda: Kakko yoku ieba, dakyoose-zu ni jibun no ikikata o tsuranuki tooshita kekka yabureta n da shi, **shooganai** to warikiru koto ga dekimashita. (see E. 13 for *kakko yoku*; E. 42 for *jibun*)

Masuda: To put it in a (self-consciously) fashionable way, I have insisted on my way of living without compromising and have failed as a consequence, so I can let go and feel that there isn't much that can be done.

b. (Taken from *Tsubasa o kudasai*, 122) Kyooka expresses a sense of futility by using *shooganai*.

偽善者。
正しいことばっかり言っててもしょうがないじゃない。

Gizensha.
Tadashii koto bakkari ittetemo **shooganai** ja-nai.

A hypocrite.
It's no use to insist on righteousness only.

c. (Taken from *Beautiful Life*, episode 2) Kyooko, because she is in a wheelchair, cannot quite reach the vending machine button she wants to push, and says the following.

杏子： ああ、もう**しかたない**な。カレーにすっかな。

Kyooko: Aa, moo **shikata nai** na. Karee ni sukka na.

Kyooko: Ah, there is no way to get around this. Maybe I should decide on curry with rice.

d. (Taken from *Tsubasa o kudasai*, 28) Kyooka reveals her feeling of desperation by *shikata nai.*

もし、私の背中に翼があったならば、私は迷わず飛んでいくだろう。
(…… 矛盾してる)
灰色の空なんかに、飛んでいっても**仕方ない**のに。

Moshi, watashi no senaka ni tsubasa ga atta naraba, watashi wa mayowa-zu tonde-iku daroo.
(……Mujun shiteru)
Haiiro no sora nanka ni, tonde-ittemo **shikata nai** noni. (see E. 15 for *nanka*)

If I had wings on my back, I would fly away without doubt.
(……This is contradictory)
There is no use flying into the gray sky.

e. (Taken from *Santaku*) Sanma muses that he cannot become an ideal father. He tells Kimura that's why he doesn't allow his daughter to call him *otoosan.*

さんま： お父さんて、父と言われるほど立派な男にはね、あのーなれない。俺もう**あきらめた**。#あかんもん、出来あがりが。

Sanma: Otoosan te, chichi to iwareru hodo rippana otoko ni wa ne, anoo nare-nai. Ore moo **akirameta**. Akan mon, dekiagari ga. (see E. 48 about inverted word order)

Sanma: I can't really become this splended role model worthy of being called *otoosan* or *chichi*. I've given up now. It's no good, what I am now.

f. (Taken from *Tsubasa o kudasai*, 39) Kyooka realizes that there is no other seat left except the one right next to Takishita and Tsubaki, the classmates Kyooka does not like. The feeling of resignation is expressed by *shikata ga nai.*

この際、**仕方がない**のだけれど、やっぱり気が進まなかった。
辺りを見回しても空いた席はもうないし、私は**あきらめて**鞄を机の上に置いた。

Kono sai, **shikata ga nai** no da keredo, yappari ki ga susuma-nakatta. (see E. 57 for *yappari*)
Atari o mimawashitemo aita seki wa moo nai shi, watashi wa **akiramete** kaban o tsukue no ue ni oita.

Under these circumstances, there is no other way, but I still didn't like the idea.
When I looked around, there was no other empty seat, so I gave up and put my bag on the desk.

g. (Taken from *Chibi Maruko-chan*, 14: 31) Maruko and Yamane, Maruko's classmate, are trying to eat some *natto* (a soybean product). Yamane is hesitant and is ready to give up by saying *akirameru*.

山根： < ... ボク .../ やっぱりよすよ /... なんか .../ 自信ないんだ>
<もう / **あきらめる**よ /... **仕方ない**さ /...... >
まる子： <ダメッ>

Yamane: ...Boku...yappari yosu yo....Nanka...jishin nai n da. (see E. 57 for *yappari*; E. 62 for *nanka*)
Moo **akirameru** yo....**Shikata nai** sa......
Maruko: Dame-tt. (see E. 18 for *dame*)

Yamane: I'm not going to do that after all. I don't have confidence, really. I'm giving up. There is no way to solve this...
Maruko: No, don't do that.

h. (Taken from *Jisshuusen chinbotsu*, Feb. 14, 2001) One resident of the city of Uwajima comments about the prime minister's handling of the tragic collision.

高橋さんは (...)「『指示を出したから問題ない』とは、本当に子どもたちのことを心配していたのか、疑問だ。彼に要求しても**仕方ない**のかな」と**あきらめた**表情で話した。

Takahashi-san wa (...) " 'Shiji o dashita kara mondai nai' to wa, hontoo ni kodomotachi no koto o shinpai shiteita no ka, gimon da. Kare ni yookyuu shitemo **shikata nai** no ka na" to **akirameta** hyoojoo de hanashita. (see E. 30 for *kodomotachi no koto*; E. 61 for *shinpai*)

Takahashi (...) said with an expression of resignation on his face, "(The prime minister's) words, 'There is no problem, because I already gave the necessary directions,' make me question if he was really concerned about those young people. But maybe there is no use making requests to him anyway."

21. Showing Surprise and Disbelief

Key Expressions

えっ	*E-tt?*	What?
(≈) うそ！	*Uso!*	You must be kidding!
(□) うそ言えよ	*Uso ie yo.*	You are lying, stop it.
(≈) ほんと？	*Honto?*	Really?
(≈) 何だって？	*Nan da tte?*	What did you say?
(≈) なに、それ	*Nani, sore.*	What (the heck) is that! What do you mean by that!
ショック	*shokku*	shock
(≈) びっくりした！	*Bikkuri shita!*	I got surprised! Boy, wasn't that a surprise!
驚く	*odoroku*	to be surprised, to be caught by surprise

Explanation

Surprise and disbelief are expressed through interjections like *E-tt* and *Uso! E-tt* is used when the speaker is simply surprised at a sudden comment, while *Uso!* challenges the unbelievable content of the news. The expression *Uso ie* (*yo*), although it literally challenges the partner to 'Go ahead and lie', is used, of course, to rebuke the person you think is not telling the truth. One also uses *Honto?* 'Really?' (or *Hontoo desu ka?*) to communicate a sense of disbelief. A certain use of *nan*(*i*) also conveys disbelief. *Nan da tte?* (or *Nan desu tte?*) is uttered in response to a surprising piece of information.

Another commonly used expression is *Nani sore*, which is not really a question but an expression of disbelief, often spoken with a tone of disgust. In certain contexts, this expression conveys the speaker's criticism. *Nan da sore* (or *Nan desu ka sore*) is used in a similar way. Although an ordinary question sentence takes the form *Sore nani?* or *Sore wa nan desu ka?,* in the disbelief expression, the order is usually inverted. Also relevant is the intonation that frequently accompanies *Nani sore.* Here *nani* is pronounced with a high tone placed on *ni*, in contrast with the question, where the high tone falls on *na.*

The English word "shock" has become a part of Japanese vocabulary and is used as an interjection when being shocked by some news, or in a phrase like *shokku o ukeru* 'to receive a shock'. *Bikkuri shita* is used as an interjection when responding to some unexpected event. For example, when someone unexpectedly and suddenly appears in front of you, you may say *Aa bikkuri shita!* 'Boy, is this a surprise!' partly as a sign of relief. In addition, *odoroku* refers to the state of being surprised at something, often in the form *Odoroita!* A speaker may inadvertently say *Odoroita!* immediately after something unexpected has happened, while she or he is regaining composure. Refer to the echo question, another rhetorical device for showing surprise and disbelief, explained in Entry 70. Also, *Maji?* 'Are you serious?' is used to show disbelief (see Entry 67.)

Examples

a. (Two girls getting excited about the price of a coat)

(≈ft1a): **ええっ**、五万円？
(≈ft2): そう。
(≈ft1b): **うっそー**！

(≈ft1a): **Ee-tt,** goman'en?
(≈ft2): Soo.
(≈ft1b): **Ussoo!** (see E. 27 for *Ussoo!*)

(≈ft1a): What? Fifty thousand yen?
(≈ft2): Yes.
(≈ft1b): You must be kidding!

b. (≈) **何だって**？あの有名な会社が倒産だって？

Nan da tte? Ano yuumeina kaisha ga toosan da tte?

What! That famous company is bankrupt?

c. (A woman confesses that she is going to get married) In this case *Nani sore* expresses not only the speaker's disbelief, but also her criticism.

(≈fy1a): 私、結婚するよ。
(≈fy2a): **うそ**！結婚するの、マジで？
(≈fy1b): まあね。この辺で適当に。
(≈fy2b): **何、それ**。そんなことでほんとにいいの？

(≈fy1a): Watashi, kekkon suru yo.
(≈fy2a): **Uso!** Kekkon suru no, maji de? (see E. 67 for *maji de*)
(≈fy1b): Maa ne. Kono hen de tekitoo ni.
(≈fy2b **Nani, sore.** Sonna koto de honto ni ii no?

(≈fy1a): I'm getting married.
(≈fy2a): No kidding! Are you really getting married, seriously?
(≈fy2b): I guess. I think it is about the right time, more or less.
(≈fy1b): What the heck is that! Are you really sure you are doing the right thing?

Authentic Examples

a. (Taken from *Majo no jooken*, episode 8) Hikaru's mother takes Michi to the airport, where Hikaru tells Michi that he is leaving for Los Angeles.

母：	光、先生にご挨拶して。
光：	ロスに、留学することにしました。
未知：	**えっ？**
光：	お元気で。
未知：	**何それ。**何でそんなこと言うの？
光：	もう、あんたの顔なんか見たくないんだよ。あんたのことなんか、好きでもなんでもないし。

haha:	Hikaru, sensei ni goaisatsu shite.
Hikaru:	Rosu ni, ryuugaku suru koto ni shimashita.
Michi:	**E-tt?**
Hikaru:	Ogenki de.
Michi:	**Nani sore.** Nande sonna koto yuu no?
Hikaru:	Moo, anta no kao nanka mitaku-nai n da yo. Anta no koto nanka, suki demo nan demo nai shi. (see E. 15 for *nanka*; E. 30 about *anta no koto*)

mother:	Hikaru. Why don't you say hello to your teacher?
Hikaru:	I've decided to go to Los Angeles to study.
Michi:	What?
Hikaru:	Take care of yourself.
Michi:	What is that? Why are you saying such a thing?
Hikaru:	I don't want to see your face any more. I don't love you any more, not at all.

b. (Taken from *Beautiful Life*, episode 1) Shuuji expresses disbelief when he discovers that he is not allowed to check out all the books he wants to from the library.

柊二：	これ全部持ち出し禁止じゃん。**何ここ。**いいよ、もう。
Shuuji:	Kore zenbu mochidashi kinshi jan. **Nani koko.** Ii yo, moo. (see E. 13 for *ii*)
Shuuji:	All these are not to be checked out. What kind of place is this? Enough is enough (I give up).

c. (Taken from *Long Love Letter Hyooryuu Kyooshitsu*, episode 10) Asami and Takamatsu see a crevasse caused by a huge earthquake and utter the following in disbelief.

浅海：　**何だこれ。**
高松：　うそだろ。

Asami: **Nan da kore.**
Takamatsu: Uso daro.

Asami: What is this?
Takamatsu: You've got to be kidding, right?

d. (Taken from *Santaku*) Kimura responds to Sanma's remark that Kimura doesn't take this kind of program seriously. Sanma is not convinced.

木村：　なあなあじゃないですよ。だって、ボク俺ほんと今出てくる前、ほんとライブより緊張しましたからね、まじで＝
さんま：　＝**うそ言えよ。**
木村：　ほんとですよ。だってもう。

Kimura: Naa naa ja-nai desu yo. Datte, boku ore honto ima dete-kuru mae, honto raibu yori kinchoo shimashita kara ne, maji de= (see E. 42 about *ore* and *boku*; E. 67 for *maji*)
Sanma: **=Uso ie yo.**
Kimura: Honto desu yo. Datte moo.

Kimura: It's not just being cozy. You know, before I, I came out now, I was tensed up, more than I get tense right before a live concert, seriously=
Sanma: =You're lying (stop that!).
Kimura: It's true. Because it's so.

e. (Taken from *Strawberry on the Shortcake*, episode 2) Yui is curious about who wrote the letter Manato received. When Manato reveals that it was Haruka, Yui comments that she was thinking so. Manato utters *Uso tsuke* in disbelief.

唯：　やっぱりねえ。そうじゃないかって思ったんだ。
まなと：　**うそつけ。**
唯：　ほんとだよ。だって彼女、まなとのこと意識してたもん。

Yui: Yappari nee. Soo ja-nai ka tte omotta n da. (see E. 57 for *yappari*)
Manato: **Uso tsuke.**
Yui: Honto da yo. Datte kanojo, Manato no koto ishiki shiteta mon. (see E. 30 for *Manato no koto*)

Yui: Just as I thought. I was thinking perhaps it was she.
Manato: You are lying (stop that!).
Yui: No, I'm not, and it's true. Because she was paying extra attention to you, Manato.

f. (Taken from *Kindaichi shoonen no jikenbo*, 5: 152) The butler is worried that one of the guests hasn't come out of the guest room and explains the situation in a supra-polite style. Another guest shows surprise in a formal style.

<お連れの / 幽月様が / 起きて来られ / ないんです！>
< ....！/ **なんですって** /？>

Otsure no Yuzuki-sama ga okite-korare-nai n desu! (see E. 72 for *n desu*)
......! **Nan desu tte?**

Ms. Yuzuki, your friend, hasn't come out of the bedroom.
What?

g. (Taken from *Jisshuusen chinbotsu*, Feb. 14, 2001) Receiving the news that civilians were on board the submarine enjoying the "tour," the high school vice-principal's reaction is described with the phrase *shokku*.

「正式に入っていないので、何とも言えないが ......」と**ショックを受けた**様子だった。

"Seishiki ni haittei-nai node, nan tomo ie-nai ga......" to **shokku o uketa** yoosu datta.

He seemed to be shocked by the news and said, " I cannot comment because I haven't heard that officially."

h. (Taken from *Strawberry on the Shortcake*, episode 3) Yui and Haruka run into each other at a supermarket.

唯： **驚いた**？
遥： 唯ちゃん。**びっくりした**よー。
唯： 買物？
遥： うん。あ唯ちゃんも？

Yui: **Odoroita?**
Haruka: Yui-chan. **Bikkuri shita** yoo.
Yui: Kaimono?
Haruka: Un. A Yui-chan mo?

Yui: Were you surprised?
Haruka: Yui. Boy, was I surprised!
Yui: Are you here shopping?
Haruka: Yes. Ah, you too, Yui?

i. (Taken from *Kitchin*, 35 [English translation, 23])

「いや、学校に来てないから、どうしたのかと思って聞いて回ってさ、そうしたらおばあちゃん亡くなったっていうだろ。**びっくりして**さ。......大変だったね。」

"Iya, gakkoo ni kite-nai kara, doo shita no ka to omotte kiite mawatte sa, soo shitara obaachan nakunatta tte yuu daro. **Bikkuri shite** sa.......Taihen datta ne. (see E. 61 for *taihen datta ne*)

"Yeah, well, you haven't been coming to classes, so I started wondering what was wrong and I asked around. They told me your grandmother had died. I was shocked. That's really rough."

j. (Taken from *Chibi Maruko-chan*, 14: 41) Maruko and her mother are surprised at each other's utterances. Note that Maruko uses an echo question to show her disbelief.

まる子：　＜おかあさん / うちは台風に / 備えて何か / してる？＞
母：　＜**えっ** .../ 特に何も / してないけど /...... ＞
まる子：　＜**ええっ**＞＜何もしてない！？＞
母：　＜そんな / **驚く**こと / ないでしょ＞

Maruko: Okaasan uchi wa taifuu ni sonaete nanka shiteru?
haha: **E-tt**... Toku ni nanimo shite-nai kedo..... (see E. 63 for *kedo*)
Maruko: **Ee-tt**. Nanimo shite-nai? (see E. 70 about echo questions)
haha: Sonna **odoroku** koto nai desho. (see E. 16 for *sonna*)

Maruko: Mom, have we prepared things for the typhoon?
mother: What? I haven't done anything in particular.
Maruko: What! You haven't done anything?
mother: There's no need to get so surprised about this, is there?

Additional Information

A number of interjections can be used to show surprise. A few of the common ones are:

1. When noticing some sudden incident:

   (≈) **あっ**、あぶない。

   A-tt, abunai.

   Ah, dangerous.

2. When discovering something unexpectedly pleasant:

   (□) **おっ**、これはうまそうだな。

   O-tt, kore wa umasoo da na.

   Oh, this looks delicious.

3. When hearing something new and unexpected:

   (≈) **へえ**、変わった人もいるもんですねえ。

   Hee, kawatta hito mo iru mon desu nee.

   I see, there are some strange people, I guess.

4. When understanding new information:

   (≈) **ふーん**、知らなかった。

   Fuun, shira-nakatta.

   Uh, I see, I didn't know that.

5. When facing something unexpected:

   (≈) **うわっ**、びっくりした。

   Uwa-tt, bikkuri shita.

   Wow, that was a surprise.

22. Being Relieved or Disappointed

Key Expressions

(≈) なんだ	*Nan da.*	That's it.
(≈) よかった！	*Yokatta!*	What a relief!
(≈) ほっとした	*Hotto shita.*	I'm relieved.
(≈) がっかり	*Gakkari.*	What a disappointment!

Explanation

When one is relieved, *Nan da* 'That's it' is used with a sigh of relief. *Nan da* presupposes that what one thought would happen differs from what did happen. *Nan da* can be positive or negative in meaning. If one's expectation was negative and an event turned out to be positive, the sense is one of relief. If, however, one's expectation was positive, and the event turned out to be negative, *nanda* indicates disappointment.

Yokatta 'What a relief' and its politer version *Yokatta desu,* are appropriate when expressing relief. If, for example, there is a potential danger, but everything turns out to be fine, the speaker says, with relief, *Yokatta. Yokatta* is often repeatedly used as an interjection, as in *Yokatta! Yokatta!* It also appears in the [V/Adj-*te yokatta*] structure, as in *Maniatte yokatta* 'What a relief to be in time'. Another expression of relief is *Hotto shita* 'I'm relieved'. *Hotto suru* is an onomatopoeic/mimetic expression resembling the "ho-tt" sound uttered in relief. It often occurs together with an interjection *A* or *Aa*, as in *Aa, hotto shita!* 'Ah, I'm relieved'.

Gakkari suru conveys disappointment. *Gakkari* by itself is also used as an interjection. In addition, *zannenna* '(lit.) regrettable' is used to show disappointment and regret, particularly toward someone else's unfortunate situation. *Zannen* often functions as an expression of compassion and sympathy (see Entry 61 for more such expressions).

Examples

a. (Two young friends chatting)

(≈my1): あっ、しまった！挨拶してくるの忘れた。
(≈fy1): **なんだ**、そんなこと？たいしたことじゃないじゃん。

(≈my1): A-tt, shimatta! Aisatsu shite-kuru no wasureta. (see E. 21 for *A-tt*; E. 18 for *shimatta*)
(≈fy1): **Nan da**, sonna koto? Taishita koto ja-nai jan. (see E. 16 for *sonna*)

(≈my1): Whoops, I'm in trouble. I forgot to say hi (to him).
(≈fy1): That's it? (I'm relieved.) That's nothing to be excited about.

b. (A man and a woman discussing a common friend who is ill)

(≈ma1a): 入院せずにすんだって。
(≈fa1a): **よかった**。
(≈ma1b): でも、けっこう長い間、通院しなければならないらしい。
(≈fa1b): そうなの。**がっかり**。すぐには、良くならないのね。

(≈ma1a): Nyuuin se-zu ni sunda tte.
(≈fa1a): **Yokatta.**
(≈ma1b): Demo, kekkoo nagai aida, tsuuin shinakereba naranai rashii. (see E. 25 for *kekkoo*)
(≈fa1b): Soo na no. **Gakkari**. Sugu ni wa, yoku nara-nai no ne.

(≈ma1a): I hear he didn't have to be hospitalized.
(≈fa1a): That's great, I'm relieved.
(≈ma1b): But it seems he will have to go see the doctor for a long while.
(≈fa1b): I see. What a disappointment! I guess you don't get well right away.

Authentic Examples

a. (Taken from *Chibi Maruko-chan*, 14: 41) Maruko is worried about the typhoon approaching that day. Maruko expresses relief with *Nan daa*.

まる子：　＜だって／貴重品は／どうするのさっ＞
母：　＜それくらいは／まとめて／ありますっ＞
まる子：　＜…あっそう／**なんだァ**／けっこう／ちゃんと／してるじゃん＞

Maruko: Datte kichoohin wa doo suru no sa-tt. (see E. 27 for *sa-tt*)
haha: Sore kurai wa matomete arimasu-tt.
Maruko: ... A-tt soo. **Nan daa.** Kekkoo chanto shiteru jan. (see E. 25 for *kekkoo*)

Maruko: But what will you do with our precious things?
mother: I have packed those things, at least.
Maruko: Is that right? That's good (I'm relieved). You are fairly well prepared, then.

b. (Taken from *Beautiful Life*, episode 4) Masao is relieved to see Sachi laugh.

正夫：　ああ、サッちゃん笑ってくれた。**よかった。**＃ああ、**よかった。**

Masao: Aa, Sat-chan waratte-kureta. **Yokatta.** Aa, **yokatta.** (see E. 24 about repetition)

Masao: Ah, Sachi, you are laughing. I'm glad (and relieved). I'm really glad!

c. (Taken from *Beautiful Life*, episode 10) Kyooko leaves the hospital to see Shuuji. Shuuji calls the hospital to explain the situation and to get permission. Kyooko is relieved to find out that she can stay overnight at Shuuji's place.

柊二：　明日もどってくればいいって。
杏子：　ほんと？
柊二：　うん。外泊扱いにしてもらったからさ。
杏子：　あ、**よかった。ほっとした。**
柊二：　ほっとしたじゃねえだろ。

Shuuji: Ashita modotte-kureba ii tte.
Kyooko: Honto?
Shuuji: Un. Gaihaku atsukai ni shite-moratta kara sa.
Kyooko: **A, yokatta. Hotto shita.**
Shuuji: Hotto shita ja-nee daro. (see E. 70 about echo responses)

Shuuji: They said it is all right if you come back tomorrow.
Kyooko: Really?
Shuuji: Yeah. They will accept this as an overnight stay.
Kyooko: Ah, that's good. I'm relieved.
Shuuji: Relieved? You shouldn't be saying that!

d. (Taken from *Beautiful Life*, episode 7) Masao and Sachi, who are in love, sometimes get into spats. They are arguing over how to address each other.

When Masao calls Sachi *omae*, Sachi responds sensitively. *Gakkari* is used as an interjection for expressing disappointment. *Unzari* 'disgusted' is used when the speaker is sick of something, with the implication of being fed up.

サチ：　あたしだってあんたって呼ぶよ。
正夫：　いいじゃん、呼べば。あんたとおまえ。
サチ：　じゃあ演歌じゃない。**がっかり**。
正夫：　こっちだってうんざり。

Sachi: Atashi datte anta tte yobu yo. (see E. 42 for *atashi*)
Masao: Ii jan, yobeba. Anta to omae. (see E. 30 for *anta* and *omae*)
Sachi: Jaa enka ja-nai. **Gakkari**.
Masao: Kotchi datte unzari. (see E. 42 for *kotchi*)

Sachi: I'm going to call you *anta*.
Masao: That's fine. Why don't you call me that. So we are *anta* and *omae*.
Sachi: Then, like the world described in old traditional Japanese songs. What a disappointment!
Masao: Me, too. I've had it.

8
When Emotion Is Intense

23. The Best and the Worst

Key Expressions

(≈) 最高！	*Saikoo!*	It's the best! Awesome!
(≈) サイテー！	*Saitee!*	The worst!
(≈) 最悪！	*Saiaku!*	The worst (situation)! The pits! The worst (case) you can think of!
一番	*ichiban*	number one, the most, the best

Explanation

Two phrases, *saikoo* 'the best' and *saitei* 'the worst', are used for pointing out two extreme, opposing evaluations. They frequently appear as interjections. The interjection *saikoo* is usually pronounced enthusiastically, whereas *saitee* sounds disgusted.

Another term, *saiaku* 'the worst situation', is used to refer to a worst-case scenario, and the adverbial *ichiban* 'the most' is used to point out a situation considered superlative, whether positively or negatively.

Authentic Examples

a. (Taken from BBS for *Beautiful Life*)

最高の感動！

Saikoo no kandoo!

The utmost sense of being moved! (see E. 1 for *kandoo*)

うああ、もう**さいこう**——っ！！

Uaa, moo **saikoo-tt**!!

Wow, truly awesome!!

b. (Taken from *Antiiku, seiyoo kottoo yoogashiten*, episode 8) Momoko talks to her friend Emiko about Antique, her favorite coffee shop.

美恵子： それで？
桃子： えっ？あ、それで、そのお店は、静かな住宅街にあって、店内はアンティークで統一されてて、で、ケーキは＃もう**サイコー**！（...）ほんとステキなお店なんだー。

Mieko: Sorede?
Momoko: E-tt? A, sorede, sono omise wa, shizukana juutakugai ni atte, tennai wa antiiku de tooitsu saretete, de, keeki wa moo **saikoo**! (...) Honto ni sutekina omise na n daa. (see E. 21 for *E-tt?*; E. 13 for *sutekina*; E. 72 for *n da*)

Mieko: And?
Momoko: Uh? Ah, uhh, that shop is located in a quiet residential neighborhood, and the interior is coordinated with antique furniture, and the cake is the very best! (...) It is really a nice shop.

c. (Taken from *SMAP x SMAP,* New Year's special) Together with Kimura, two guests, Tsutsumi and Fukatsu, praise Kyoto and Gion, where all had been recently. Nakai, taken aback by their enthusiasm, comments.

堤： 京都、**最高**！
木村： 京都、**最高**！
深津： 京都、**最高**！（堤と深津、さらに繰り返す）
堤： 祇園、**最高**！
深津： **最高**！
中居： 祇園、行かれたんですか。
堤： 行きました。
中居： 祇園、でも、撮影ないですよね。
堤： ない。＃お酒、**最高**！
中居： お酒、**最高**！

Tsutsumi: Kyooto, **saikoo**!
Kimura: Kyooto, **saikoo**! (see E. 24 about repetition)
Fukatsu: Kyooto, **saikoo**! (*Tsutsumi to Fukatsu, sara ni kurikaesu.*)
Tsutsumi: Gion, **saikoo**!
Fukatsu: **Saikoo**!
Nakai: Gion, ikareta n desu ka.
Tsutsumi: Ikimashita.

Nakai: Gion, demo, satsuei nai desu yo ne.
Tsutsumi: Nai. Osake, **saikoo**!
Nakai: Osake, **saikoo**!

Tsutsumi: Kyoto is the best!
Kimura: Kyoto is the best!
Fukatsu: Kyoto is the best! (*Tsutsumi and Fukatsu repeat the expression a few more times.*)
Tsutsumi: Gion is the best!
Fukatsu: The best!
Nakai: You went to Gion?
Tsutsumi: Yes, we did.
Nakai: At Gion, there was no shooting of the movie there, was there?
Tsutsumi: No. The sake is the best!
Nakai: Yeah, the sake is the best!

d. (Taken from *Chibi Maruko-chan*, 14: 102) Maruko's sister is upset about her father's smoking habit.

父： ＜どうだ / うまそうな / においだろ＞
姉： **＜サイテー＞**
とお姉ちゃんは / カンカンに怒りますが。

chichi: Doo da umasoona nioi daro.
ane: **Saitee.**
to oneechan wa kankan ni okorimasu ga. (see E. 10 for *kankan ni okoru*)

father: See, doesn't the cigarette smell delicious?
sister: It's the worst.
So saying, my sister gets extremely mad.

e. (Taken from *Majo no jooken*, episode 10) Masaru confesses to Michi that he is unable to say anything against his boss. He reveals that he despises himself.

大： (…) 上司にさんざんイヤミ言われても、反論ひとつできないんだ、俺は。(…) **最悪**だよ、俺は。#結婚しなくて正解だよ、未知。

Masaru: (…) Jooshi ni sanzan iyami iwaretemo, hanron hitotsu deki-nai n da, ore wa. (…) **Saiaku** da yo, ore wa. Kekkon shi-nakute seikai da yo, Michi. (see E. 48 about inverted word order)

Masaru: (…) Even when my boss repeatedly makes nasty remarks about me, I cannot fight back with a single argument. (…) The worst, that's me, for sure. Michi, you got the right idea, not marrying me.

f. (Taken from *Long Love Letter Hyooryuu Kyooshitsu*, episode 1) Yuka criticizes Asami's behavior as a teacher, and they begin to argue.

結花：　あたしの方こそあなたみたいな**最悪**の教師に、あんたなんて呼ばれるすじあいはありません。
浅海：　あんたが**最悪**だよ。
結花：　なにそれ！
浅海：　**サイアク**、**サイアク**、まじ、**サイアク**だよ。

Yuka: Atashi no hoo koso anata mitaina **saiaku** no kyooshi ni, anta nante yobareru sujiai wa arimasen. (See E. 30 for *anta*)
Asami: Anta ga **saiaku** da yo.
Yuka: Nani sore! (see E. 21 for *Nani sore*)
Asami: **Saiaku**, **saiaku**, maji **saiaku** da yo. (see E. 67 for *maji*; E. 24 about repetition)

Yuka: Really, there is no reason that I'm the one who has to be called *anta* by a teacher like you, the worst.
Asami: You are the worst.
Yuka: What are you talking about!
Asami: Worst, worst. Seriously you are the worst.

g. (Taken from interview #80, with Ukon Ichikawa, kabuki actor)

市川：　(...) だいたいはおっしゃらない。自分で考えさせる。「あんた、悪くはないけど、よくはないね」というのが多いです。
林：　そういうのって**いちばん**つらいかもしれないですね。

Ichikawa: (...) Daitai wa osshara-nai. Jibun de kangaesaseru. "Anta, waruku wa nai kedo, yoku wa nai ne" to yuu no ga ooi desu. (see E. 30 for *anta*)
Hayashi: Soo yuu no tte **ichiban** tsurai kamo shirenai desu ne. (see E. 47 for *tte*; E. 7 for *tsurai*)

Ichikawa: (...) In most cases, he does not specify. He makes me think myself. He often says, "Your performance is not bad, but it is not good either."
Hayashi: That kind of comment is perhaps the most painful, isn't it?

h. (Taken from *Dokkin paradaisu*, 234) Ai confesses that she is the happiest girl in the world.

亜衣は、今、
世界で**いちばん**、幸せな女の子 ...... です！

Ai wa, ima,
sekai de **ichiban**, shiawasena onna no ko......desu! (see E. 42 about the use of a personal name as a strategy for self-reference; E. 5 for *shiawasena*)

Ai is, now,
the happiest girl in the world!

24. Adding Extra Emphasis

Key Expressions

(≈) すごく，すごい	*sugoku, sugoi*	extremely
とても	*totemo*	very much
(≈) メチャクチャ	*mechakucha*	extremely
(v) めちゃ，めっちゃ	*mecha, metcha*	extremely
(≈) 超	*choo*	super
[繰り返し]	*kurikaeshi*	repetition

Explanation

When people are emphasizing their views and feelings, they use emphatic adverbs like *sugoku* and *totemo. Sugoi* is an *i*-type adjective and means 'extraordinary', but in casual speech it is also used as an adverb, as in *sugoi shiawase* 'extremely and extraordinarily happy'. Sometimes these phrases are also emphasized through sound change, resulting in *suggoku* and *tottemo* (see Entry 27).

As a casual expression, the adverb *mechakucha* is used for emphasis. A similar expression, *muchakucha,* functions in a similar way. The prefixes *mecha* and *choo* can also be added. *Mecha* can be affixed to all parts of speech, although it appears most frequently with adverbs and adjectives. For example, *mecha kawaii* means 'extremely cute'. *Mecha* (or the more emphatic *metcha*) is a shortened version of the emphatic adverb *mechakucha*. *Mecha* and *metcha* are used most frequently, though not exclusively, by youth in very casual style.

Choo 'super, extremely, exceeding' can also be affixed to all parts of speech, and it is quite versatile. For example, *choo kakko ii* 'extremely cool', *choo benkyoo suru* 'to study really hard', and so on. Although originally the use of these emphatic prefixes was limited to youth, their use has spread to the general public, at least in casual conversation. *Mechakucha*, *mecha*, and *choo* should be avoided in formal situations.

When a speaker is overwhelmed by emotion, the use of repetition increases the degree of expressivity. Repeating twice, three times, or even more conveys an overall emphasis.

Examples

a. (A man commenting on a movie he saw; a younger female friend responds)

(ma1): あの映画、**とっても**感動しました。私にしては珍しく。
(fy1): そう、そうなんです。私も**すごく**感激して、何度も泣いてしまったんです。

(ma1): Ano eiga, **tottemo** kandoo shimashita. Watashi ni shite wa mezurashiku. (see E. 1 for *kandoo shimashita*)
(fy1): Soo, soo na n desu. Watashi mo **sugoku** kangeki shite, nando mo naite-shimatta n desu. (see E. 1 for *kangeki*; E. 17 for *naite-shimatta*; E. 72 for *n desu*)

(ma1): That movie, I was moved. It was a rare thing for me.
(fy1): Yes, exactly so. I was very deeply moved and I cried many times.

b. (Two teenage girls shopping together) *Mecha*, *choo*, and repetition are used to express strong emotion and enthusiasm.

(≈ft1a): ねえ、この帽子、良くない？
(≈ft2): どれ、見せて。やだ、**めちゃ**かわいい！
(≈ft1b): えっ、1200 円？　**超**安いじゃん。買っちゃおう。買っちゃおう。

(≈ft1a): Nee, kono booshi, yoku-nai?
(≈ft2): Dore, misete. Ya da, **mecha** kawaii! (see E. 31 for *kawaii*)
(≈ft1b): E-tt, sennihyakuen? **Choo** yasui jan. Katchaoo. Katchaoo. (see E. 21 for *E-tt*; E. 17 for *katchaoo*)

(≈ft1a): Say, isn't this hat nice?
(≈ft2): Which one, let me see. Wow, totally cute!
(≈ft1b): What, only 1200 yen? Unbelievably inexpensive! I'm going to buy this, for sure.

Authentic Examples

a. (Taken from BBS for *Beautiful Life*) Although *choo* and *mecha* are colloquial expressions, they appear in the written media as well, particularly when a writer is directly revealing or confessing his or her inner feelings.

超感動した。

Choo kandoo shita. (see E. 1 for *kandoo shita*)

I was extremely moved.

めちゃ感動しました。

Mecha kandoo shimashita.

I was totally (or completely) moved.

めちゃめちゃ寂しい。

Mecha mecha sabishii. (see E. 8 for *sabishii*)

I am so totally lonely.

b. (Taken from *Long Love Letter Hyooryuu Kyooshitsu*, episode 4) Takamatsu tells how much he loved Ichinose by using *suggee*. *Suggee* is a blunt, emphatic version of *sugoi* (see Chapter 2 and Entry 27).

「俺、**すっげえ**好きだったんだよね。#いつも一緒にいてさ」

"Ore, **suggee** suki datta n da yo ne. Itsumo issho ni ite sa. (see E. 32 for *suki*; E. 72 for *n da*)

"I loved her so so much. We were together all the time."

c. (Taken from *SMAP x SMAP*, special live show) Tsuyoshi comments on how he felt during the time when Goroo was unable to participate in the group activities.

剛： だから本当に、悪かったことなんだけど、あの僕の中では**すごく**、ほんとにあの改めて再確認する、あの、こと、が多かったりとかして。#なんか自分自身も**すごく**考えた、この何ヶ月でした。

Tsuyoshi: Dakara hontoo ni, warukatta koto na n da kedo, ano boku no naka de wa **sugoku**, honto ni ano aratamete saikakunin suru, ano, koto, ga ookattari toka shite. Nanka jibun jishin mo **sugoku** kangaeta, kono nankagetsu deshita. (see E. 42 for *boku*; E. 63 for *tari [toka] shite*; E. 62 for *nanka*; E. 42 for *jibun*)

Tsuyoshi: So, it was an unfortunate incident, but in myself, I reconfirmed how I felt about things intensely (and) many times. During these several months I myself also thought about a lot of things over and over.

d. (Taken from interview #86, with Mayumi Narita, winner of the Special Olympics gold medal in swimming)

林： いいスケジュールでよかったですね。
成田： そうですね。一緒にやってるおばさんたちが**メッチャクチャ**いい人たちで、お母さんが何人もいるみたいで、(...).

Hayashi: Ii sukejuuru de yokatta desu ne. (see E. 22 for *yokatta*)
Narita: Soo desu ne. Issho ni yatteru obasantachi ga **metchakucha** ii hitotachi de, okaasan ga nannin mo iru mitai de, (...).

Hayashi: It was nice that your schedule worked out fine.
Narita: Indeed. The older women with whom I work out are extremely nice, and it is like I have many mothers (...).

e. (Taken from *Kitchin*, 52–53 [English translation, 34])

顔がそっくりなので孫らしい彼女は、道もバスも混んでいるので**むちゃくちゃ**に機嫌が悪いらしく、身をよじらせて怒って言った。
「知らない。あれ飛行船じゃないもん。」

Kao ga sokkuri na node mago rashii kanojo wa, michi mo basu mo kondeiru node **muchakucha** ni kigen ga warui rashiku, mi o yojirasete okotte itta. (see E. 10 for *okoru*) "Shira-nai. Are hikoosen ja-nai mon."

The little girl, whose face epitomized "grandchild," was in a very bad mood, perhaps because of the traffic jam and crowdedness. She said angrily, fidgeting, "I don't care. And it's not a dirigible!"

f. (Taken from *Muko-dono*, episode 1) Yuuichiroo is elated when receiving a gift.

祐一郎：　ありがと！**めっちゃ**うれしい！

Yuuichiroo: Arigato! **Metcha** ureshii! (see E. 5 for *ureshii*)

Yuuichiroo: Thank you! I am totally delighted!

g. (Taken from *SMAP x SMAP*, special live show) *Choo* is affixed to a verb. This interaction contains frequent occurrences of listener responses, illustrating how interactive a conversation is. *Chau* is a shortened version of *chigau*.

木村：　あれ、俺、知ってる？
慎吾：　なに。
木村：　**超**挑戦したの、俺。
中居：　なに。
木村：　オーナーやってる時。
中居：　これを？
木村：　ちゃう。おいしいってやつ。
中居：　おいしい、うんうん。
木村：　だから慎吾の「う」っていうやつの、
中居：　うん。
木村：　あれとして。
中居：　うん。
木村：　やったの。ね、二回ぐらいね。
中居：　うん。

Kimura: Are, ore, shitteru?
Shingo: Nani.
Kimura: **Choo** choosen shita no, ore. (see E. 48 about inverted word order)
Nakai: Nani.
Kimura: Oonaa yatteru toki.
Nakai: Kore o?
Kimura: Chau. Oishii tte yatsu.

Nakai: Oishii, un un.
Kimura: Dakara Shingo no “u” tte yuu yatsu no,
Nakai: Un.
Kimura: are to shite.
Nakai: Un.
Kimura: Yatta no. Ne, nikai gurai ne.
Nakai: Un.

Kimura: That, I did, do you know that?
Shingo: What?
Kimura: I tried it really hard.
Nakai: What?
Kimura: When I was the owner (of the Bistro SMAP).
Nakai: You mean this?
Kimura: No, not that. The one you say “*Oishii* (Delicious).”
Nakai: I see, that *oishii.*
Kimura: I mean the one that Shingo goes “Whh,”
Nakai: Uh-huh.
Kimura: that one.
Nakai: Uh-huh.
Kimura: I did it, about twice, right?
Nakai: Yeah.

h. (Taken from *Kindaichi shoonen no jikenbo*, 5: 74) Hajime comments on the food, and Miyuki responds. *Umee-tt* is an emphatic version of *umee.* See Chapter 2 about the use of *umee* instead of *umai.*

はじめ： ＜このボルシチ / **ちょー** / うめえーっ＞
美雪： ＜はじめちゃん …… ＞ ＜お願いだから / 盛大に音をたてて / すするのはやめて！！＞

Hajime: Kono borushichi **choo** umee-tt.
Miyuki: Hajime-chan…… Onegai da kara seidai ni oto o tatete susuru no wa yamete!! (see E. 59 for *Onegai da kara*)

Hajime: This borscht stew is super, super good.
Miyuki: Hajime… I beg you, please do not so noisily slurp up the stew!!

i. (Taken from interview #87, with Muneaki Masuda, company president)

増田： それでよけいに家族が僕を大事にしたわけね。**超**過保護で、中学校のときにいじめられっ子になっちゃって (…)。

Masuda: Sorede yokei ni kazoku ga boku o daiji ni shita wake ne. **Choo** kahogo de, chuugakkoo no toki ni ijimerarekko ni natchatte (…). (see E. 17 for *natchatte*)

Masuda: So, my family were even more concerned about me. They were super protective, and I ended up being bullied during my junior high school days (…).

j. (Taken from *Long Vacation*, episode 7) Sena expresses Ryooko's feelings by repeating a phrase many times.

瀬名： **会いたくて。会いたくて。もう会いたくて、会いたくて、会いたくて。**#好きんなるとそうなんだろね。

Sena: **Aitakute. Aitakute.** Moo **aitakute, aitakute, aitakute.** Suki n naru to soo na n daro ne. (see E. 32 for *suki*)

Sena: Want to see, want to see him. Really want to see, want to see, want to see him. When you love someone, it must be like that.

Note

The prefix *choo* may be used in a slightly different way as well. For example, *choo shizen* does not mean 'it is extremely natural', but rather that something is supernatural, in the sense of being beyond nature, as in the case of a mystery unexplained by the laws of nature. However, in casual speech, particularly among youth, *choo* is understood to be an emphatic marker. According to A. Ikegami (2000), *choo* was originally a local idiom in Shizuoka that spread first into Kanagawa and then nationwide through the media.

25. Expressing Considerable Emotion

Key Expressions

かなり	*kanari*	considerably, very much
(≈) わりと	*warito*	comparatively, relatively
(≈) けっこう	*kekkoo*	rather, more than expected, considerably

Explanation

Kanari, *warito*, and *kekkoo* are three of the many adverbs that describe heightened degrees of intensity. *Kanari* 'considerably' is used to describe a high degree or extent of things, without specificity. *Warito* 'comparatively, relatively' is used as a qualification, as in *warito kantanna* 'relatively simple'.

These terms not only refer to actual degree of intensity, but also—and more important—add a certain vagueness and softness to the sentence. A statement of the approximate degree of intensity of something becomes less specific, and therefore leaves room for potential vagueness. A third important and frequently used word for this purpose is *kekkoo* 'rather, more than expected, considerably'.

Kekkoo implies that the degree is more than expected and is in some way a surprise. Because of this additional sense of unexpectedness and surprise, *kekkoo* is frequently used in conversation to decrease the speaker's responsibility for the utterance. When a speaker uses *kekkoo* in reference to his or her own situation, it gives an impression of talking from someone else's perspective, creating a sense of distance with a somewhat alienating effect. For example, the expression *Atashi tte kekkoo ganbariya na n desu* conveys: "You may find it surprising, but I am a hardworking person, and I'm sort of surprised at this myself." (See Chapter 2, where youth language is discussed, for more on this.)

Quite a few adverbs describe different degrees of intensity. A selection ranging from most to least intense includes:

なかなか	*nakanaka*	more than thought
まあまあ	*maamaa*	more or less, so-so
比較的	*hikakuteki*	comparatively
若干	*jakkan*	somewhat
少し	*sukoshi*	a little
ちょっと	*chotto*	a bit
わずかに	*wazuka ni*	very little, slightly

It is important to note that some degree words implying the speaker's surprise cannot be used when praising someone. For example, one should avoid using *warito* 'relatively' when appreciating one's host's cooking, as in **Warito oishikatta* 'This was relatively good'. *Kekkoo* should be avoided for the same reason, as in **Kore kekkoo oishii desu* 'This is rather good (better than I expected)' when someone went to the trouble to prepare food for you.

Examples

a. (Two youths chatting about learning to play chess)

(≈my1a): チェスって、**けっこう**難しいんだろ？
(≈my2): うん、**かなり**。
(≈my1b): じゃ、やめとこ。俺には無理だ。

(≈my1a): Chesu tte, **kekkoo** muzukashii n daro? (see E. 47 for *tte*)
(≈my2): Un, **kanari**.
(≈my1b): Ja, yametoko. Ore ni wa muri da.

(≈my1a): Isn't chess rather difficult?
(≈my2): Yes, very.
(≈my1b): Well then, I won't play. It's too much for me.

b. (Two teens talking about a man) One speaker notices the partner's closeness to the man.

(≈ft1a): **けっこう**楽しそうに話してたじゃない？親しい人？
(≈ft2a): **ちょっと**。そんなに親しいって程でもないんだ。
(≈ft1b): あの人、誰なのよ。
(≈ft2b): へへ、秘密。

(≈ft1a): **Kekkoo** tanoshisoo ni hanashiteta ja-nai? Shitashii hito?
(≈ft2a): **Chotto**. Sonna ni shitashii tte hodo demo nai n da. (see E. 72 for *n da*)
(≈ft1b): Ano hito, dare na no yo.
(≈ft2b): He he, himitsu.

(≈ft1a): You seem to have been rather enjoying talking with him. Is he someone close?
(≈ft2a): A bit, I must say. We aren't really that close.
(≈ft1b): Who is that guy?
(≈ft2b): Heh heh, it's a secret.

Authentic Examples

a. (Taken from *SMAP x SMAP*, special live show) Kimura is asked how he feels, now that Goroo is coming back to the show. Kimura adds *un* to indicate the end of his utterance.

木村： とにかく待ってたからね俺は。**かなり**うれしいね、うん。

Kimura: Tonikaku matteta kara ne ore wa. **Kanari** ureshii ne, un. (see E. 48 about inverted word order)

Kimura: Anyway, I've been waiting for him. So, I'm very pleased, yes indeed.

b. (Taken from Shooji 2003a, 55) In this essay, titled "Hyaku-en no udon o tabe ni iku" (Going to eat a 100-yen udon noodle dish), the writer comments on the noodle dish.

うどんは**かなり**太目、モチモチとコシがあって**なかなか**おいしい。

Udon wa **kanari** futome, mochimochi to koshi ga atte **nakanaka** oishii.

The *udon* noodles are nicely fat; they are chewy and firm *(al dente)* and more delicious than I thought.

c. (Taken from *Long Love Letter Hyooryuu Kyooshitsu*, episode 7) Asami suggests that he and Yuka have a date.

浅海： あのー。（結花、振り向く）突然なんですけど、#今日とか、明日とか、あさってとか週末とかいつか暇ですか。（結花、びっくりした表情）あのー、すいません。あの、**ちょっと**今、言ってみようかなと思っただけです。

結花： あの、#暇です、**わりと**。#ていうか、とても。（浅海と結花、お互いに微笑みあう）

Asami: Anoo. (*Yuka, furimuku*) Totsuzen na n desu kedo, kyoo toka, ashita toka, asatte toka shuumatsu toka itsuka hima desu ka. (see E. 69 for *totsuzen na n desu kedo*) (*Yuka, bikkurishita hyoojoo*) Anoo, suimasen. Ano, **chotto** ima, itte-miyoo ka na to omotta dake desu.

Yuka: Ano, hima desu, **warito**. Te yuu ka, totemo. (see E. 44 for *te yuu ka*; E. 24 for *totemo*) (*Asami to Yuka, otagai ni hohoemi au*)

Asami: Uhh, excuse me. (*Yuka turns her head [toward Asami]*) It's sudden, but are you free today, tomorrow, the day after tomorrow, the weekend, or some other time? (*Yuka shows surprise*) Sorry. I just thought I would try it (a bit) anyway.

Yuka: Yes, I am relatively free. Uhh, to tell you the truth, very free. (*Asami and Yuka look at each other and smile*)

d. (Taken from *Chibi Maruko-chan*, 13: 76) The father comments on the sushi. His use of *kekkoo* indicates that his expectations were low, but that the sushi he is eating is surprisingly good.

父： ＜このスシ**けっこう**/うまいなァ＞

chichi: Kono sushi **kekkoo** umai naa.

father: This sushi (surprisingly), this is rather good.

e. (Taken from *Strawberry on the Shortcake*, episode 1) The mother tells Yui to be friendly to Manato. Manato is the son of the man the mother is marrying. Yui responds that, unbeknownst to her mother (surprisingly, and to a certain degree), she and Manato are friends.

母： なかよくしてね。
唯： もう**けっこう**なかいいよ。

haha: Nakayoku shite ne.
Yui: Moo **kekkoo** naka ii yo.

mother: Be good friends with him.
Yui: We are already pretty good friends.

f. (Taken from interview #79, with Nobuyuki Matsuhisa, owner and chef of Nobu Tokyo)

林：　厨房では**けっこう**怖いんですか。
松久：　仕事をしてるときは**けっこう**怖いですよ。

Hayashi: Chuuboo de wa **kekkoo** kowai n desu ka. (see E. 11 for *kowai*; E. 72 for *n desu ka*)
Matsuhisa: Shigoto o shiteru toki wa **kekkoo** kowai desu yo.

Hayashi: Aren('t) you rather severe and threatening in the kitchen?
Matsuhisa: Yes, while I am working, I am rather (unexpectedly) threatening (and make people feel fearful of me).

g. (Taken from *Kitchin*, 59 [English translation, 38])

「あっそれ知ってる。何だっけ。**けっこう**好き。誰のうただっけ。」私は言った。

"A-tt sore shitteru. Nan dakke. **Kekkoo** suki. Dare no uta dakke." (see E. 21 for *A-tt*)
Watashi wa itta.

"Oh!" I said. "I know that song. What's it called again? I love that song. Who was it that sang it?"

Additional Information

The adverb *chotto* 'a bit' is also used as a degree word. Its function, however, extends far beyond this basic meaning. It can be used:

1. To mean 'a bit, a little, slightly, somewhat' when diminishing a favor to the partner, as in *Honno chotto desu kedo* 'This is just a little bit, but...'.
2. When the speaker does something incidentally or just in passing, as in *Kaerigake ni chotto yotte-mimashoo ka* 'Shall we stop by on our way home?'.
3. As an attention-getting device. For example, *Chotto!* 'Hey!' *Nee chotto* 'Say', and *Chotto Ueda-san* 'Hey, Ueda'.
4. When gently refusing a request. In this case, *chotto* really means 'rather'. For example, *Uun, chotto muzukashii naa, kore wa* 'Uhh, this is rather difficult, I'm afraid'.
5. When refusing to answer a question straightforwardly or being unwilling to provide information. For example, in response to the question *Doko itteta no?* 'Where have you been?' one may answer *Chotto* 'Uh, well'.

26. Cannot Stop Feeling

Key Expressions

さびしくてしかた(が)ない	*sabishikute shikata (ga) nai*	cannot bear the overwhelming feeling of loneliness
会いたくてたまらない	*aitakute tamaranai*	cannot help really wanting to see (him)
たまんない	*tamannai*	unbearable
くやしいったらない	*kuyashii ttara nai*	regrettable beyond belief, too regrettable for words

Explanation

The out-of-control feelings that individuals sometimes experience can be conveyed by the sentence structures introduced here, as well as by others. One structure is the idiomatic expression *shikata (ga) nai. Shikata (ga) nai* literally means 'there is no way of solving the problem'. It expresses the feeling that something is beyond one's control, and it expresses the attitude that no matter how hard one tries, the situation is impossible to escape or to be done with. *Shikata (ga) nai* takes [Adj-*te* + *shikata (ga) nai*] and [V stem + *takute* + *shikata (ga) nai*]. *Ga* is optional; when used, it conveys a more formal tone. (Note that *shikata* [*ga*] *nai* may also be used independently to communicate resignation, as discussed in Entry 20.)

The expression *tamaranai* literally means 'cannot bear' or 'cannot stand.' The formal version *tamarimasen* and the more colloquial *tamannai* are also used. *Tamaranai* takes the structure [Adj-*te* + *tamaranai*] and [V stem + *takute* + *tamaranai*]. Since *tamaranai* implies that something cannot be borne, it is usually used with phrases that refer to feelings and senses. *Tamaranai* or *tamannai* and *tamaranaku* are also used as two independent adjectives and an adverb, respectively, to express an unbearable intensity, as in *tamannai kimochi* 'unbearable feeling' and *tamaranaku sabishii* 'unbearably lonesome'.

Another sentence structure for overwhleming emotions is [Adj basic + *ttara nai*]. This structure implies feelings so strong and beyond belief that one cannot find words for them. The repetition of [Adj-*te*] can also be used to emphatically express feelings, as in *Ureshikute, ureshikute* 'so very, very delighted'. When using these structures and phrases, keep in mind that they cannot directly convey someone else's feelings.

Examples

a. (≈) 妻に先立たれて、**さびしくてしかたがない**。

Tsuma ni sakidatarete, **sabishikute shikata ga nai.**

My wife has passed away, and I'm overwhelmed by this feeling of loneliness.

b. 母は海外旅行を**したくてたまらない**らしいんですよ。

Haha wa kaigai ryokoo o **shitakute tamaranai** rashii n desu yo.

It seems that my mother really wants to travel abroad.

c. (Two young women talking about a common friend)

(≈fy1a): 彼女、飛び跳ねてたわね。
(≈fy2): 彼に会えて**うれしくてしかたがない**んじゃない？
(≈fy1b): そうでしょ、三ヶ月ずっと**会いたくてたまらなかった**らしいから。

(≈fy1a): Kanojo, tobihaneteta wa ne.
(≈fy2): Kare ni aete **ureshikute shikata ga nai** n ja-nai?
(≈fy1b): Soo desho, sankagetsu zutto **aitakute tamaranakatta** rashii kara.

(≈fy1a): She was jumping with joy, wasn't she?
(≈fy2): She is totally overwhelmed with joy that she can see him.
(≈fy1b): Right, she seemed to have been really wanting to see him all during the past three months.

d. (≈) この間買ったばかりの傘を電車の中に忘れてきちゃった。**ほんとくやしいったらない**よ。

Kono aida katta bakari no kasa o densha no naka ni wasurete-kitchatta. Honto **kuyashii ttara nai** yo. (see E. 19 for *kuyashii*)

I left the umbrella I just bought in the train. It's upsetting beyond belief.

Authentic Examples

a. (Taken from *Tsubasa o kudasai*, 83) Kyooka expresses her desire to get away from school.

六限終了の鐘が鳴った時、正直言ってホッとした。
一刻も早く、教室……学校から**抜け出したくてたまらなかった**。

Rokugen shuuryoo no kane ga natta toki, shoojiki itte hotto shita. (see E. 44 for *shoojiki itte*; E. 22 for *hotto shita*)
Ikkoku mo hayaku, kyooshitsu……gakkoo kara **nukedashitakute tamaranakatta.**

When the chime for the end of sixth period rang, to be honest, I was relieved. As soon as possible, from the classroom—actually from school—I desperately wanted to get away.

b. (Taken from *Chibi Maruko-chan*, 13: 41) Maruko talks to her grandfather about the letter he has received. Note that the expression *nan ja yo* is in an imagined speech style (called *roojingo* 'old-man-style'). It is not likely that Japanese senior speakers would use this form, but it appears in the Japanese mass media to stereotype someone as an old man. (See Entry 76 regarding this style.)

まる子： (…)＜お見舞いのとき/持ってった手紙の/返事くれたの？＞
祖父： ＜そうなんじゃよ/わしゃうれしくて＞＜もう**たまらん**よ＞

Maruko: (…) Omimai no toki mottetta tegami no henji kureta no?
sofu: Soo na n ja yo. Washa ureshikute. Moo **tamaran** yo. (see E. 5 for *ureshii*)

Maruko: (…) Did he send you a letter in response to your letter? The letter I delivered to him when he was sick at home?
grandfather: That's right. I am so delighted, I'm totally overwhelmed!

c. (Taken from *Beautiful Life*, episode 8) Shuuji confesses how much he cares about Kyooko.

杏子： 正直だね。正直すぎるよ。
柊二： や、あんたにうそをつきたくねえしさ。ってか、ついてもどうせすぐ見抜くでしょ。や、俺、あんたがいなくなるって思ったら、#胸つかまれたみたいに痛くなってさあ。今こうやって、一緒にいても、なんか、けっこう**たまんない**感じだし。#ごめん俺、あんたが好きだわ。どういうふうに言われても、俺杏子じゃないとだめだわ。

Kyooko: Shoojiki da ne. Shoojiki sugiru yo.
Shuuji: Ya, anta ni uso o tsukitaku-nee shi sa. Tte ka, tsuitemo doose sugu minuku desho. Ya, ore, anta ga i-naku naru tte omottara, mune tsukamareta mitai ni itaku natte saa. Ima koo yatte, issho ni itemo, nanka, kekkoo **tamannai** kanji da shi. Gomen ore, anta ga suki da wa. Doo yuu fuu ni iwaretemo, ore Kyooko ja-nai to dame da wa. (see E. 44 for *tte ka*; E. 57 for *doose*; E. 7 for *itai*; E. 62 for *nanka*; E. 25 for *kekkoo*; E. 32 for *suki*; E. 18 for *dame*)

Kyooko: You are honest. Too honest.
Shuuji: Well, I don't want to tell you lies. More truthfully, if I lie, you will know it right away anyway. When I thought that you would no longer be with me, my heart began to ache as if it were

squeezed (by someone). Even now, I'm overwhelmed with unbearable feelings. I love you. No matter what people say, I cannot be all right without you, Kyooko.

27. Emotional Emphasis through Sound

Key Expressions

(≈) よーく	*yooku*	very well
(≈) にほんじーん	*nihonjiin*	(really) Japanese
(≈) ぜんっぜん	*zen-tt-zen*	absolutely (not), whatsoever
(≈) うれしーっ！	*Ureshiii-tt!*	I'm so delighted
(□) そんなこと言うなっ	*Sonna koto yuu-na-tt.*	Don't ever say such a thing.

Explanation

Emotion is expressed not only in phrases and sentence structures, but also by sound. Usually an increase in volume and length indicates emphasis in meaning. Elongation of vowels causes an emphatic effect, as in *yooku* 'really well' instead of *yoku* 'well'.

Another sound change is inserting a glottal stop (the sound usually transcribed as a small *tsu* in hiragana and katakana), which creates a more emphatic and/or more emotive effect. For example, *zen-tt-zen* instead of *zenzen* '(not) at all' means 'absolutely not'. The glottal stop can be added at the end of an utterance (written as *ureshiii-tt* and *yuu-na-tt*, for example) when the speaker wants to express an exceptionally assertive attitude.

Examples

a. はいはい、**よーく**わかりました。(*yooku* instead of *yoku*)

Hai hai, **yooku** wakarimashita. (see E. 66 for *wakarimashita*)

Yes, sure, I got it really well.

b. これからも**ずーーっと**続けますから。(*zuuutto* instead of *zutto*)

Kore kara mo **zuuutto** tsuzukemasu kara.

I will continue from now on for a very, very long time.

c. (≈) **ねえ**、行こうよ、**ねえ**。(*nee* instead of *ne*)

Nee, ikoo yo, **nee**. (see E. 54 for *nee*)

Say, let's go, won't you, please?

d. (≈) あの人ほんと**にほんじーん**って感じだねえ。(*nihonjiin* instead of *nihonjin*)

Ano hito honto **nihonjiin** tte kanji da nee.

He gives the impression that he really is Japanese.

e. (≈) あの人のこと、**ぜんっぜん**わかんない。(*zen-tt-zen* instead of *zenzen*)

Ano hito no koto, **zen-tt-zen** wakan-nai. (see E. 66 for *wakan-nai*)

About him, I don't understand him at all.

Authentic Examples

a. (Taken from *Muko-dono*, episode 2) Yuuichiroo, who is on the phone, describes his nephew Ryoo. *Mecha* is elongated and accompanied by the glottal stop, resulting in *meeetcha*.

亮、**め——っちゃ**いいやつなんで、これからも仲良くしてやってね。

Ryoo, **meeetcha** ii yatsu na n de, kore kara mo nakayoku shite-yatte ne. (see E. 30 for *yatsu*)

Ryoo is such a good guy, so will you please continue to be good friends with him?

b. (Taken from *Ren'ai hakusho*, 14: 52) Kaho describes her friend, Sumire.

自分がかわいいことを、自分で**よーく**わかっていて。

Jibun ga kawaii koto o, jibun de **yooku** wakatteite. (see E. 42 for *jibun*; E. 31 for *kawaii*; E. 66 for *wakatteite*)

She herself knows very well how cute she is.

c. (Taken from *Ren'ai hakusho*, 14: 9) Kaho expresses her feelings for her friend Sumire. First she says *chotto*, but in fact she dislikes Sumire quite a bit.

ちょっと……。
ていうか。
ううん。
かなーり苦手な、
同級生の伊藤すみれちゃん。

Chotto. (see E. 25 for *chotto*)
Te yuu ka. (see E. 44 for *te yuu ka*)
Uun.
Kanaari nigatena,
Dookyuusei no Itoo Sumire-chan.

A bit.
To tell the truth.
No.
Very unlikable,
classmate Sumire Itoo.

d. (Taken from *Chibi Maruko-chan*, 14: 136) Maruko emphatically denies bad memories.

<そんなこと / **ぜんっぜん** / 覚えてないや .../ 潮干狩りが / 楽しかったことしか ... >

Sonna koto **zen-tt-zen** oboete-nai ya...Shiohigari ga tanoshikatta koto shika...

I don't remember that at all...(I remember) only the fun things about hunting for clams on the beach.

e. (Taken from *Kitchin*, 33 [English translation, 22])

いっつも、そうだ。私はいつもギリギリにならないと動けない。

Ittsumo, soo da. Watashi wa itsumo girigiri ni nara-nai to ugoke-nai.

I've always been like that. Unless I'm pushed to the edge, I won't make a move.

f. (Taken from *Himawari nikki*, 188) Konomi expresses how she feels when she and her boyfriend Satoo go out for a festival and have a certain soft drink together.

「**おいしーっ**！ラムネ好き！」
思わず本音がでちゃう！

"**Oishiii-tt!** Ramune suki!"
Omowazu honne ga dechau! (see Chapter 3 for *honne*; E. 17 for *dechau*)

"Delicious! I love *Ramune* soda."
Inadvertently, I express my *honne* (true feelings).

g. (Taken from *Chibi Maruko-chan*, 14: 16) Maruko complains that she wants to eat something special at a Chinese restaurant, to which her father angrily responds.

父：	<うるさいっ / 金のかかること / 言うなっ>
chichi:	**Urusai-tt.** Kane no kakaru koto **yuu-na-tt.** (see E. 39 for *urusai*)
father:	Be quiet. Don't say things that will cost me money.

Additional Information

In casual spoken Japanese, *i* in some *i*-type adjectives may be deleted, as shown below. These sound changes convey an air of casualness, but they are not necessarily emphatic in meaning.

ふるい	*furu-tt,* instead of *furui*
恐い	*kowa-tt,* instead of *kowai*
暑い	*atsu-tt,* instead of *atsui*

Note the use of *kowa-tt* in the following authentic example.

1. (Taken from Konishi, 16) In this essay, Konishi critiques the fashion of a British politician's wife. The short essay accompanying her photograph is titled *Naimen no takumashisa mo fukumete fasshon. Sonna jidai, shushoo fujin no suutsu wa, otokomono?* (Fashion that includes inner strength. In such an era, the suit worn by the wife of the prime minister is one tailored for men?) Curiously, the writer refers to himself as *atashi*, an expression stereotypically associated with a female speaker. It seems that by referring to himself as *atashi*, he playfully identifies himself as a stereotypically "feminine" obedient person.

   で、時代の女というのは、彼女のような人ってことになるんだろうな。つまり強く、たくましく、男を支え……。**コワッ**。とりあえず、今日はアタシも早く帰ろーっと。

   De, jidai no onna to yuu no wa, kanojo no yoona hito tte koto ni naru n daroo na. Tsumari tsuyoku, takumashiku, otoko o sasae……**Kowa-tt.** Toriaezu, kyoo wa atashi mo hayaku kaeroo-tt to.

   So, the woman representing today's woman would be someone like her. In other words, she is strong, reliable, and supports her man....Scary, isn't it? For now, today, I think I'm going back home early.

9
Falling in and out of Love

28. Proclaiming the Bond of "the Two of Us"

Key Expressions

ふたり	*futari*	(lit.) two people, the two of us
俺達	*oretachi*	we
私達	*watashitachi*	we

Explanation

The awareness of two people in love is often expressed by *futari,* which literally means two people. In certain contexts, it refers to the unit of (two) lovers. For example, lovers may refer to their life together as *korekara no futari no shoorai* 'the future for the two of us'.

Oretachi is used by a male speaker in reference to his group members, but in the context of the love relationship, *oretachi* (echoing the "masculine" voice) adds a meaning of the bond unifying the "two of us." Likewise, *watashitachi* may refer to that "us"-ness, the strong bond between lovers.

Examples

a. (≈) これからは、**ふたりで**生きていこう。

Kore kara wa, **futari de** ikite-ikoo.

From now on, the two of us (we) will spend our lives together.

b. (≈) **私達**、幸せになろうね。

Watashitachi, shiawase ni naroo ne. (see E. 5 for *shiawase*)

We, we will be happy together, won't we?

Authentic Examples

a. (Taken from *Long Vacation*, episode 3) Minami invites Sena and Ryooko to the bar where Minami's brother works. Minami emphasizes that the two of them should come together.

南：　ねえ、この間のおわびに、いいお店招待する。
瀬名：　なに、おわびって。
南：　(…) 涼子ちゃんにもこの間のことあやまりたいし。ねえ、一緒においでよ。涼子ちゃんと。＃**ふたりで**。
瀬名：　**ふたりで？**

Minami: Nee, kono aida no owabi ni, ii omise shootai suru.
Sena: Nani, owabi tte. (see E. 70 about echo questions)
Minami: (…) Ryooko-chan ni mo kono aida no koto ayamaritai shi. Nee, issho ni oide yo. Ryooko-chan to. **Futari de.** (see E. 63 about the use of *shi*)
Sena: **Futari de?**

Minami: Say, I want to invite you to a nice place as part of my apology to you.
Sena: What do you mean by apology?
Minami: (…) I want to apologize to Ryooko about what happened the other day. So, will you come together? Ryooko and you. The two of you.
Sena: You mean the two of us?

b. (Taken from *Majo no jooken*, episode 3) Hikaru uses the term *oretachi* in front of his mother. She responds in disgust.

光：　何でだよ。
母：　何が？
光：　ふざけんなよ。あんたのせいで、**俺達**がどんな思いしてるか分かってんのかよ。
母：　＃「**俺達**」＃＃光、もうこれ以上あの先生に関わるのは、やめなさい。

Hikaru: Nande da yo.
haha: Nani ga?

Hikaru: Fuzaken-na yo. Anta no sei de, **oretachi** ga donna omoi shiteru ka wakatten no ka yo. (see E. 66 for *wakaru*)
haha: "**Oretachi.**" Hikaru, moo kore ijoo ano sensei ni kakawaru no wa yamenasai. (see E. 70 about echo responses)

Hikaru: Why?
mother: What about?
Hikaru: Don't behave like an idiot. Do you have any idea as to how much of a trouble we are in because of you?
mother: "We"? Hikaru, stop being involved with that teacher right now.

c. (Taken from *Suna no ue no koibitotachi*, episode 6) Akira and Reiko are beginning to realize that they are in love. Note that the term *oretachi* becomes the topic of conversation.

朗： 乗り越えなくちゃいけないんだ。#ひとみの死を、乗り越えなくちゃいけないんだよ、**俺達**は。
黎子： (びっくりして朗をみつめ)「**俺達**」(朗うなずく)忘れるんじゃなくて。
朗： (うなずいて)ああ。
黎子： 分からない、どうしていいのか。
朗： だから**俺達**が向き合うんだ。

Akira: Norikoenakucha ikenai n da. Hitomi no shi o, norikoenakucha ikenai n da yo, **oretachi** wa. (see E. 48 about inverted word order)
Reiko: (*bikkurishite Akira o mitsume*) "**Oretachi**" (see E. 70 about echo responses) (*Akira unazuku*) Wasureru n ja-nakute.
Akira: (*unazuite*) Aa.
Reiko: Wakara-nai, doo shite ii no ka. (see E. 66 for *wakara-nai*; E. 48 about inverted word order)
Akira: Dakara **oretachi** ga mukiau n da. (see E. 72 for *n da*)

Akira: We must overcome. Hitomi's death, we must overcome it.
Reiko: (*surprised, looking at Akira*) "We," you mean. (*Akira nods*) Do you mean that we should overcome, instead of forgetting about her?
Akira: (*Akira nods*) Yes.
Reiko: I don't know what to do.
Akira: So we should face reality, that is, us.

29. To Feel like Falling in Love

Key Expressions

[誘いの表現]	*sasoi no hyoogen*	invitation (expressions)
気がある	*ki ga aru*	to begin to love
ナンパする	*nanpa suru*	to seduce (a stranger), to make advances
つきあう	*tsukiau*	to go steady
デートする	*deeto suru*	to have a date

Explanation

As people begin to fall in love, they suggest getting together. These invitations are realized by a variety of strategies, two of which are shown in examples (a) and (b). In (a), a negative question, *Oiwai shi-nai?* 'Shall we celebrate?' is used as an invitation, and in (b), prefacing expressions like *Kyoo hima?* 'Are you free today?' and *Moshi yokattara* 'If it's O.K.' are used when making a suggestion.

Verbs that describe actions associated with the beginning of a romantic relationship include *ki ga aru, nanpa suru, tsukiau,* and *deeto suru. Ki ga aru* refers to the initial sense of falling in love, of having the kind of interest in a person that anticipates a love relationship.

Nanpa suru means to seduce someone into entering a man-woman relationship, often a physical and sexual relationship. *Nanpa* mostly, but not exclusively, refers to situations in which a man makes advances toward a woman. *Nanpa* relationships are usually considered casual, frivolous, and merely physical, but two people who come to know each other through *nanpa* may develop a serious relationship. *Nanpa* is a phrase used primarily in casual speech; it should be avoided in formal situations.

Tsukiau, when used in reference to romantically involved parties, refers to being in a steady relationship. *Tsukiau* is also used for the general social interaction with friends and acquaintances. *Koosai suru* is a more formal version of *tsukiau. Deeto suru* refers to having a date, usually with a person with whom one is romantically involved.

Authentic Examples

a. (Taken from *Beautiful Life*, episode 1) Kyooko suggests to Shuuji that they meet again.

杏子：　雑誌に載ったら、今日の、雑誌に載ったらお祝いしない？
柊二：　お祝い？
杏子：　うん。＃＃しないか。
柊二：　いやいやいや、じゃお祝いやろうか。
杏子：　ほんと？

Kyooko: Zasshi ni nottara, kyoo no, zasshi ni nottara oiwai shi-nai?
Shuuji: Oiwai? (see E. 70 about echo questions)
Kyooko: Un. Shi-nai ka.
Shuuji: Iya, iya, iya, ja oiwai yaroo ka. (see E. 24 about repetition)
Kyooko: Honto?

Kyooko: If the photos taken today appear in the magazine, shall we celebrate?
Shuuji: Celebrate?
Kyooko: Yeah. I guess not.
Shuuji: Right, O.K., let's celebrate.
Kyooko: Really?

b. (Taken from *Strawberry on the Shortcake*, episode 6) Naoto invites Haruka to go out with him, although Haruka refuses him right away. Haruka says "no" by apologizing and offers the reason for her refusal.

なおと：　あ、今日ひま？もしよかったらこれから＝
遥：　＝ごめん、約束あるの。
なおと：　ああ、そうなんだ。
遥：　じゃ。
なおと：　う、あ、じゃあ。

Naoto: A, kyoo hima? Moshi yokattara kore kara=
Haruka: =Gomen, yakusoku aru no.
Naoto: Aa, soo na n da. (see E. 46 for *soo na n da*)
Haruka: Ja.
Naoto: U, a, jaa.

Naoto: Uh, are you free today? If it's O.K., from now=
Haruka: =Sorry, I have an appointment.
Naoto: Oh, I see.
Haruka: See you.
Naoto: Uh, ah, well, then.

c. (Taken from *Beautiful Life*, episode 5) Masao hesitantly asks Sachi if she likes him.

正夫：　失礼なこと言うけど、百万回ごめんね。さっちゃん俺のこと、お、俺に、**気がある**のかなあ。
サチ：　#あっ、#バリバリ好き。

Masao: Shitsureina koto yuu kedo, hyakumankai gomen ne. Satchan ore no koto, o, ore ni, **ki ga aru** no ka na. (see E. 30 for *ore no koto*)
Sachi: A-tt, baribari suki. (see E. 32 for *suki*)

Masao: Excuse me for saying something rude, and I apologize for it a million times. Sachi, do you like me?
Sachi: Yes, I like you like crazy.

d. (Taken from *Beautiful Life*, episode 1) Shuuji explains how Miyama feels about Kyooko, who doesn't quite understand the situation. Kyooko uses *Ha?* 'Huh?' (with a rising tone) to request that Shuuji clarify the point.

柊二：　**ナンパ**でしょ。
杏子：　は？
柊二：　あんたのこと好きなんじゃないの？だからこう**デート**にさそってる？
杏子：　なわけないでしょ。
柊二：　だって、持ってたよなんか、チケット。だから映画じゃない？二枚。
杏子：　うそ。

Shuuji: **Nanpa** desho.
Kyooko: Ha?
Shuuji: Anta no koto sukina n ja-nai no? Dakara koo **deeto** ni sasotteru? (see E. 30 for *anta no koto*; E. 32 for *suki*)
Kyooko: Na wake nai desho.
Shuuji: Datte, motteta yo nanka, chiketto. Dakara eiga ja-nai? Nimai.
Kyooko: Uso. (see E. 21 for *Uso*)

Shuuji: So, he's making advances toward you.
Kyooko: Huh?
Shuuji: Isn't it that he likes you? That's why he is inviting you for a date.
Kyooko: That can't be.
Shuuji: But he was holding tickets or something. I think they are movie tickets. Two of them.
Kyooko: You must be kidding.

e. (Taken from *Beautiful Life*, episode 2) Miyama confesses that he likes Kyooko.

美山：	杏子さん、おれ、杏子さんが好きです。**つきあってくれませんか。**
Miyama:	Kyooko-san, ore, Kyooko-san ga suki desu. **Tsukiatte**-kuremasen ka.
Miyama:	Kyooko, I like you. Will you go steady with me?

f. (Taken from *Majo no jooken*, episode 5) Hikaru emphasizes that Hikaru and Michi are in a steady love relationship by the expression *tsukiatteru*.

光：	そっちがやめんなら、俺もやめるから。
未知：	やめてよそんなの。
光：	だったら、二度とつまんないこと言うなよ。
未知：	でも。
光：	どうどうとしてりゃいいじゃん。俺達**つきあってん**だからさ。
Hikaru:	Sotchi ga yame n nara, ore mo yameru kara.
Michi:	Yamete yo sonna no. (see E. 16 for *sonna*; E. 48 about inverted word order)
Hikaru:	Dattara, nido to tsumannai koto yuu na yo.
Michi:	Demo.
Hikaru:	Doodoo to shiterya ii jan. Oretachi **tsukiatte n** da kara sa.
Hikaru:	If you are quitting, I'll also quit school.
Michi:	Stop such nonsense.
Hikaru:	If you feel that way, don't say silly things ever again.
Michi:	But...
Hikaru:	We should be proud and firm. We are in a steady relationship, aren't we?

g. (Taken from *Long Vacation*, episode 2) Sena, who secretly loves Ryooko, takes her to a nearby amusement park. Ryooko tells him that going to an amusement park is like having a date, which is what Sena had in mind.

涼子：	(...)ディズニーランドも、**デート**みたいになっちゃうし。#ほら、こういうのも**デート**みたい。
瀬名：	えっ。これって**デート**じゃないの？
涼子：	##**デート**なんですか？
Ryooko:	(...) Dizuniirando mo, **deeto** mitai ni natchau shi. Hora, koo yuu no mo **deeto** mitai. (see E. 17 for *natchau*)
Sena:	E-tt. Kore tte **deeto** ja-nai no? (see E. 47 for *tte*)
Ryooko:	**Deeto** na n desu ka?
Ryooko:	Going to Disneyland will be like having a date. You see, this is like having a date.
Sena:	What? Isn't this a date?
Ryooko:	Oh, is this a date?

30. Intimate Vocatives and References to Lovers

Key Expressions

あなた	*anata*	you
(≈) あんた	*anta*	you
(≈) おまえ	*omae*	you
美知子	*Michiko*	
(≈) みっちゃん	*Mit-chan*	
彼氏	*kareshi*	boyfriend, (male) lover
彼のこと	*kare no koto*	(things about) him

Explanation

How one calls to or refers to someone expresses one's feelings toward that person. Choosing the appropriate vocative and reference forms is important both personally and socially. Various forms indicate different levels of formality and intimacy.

Second person pronouns are used not only as reference forms but also for the purpose of addressing someone in a limited way. Note that all of the following forms, except *otaku*, should not be used to a person to whom one should be polite.

あなた	*anata*	Used toward a person with whom one is not intimate; also used by wives toward husbands (with intimacy) (In recent years, *anata* has occasionally been used as a polite form.)
あんた	*anta*	In casual speech only; may be derogatory
おたく	*otaku*	Toward an unfamiliar party, in formal speech
キミ	*kimi*	Used in a friendly manner
おまえ	*omae*	Primarily used by male speakers toward female speakers; can either imply intimacy or be derogatory
そっち	*sotchi*	Used to show some distance, mostly in casual speech

Except for *omae*, these pronouns are used by both male and female speakers. In the less assertive "feminine" style, however, *anata* is preferred to *anta,* especially in less casual situations. Likewise, between spouses, the husband may use *omae*, but the wife is likely to use *anata*. Men sometimes call women *omae* to indicate a feeling of intimacy, although some women may not like the term, pointing out that it has a derogatory connotation.

Vocative and reference forms include (1) full name or last name plus *-sama/ -san/-kun*, (2) last name only, (3) shortened last name, (4) first name with *-sama/ -san/-kun*, (5) first name only, (6) shortened first name, and (7) use of diminutive *-chan*, among others.

As intimacy increases, how lovers address each other changes. One uses [last name + *-san*] in formal situations. Increasing closeness may encourage use of [first name + *-san*] or the first name only. When two people realize that they are lovers, the preferred vocative among youth is the first name only. One also uses the first name in reference to the second person (you). For example, *Masao iku?* means 'Are you going, Masao?'

If you wish to show politeness toward a person or maintain a social distance, calling him or her by his or her first name is considered rude. Calling someone by first name only is not necessarily a friendly expression.

The pronouns *kare* and *kanojo* may mean more than 'he' and 'she'. Use of pronouns is rather limited in Japanese; when they do occur they tend to have special overtones. *Kare* (also *kareshi*, often pronounced with a flat tone instead of a high tone placed on *ka*) is used to refer to a boyfriend or male lover, and *kanojo* (sometimes also pronounced with a flat tone) to a girlfriend or a female lover. These expressions are particularly popular among youth in casual conversation.

When a person is the target of one's thought and emotion, *no koto* is often added. Kyooko, for example, becomes *Kyooko no koto*. By adding *no koto*, which may be translated as 'things about Kyooko,' one conveys a sense that one is referring to additional inner thoughts and feelings about Kyooko. Also, by adding *koto*, one makes the preceding noun less specific and the meaning more diffuse, indirect, and yet potentially more significant (because it focuses on inner thoughts and feelings). *No koto* is added to pronouns as well, as in *kare no koto* 'things about him'.

No koto is added when the person becomes the target of one's psychological process as well, as in *ano hito no koto o omou* 'to think about that person'. Note, however, that because of the "about"-ness associated with *koto*, many nouns cannot take *no koto* when the verb acts on the object directly, as in **Otoko wa ano hito no koto o koroshita* 'The man murdered about him'.

Authentic Examples

a. (Taken from *Beautiful Life*, episode 3) Mayumi is upset with Kyooko and criticizes her. She maintains a certain formality and distance that are conveyed in part by *anata*.

真弓：　**あなた**は一体何考えてるの？

Mayumi: **Anata** wa ittai nani kangaeteru no?

Mayumi: What in the world are you thinking about?

b. (Taken from *Majo no jooken*, episode 6) Hikaru and Michi escape from the high school and are in the train heading toward the suburbs. In this scene Michi uses *sotchi* and *anata* when addressing Hikaru.

光：　大丈夫？後悔してない？
未知：　#**そっち**は？
光：　俺は先生と一緒なら。
未知：　#あたしはもう、教師じゃない。#**あなた**も、生徒じゃない。

Hikaru: Daijoobu? Kookai shite-nai? (see E. 19 for *kookai suru*)
Michi: **Sotchi** wa?
Hikaru: Ore wa sensei to issho nara.
Michi: Atashi wa moo, kyooshi ja-nai. **Anata** mo, seito ja-nai.

Hikaru: Are you all right? You are not regretting (it), are you?
Michi: How about you?
Hikaru: I'm fine if I'm with you, (*sensei*).
Michi: I'm no longer your teacher. You are no longer my student.

c. (Taken from *Beautiful Life*, episode 1) Note Kyooko's use of *anta* toward Shuuji when she is a bit upset.

杏子：　ちょっと**あんた**、さっきから何やってんの？

Kyooko: Chotto **anta,** sakki kara nani yatten no?

Kyooko: Hey, you, what have you been doing there?

d. (Taken from *Beautiful Life*, episode 2) Shuuji calls Mayumi *omae*, partly because they have been intimately involved.

真弓：　ねえわたしワイン飲んじゃおうかな。
柊二：　朝から飲むなよ**おまえ**ほんとに。

Mayumi: Nee watashi wain nonjaoo ka na.
Shuuji: Asa kara nomu na yo **omae** honto ni.

Maymi: Say, maybe I'll have some wine.
Shuuji: Don't you start drinking in the morning, seriously.

e. (Taken from *Dokkin paradaisu* 3: 88–89) One of Ai's brothers talks to Akira. *Akira* is used as a vocative and *omae* as a reference form.

竜兄がさっきから黙りこくっている暁兄に声をかける。
「おい**暁**、**お前**も黙ってないで、亜衣に何か言ってやったらどうなんだよ？」

Ryuu-nii ga sakki kara damari kokutteiru Akira-nii ni koe o kakeru.
"Oi **Akira**, **omae** mo damatte-naide, Ai ni nanika itte-yattara doo na n da yo?"

Brother Ryuu talks to Akira, who has remained silent for a while.
"Hey, Akira, why don't you quit being silent and say something to Ai ?"

f. (Taken from *Beautiful Life*, episode 7) Sachi does not like to be called *omae*, which has a derogatory tone.

サチ：　あっ。
正夫：　なに？
サチ：　今**おまえ**って言ったね。
正夫：　何が。
サチ：　正夫さんてほんとは、そうやって女の人に**おまえ**とか言う人なんだ。
正夫：　何だ。
サチ：　**おまえ**だって。
正夫：　**おまえ、おまえ、おまえ、おまえ、おまえ**。どこが悪い？
サチ：　男尊女卑。
正夫：　そういう問題か。
サチ：　そういう問題よ。

Sachi: A-tt.
Masao: Nani?
Sachi: Ima **omae** tte itta ne.
Masao: Nani ga.
Sachi: Masao-san te honto wa, soo yatte onna no hito ni **omae** toka yuu hito na n da. (see E. 72 for *n da*)
Masao: Nan da.
Sachi: **Omae** da tte.
Masao: **Omae, omae, omae, omae, omae**. Doko ga warui? (see E. 24 about repetiton)
Sachi: Danson johi.
Masao: Soo yuu mondai ka.
Sachi: Soo yuu mondai yo.

Sachi: Ah.
Masao: What is it?
Sachi: You just said "*omae*."
Masao: What!

Sachi:	Masao, you're the kind of person who would call a woman *omae*.
Masao:	So what!
Sachi:	You're saying "*omae.*"
Masao:	*Omae, omae, omae, omae, omae*. What's wrong with that?
Sachi:	Discrimination against woman.
Masao:	Is this that kind of problem?
Sachi:	Yes, it is that kind of problem, for sure.

g. (Taken from *Majo no jooken*, episode 11) In this scene, Hikaru uses *Michi* as a vocative for the first time. Up to this point he has always called her *sensei* 'teacher.' Hikaru and Michi now call each other by first name only, confirming their intimate relationship.

未知：	ねえ、お願いがあるんだけど。
光：	なに？
未知：	先生って言うの、もうやめない？
光：	(未知を抱いてささやく) **未知。未知。**
未知：	**光。**

Michi:	Nee, onegai ga aru n da kedo.
Hikari:	Nani?
Michi:	Sensei tte yuu no, moo yame-nai?
Hikari:	(*Michi o daite sasayaku*) **Michi. Michi!**
Michi:	**Hikaru!**

Michi:	Say, I have a request to make.
Hikaru:	What is it?
Michi:	Why not stop calling me *sensei*?
Hikaru:	(*Hikaru whispers while holding Michi*) Michi. Michi!
Michi:	Hikaru!

h. (Taken from *Beautiful Life*, episode 11) Shuuji first refers to Kyooko by first name only, but realizing that he is talking to her brother, he rephrases, saying *Kyooko-san*. Curiously, Masao immediately comments that it is O.K. to call her Kyooko. This is an important moment in the drama. Masao has been against the romantic relationship between his sister and Shuuji, but now he is convinced of Shuuji's sincerity.

正夫：	俺とサッちゃんのお祝い？
柊二：	ええ、俺と話しててそういうふうにしたいって。**杏子**もほら、あのー、ね、#**杏子さん**も、外泊扱いしてもらえれば、OKじゃないですか。
正夫：	いいよ、杏子で。

Masao: Ore to Sat-chan no oiwai?
Shuuji: Ee, ore to hanashitete soo yuu fuu ni shitai tte. **Kyooko** mo hora, anoo, ne, **Kyooko-san** mo, gaihaku atsukai shite-moraereba, O.K. ja-nai desu ka.
Masao: Ii yo, Kyooko de.

Masao: You mean a celebration for me and Sachi?
Shuuji: Yes, when she was talking with me, she said she wanted to do it. About Kyooko, I mean, Kyooko-san, it will be O.K. for her if we ask the hospital to allow an outside overnight stay.
Masao: It's O.K. for you to call her Kyooko.

i. (Taken from *Beautiful Life*, episode 6) Shuuji who is meeting with a female headhunter at a coffee shop notices that Kyooko is having coffee with a young man. Shuuji follows Kyooko to the restroom and asks about the young man. They end up getting into an argument and end the conversation as below.

杏子： かわいい**彼女**が待ってるよ。早く戻った方がいいんじゃない？
柊二： **彼女**じゃないです。
杏子： あ、そう。あたしのは**彼氏**なの。じゃあね。

Kyooko: Kawaii **kanojo** ga matteru yo. Hayaku modotta hoo ga ii n ja-nai?
Shuuji: **Kanojo** ja-nai desu.
Kyooko: A, soo. Atashi no wa **kareshi** na no. Jaa ne.

Kyooko: Your cute girlfriend is waiting for you. Better return to your seat for her.
Shuuji: She is not my girlfriend.
Kyooko: I see. The person with me is my boyfriend. Bye!

j. (Taken from *Long Love Letter Hyooryuu Kyooshitsu*, episode 9) Takamatsu and Yuka talk about a dream that Oonishi told them that she had. In the dream, Takamatsu's girlfriend, Ichinose, and Yuka's father were together, looking for them.

結花： 一ノ瀬さんて。
高松： **彼女**。
(...)
結花： でももしあの夢が本当だったとしたら (...) 何で**高松君の彼女**といっしょにいたんだろう。
高松： 知らねえ。# でも、何となく信じてる。あの夢の話本当かもって。

Yuka: Ichinose-san te.
Takamatsu: **Kanojo.**
(…)
Yuka: Demo moshi ano yume ga hontoo datta to shitara (…) nande **Takamatsu-kun** no **kanojo** to issho ni ita n daroo.
Takamatsu: Shira-nee. Demo, nantonaku shinjiteru. Ano yume no hanashi hontoo kamo tte. (see Chapter 2 for *shira-nee* instead of *shira-nai*)

Yuka: Who is Ichinose?
Takamatsu: My girlfriend.
(…)
Yuka: But, if that dream was real, (…) why was my father with your girlfriend?
Takamatsu: I don't know. But for some reason I believe that the dream may be real.

k. (Taken from *Taiyoo wa shizuma-nai*, episode 3) Ami confesses that she loves Nao by using his last name, Masaki.

亜美： **真崎さんのこと**、好きです。
直： えっ？
亜美： 好きです。＃私は＃真崎さんの味方ですから。(直、下を向いて何も言わない)すいません。
直： あやまることはないけど。
亜美： すいません。(亜美、その場を走り去る)

Ami: **Masaki-san no koto,** suki desu. (see E. 32 for *suki*)
Nao: E-tt? (see E. 21 for *E-tt?*)
Ami: Suki desu. Watashi wa Masaki-san no mikata desu kara. (*Nao, shita o muite nani mo iwa-nai*) Suimasen.
Nao: Ayamaru koto wa nai kedo. (see E. 63 for *kedo*)
Ami: Suimasen. (*Ami, sono ba o hashirisaru*)

Ami: I love you, Masaki.
Nao: What?
Ami: I love you. I am on your side. (*Nao looks downward and says nothing*) Sorry.
Nao: No need for apology, but…
Ami: Sorry. (*Ami runs away*)

l. (Taken from *Ren'ai hakusho* 14: 108) Kaho wonders about Sumire, who may be interested in Kaho's boyfriend. She knows that Sumire loves another boy, Rihito.

それは……あたしも気がついてたけど。
「でも、すみれちゃん、**リヒトのこと**好きなんだし」

Sore wa……atashi mo ki ga tsuiteta kedo.
"Demo, Sumire-chan, **Rihito no koto** sukina n da shi." (see E. 32 for *suki*; E. 72 for *n da*; E. 63 about the use of *shi*)

That…I have been noticing, too, but…
"But, Sumire loves Rihito, so."

Note

How to refer to another person differs depending on multiple factors, including situation, personal relationship, topic of conversation, and feelings. For example, in *Santaku*, Sanma, in reference to Kimura, uses varied expressions—*omae*, *kimi*, *otaku*, and *Kimura-kun*. His most frequent choice is *omae*, showing that he feels close to Kimura but treats him as his junior. Kimura, however, uses only *Sanma-san* and avoids using second person pronouns altogether. Sanma, as the senior in the relationship, has access to different forms and mixes different expressions that communicate different degrees of intimacy and power.

Additional Information

A few additional forms should be particularly noted, because they are blunt and convey the speaker's attitude.

(口) あいつ	*aitsu*	that person, the guy you also know (may be derogatory)
(口) こいつ	*koitsu*	this person (may be derogatory)
(口) そいつ	*soitsu*	that person, the guy I'm talking about (may be derogatory)
(口) やつ	*yatsu*	guy, fellow, person, mostly in reference to a male person (may be derogatory)
(口) 野郎（やろう）	*yaroo*	idiot, idiotic guy (very blunt and used in curses, as in *Kono yaroo!* 'This idiot!')

The expressions above are often used for derogatory effect. However, depending on the context, these expressions may also be used (almost teasingly) for showing intimacy. (See Entry 58 about good-natured teasing.)

1. (Taken from *Iruka to tsuiraku*, 142) In this part, the author is ordered to throw out the cargo (including the luggage) from the airplane, which was about to crash. *Kono yaroo* is used to express anger and contempt.

——この**野郎**、この**野郎**。
心の中でつぶやきながら捨てていった。

—Kono **yaroo**, kono **yaroo**.
Kokoro no naka de tsubuyaki nagara sutete-itta.

—Idiot, this idiot.
Thus mumbling in my heart, I threw those things out (one by one).

31. Feelings of One's Aching Heart

Key Expressions

せつない	*setsunai*	heart-aching
いとしい	*itoshii*	dearly loved
恋しい	*koishii*	romantically loving
かわいい	*kawaii*	endearing, cute, sweet

Explanation

Of the adjectives that describe an aching heart, *setsunai* is perhaps used most frequently. *Setsunai* describes an overwhelming love and desire with a touch of sadness. *Itoshii* refers to tenderness to a person one cares about very much. It is often used toward someone who is weaker or younger, as in *itoshii wagako* 'dear child of mine'.

Koishii is primarily reserved for romantic relationships, although it is not totally restricted to them. *Koishii* conveys a pining for the person with whom one is romantically involved. For example, if the lover is absent, *Ano hito ga koishii* 'I miss him/her lovingly' is appropriate.

Kawaii refers to affection for someone who (or something that) is cute, small, lovable, sweet, and vulnerable. In intimate relationships, *kawaii* is frequently used in reference to females, as in *kawaii onna* 'a sweet woman I love tenderly'. *Kawaii* can be used toward males as well.

Examples

a. (Two women chatting)

(≈fy1): プレゼント買いに行くんだ。彼の。
(≈fy2): そう、**いとしい**彼のためだもんね。

(≈fy1): Purezento kai ni iku n da. Kare no.
(≈fy2): Soo, **itoshii** kare no tame da mon ne.

(≈fy1): I'm going to buy a present. For him.
(≈fy2): I see, for him whom you dearly love.

b. 私は旅に出ると、ほとんど毎日のように**恋しい**人に手紙を書くことにしています。

Watashi wa tabi ni deru to, hotondo mainichi no yoo ni **koishii** hito ni tegami o kaku koto ni shiteimasu.

When I travel, I write a letter to the person I love dearly (and romantically) almost every day.

Authentic Examples

a. (Taken from BBS for *Beautiful Life*)

あまりにも**せつなくて**悲しくて、涙が自然とあふれ出てきました。
Amarinimo **setsunakute** kanashikute, namida ga shizen to afuredete-kimashita. (see E. 2 for *namida*)
It was so heart-aching and sad that, without my knowing it, tears began to well up in my eyes.

せつなすぎました。
Setsunasugimashita.
I felt so much heartache.

あったかくて**切ない**きもち。
Attakakute **setsunai** kimochi. (see E. 6 for *attakai*)
A warm and heart-aching feeling.

最終回とっても**切なかった**です。
Saishuukai tottemo **setsunakatta** desu. (see E. 24 and E. 27 for *tottemo*)
The final episode was so heart-aching.

b. (Taken from *Long Vacation*, episode 7) Through the use of *setsunai*, Sugisaki reveals his love for Minami.

杉崎： 南ちゃんはいつもせいいっぱいだ。#切れそうに、張り詰めた糸みたいだ。#見てて**切ない**よ。
南： **切ない**？
杉崎： 見てて**切ない**のは、俺が南ちゃん好きなせいだけど。

Sugisaki: Minami-chan wa itsumo seiippai da. Kiresoo ni, haritsumeta ito mitai da. Mitete **setsunai** yo.
Minami: **Setsunai**? (see E. 70 about echo questions)
Sugisaki: Mitete **setsunai** no wa, ore ga Minami-chan sukina sei da kedo. (see E. 32 for *sukina*)

Sugisaki: Minami, you are always doing all your best. You are like a tightly strung line of thread. My heart aches to see you like that.
Minami: Your heart aches?
Sugisaki: Well, the reason my heart aches is that I love you.

c. (Taken from *Long Vacation*, episode 6) Sugisaki shows his affection by saying that Minami is *kawaii*.

杉崎： ま、もっとも俺は、例えば南ちゃんが百社面接落ちても、カッコよくて、**かわいい**と思うけど。
南： えっ。

Sugisaki: Ma, mottomo ore wa, tatoeba Minami-chan ga hyakusha mensetsu ochitemo, kakko yokute, **kawaii** to omou kedo. (see E. 13 for *kakko ii*; E. 63 for *kedo*)
Minami: E-tt.

Sugisaki: Well, anyway, even when you, Minami, fail job interviews a hundred times over, I think you are neat and cute.
Minami: What?

d. (Taken from *Long Vacation*, episode 5) Sena and Minami discuss how they feel when people who are close have differing opinions. Here Sena is talking about Ryooko.

瀬名： あのねそれだけじゃなくて、笑うとこも違うんですよ。僕がおかしくないのに横で笑ってるの。
南： わかる。あるある。自分が全然おかしくないのに人が笑ってるとムカつくよね。
瀬名： ムカつかない。涼子ちゃん**かわいい**から。

Sena: Ano ne sore dake ja-nakute, warau toko mo chigau n desu yo. Boku ga okashiku-nai noni yoko de waratteru no.
Minami: Wakaru. Aru aru. Jibun ga zenzen okashiku-nai noni hito ga waratteru to mukatsuku yo ne. (see E. 66 for *wakaru*; E. 24 about repetition; E. 42 for *jibun*; E. 10 for *mukatsuku*)
Sena: Mukatsuka-nai. Ryooko-chan **kawaii** kara.

Sena: And that's not all. We laugh at different things. Even when I don't find it funny, she is laughing right next to me.
Minami: I know. I know that those things happen. Although you yourself

don't find it funny at all, someone else is laughing. Isn't it disgusting?

Sena: I don't find it so disgusting. Because Ryooko is cute and sweet.

Note

Kawaii, particularly when it is written in *katakana*, may mean more than the traditional meaning of love for someone or something cute, small, lovable, sweet, and vulnerable. It can also show personal preferences and likings, as in *Kore kawaii* in reference to some ordinarily ugly object. Whatever it may be and however weird a thing may be, as long as it is the speaker's personal favorite, *kawaii* may be used.

Additional Information

Vocabulary for different kinds of love:

愛	*ai*	love
愛情	*aijoo*	love
純愛	*jun'ai*	true love, pure romantic love
恋愛	*ren'ai*	love affair
親愛	*shin'ai*	intimacy (of a friendship), affection

Vocabulary related to love affairs:

初恋	*hatsukoi*	first love, puppy love
片思い	*kataomoi*	one-sided love, unrequited love
カップル	*kappuru*	(from English *couple*) lovers, married couple
恋	*koi*	love (usually between people of opposite sexes)
恋人	*koibito*	lover
恋心	*koigokoro*	(lit., love heart) feelings of love
恋女房	*koinyooboo*	(lit., beloved wife) a wife who married for love and who is still loved by her husband
相思相愛	*sooshi sooai*	(lit., think together, love together) to love and to be loved in return
ツーショット	*tsuu shotto*	(related to English *two* and *shot*) two lovers in a picture taken together in general use, two people taken together in a picture or two people witnessed together

1. (Taken from *Ainori*) In this show, *Saigo no machi de gyooten koodoo onna* (Surprising female member's action at the final destination), Miyaken shows concern for Saki, and asks her if she is all right. Note the use of the word *ren'ai*. *Un* in parentheses represents the listener's backchannel response.

宮ケン： こないだ、とかさ、すごい、悩んでたじゃん。（うん）でワゴンで話して、どうよ、あれから。
サキ： ##話してたらさあ（うん）、**恋愛**の話になって（うん）そしたら何か、**恋愛**を、進められてないんだよねって、言われちゃって。自分なりには、アピールしてきてるつもりだし（うん）でも何か、そういうふうに言われちゃったらやっぱり、もしかしたら、１パーセントも想ってくれないかも、しれないし（うん）。分からな過ぎてなんか、へコんだね。

Miyaken: Konaida, toka sa, sugoi, nayandeta jan. (un) De wagon de hanashite, doo yo, are kara. (see E. 62 for *toka*; E. 24 for *sugoi*)
Saki: Hanashitetara saa (un), **ren'ai** no hanashi ni natte (un) soshitara nanka, **ren'ai** o, susumerarete-nai n da yo ne tte, iwarechatte. Jibun nari ni wa, apiiru shite-kiteru tsumori da shi (un) demo nanka, soo yuu fuu ni iwarechattara yappari, moshikashitara, ichi paasento mo omotte-kure-nai kamo, shirenai shi (un). Wakara-na sugite nanka, hekonda ne. (see E. 57 for *yappari*; E. 62 for *nanka*; E. 18 for *hekomu*)

Miyaken: The other day, you were really troubled, right? (uh-huh) Then you two talked in the van; how are things, since then?
Saki: While we were talking (uh-huh), the topic turned to love affairs (in general) (uh-huh), then I was told that his relationship isn't progressing. I think I am making every effort I can make to appeal to him (uh-huh), but somehow, when I was told it wasn't going anywhere, I thought, after all it may be that his love for me may not even be one percent (yeah). I just don't understand, and I felt defeated and disappointed.

32. Confessing and Declaring Love

Key Expressions

好き	*suki*	to like, to love
愛してる	*aishiteru*	to love
(v) ラブラブ	*raburabu*	(lit. love-love) in a loving relationship, lovey-dovey
告白する	*kokuhaku suru*	to confess love
(≈) 結婚しよう	*Kekkon shiyoo.*	Let's get married.

Explanation

Once the romantic relationship is established, there are many ways in which lovers express their passion. Most typically, *suki* or *suki da* 'to like, to love' is used to express the feeling that one likes or loves something or someone. Although *suki* has common uses like *Pasuta ga suki* 'I like pasta', in intimate human relationships, *suki* really means love. Another expression, *aishiteru* 'to love' is used in reference to a deeper, more serious love. When two people love each other, *aishiau* 'to love each other' is used.

Regarding *suki* (*da*) and *aishiteru*, it should be noted that, as mentioned in Entry 30, when one is expressing love, the object of that love is often described with *no koto*. For example, *Anata no koto aishiteru* '(lit.) I love (things about) you' is often used instead of *Anata o aishiteru* 'I love you'. When the phrase *no koto* is used, *anata* is presented softly; at the same time, the speaker's inner thoughts and feelings about the person are focused.

Raburabu, borrowed from the English word *love* and augmented, is a recent innovation almost always used by youth and young adults in very casual style. It describes a situation in which both lovers are in the middle of a romantic relationship. *Kokuhaku suru* refers to making a confession of love toward someone. In casual, slang-like youth speech, *kokuru* is also used. The most direct marriage proposal is the straightforward *Kekkon shiyoo* 'Let's get married'.

Authentic Examples

a. (Taken from *Long Love Letter Hyooryuu Kyooshitsu*, episode 7) Yuka is in a bad mood and complains about their relationship to Asami, but soon they make up.

結花：　ていうか、私とつきあったのだってどうせ年上の女とつきあってみたかったっていうだけでしょ。いいよ。誰にだってそういう時期ってあるし。
浅海：　**好き**だからでしょ。#**好き**だからここにいるし、**好き**だから他の男に嫉妬だってするし別にふつうじゃん。
(長い沈黙の後)
結花：　かも。##ふつうかも。

Yuka: Te yuu ka, watashi to tsukiatta no datte doose toshiue no onna to tsukiatte-mitakatta tte yuu dake desho. Ii yo. Dare ni datte soo yuu jiki tte aru shi. (see E. 44 for *Te yuu ka*; E. 57 for *doose*; E. 63 for *aru shi*)
Asami: **Suki** da kara desho. **Suki** da kara koko ni iru shi, **suki** da kara hoka no otoko ni shitto datte suru shi betsu ni futsuu jan. (see E. 12 for *shitto suru*)
(*nagai chinmoku no ato*) (see E. 75 about silence)
Yuka: Kamo. Futsuu kamo.

Yuka: Truthfully, you have a relationship with me simply because you want to be involved with an older woman. It's O.K. Everyone goes through a stage like that.
Asami: It's because I love you. Because I love you, I am here, and because I love you, I get jealous about other men. I think that's natural (and expected).
(*after a long silence*)
Yuka: Perhaps. Maybe that is natural.

b. (Taken from *Suna no ue no koibitotachi*, episode 1) Hitomi and Akira are lovers who are traveling together and relaxing at a hotel. Hitomi uses *suki* and *aishiteru*, hoping to confirm Akira's long-lasting love.

ひとみ： 私のこと**好き**？**愛してる**。
朗： だからこうしてんじゃん。
ひとみ： ううん。ずっと**好き**？永遠に**愛してる**？
朗： 今が永遠に続けばいいと思ってるよ。

Hitomi: Watashi no koto **suki**? **Aishiteru**. (see E. 30 for *watashi no koto*)
Akira: Dakara koo shite n jan.
Hitomi: Uun. Zutto **suki**? Eien ni **aishiteru**?
Akira: Ima ga eien ni tsuzukeba ii to omotteru yo.

Hitomi: Do you like me? You love me, right?
Akira: That's why we are here like this.
Hitomi: No, that's not it. Will you always like me? Love me forever?
Akira: I'm thinking that it would be nice if this moment could continue on into eternity.

c. (Taken from *Ainori*) In the show *Chikyuu isshuu daigookyuu ketsumatsu* (A big cry at the end of the around-the-world tour), Saki confesses her love for Dobo.

サキ： なんか私さ（うん）始めは仲間にも、旅にも、慣れることができなくて（うん）恋もできなくて（うん）それがつらくて。だけど、私は絶対ここで＃＃ほんとに大事な人を見つけて帰れるって諦めずに信じて旅を続けてたのね。（うん）そしたらドボくんに会えたの。
＃＃今までずっと言いたかったことがやっと言えるかな。＃私はドボくんが、**大好きです**。＃＃ずっと私のそばにいてもらいたいから。＃＃これチケット。
ドボ： ありがとう。
サキ： じゃ明日待ってるね。
ドボ： ああ、わかった。

Saki: Nanka watashi sa (un) hajime wa nakama nimo, tabi nimo, nareru koto ga deki-nakute (un) koi mo deki-nakute (un) sore ga tsurakute. Dakedo, watashi wa zettai koko de honto ni daijina hito o mitsukete kaereru tte akirame-zu ni shinjite tabi o tsuzuketeta no ne. (un) Soshitara Dobo-kun ni aeta no. (see E. 31 for *koi*; E. 7 for *tsurai*; E. 20 for *akirameru*)
Ima made zutto iitakatta koto ga yatto ieru ka na. Watashi wa Dobo-kun ga, **daisuki desu**. Zutto watashi no soba ni ite-moraitai kara. Kore chiketto.

Dobo: Arigatoo.

Saki: Ja ashita matteru ne.

Dobo: Aa, wakatta. (see E. 66 for *wakatta*)

Saki: Uh, you know, (uh-huh) I couldn't feel comfortable with the members or about the trip (uh-huh), and I couldn't find someone to be in love with (uh-huh), and it was painful. But, I didn't give up and continued with the tour, believing that I would be able to find someone truly precious, and then the two of us could return to Japan (uh-huh). Then, I finally met you, Dobo.
Now maybe I can finally say what I've always wanted to say. I really love you, Dobo. I want you to be by my side forever, so. This is the ticket.

Dobo: Thank you.

Saki: I'll be waiting for you tomorrow.

Dobo: Yes, I got it.

d. (Taken from *Santaku*) Sanma comments on how difficult it is to be a good father. He says he cannot use words like *father* and *daughter* lightly because he takes them seriously. He confesses that there are many other words he uses lightly, though.

木村： まじですか。

さんま： うん、**好き**っていう字はなんぼでも書けるけどね、**愛してる**とか。

木村： **好き**とハートマークでしょ＝

さんま： ＝**好き**とハートマークと、電話番号は、とか。

Kimura: Maji desu ka. (see E. 67 for *maji*)

Sanma: Un, **suki** tte yuu ji wa nanbo demo kakeru kedo ne, **aishiteru** toka. (see E. 62 for *toka*)

Kimura: **Suki** to haato maaku desho.

Sanma: **Suki** to haato maaku to, denwa bangoo wa, toka.

Kimura: Are you serious?
Sanma: Yeah, I can use the character for "like" as many times as I want, and like the character for "love."
Kimura: You mean "like" and the heart icon, right?
Sanma: Right, "like," the heart icon, and "What's your phone number?" and so on.

e. (Taken from *Dokkin paradaisu*, 142) Ai reveals her love for Akira.

「おじいちゃん、亜衣ね、暁兄のことが**好きだった**の。妹としてじゃなくて、暁兄に恋してたの」
「亜衣ちゃん？」
薫さんのやさしい声。

"Ojiichan, Ai ne, Akira-nii no koto ga **suki datta** no. Imooto to shite janakute, Akira-nii ni koishiteta no." (see E. 42 about the use of personal name as a strategy for self-reference; E. 30 for *Akira-nii no koto*; Additional Information for *koi shiteta*)
"Ai-chan?"
Kaoru-san no yasashii koe. (see E. 6 for *yasashii*)

"Dear Grandfather, Ai (I) loved Akira. Not as a brother. I was in love with him.
"Ai, really?"
Kaoru responds in a soft voice.

f. (Taken from interview #86, with Mayumi Narita, winner of the Special Olympics gold medal in swimming) Narita uses *raburabu* to describe her relationship with her new husband.

成田： 全然**ラブラブ**とかじゃないんですよ。これってほんとに新婚生活なの？と思うくらい。昨日も友達が夜、電話してきて、「ごめんね、**ラブラブ**タイムなのに」って言うから、「全然**ラブラブ**じゃないよ。なに？」って長電話しちゃって (...).

Narita: Zenzen **raburabu** toka ja-nai n desu yo. Kore tte honto ni shinkon seikatsu na no? to omou kurai. Kinoo mo tomodachi ga yoru, denwa shite-kite, "Gomen ne, **raburabu** taimu na noni" tte yuu kara, "Zenzen **raburabu** ja-nai yo. Nani?" tte nagadenwa shichatte (...). (see E. 47 for *tte*; E. 17 for *shichatte*)

Narita: It's not love-love (lovey-dovey) at all. To the extent that I wonder if this really is a newlywed's life style. For example, yesterday a friend of mine called and said, "Sorry for bothering you during your love-love time." So I said, "Not love-love at all. What is it?" and ended up talking to her for a long time on the phone.

g. (Taken from *Long Love Letter Hyooryuu Kyooshitsu*, episode 7) One of the students, Ikegaki, tells his friends that he has confessed his love to a girl named Andoo. Note *kokuru*, the use of which is limited to youth.

池垣：	俺さあ、きのうの夜、安藤に**コクった**んだ。
高松：	うそ。まじで？で、どうだったんだよ。
池垣：	それがさ、ちょっと待ってとか言われたんだけど、それってどう思う？
高松：	＃＃バーカ。女はなあ、ノーって言わねえ限りＯＫなんだよ。

Ikegaki:	Ore saa, kinoo no yoru, Andoo ni **kokutta** n da. (see E. 72 for *n da*)
Takamatsu:	Uso. Maji de? De, doo datta n da yo. (see E. 67 for *Maji de?*)
Ikegaki:	Sore ga sa, chotto matte to ka iwareta n da kedo, sore tte doo omou? (see E. 47 for *tte*)
Takamatsu:	Baaka. Onna wa naa, noo tte iwa-nee kagiri O.K. na n da yo. (see E. 58 about the use of *Baaka*; Chapter 2 for *iwa-nee* instead of *iwa-nai*)

Ikegaki:	I confessed my love to Andoo last night.
Takamatsu:	No kidding. Seriously? And, what happened?
Ikegaki:	She said that she wants me to wait. What do you think?
Takamatsu:	You idiot. As long as a woman does not say no, she means O.K.

h. (Taken from *Majo no jooken*, episode 10) Hikaru makes a marriage proposal by using a very direct strategy.

光：	**結婚しよう**、今すぐ。
未知：	えっ？
光：	俺が18になってからなんて言ってられねえよ。みんなが反対しても、かまわない。

Hikaru:	**Kekkon shiyoo**, ima sugu. (see E. 48 about inverted word order)
Michi:	E-tt?
Hikaru:	Ore ga juuhachi ni natte kara nante itte rare-nee yo. Minna ga hantai shitemo, kamawa-nai. (see Chapter 2 for *rare-nee* instead of *rare-nai*)

Hikaru:	Let's get married, right now.
Michi:	What?
Hikaru:	I can't wait until I'm eighteen years old. I don't care if everyone opposes it.

Additional Information

Other verbs for different aspects of being in love include:

あこがれる	*akogareru*	to be infatuated with, to dream about
恋に落ちる	*koi ni ochiru*	to fall in love
恋する	*koi suru*	to love romantically
恋焦がれる	*koikogareru*	(lit. to be in burning love) to be crazily in love
口説く	*kudoku*	to persuade someone to accept love
熱を上げる	*netsu o ageru*	(lit., to raise the heat) to be hot for, to be crazy about
思いを寄せる	*omoi o yoseru*	(lit., to collect thoughts) to think about someone lovingly in one's heart
慕う	*shitau*	to adore, to long for

33. Shifting Styles as Love Grows

Key Expression

[スタイルシフト] *sutairu shifuto* style shift

Explanation

Politeness levels and styles (supra-polite, formal, casual, and so on) depend not only on social convention but also on personal feelings. In this sense, stylistic choice is an expressive strategy. While styles reflect personal relationships in progress, they also establish and confirm those relationships. For example, a changing relationship between a man and a woman leads to a certain style shift, which in turn forces the lovers (and the people around them) to realize that their relationship is in transition. Speech style not only reflects but also enacts and reinforces lovers' emerging feelings.

As a relationship deepens, sometimes the speech style itself becomes the topic of conversation. Although on the surface the discussion may seem to be only the speech style, beneath the words are the speaker's feelings about the relationship itself.

Authentic Examples

a. (Taken from *Majo no Jooken*, episode 4) After they spend the night together at the school library, Michi and Hikaru exchange greetings (*Ohayoo*) in casual style. Contrast this encounter with their earlier encounter, example (b). The reciprocal greeting style in (a) illustrates how the choice of speech style reflects and reinforces Michi and Hikaru's emerging feelings.

未知： **おはよう。**
光： **おはよう。**
未知： 急いで。もうすぐ警備の人来るから。

Michi: **Ohayoo.**
Hikaru: **Ohayoo.**
Michi: Isoide. Moo sugu keibi no hito kuru kara.

Michi: Good morning.
Hikaru: Good morning
Michi: Please hurry. The guard will come around soon.

b. (Taken from *Majo no jooken*, episode 2) Earlier Hikaru spots Michi on campus and runs to her. They exchange the following greetings. Here Hikaru uses the formal greeting (*Ohayoo gozaimasu*) expected of a student toward a teacher.

未知： **おはよう。**
光： **おはようございます。**（「ございます」のところで目を伏せて会釈する）ねえ、こないださ、どうだった？

Michi: **Ohayoo.**
Hikaru: **Ohayoo gozaimasu.** (*"Gozaimasu" no tokoro de me o fusete eshaku suru*) Nee, konaida sa, doo datta? (see E. 54 for *nee*)

Michi: Good morning.
Hikaru: Good morning. (*bowing quickly when he says* "Gozaimasu") Say, how did it go the other day?

c. (Taken from *Long Vacation*, episode 11) Toward the end of the drama series, Minami and Sena meet at a noodle shop they used to frequent. Minami, as she always has, speaks in the casual style. Sena, who used to speak predominantly in the formal style, now speaks in the casual style as well. This shift is obvious when compared with another conversation that took place in the same noodle shop in episode 1 (given in example [d]). Then Sena used the formal style. In (c), the casual speech style is reciprocated, reflecting and confirming their intimate relationship.

南： あのレコード会社は？
瀬名： ああ**断っちゃった**よ。
南： ふう、へええ。(...)

瀬名：	でもねもう、#お休みは、終り**だから。**長いお休み↑、はもう、終り**だからね。**もう25 **だしさ**俺。そろそろ**決着つけないと。**
南：	#しばらく見ないうちに、大人になったね。
瀬名：	#とにかく**渡したからね。**

Minami:	Ano rekoodo gaisha wa?
Sena:	Aa **kotowatchatta** yo. (see E. 17 for *kotowatchatta*)
Minami:	Fuu, heee. (...) (see E. 21 for *hee*)
Sena:	Demo ne moo, oyasumi wa, owari **da kara.** Nagai oyasumi ↑, wa moo, owari **da kara** ne. Moo nijuugo **da shi** sa ore. Sorosoro **ketchaku tsukenai** to. (see E. 65 for rising intonation)
Minami:	Shibaraku mi-nai uchi ni, otona ni natta ne.
Sena:	Tonikaku **watashita kara** ne.

Minami:	What happened with that record company?
Sena:	Ah, I declined their offer.
Minami:	Oh, I see. (...)
Sena:	But, you know, the vacation is over. The long vacation is now over. I'm already twenty-five years old, you know. I must make up my mind.
Minami:	You've grown up a lot while I haven't see you.
Sena:	Anyway, I handed it to you, O.K?

d. (Taken from *Long Vacation*, episode 1) At the noodle shop, Minami and Sena ask each other what they do (for a living). Sena lies, saying that he is a pianist, and Minami also lies, saying that she is a model for *AnAn*, a popular women's fashion magazine. Note the formal *ja-nai desu ka* Sena uses.

南：	すごいんだね。
瀬名：	自分だってアンアンのモデル**じゃないですか。**
南：	う、うーん、ふっ。

Minami:	Sugoi n da ne. (see E. 13 for *sugoi*)
Sena:	Jibun datte AnAn no moderu **ja-nai desu ka.** (see E. 42 for *jibun*)
Minami:	U, uun, fu-tt.

Minami:	Wow, you are something.
Sena:	You are a model for *AnAn*, right?
Minami:	Uh, huh, humph.

e. (Taken from *Taiyoo wa shizuma-nai*, episode 11) In this scene, Nao suggests that Ami change her speech style. Commenting on the partner's speech style is an indirect way of revealing one's inner feelings.

直：　なんでこんなとこにいんだよ。
亜美：　どこにいようと私の勝手です。
直：　そういう学級委員みたいな**ですます調いいかげんやめたら。**

Nao: Nande konna toko ni i n da yo.
Ami: Doko ni iyoo to watashi no katte desu.
Nao: Soo yuu gakkyuu iin mitaina **desumasuchoo iikagen yametara.**

Nao: Why are you here?
Ami: Wherever I am, it's up to me.
Nao: Say, why don't you quit using the *desu/masu* style like a student council member?

f. (Taken from *Beautiful Life*, episode 4) Shuuji and Kyooko find themselves in an awkward conversation. When the mutually acknowledged casual speech style shifts back to a formal style, that shift conveys distance. Note Kyooko's unusually formal apology. And the distance that the formal style expresses becomes the topic of the conversation.

柊二：　ジャケットさあ、クリーニング済みで送られてきたわ。
杏子：　**すみませんでした**、長い間借りたまんまで。
柊二：　誰としゃべってんの？
杏子：　えっ？
柊二：　なに、その他人行儀。
杏子：　##だって他人じゃん。
柊二：　##あっ、そう。#うん、分かった。

Shuuji: Jaketto saa, kuriiningu zumi de okurarete-kita wa.
Kyooko: **Sumimasen deshita**, nagai aida karita manma de.
Shuuji: Dare to shabetten no?
Kyooko: E-tt? (see E. 21 for *E-tt?*)
Shuuji: Nani, sono tanin gyoogi. (see E. 21 for the use of *nani* expressing disbelief)
Kyooko: Datte tanin jan.
Shuuji: A-tt, soo. Un, wakatta. (see E. 21 for *A-tt*; E. 66 for *wakatta*)

Shuuji: The jacket, it was sent to me after being cleaned (by a cleaner).
Kyooko: Thank you, and sorry that I didn't return it for a long time.
Shuuji: Who are you talking with?
Kyooko: What?
Shuuji: What is that distant relation-less manner (of speech)?
Kyooko: We are not in a relationship, right?
Shuuji: Oh, I see. I got it.

34. Refusing Advances

Key Expressions

(≈) 他に好きな人がいる	*Hoka ni sukina hito ga iru.*	There is someone else I love.
(≈) 君にはもっとふさわしい人がいる	*Kimi ni wa motto fusawashii hito ga iru.*	There is someone else more suited for you.
いいお友達でいましょう	*Ii otomodachi de imashoo.*	Let's be just good friends.

Explanation

When someone makes unwelcome romantic advances to you, how do you deter the person? In such a sensitive situation, it is obviously wise to avoid enumerating the person's bad points. Instead, a more benign strategy seems to make sense, for example, by saying something like *Hoka ni sukina hito ga iru n desu* 'There is someone else I love'. This statement, whether true or not, lets a person down more easily.

Another indirect way of refusing advances is to suggest that someone else is better for him/her (implying that the speaker is not good enough). Expressions such as *motto fusawashii hito* 'a person more suited for' and *motto oniai no hito* 'a person who is more appropriate and suitable' are useful here. This strategy also conveys the sense that one does not deserve such love. This is a face-saving device that minimizes the partner's shame and hurt.

To let one's partner know that romance is not an option, one may emphasize something else. For example, one may suggest that the relationship is a friendship, not a romantic affair, by saying something like *Ii otomodachi de imashoo* 'Let's be just good friends'.

Example

a. (A man breaking up with a woman)

(my1a): 真理さん、あなたには僕じゃなくて、**きっともっとふさわしい人がいます**よ。
(fy1a): えっ？
(my1b): きっと**お似合いの人が**。
(fy1b): そんな。

(my1a): Mari-san, anata ni wa boku ja-nakute, **kitto motto fusawashii hito ga imasu** yo.
(fy1a): E-tt? (see E. 21 for *E-tt?*)
(my1b): Kitto **oniai no hito** ga.
(fy1b): Sonna. (see E. 16 for *Sonna*)

(my1a): Mari, for you, there is someone more suited to you than I am, for sure.
(fy1a): What?
(my1b): Someone more suitable, for sure.
(fy1b): Such a thing you say, but…

Authentic Examples

a. (Taken from *Long Vacation*, episode 5) Sena comes to see Ryooko, but Ryooko finds it difficult to say anything. Worried, Sena asks what the matter is and is told that Ryooko is in love with someone else.

瀬名： どうしたの？＃＃こっち向いてよ。
涼子： ごめん。＃＃ごめんなさい。＃＃私、**他に好きな人がいる**。

Sena: Doo shita no? Kotchi muite yo.
Ryooko: Gomen. Gomennasai. Watashi, **hoka ni sukina hito ga iru**.

Sena: What's wrong? Look at me.
Ryooko: Sorry. I'm sorry. I have someone else that I love.

b. (Taken from *Strawberry on the Shortcake*, episode 3) Saeki tells Yui directly that he loves someone else.

佐伯： じゃ、はっきり言うね。僕には**好きな人がいる**。好きと言うより愛していると言った方がいいのかもしれない。
唯： そうなんだ。
佐伯： 分かってくれた？

Saeki: Ja, hakkiri yuu ne. Boku ni wa **sukina hito ga iru**. Suki to yuu yori aishiteiru to itta hoo ga ii no kamo shirenai. (see E. 69 for *hakkiri yuu*; E. 32 for *aishiteru*)
Yui: Soo na n da. (see E. 46 for *Soo na n da*)
Saeki: Wakatte-kureta? (see E. 66 for *wakaru*)

Saeki: Well, I must put it frankly. I have someone I like. Perhaps it is better to say that it is someone I love.
Yui: I see.
Saeki: You understand me now, right?

c. (Taken from *Beautiful Life*, episode 2) Miyama confesses to Kyooko that he loves her. Kyooko refuses Miyama's advance by suggesting that there is someone more suited for him.

美山： 杏子さん、俺、杏子さんが好きです。つきあってくれませんか。
杏子： ごめんなさい。#美山さん、**私なんかじゃなくて、ふつうに健康でかわいい女の子がいる**よ。普通にデートできて、普通に …

Miyama: Kyooko-san, ore, Kyooko-san ga suki desu. Tsukiatte-kuremasen ka. (see E. 32 for *suki*; see E. 29 for *tsukiau*)
Kyooko: Gomennasai. Miyama-san, **watashi nanka ja-nakute, futsuu ni kenkoo de kawaii onna no ko ga iru** yo. Futsuu ni deeto dekite, futsuu ni… (see E. 15 for *nanka*; see E. 31 for *kawaii*; E. 29 for *deeto*)

Miyama: Kyooko, I love you. Will you go steady with me?
Kyooko: I'm sorry. Miyama, I'm not right for you; a healthy cute girl is more suited for you. A girl you can go with on a date as everyone else does…

35. Breaking Up

Key Expressions

(≈) 別れよう	*Wakareyoo.*	Let's break up. Let's be separated.
別れ話	*wakare banashi*	separation talk, discussion of a breakup
ふられる	*furareru*	to be dumped
棄てる	*suteru*	to mercilessly dump (a lover)
捨てられる	*suterareru*	to be dumped (by a lover)

Explanation

When one wants to break off a relationship, one may simply cut off all communication, or indicate the breakup through various phrases that clearly convey the message that "it's over."

Wakareru means to break up, to be separated, and to go different ways. This expression can be used for both unmarried and married couples. *Wakare banashi* is the phrase that refers to discussion of the breakup. *Wakare banashi o kiridasu* means to initiate a talk about separation, for example.

Furareru is a passive of *furu* 'to dump (a lover)'. *Furareru* is used when you break up with your lover because your lover doesn't love you any longer. The verb *suteru* '(lit.) to discard' and its passive *suterareru* 'to be discarded' (written in either kanji as shown above) are similarly used in reference to the dumping of someone and to being dumped mercilessly by someone in a love relationship.

Example

a. (A girl is concerned about her sad-looking friend)

(≈ft1): なに、**フラれた**の、そんな悲しそうな顔して。
(≈ft2): うん、そうみたい。

(≈ft1): Nani, **furareta** no, sonna kanashisoona kao shite. (see E. 16 for *sonna*; E. 7 for *kanashii*)
(≈ft2): Un, soo mitai.

(≈ft1): What, are you dumped, you look so sad.
(≈ft2): It appears so, I'm afraid.

Authentic Examples

a. (Taken from *Antiiku, seiyoo kottoo yoogashiten*, episode 9) Tachibana is told by his girlfriend that their relationship is over.

恋人：橘。
橘：うん？＃何だ。どうした。
恋人：**別れよう**か。
橘：えっ？＃何で？
恋人：疲れる。キミといると疲れる。
橘：どうして？
恋人：無理してるんだよ、キミは。

koibito: Tachibana.
Tachibana: Un? Nan da. Doo shita.
koibito: **Wakareyoo** ka.
Tachibana: E-tt? Nande? (see E. 21 for *E-tt?*)
koibito: Tsukareru. Kimi to iru to tsukareru. (see E. 30 for *kimi*)
Tachibana: Doo shite?
koibito: Muri shiteru n da yo, kimi wa. (see E. 48 about inverted word order)

lover: Tachibana.
Tachibana: Yes. What is it? What's wrong?
lover: We should break up.
Tachibana: What? Why?

lover: I get tired. Being with you makes me feel tired.
Tachibana: Why?
lover: You are forcing yourself (to be with me).

b. (Taken from *Majo no jooken*, episode 11) After their breakup, Hikaru and Michi run into each other at a museum. Hikaru confronts Michi about their relationship.

光： 俺と**別れて**良かったってわけだ。
未知： えっ。
光： 俺なんかいない方が幸せってことだろ。
未知： そういうことじゃないの！
光： 先生は勝手だよ！(...) 俺のことなんかもう愛してないんだろ。そうなんだろ。##答えろよ。
未知： 愛してる。
光： じゃなんで**別れなきゃ**いけないんだよ。

Hikaru: Ore to **wakarete** yokatta tte wake da.
Michi: E-tt.
Hikaru: Ore nanka i-nai hoo ga shiawase tte koto daro. (see E. 15 for *nanka*; E. 5 for *shiawase*)
Michi: Soo yuu koto ja-nai no! (see E. 72 for *no*)
Hikaru: Sensei wa katte da yo! (...) Ore no koto nanka moo aishite-nai n daro. Soo na n daro. Kotaero yo. (see E. 30 for *ore no koto*; E. 15 for *nanka*)
Michi: Aishiteru. (see E. 32 for *aishiteru*)
Hikaru: Ja nande **wakarenakya** ikenai n da yo.

Hikaru: So, it was good to be separated from me.
Michi: What?
Hikaru: You are happier without me, right?
Michi: That's not it!
Hikaru: You are selfish! You no longer love me, right? That's it. Answer me.
Michi: I love you.
Hikaru: Then why do we have to break up?

c. (Taken from *Beautiful Life*, episode 3) Sachi is impressed that Miyama continues to come to see Kyooko, even though Kyooko has refused Miyama's request for a date.

サチ： しかし勇気あるよね。**ふられても**また来るあの根性。
杏子： 私には無理だな。
サチ： うん。
杏子： **ふられたらふられっぱなし**。
サチ： えっ、**ふられた**の？

Sachi: Shikashi yuuki aru yo ne. **Furaretemo** mata kuru ano konjoo.
Kyooko: Watashi ni wa muri da na.
Sachi: Un.
Kyooko: **Furaretara furareppanashi.**
Sachi: E-tt, **furareta** no? (see E. 21 for *E-tt*)

Sachi: But he is courageous, isn't he? Even when he is refused, he has the guts to come again.
Kyooko: It's impossible for me to do it.
Sachi: Yeah.
Kyooko: If I'm dumped, I'm dumped, and I won't do anything about it.
Sachi: What? You've been dumped?

d. (Taken from *Long Vacation*, episode 6) Sena explains to Momoko that she has broken up with Ryooko.

瀬名： もう、関係ないからさ。
桃子： えっ、関係ないって？
瀬名： **フラれちゃった**から。
桃子： どうして？
瀬名： 他にね、好きな人が、できたんだって。
桃子： 他に好きな人ってだれ。ねだれだれだれだれ。

Sena: Moo, kankei nai kara sa.
Momoko: E-tt, kankei nai tte? (see E. 21 for *E-tt*; E. 70 about echo questions)
Sena: **Furarechatta** kara. (see E. 17 for *furarechatta*)
Momoko: Doo shite?
Sena: Hoka ni ne, sukina hito ga, dekita n datte. (see E. 34 for *hokani sukina hito ga dekita*)
Momoko: Hoka ni sukina hito tte dare. Ne dare dare dare dare. (see E. 24 about repetition)
Sena: I have nothing to do with her anymore.
Momoko: What? What happened?
Sena: I was dumped by her.
Momoko: How come?
Sena: She has someone else she is in love with.
Momoko: Who is that someone else she loves? Who, who, who, who is it?

e. (Taken from *Shiretoko rausudake satsujin bojoo*, 86) Shimon meets Kimiko, a friend of Taeko (who has committed suicide).

「前の人と**別れた**原因は、なんだったんでしょうね？」
「多恵子はその人に**棄てられた**みたいです」
「というと、彼に新しい恋人ができた？」
「そうだと思います」

"Mae no hito to **wakareta** gen'in wa, nan datta n deshoo ne?"
"Taeko wa sono hito ni **suterareta** mitai desu."
"To yuu to, kare ni atarashii koibito ga dekita?" (see E. 31 for *koibito*)
"Soo da to omoimasu."

"I wonder what the reason was that she got separated from her former lover."
"It seems that Taeko was dumped by him."
"You mean that he has someone new that he loves?"
"I think so."

Additional Information

There is abundant vocabulary for the complexities of love affairs. Some well-known examples are:

不倫	*furin*	an adulterous affair
冷める	*sameru*	(lit,. to get cold) to stop loving, to fall out of love
三角関係	*sankaku kankei*	(lit., triangle relationship) a love triangle
浮気	*uwaki*	being unfaithful to a spouse or lover
よろめく	*yoromeku*	(lit., to stagger) to stray, to cheat on a spouse

10
Emotion in Conflict Situations

36. Defiance

Key Expressions

(≈) 文句ある？	*Monku aru?*	You have a problem with that?
(□) 見てろ！	*Mitero!*	Wait and see (what happens)!
(□) やれるならやってみな！	*Yareru nara yatte-mina!*	If you can, let's see you do it!

Explanation

As a prelude to a conflict, obvious defiance may be exhibited through overtly challenging expressions. Such expressions should be avoided unless either the *amae* relationship is established or the risk is worth taking. Frequently used defiant expressions include the expression *Monku aru?* 'You have a problem with that?'.

The command form *miteiro* or *mitero* 'wait and see' is uttered as a defiant exclamative, as in *Ima ni miteiro!* 'Just you wait and see!' communicating a defiant threat. The [V-*te-miro/mina*], command form of [V-*te-miru*], as in *Yareru nara yatte-mina!* 'If you can, let's see you do it!', is a challenge that puts the partner on the spot. The speaker's presumption is that the partner is in fact incapable of proving himself or herself, which adds to the sense of defiance.

Note that these command forms are not made in a literal sense, but as rhetorical commands. You do not really expect your partner to do anything. Rather, you shout these phrases as an expression of your defiance.

Examples

a. (Two girls in a fight)

(≈ft1): **文句ある**？あんたに関係ないでしょ！
(≈ft2): 何よ。変なことばっかり言って。

(≈ft1): **Monku aru**? Anta ni kankei nai desho! (see E. 39 for *kankei nai*)
(≈ft2): Nani yo. Henna koto bakkari itte. (see E. 37 for *nani*)

(≈ft1): You have a problems with that? None of your business!
(≈ft2): What? All you say is simply nonsense.

b. (□) **見てろよ**、今度痛い目にあわせてやるからな。

Mitero yo, kondo itai me ni awasete-yaru kara na. (see E. 71 for *awasete-yaru*)

Just you wait and see, next time I'll make sure that you'll be badly hurt.

c. (□) そんなことが、**やれるならやってみな**。

Sonna koto ga, **yarerunara yatte-mina**. (see E. 16 for *sonna*)

If you can do that, let's see you do it (and prove it to me).

Authentic Examples:

a. (Taken from *Beautiful Life*, episode 11) In preparation for a party celebrating Masao and Sachi's romance, Masao and Shuuji are decorating the room.

正夫： ふ、踏んでる、踏んでる。
柊二 すみません。#でもこういうなんか、幼稚園チックで、大丈夫なんすか。
正夫： な、なになに、**なんか文句ある**？
母： ケンカしないで。さっさとやんないと帰ってきちゃうよ。

Masao: Fu, funderu, funderu.
Shuuji: Sumimasen. Demo koo yuu nanka, yoochienchikku de, daijoobu na n su ka.
Masao: Na, nani nani, **nanka monku aru**?
haha: Kenka shi-naide. Sassa to yan-nai to kaette-kichau yo. (see E. 17 for *kichau*)

Masao: Stepping on it, you are stepping on it!
Shuuji: Sorry. But, with this kind of kindergarten-like decoration, is it really O.K?
Masao: Wha, what! You got a problem with it?
mother: Don't get into a fight. Unless you get things ready right away, she'll be here in no time.

b. (Taken from *Chibi Maruko-chan*, 14: 11) Maruko and her sister are in a fighting mood.

姉：　＜…なに/今の歌…/だっさー…＞
まる子：　＜なにっ/**文句/あるっ**＞
祖父：　＜こら/こら＞　＜お願いだから/ケンカしないで/おくれ＞

ane: …Nani ima no uta…dassaa… (see E. 13 for *dasai*; E. 27 for *dassaa* instead of *dasai*)
Maruko: Nani-tt, **monku aru-tt**. (see E. 37 for *nani-tt*)
sofu: Kora kora. Onegai da kara kenka shi-naide okure…. (see E. 59 for *onegai da kara*)

sister: What is that song! It's silly and out of style.
Maruko: What! You got a problem with it?
grandfather: Now, now. Please don't get into a fight.

c. (Taken from *Chibi Maruko-chan*, 14: 111) Maruko's sister is upset about their father's smoking habit. Curiously, the sister shows defiance by saying *Monku ooari yo* to her father's defiant utterance. Obviously, among family members these half-teasing spats occur frequently without serious consequences.

姉：　＜また/タバコ/吸ってる＞＜あー/やだ/やだ＞
父：　＜なんだよ/**文句ある**か＞
姉：　＜**文句/大あり**よ＞

ane: Mata tabako sutteru. Aa ya da ya da. (see E. 9 for *ya da*; E. 24 about repetition)
chichi: Nan da yo. **Monku aru** ka. (see E. 37 for *Nan da yo*)
ane: **Monku ooari** yo.

sister: You are smoking again. Ah, I can't stand it.
father: What! You got a problem with it?
sister: Yes, definitely, I've got a major problem with it!

d. (Taken from *Kindaichi shoonen no jikenbo*, 5: 70) One of the guests staying in an old mansion shows defiance. The guests are fighting over an inheritance.

＜こうなったら/なにがなんでも/テメーの財産/ぶん取ってやるぜ！＞
＜**見てろよ**/——！！＞

Koo nattara nani ga nan demo temee no zaisan bundotte-yaru ze! (see E. 71 for *bundotte-yaru*)
Mitero yooo!!

All right now, no matter what, I'm going to make sure to get my share of the assets.
Just wait and see!!

e. (Taken from *Suna no ue no koibitotachi*, episode 3) Akira did not show up at a business meeting, and Noguchi, his boss, is upset. *Nagutte-miro yo* is used as a rhetorical command.

野口： おまえなあ、#会社やめろ。#女が死んだぐらいでいつまでもメソメソしてんじゃねえよ。(朗、握りこぶしをつくって怒りの表情) **なぐってみろよ。**

Noguchi: Omae naa, kaisha yamero. Onna ga shinda gurai de itsumade mo mesomeso shite n ja-nee yo. (see E. 30 for *omae*) (*Akira, nigiri kobushi o tsukutte ikari no hyoojoo*) **Nagutte-miro yo.**

Noguchi: You, why don't you quit the job. Just because your woman has passed away, stop crying over her so long. (*Akira, forming a fist, shows an angry expression*) Come on, hit me if you can!

f. (Taken from *Naku yo Uguisu*, 3: 149) During the baseball game, Soga expresses defiance toward Uguisu.

＜打てるもん/なら/**打ってみな**＞

Uteru mon nara **utte-mina.**

If you can get a hit, let's see you do it (and prove it to me).

Additional Information

A few of the frequently used defiant interjections follow.

1. Defiance

(≈) **ふん**、なまいきな。

Fun, namaiki na.

Humph, you got a lot of nerve.

2. Disgust

(≈) **ちぇっ**，ケチだなあ。

Che-tt, kechi da naa.

Ugh, stingy you.

3. Challenging the partner

   (≈) へん、何も知らないくせに。

   Hen, nani mo shira-nai kuse ni.

   Heck, you don't know anything about it.

4. Being dismissive

   (≈) なにさ、子供のくせに。

   Nani sa, kodomo no kuse ni.

   What the hell, you are just a child.

5. Calling angrily

   (□) やい、静かにしろ。

   Yai, shizukani shiro.

   Hey, be quiet.

37. Interjections in Conflict Situations

Key Expressions

(□) 何だと！	*Nan da to!*	What (are you talking about)!
(□) なに！	*Nani!*	What!
(□) 何を！	*Nani o!*	What (the hell)!
(≈) 何さ！	*Nani sa!*	What! Don't give me that!
何ですって！	*Nan desu tte!*	What (are you saying!)

Explanation

Interjections using *nan*(*i*) frequently appear in conflict situations. They signal the speaker's anger and resentment. In such contexts, *nani* is pronounced clearly and strongly, showing strong opposition. In conflict, *Nani!* is often pronounced with the higher tone placed on *ni*, unlike the interrogative *nani,* which is said with the higher tone on *na*.

Interjections such as *Nan da to!* 'what (are you talking about)!'; *Nani o!* 'What (the hell)!'; and *Nani sa!* 'What! Don't give me that!' convey accusatory, challenging, defiant, and fighting attitudes. They do not expect the answer that the use of *nan*(*i*) implies. *Nan desu tte!* 'What (are you saying!)' also shows defiance, although *Nan desu tte?* (with sharp rising tone at the final *e*) is used to show surprise (as discussed in Entry 21). Often *nan*(*i*) interjections are countered by *nan*(*i*) responses.

Examples

a. (Two women in conflict)

(≈fy1a): あんた、また、私にウソついたのね。
(fy2a): **何ですって！**
(≈fy1b): **何さ！**土曜日、勉強するって、あれウソじゃない。男の人と一緒に、渋谷行ったでしょ。
(fy2b): えっ？

(≈fy1a): Anta, mata, watashi ni uso tsuita no ne.
(fy2a): **Nan desu tte!**
(≈fy1b): **Nani sa!** Doyoobi, benkyoo suru tte, are uso ja-nai. Otoko no hito to issho ni, Shibuya itta desho.
(fy2b): E-tt?

(≈fy1a): You lied to me again.
(fy2a): What are you saying!
(≈fy1b): Don't give me that! You said you were going to study on Saturday. That's a lie. You went to Shibuya with a man.
(fy2b): What?

b. (Two men in conflict)

(□my1a): いい加減にしろよ。
(□my2): **何だと！**
(□my1b) **なに！**

(□my1a): Ii kagen ni shiro yo. (see E. 41 for *ii kagen ni shiro*)
(□my2): **Nan da to!**
(□my1b): **Nani!**

(□my1a): Behave yourself.
(□my2): What are you talking about!
(□my1b): What are **you** saying!

Authentic Examples

a. (Taken from *Beatiful Life*, episode 8) Shuuji visits Kyooko's home and gets in a fight with Masao.

正夫： 杏子ならいないよ。帰んな。
柊二： いや、いるんでしょ。（ここから正夫と柊二はつかみ合い押し合う）
正夫： いない。
柊二： いるんでしょ。
正夫： いない。

柊二：　俺達の問題なんですから、会わしてくださいよ。
正夫：　**何を！**（ふたりで取っ組み合いのけんかになりそうになる）

Masao: Kyooko nara i-nai yo. Kaenna. (see E. 47 for *nara*)
Shuuji: Iya, iru n desho. (*Koko kara Masao to Shuuji wa tsukamiai oshiau*)
Masao: I-nai.
Shuuji: Iru n desho.
Masao: I-nai.
Shuuji: Oretachi no mondai na n desu kara, awashite-kudasai yo.
Masao: **Nani o!** (*Futari de tokkumiai no kenka ni narisoo ni naru*)

Masao: Kyooko isn't home. So leave.
Shuuji: That's not true, she's here. (*Masao and Shuuji grab and push each other*)
Masao: She is not here.
Shuuji: She is.
Masao: She is not.
Shuuji: It's our business, so let me see her.
Masao: What (the hell)! (*The two are about to get into a physical fight*)

b. (Taken from *Long Love Letter Hyooryuu Kyooshitsu*, episode 4) Yuka is upset that she cannot take the place of a student because, she is told, she is not young enough.

結花：　その子を離して。私が身代わりになります。
関谷：　あなたはいいわ。若くないから。
結花：　**何ですって！**
舞岡：　離してよ！

Yuka: Sono ko o hanashite! Watashi ga migawari ni narimasu.
Sekiya: Anata wa ii wa. Wakaku-nai kara. (see E. 13 for *ii*)
Yuka: **Nan desu tte!**
Maioka: Hanashite yo!

Yuka: Release that student. I will be in her place.
Sekiya: I don't need you. Because you are no longer young.
Yuka: What (are you saying)!
Maioka: Please let me go!

c. (Taken from *Majo no jooken*, episode 4) In this interaction, Michi and Hikaru are playfully fighting. Michi complains about the sketch Hikaru drew of her. Playful fights are created in part by using *nan(i)*, but the verbal expressions are not necessarily literally interpreted. In this situation, tone of voice, facial expressions, gesture, and so on, all convey that the two are not really fighting, but teasing each other.

未知：　ねえ、やっぱり私の顔変だよ。
光：　うるせえなあ。(光、スケッチブックを取り返そうとする)
未知：　**何**、ちょっと、やめてよ。(ふたりで奪い合う)
光：　**何**だよ。
未知：　ちょっと。
光：　離せよ。(スケッチが破れる)
未知：　ああっ。##もう何すんのよ。
光：　そっちが悪いんだろ。

Michi: Nee, yappari watashi no kao hen da yo. (see E. 57 for *yappari*)
Hikaru: Urusee naa. (see Chapter 2 for *urusee* instead of *urusai*) (*Hikaru, suketchi bukku o torikaesoo to suru*)
Michi: **Nani,** chotto, yamete yo. (*Futari de ubaiau*)
Hikaru: **Nan** da yo.
Michi: Chotto. (see E. 25 for *chotto*)
Hikaru: Hanase yo. (*Suketchi ga yabureru*)
Michi: Aa-tt. Moo nani sun no yo. (see E. 40 for *nani sun no*)
Hikaru: Sotchi ga warui n daro. (see E. 30 for *sotchi*)

Michi: Say, this face of mine, it is strange.
Hikaru: Forget it, will you? (*Hikaru tries to grab the sketch book*)
Michi: What! Stop that! (*Hikaru and Michi fight over the sketchbook*)
Hikaru: What do you want!
Michi: Wait.
Hikaru: Let it go. (*The sketch is torn*)
Michi: Oh no. See what you've done.
Hikaru: You are the one to be blamed, you know.

38. Cursing and Offensive Language

Key Expressions

(□) ばか	*Baka.*	Fool. Idiot.
(□) ばかやろう！	*Baka yaroo!*	Idiot!
(□) くそ！	*Kuso!*	Shit!
(□) ちくしょう！	*Chikushoo!*	(lit., beast) Hell! Damn! Fuck!

Explanation

Every language is equipped with words that are considered offensive. In Japanese, phrases such as *baka* 'fool', *kuso* 'shit', and *chikushoo* 'hell, damn, fuck' are used for such purposes.

As an interjection, *baka* expresses the speaker's anger and frustration. When used with a specific pronoun or a name, *no baka* is added, as in *Masao no baka!* 'Masao, you idiot!' *Bakayaroo*, more derogatory than *baka*, combines *baka* and *yaroo* 'idiot, idiotic guy (derogatory)' (see Entry 30, Additional Information) and expresses hatred and anger toward a person.

Kuso is uttered as an interjection, as a cursing word, when someone is very upset and frustrated. *Kuso* is also used in combination with other phrases, such as *kuso muzukashii* '(lit.) shit difficult'. Also, in reference to someone to whom the speaker wants to show strong anger, *kusottare* 'shithead' is used. In all cases, *kuso* signals a derogatory attitude combined with anger, strong dislike, and frustration. *Chikushoo* refers to animals; when used in cursing, it emphasizes that someone or something is beastly and below human dignity.

In general, cursing words occur frequently in the more assertive "masculine" style, but female speakers use them if the situation warrents and allows them. These straightforward emotives are more likely to be tolerated among *amae*-established *uchi* members. They are used exclusively in casual situations. Using them in a formal situation would result in an almost irrevocably unpleasant and confrontational relationship.

Authentic Examples

a. (Taken from *Chibi Maruko-chan*, 14: 73) Maruko and her grandfather have run after a roasted sweet potato vendor, but the grandfather forgot to bring his wallet. Maruko yells angrily at her grandfather.

まる子： <せっかく走って/行ったのにい/おじいちゃんの**ばか**>

Maruko: Sekkaku hashitte-itta nonii ojiichan no **baka.** (see E. 14 for *sekkaku*)

Maruko: We ran all the way. You silly grandpa.

b. (Taken from *Chibi Maruko-chan*, 14: 167) Kosugi curses in his heart.

小杉： < ... **くそう** / 永沢君も / 藤木君も / 今にみていろ ... >

Kosugi: **Kusoo**, Nagasawa-kun mo Fujiki-kun mo ima ni miteiro. (see E. 36 for *miteiro*)

Kosugi: Shit. Nagasawa and Fujiki, just you wait and see.

c. (Taken from *Kindaichi shoonen no jikenbo*, 5: 147) Hajime curses as he realizes that he has been drugged.

はじめ：　＜**くそ** ....../ 注意してたん / だが ....../ やっぱり夕食に / 睡眠薬が ....！？＞
(...)
＜**く.. くそ**！ / だ .. だめだ /...... ＞
＜もう .... ＞

Hajime: **Kuso**......chuuishiteta n da ga......yappari yuushoku ni suimin' yaku ga....!? (see E. 57 for *yappari*)
(...)
Ku..kuso! Da..dame da!......
Moo....

Hajime: Shit. I was cautious, but I'm afraid that as suspected sleeping pills were in the supper!?
(...)
Sh...shit! I can't bear it...
Any longer....

d. (Taken from *Kindaichi shoonen no jikenbo*, 5: 70) One of the guests yells out.

＜**くそっ山之内**！ / あのインケン / 野郎っ！！＞

Kuso-tt Yamanouchi! Ano inken yaroo!! (see E. 30 for *yaroo*)

Shitty Yamanouchi. That cunning weasel!!

e. (Taken from *Chibi Maruko-chan*, 13: 43) Maruko and her friend are in charge of cleaning the classroom. They try to force their classmates to get involved in the cleaning. The classmates are upset, and Maruko and her friend become the target of the curses.

生徒１：　＜**くそったれ**＞
生徒２：　＜死ねっ　掃除係＞
生徒３：　＜**ばーか**＞

seito 1: **Kusottare.**
seito 2: Shine-tt, Soojigakari.
seito 3: **Baaka.**

student 1: Shithead!
student 2: Die, you, the cleaning group!
student 3: Idiot!

f. (Taken from *Taiyoo wa shizuma-nai*, episode 1) Nao's father, frustrated that he cannot make the repairs that his wife had asked him to do, screams to Nao.

父：　頼まれたんだよ、母さんに。#直しといてって、言ったんだ。(直そうとするがうまくいかない)直してくれって、言われたんだよ。**くそー！くそ！ちきしょう！**

chichi: Tanomareta n da yo, kaasan ni. Naoshitoite tte, itta n da. (see E. 72 for *n da*) (*Naosoo to suru ga umaku ika-nai*) Naoshite-kure tte iwareta n da yo. **Kusoo! Kuso! Chikishoo!**

father: I was asked by your mother. She told me to repair this. (*He tries in vain*) She told me to repair this. Shit. Damn! To hell with it!

g. (Taken from *Long Love Letter Hyooryuu Kyooshitsu*, episode 6) Asami gets sick because of an infected wound. Asami incurred the wound fighting against invaders to protect Ootomo, so Ootomo feels bad and vents his feelings accordingly.

大友：　このいだの傷のせいだ。#**ちくしょう。**俺のせいだよ。
愛川：　違うよ。私の消毒の仕方が悪かったのよ。

Ootomo: Konaida no kizu no sei da. **Chikushoo.** Ore no sei da yo.
Aikawa: Chigau yo. Watashi no shoodoku no shikata ga warukatta no yo.

Ootomo: It's because of the wound he suffered the other day. Damn! It's because of me.
Aikawa: No, it's not. It's because I didn't disinfect the wound correctly.

Additional Information

The derogatory *baka* may also be used in reference to oneself when a speaker or writer is self-consciously critical of himself or herself. Two examples follow.

1. (Taken from Iijima, 149) In this essay, *Shanhai* (Shanghai), the writer mentions how ignorant she would be if the news program she regularly watches were canceled.

   私は、この番組がなければ何も知らずに生活をしている、**ばか三十歳**だ。この番組がなければ私は何も知らない。本当だよ。

   Watashi wa, kono bangumi ga nakereba nanimo shira-zu ni seikatsu o shiteiru, **baka sanjussai** da. Kono bangumi ga nakereba watashi wa nanimo shira-nai. Hontoo da yo.

   If this program didn't exist, I would be living without knowing anything; I'm such a thirty-year-old idiot. If this program didn't exist, then I wouldn't know about anything. It's true.

2. (Taken from Oomori, 119) In this essay about movies, the writer reminisces about his childhood. When he was a boy, a friend told him how

great one of the famous local movie theaters was, and this made a big impression on him, particularly because the movie theater had a chime just like his school's. The writer realizes how silly he was then, and expresses his feelings by using *Baka*.

「グランドはよ、始まる前にブーッて音じゃなくて、キンコンカンコンって鳴るのよ」なんて話している近所の不良中学生の声を耳にして、「すげえ、学校みたいじゃん」と思ったことがある。**馬鹿**。

"Gurando wa yo, hajimaru mae ni bu-tte oto ja-nakute, kinkonkankon tte naru no yo" nante hanashiteiru kinjo no furyoo chuugakusei no koe o mimi ni shite, "Sugee, gakkoo mitai jan" to omotta koto ga aru. **Baka.** (see E. 13 and Chapter 2 for *sugee*)

When I heard this junior high school delinquent in the neighborhood say, "You know the Grand, they use the chime that goes *kinkonkankon* instead of the buzzer when the movie starts," I thought, "Wow, how cool, that must be like our school's chime!" What an idiot (I was)!

39. Denying Relevance

Key Expressions

(≈) 関係ない	*Kankei nai.*	(lit., unrelated) None of your business. That has nothing to do with me.
(≈) うるさい！	*Urusai!*	Be quiet!
(□) 勝手にしろ	*Katte ni shiro.*	Do whatever you like (but don't bother me).
(□) 黙れ！	*Damare!*	Shut (the fuck) up!
(≈) ほっといて！	*Hottoite!*	Leave me alone!

Explanation

One defense mechanism in conflict situations is simply to deny the relevance of what has been said. Telling the partner that it's none of the partner's business, for example, is an example of this denial. *Kankei nai* literally states that there is no relationship. *Urusai* 'Be quiet' orders other people to shut up. *Katte ni shiro* communicates the speaker's wish to be left alone, with the implication that whatever the person does is irrelevant.

Damare is an abrupt command form of the verb *damaru* 'to shut up'. *Hottoite* is associated with *hottoku* (or *hootte-oku*), which literally means to leave something alone. *Hottoite* indicates an angry desire to get away from someone who is a nuisance.

Examples

a. (A husband and wife are fighting)

(fa1): 私がどこに行こうと、あんたに**関係ないでしょ**。
(□ma1): またわけのわからないこと言って。もういい！**勝手にしろ**！

(fa1): Watashi ga doko ni ikoo to, anta ni **kankei nai desho.**
(□ma1): Mata wake no wakara-nai koto itte. Moo ii! **Katte ni shiro!** (see E. 13 for *ii*)

(fa1): Wherever I go, that has nothing to do with you, does it?
(□ma1): You are saying unreasonable things again. Enough is enough. Do whatever you want to do!

b. (□) お前は**黙ってろ**。

Omae wa **damattero.**

You, just shut (the fuck) up.

Authentic Examples

a. (Taken from *Beautiful Life*, episode 11) Satoru, who used to work with Shuuji at Hotlip, visits Shuuji. Shuuji has given up his job, and Satoru wants to encourage him to work again. Shuuji refuses angrily.

柊二： **かんけえねえだろ**！な、**ほっとけ**よ。悪いけど今、俺あんたの顔、見たくねえからさ。早く帰って。早く！

Shuuji: **Kankee nee daro.** Na, **hottoke** yo. Warui kedo ima, ore anta no kao, mitaku-nee kara sa. Hayaku kaette. Hayaku! (see Chapter 2 for *mitaku-nee* instead of *mitaku-nai*)

Shuuji: It's none of your business. Leave me alone, will you? Sorry, but I don't want to see your face now. Leave right away. Now!

b. (Taken from *Majo no jooken*, episode 5) Hikaru gets mad at Michi, who refuses to see him. Hikaru yells *Kankee nee daro!* and violently hangs up the phone.

光： それじゃあその辺の大人といっしょじゃねえかよ。#分かった。もう会わねえよ。
未知： どういうこと？
光： **かんけえねえだろ**！

Hikaru:	Sore jaa sono hen no otona to issho ja-nee ka yo. Wakatta. Moo awa-nee yo. (see E. 66 for *Wakatta*; Chapter 2 for *ja-nee* and *awa-nee*)
Michi:	Doo yuu koto?
Hikaru:	**Kankee nee daro!**

Hikaru:	Then you are the same as other grown-ups around here. I got it. I won't see you any more.
Michi:	What do you mean?
Hikaru:	It's none of your business!

c. (Taken from *Antiiku, seiyoo kottoo yoogashiten*, episode 4) A girl named Kayoko complains about the cake Eiji has delivered.

エイジ：	どう、すごいだろ。
加代子：	（沈黙の後）違う。
エイジ：	ちょっと待ってよ。ほら、ちゃんと見てよ。このどこがいけないの？何が違うの？
母：	加代子。
加代子：	**うるさいな。**違うの！
エイジ：	ほら、もう一回ちゃんと見て。ほらこれすげえだろ、ほらここんとことかさ＝
加代子：	＝違うったら違うの！

Eiji:	Doo sugoi daro. (see E. 13 for *sugoi*)
Kayoko:	(*chinmoku no ato*) (see E. 75 about silence) Chigau.
Eiji:	Chotto matte yo. Hora, chanto mite yo. Kono doko ga ike-nai no? Nani ga chigau no?
haha:	Kayoko.
Kayoko:	**Urusai na.** Chigau no! (see E. 72 for *no!*)
Eiji:	Hora, moo ikkai chanto mite. Hora kore sugee daro, hora koko n toko toka sa= (see Chapter 2 for *sugee* instead of *sugoi*; E. 13 for *sugoi*; E. 48 about inverted word order)
Kayoko:	=Chigau ttara chigau no!

Eiji:	How is it? Isn't this great?
Kayoko:	(*after a silence*) This isn't it.
Eiji:	Wait a second. See, look carefully. What's wrong with this? What's wrong?
mother:	Kayoko.
Eiji:	See, look one more time. Look, right here, isn't this great?=
Kayoko:	=It's wrong, I'm telling you, it's wrong.

d. (Taken from *Muko-dono*, episode 8) The father is angry at his son, Masaki, and scolds him. Masaki responds angrily.

父：	何度警察の世話になったら気が済むんだ。
まさき：	いちいち**うるせえんだよ。かんけえねえだろ**！
chichi:	Nando keisatsu no sewa ni nattara ki ga sumu n da. (see E. 40 about rhetorical questions)
Masaki:	Ichiichi **urusee n da yo. Kankee nee daro**! (see Chapter 2 for *urusee* instead of *urusai*, and *nee* instead of *nai*)
father:	How many times do you want to be arrested by the police?
Masaki:	Shut up! It's none of your business! (It has nothing to do with you!)

e. (Taken from *Tsubasa o kudasai*, 122) Kyooka is frustrated and angry at Tsubasa.

「**ほっといて**。あんたなんか大嫌いよ。出てって。顔も見たくない！」

Hottoite. Anta nanka daikirai yo. Dete-tte. Kao mo mitaku-nai! (see E. 15 for *nanka*; E. 9 for *daikirai*)

Leave me alone. I hate you. Leave. I don't want to see your face!

40. Criticizing Angrily: *Nani* and Rhetorical Questions

Key Expressions

(≈) 何寝ぼけてんの！	*Nani neboketen no!*	What the hell! You are behaving like you're half-asleep!
(≈) 何やってんの！	*Nani yatten no!*	What (in the world) are you doing!
(≈) 何言ってんの！	*Nani itten no!*	What are you talking about!
(≈) 何ができるって言うの！	*Nani ga dekiru tte yuu no!*	What are you saying that you can do!
(□) そんなことできるものか！	*Sonna koto dekiru mono ka!*	There is no way that you can do that!

Explanation

In addition to its use as an interjection for expressing anger and resentment discussed in Entry 37, *nan*(*i*) is frequently used in rhetorical questions. The rhetorical question has an interrogative word—such as *nan*(*i*)—within a question sentence, and it usually ends with the *n*(*o*) *da* form. Rhetorical questions are interpreted as a strong negation of the statement implied by the question. No answers are expected.

Another structure often occurring in rhetorical questions is utterance-final *mon*(*o*) *ka*. Again, no literal interpretation is required. For example, as a strong negative response to a request, one may answer *Sonna tokoro e ikeru mono ka!* meaning '(Of course not) How could I go to such a place!'.

Examples

a. (A man is angry at his wife)

(□ma1): おまえに**何ができるんだ**！
(fa1): ……

(□ma1): Omae ni **nani ga dekuru n da!**
(fa1): .... (see E. 75 about silence)

(□ma1): What in the world can you do! You can't do anything.
(fa1): (silence)

b. (□) やりがいのある仕事のためでなければ東京なんかに住む**ものか**。

Yarigai no aru shigoto no tame de-nakereba Tookyoo nanka ni sumu **mono ka.** (see E. 15 for *nanka*)

Unless it is for a rewarding job, who would live in a place like Tokyo?

c. (A man challenges the partner's request for a time-out)

(≈my1): ちょっとタイム！
(□my2): **何が**タイムだ！冗談じゃないよ。

(≈my1): Chotto taimu! (see E. 25 for *chotto*)
(□my2): **Nani** ga taimu da! Joodan ja-nai yo.

(≈my1): A time-out!
(□my2): A time-out? What are you talking about! Don't joke around with me!

Authentic Examples

a. (Taken from *Kookaku kidootai*, 37 [English translation, 41]) One of Major Kusanagi's subordinates yells out in frustration.

＜イシカワ / イシカワ！＞　＜**何 / 寝ボケて / やがるッ！！**＞

Ishikawa. Ishikawa! **Nani nebokete yagaru-tt!!**

<Ishikawa!/ Ishi/kawa!> <What/ the hell/ are you/ doing?!>

b. (Taken from *Kookaku kidootai*, 138 [English translation, 140]) Ishikawa angrily criticizes Togusa.

＜**何 / ズレた事 / やってんだよ** / おめーはっ＞

Nani zureta koto yatten da yo omee wa-tt. (see E. 48 about inverted word order; E. 30 for *omae*)

<What/ the hell/ do you/ think/ you're/ doing,/ Togusa?>

c. (Taken from *Muko-dono*, episode 4) Satsuki is upset about her sister, Kaede. Kaede often borrows Satsuki's things without permission. One day Kaede accidentally finds a few pictures. When Kaede confronts Satsuki about the pictures, Satsuki is outraged.

さつき：　勝手に私のひきだし開けたの？
かえで：　ひきだしなんか開けてないわよ。洋服の間にはさまってたのよ！＝
さつき：　＝**何言ってんの**？同じことじゃない。勝手なことしないで。

Satsuki: Katte ni watashi no hikidashi aketa no?
Kaede: Hikidashi nanka akete-nai wa yo. Yoofuku no aida ni hasamat-teta no yo!= (see E. 15 for *nanka*)
Satsuki: =**Nani itten no**? Onaji koto ja-nai. Kattena koto shi-naide.

Satsuki: Did you open the drawer (of my desk) without permission?
Kaede: I haven't opened the drawer. I found them inserted between your clothing items.=
Satsuki: =What are you saying! The same thing, isn't it? Don't do things without my permission.

d. (Taken from interview #154, with Masahiro Takashima, actor) Takashima comments about his mother, who was heartbroken about his father's illness. He recalls the time that he scolded his mother.

高嶋：　マイナス思考のことばかり言うんで、「**何を言ってるんだ**」って怒ったんです。

Takashima: Mainasu shikoo no koto bakari yuu nde, "**Nani o itteru n da**" tte okotta n desu. (see E. 10 for *okoru*; E. 72 for *n desu*)

Takashima: Because all she ever says is negative things, I got angry and blurted out "What are you saying! (Stop the nonsense!)".

e. (Taken from *Beautiful Life*, episode 3) Mayumi, Shuuji's ex-girlfriend, is upset that Kyooko brought Shuuji a scrapbook of haircut designs. Earlier, because of Kyooko's mistake, Shuuji's haircut designs were stolen by Satoru, Shuuji's colleague and rival, and Kyooko is trying to make up for it. Mayumi uses *nan*(*i*) twice to express her strong accusatory attitude.

真弓：　いい加減にしなさいよ、素人が。柊二がこんなに苦しんでるの、あんたのせいなんだよ。それを**何**よ能天気にこんなもん持ってこれるわけ？
柊二：　いい加減にしろよ。
真弓：　柊二も柊二よ。
柊二：　何だよ。
真弓：　**何**こんな幼稚園児の工作みたいなのにつきあってんのよ。

Mayumi: Ii kagen ni shinasai yo, shirooto ga. Shuuji ga konna ni kurushinderu no, anta no sei na n da yo. Sore o **nani** yo nootenki ni konna mon motte-koreru wake? (see E. 41 for *Ii kagen ni shinasai*; E. 16 for *konna ni*)
Shuuji: Ii kagen ni shiro yo. (see E. 41 for *ii kagen ni shiro*)
Mayumi: Shuuji mo Shuuji yo. (see E. 74 about the tautological effect)
Shuuji: Nan da yo.
Mayumi: **Nani** konna yoochienji no koosaku mitaina no ni tsukiatten no yo.

Mayumi: Stop fooling around. What does a layperson know? It is because of you, you know, that Shuuji is in this much trouble. How silly can you be to bring this thing over here so thoughtlessly?
Shuuji: Stop that.
Mayumi: Shuuji, you are behaving strangely, too.
Shuuji: What (do you mean)?
Mayumi: Why are you paying attention to this arts-and-craft stuff that looks like a kindergartner's work?

f. (Taken from *Majo no jooken*, episode 6) Dr. Godai shows anger and frustration to Hikaru's mother. He argues vehemently with her, insisting that her son, Hikaru, cannot do much to help her.

母：　この病院を継ぐのは、光だけです！
五代：　彼に、**何ができるんです**！大学出て医師免許とるまであと何年かかります？その間あなたがこの病院を一生懸命守っていくわけですか。それだって、**いつまで続くものか**。

haha: Kono byooin o tsugu no wa, Hikaru dake desu!
Godai: Kare ni, **nani ga dekiru n desu**! Daigaku dete ishi menkyo toru made ato nannen kakarimasu? Sono aida anata ga kono byooin

o isshookenmei mamotte-iku wake desu ka. Sore datte, **itsu made tsuzuku mono ka**.

mother: The person to take over this hospital is Hikaru and only Hikaru!

Godai: What can he do! How many years will it be before he graduates from a medical school and obtains his medical license? Are you going to be responsible for this hospital all during that time? Even then, how long will you be able to sustain that? (Not too long at all!)

g. (Taken from *Kindaichi shoonen no jikenbo*, 5: 51) One of the guests is angry and frustrated.

<やる気でなければ / こんな北海道の / 山奥くんだりまで / **来るものか**! >

Yaru ki de-nakereba konna Hokkaidoo no yamaoku kundari made **kuru mono ka**! (see E. 16 for *konna*)

Unless I intend to do all I can, who would come (all the way) to these deep mountains of Hokkaido? (Nobody would!)

41. When Trying to End the Conflict

Key Expressions

まあまあ	*maa maa*	now, now; well, well
(≈) 気にしない	*Ki ni shi-nai.*	Don't worry about it.
(□) やめろよ	*Yamero yo.*	Stop that, will you?
もういい加減にしなさい	*Moo ii kagen ni shi-nasai.*	Behave yourself. Stop it now. Enough is enough.

Explanation

To calm an angry partner, the most useful phrase is *maa maa*. It is used as an interjection in conflict situations with the clear intent to calm down the people involved.

When the partner is upset by someone else's comment, *Ki ni shi-nai* 'Don't worry about it' is frequently used. *Ki ni shi-nai* expresses the speaker's suggestion that the upsetting thing does not deserve sincere attention. This is similar to the English "It's nothing to get upset about" and "Forget about it." When trying to stop a fight, one uses command forms like *Yamero!* 'Stop it!'.

Ii kagen ni shinasai literally means 'Behave yourself and do things only to a reasonable degree'. It is a formulaic expression used to appeal to reason. This expression implies something similar to "Enough is enough" or "That's enough." A blunt version, *Ii kagen ni shiro (yo)!* is used when the speaker is angry about the bad situation; it shows greater frustration. Although this expression shows more anger than desire for reconciliation, because it is used as an ultimatum, it may encourage some effort toward reconciliation.

Examples

a. (A man trying to calm his friend down)

(≈my1a): 田中のやつ、また変なこと言い出したんだ。
(≈my2a): あいつの言うことは、**気にしない、気にしない**。
(≈my1b): でも、頭に来るよな、勝手なことばかり言って。
(≈my2b): **まあまあ**、そう興奮するなよ。

(≈my1a): Tanaka no yatsu, mata henna koto iidashita n da. (see E. 30 for *yatsu*)
(≈my2a): Aitsu no yuu koto wa, **ki ni shi-nai, ki ni shi-nai.** (see E. 30 for *aitsu*; E. 24 about repetition)
(≈my1b): Demo, atama ni kuru yo na, kattena koto bakari itte. (see E. 10 for *atama ni kuru*; E. 48 about inverted word order)
(≈my2b): **Maa maa**, soo koofun suru-na yo.

(≈my1a): That guy, Tanaka, is mumbling about something absurd again.
(≈my2a): Whatever he says, don't worry about it, not at all.
(≈my1b): But he makes me mad. He always says unreasonable things.
(≈my2b): Well, well, don't get so charged up.

b. **やめなさい**、つまんないことで言い争うのは。

Yamenasai, tsumannai koto de iiarasou no wa. (see E. 48 about inverted word order)

Stop it, don't go on arguing about silly points.

Authentic Examples

a. (Taken from *Beautiful Life*, episode 9) Shuuji is upset to find out that his assistant, Takumi, is about to steal the client list from Hotlip. Satoru tries to end the fight. Here *yamete-yare* conveys Satoru's awareness of Shuuji's kindness toward Takumi in stopping the fight.

柊二　　こんなことまでしてこんなこそどろみてえなことまでしておまえ行きたかったんだろ。行けよ、じゃあ。
サトル：おい**やめてやれよ**、もう。

Shuuji: Konna koto made shite, konna kosodoro miteena koto made shite omae ikitakatta n daro. Ike yo, jaa. (see Chapter 2 for *miteena* instead of *mitaina*)
Satoru: Oi **yamete-yare yo**, moo.

Shuuji: Doing a thing like this, stealing things from us like a thief. You wanted to go over there, right? Why don't you go there, then.
Satoru: Stop that, right now.

b. (Taken from *Muko-dono*, episode 9) Two sisters, Kaede and Satsuki, get into fights often. Most of the time, Kaede borrows things from Satsuki without permission. Observing the fight between his two daughters, their father orders them to stop.

さつき： 返してよ。この時計私が持ってる中で一番高いんだからね！
かえで： だから借りたんじゃないの。
さつき： なに！（かえでとさつき、時計をとりあう）
父： ふたりとも**いい加減にしなさい**。

Satsuki: Kaeshite yo. Kono tokei watashi ga motteru naka de ichiban takai n dakara ne! (see E. 23 for *ichiban*)
Kaede: Dakara karita n ja-nai no.
Satsuki: Nani! (see E. 37 for *nani*) (*Kaede to Satsuki, tokei o toriaru*)
chichi: Futari tomo **ii kagen ni shinasai.**

Satsuki: Give it back to me. That watch is the most expensive of all the watches I have.
Kaede: That's why I borrowed it from you.
Satsuki: What! (*Kaede and Satsuki try to grab at the watch*)
father: Both of you, stop that right now.

c. (Taken from *Dokkin paradaisu*, 92) Ai's brother orders a stop to the fight.

「そこまでだ！**いいかげんにしろ**！ふたりとも」

Soko made da! **Ii kagen ni shiro**! Futari tomo.

That's it! That's enough! Both of you!

d. (Taken from *Taiyoo wa shizuma-nai*, episode 2) Nao is frustrated when the hospital telephone operator fails to connect him to Dr. Minami with whom Nao needs to talk. Note the mixture of the formal *Ii kagen ni shite-kudasai yo* and the blunt *Ii kagen ni shiro yo!*. The formal expression is directed toward the telephone operator, but the blunt style is used to show intense emotion. See Entry 76 for further explanation of style mixture.

直：　だから、母のことで聞きたいことがあるんです。(...) **いい加減にしてくださいよ。#いい加減にしろよ**！遺骨ん中にお宅のメスが入ってたんだよ！

Nao: Dakara, haha no koto de kikitai koto ga aru n desu. (...) **Ii kagen ni shite-kudasai yo. Ii kagen ni shiro yo!** Ikotsu n naka ni otaku no mesu ga haitteta n da yo! (see E. 72 for *n da*; E. 55 for the use and non-use of *yo*)

Nao: As I've been saying, I want to ask something about my mother. (...) Please, enough is enough. Hell, that's enough! A surgical knife was found in my mother's ashes, I'm telling you!

III

Empathy

11
Revealing Oneself Softly

42. Identifying Oneself

Key Expressions

私	*watashi*	I
あたし	*atashi*	I
(ロ) 俺	*ore*	I
僕	*boku*	I
自分	*jibun*	self, inner self

Explanation

Self-referencing terms in Japanese are varied, and their specific form depends on how the speaker wants to present the self to a particular partner. For female speakers, the usual choices are *watakushi*, *watashi*, and *atashi*. For male speakers, *watakushi*, *watashi*, *boku*, and *ore* are options.

(≠) 私	*watakushi*	very formal
私	*watashi*	formal in "masculine" style, formal and casual in "feminine" style
あたし	*atashi*	casual, mostly used by a female speaker
(ロ) 俺	*ore*	blunt, almost always used by a male speaker
僕	*boku*	casual, almost always used by a male speaker

Another self-reference term is *jibun* 'self'. *Jibun* is gender-free and is used in referring to one's inner sense of self. Although pronouns are usually chosen on the basis of situation, for example, the speaker's gender and to whom the reference is made, *jibun* is immune from these situational factors. *Jibun* is always *jibun*; it refers to the inner, private, and firm sense of self.

Jibun is also used when the sense of self is focused or contrasted with someone else's. *Jibunra* 'we, us' is sometimes used to refer to a group, with a strong sense of *uchi* membership. It is used synonymously with *uchira* 'we, the *uchi* members'. (See Chapter 3 about *uchi* and *soto*.)

When *jibun* refers to someone already mentioned in a sentence, it highlights the sense of inner self. Contrast the two sentences below.

1. (≈) 彼は**自分**のことが分からなくなった。

   Kare wa **jibun** no koto ga wakara-naku natta.

   He (became confused and) did not understand his inner self.

2. (≈) 彼は彼のことが分からなくなった。

   Kare wa kare no koto ga wakara-naku natta.

   He (became confused and) did not understand (about) himself.

Jibun no koto is relatively subjective and internal, whereas *kare no koto* is more objective and distant. *Jibun no koto* encourages the partner to align with the speaker's internal perspective. Because *jibun* reaches for the inner self, it engenders a sense of shared empathy.

Jibun can also refer to a generic sense of self, as in example (3). There *jibun* does not refer to a specific person, but comments on the self in general. In contrast, *anata no koto* in example (4) is comparatively more specific and focuses on the partner.

3. (≈) **自分**のことは**自分**で考えなければね。

   Jibun no koto wa **jibun** de kangaenakereba ne.

   (lit.) The self must think about one's self by oneself.

4. (≈) あなたのことはあなたが考えなければね。

   Anata no koto wa anata ga kangaenakereba ne.

   You must think about your self by yourself.

Jibun occasionally serves as a first person pronoun. In such cases it conveys a sense of traditional masculinity that sometimes reflects military and regional identities.

Examples

a. (Two young people trying to understand each other)

   (≈fy1): **あたし**の気持ち、分かってくれる？
   (≈my1): うん、分かるけど、**僕**のことも理解してくれよ。

(≈fy1): **Atashi** no kimochi, wakatte-kureru?
(≈my1): Un, wakaru kedo, **boku** no koto mo rikai shite-kure yo. (see E. 66 for *wakaru*; E. 30 for *boku no koto*)

(≈fy1): Will you please understand my feelings?
(≈my1): Sure, I understand. But you've got to understand how I feel, too.

b. (A man expresses his dissatisfaction)

(□ma1): **俺**はやっぱ、そういうの気に入らねえな。
(my1): すみません。

(□ma1): **Ore** wa yappa, soo yuu no ki ni ira-nee na. (see E. 57 for *yappa*)
(my1): Sumimasen.

(□ma1): After all, I don't really like things like that.
(my1): I'm sorry.

c. (≈) 他人のことは余り気にせず**自分**のことだけはきちんとしたい。

Tanin no koto wa amari ki ni sezu **jibun** no koto dake wa kichin to shitai. (see E. 30 for *jibun no koto*)
Not paying too much attention to other people, I want to make sure to take care of my own things correctly.

d. (≈) どんなことがあっても、**自分**は大切にしたい。

Donna koto ga attemo, **jibun** wa taisetsu ni shitai.

Whatever happens, I want to cherish my (own) self.

e. (A man identifies himself in a traditional style)

はい、**自分**は広島出身です。
Hai, **jibun** wa Hiroshima shusshin desu.

Yes, I am from Hiroshima.

Authentic Examples

a. (Taken from *Long Vacation*, episode 7) Shinji is confused and unable to decide how to identify himself, particularly because he is talking to Ryooko, a girl from a good family.

涼子： はい、もしもし。
真二： あ、**俺**。あ、いや、**僕**。い、いや。あ、じゃなくて、**俺**、**俺**。あ、いや、あの**俺**、**わた**、**私**、**俺**。
涼子： 真二さん？

Ryooko:	Hai, moshi moshi.
Shinji:	A, **ore**. A, iya, **boku**. I, iya. A, ja-nakute, **ore**, **ore**. A, iya, ano **ore**, **wata- watashi**, **ore**.
Ryooko:	Shinji-san?

Ryooko:	Hello.
Shinji:	Oh, it's *ore*. I mean, *boku*. No, uh, not so, *ore, ore*. Ah, no, uh, *ore, wata- watashi*, no, *ore*.
Ryooko:	Shinji?

b. (Taken from *Santaku*) Kimura responds to Sanma's comment that Kimura doesn't take this kind of program seriously. He can afford to be relaxed about it, because he has other sources of income. Note that Kimura starts to say *boku*, but instantly rephrases it to *ore* (see additional information about this).

木村：	なあなあじゃないですよ。だって、**ボク俺**ほんと今出てくる前、ほんとライブより緊張しましたからね、まじで＝
さんま：	＝うそ言えよ。
木村：	ほんとですよ。だってもう。
さんま：	俺はいつも段取りとか考えていたら、うわ仕事の顔してるって。

Kimura:	Naa naa ja-nai desu yo. Datte, **boku ore** honto ima dete-kuru mae, honto raibu yori kinchoo shimashita kara ne, maji de=
Sanma:	=Uso ie yo. (see E. 21 for *uso ie yo*)
Kimura:	Honto desu yo. Datte moo.
Sanma:	Ore wa itsumo dandori toka kangaetetara, uwa shigoto no kao shiteru tte. (see E. 21 for *uwa*, a variety of *uwa-tt*)

Kimura:	It's not just being cozy. You know, before I, I came out now, I was tensed up, more than I get tense right before a live concert, seriously=
Sanma:	=You're lying (stop that!).
Kimura:	It's true. Because, it's so.
Sanma:	I was thinking about the procedures, and then you say, "Wow, you look really serious with your 'business face'."

c. (Taken from *Tsubasa o kudasai*, 57) Kyooka realizes that she knew that her friend Hatano was being bullied by some other classmates. She refers to herself as her inner sense of *jibun* as well as *watashi*.

「言われなくても …… **自分**が一番よくわかってんのよ ……」
吐き出すように言って、**私**は枕を握り締めた。

"Iware-nakutemo……**jibun** ga ichiban yoku wakatten no yo….." (see E. 23 for *ichiban*; E. 66 for *wakatteru*)
Hakidasu yoo ni itte, **watashi** wa makura o nigirishimeta.

"Even when I am not told so, I myself am the one who understands that more than anyone else."
Saying so in disgust, I grabbed my pillow tight.

d. (Taken from *Kitchin*, 51 [English translation, 33]) Here, the narrator uses *jibun o omou* 'to think of my (inner) self'. The focus is on the sense of self as the narrator's self-reflections are presented.

最後の荷物が**私**の両足のわきにある。**私**は今度こそ身一つになりそうな**自分**を思うと、泣くに泣けない妙にわくわくした気持ちになってしまった。

Saigo no nimotsu ga **watashi** no ryooashi no waki ni aru. **Watashi** wa kondo koso mihitotsu ni narisoona **jibun** o omou to, naku ni nake-nai myoo ni wakuwaku shita kimochi ni natte-shimatta. (see E. 17 for *natte-shimatta*)

I carried the last of my things in both hands. When I thought, now at last I won't be torn between two places, I began to feel strangely shaky, close to tears.

e. (Taken from *Taiga no itteki*, 77) Note the author's choice of *watashi* and *jibun*. He takes the position that inside *watashi* there are two senses of inner *jibun*.

私という**自分**が二つある、というのは、そういうことである。すべての人間と共通している**自分**と、だれとも異なるただひとりの**自分**、その二つの**自分**は、ときとして対立し、ときとして同調する。

Watashi to yuu **jibun** ga futatsu aru, to yuu no wa, soo yuu koto dearu. Subete no ningen to kyootsuu shiteiru **jibun** to, dare to mo kotonaru tada hitori no **jibun**, sono futatsu no **jibun** wa, toki to shite tairitsu shi, toki to shite doochoo suru.

This is what I mean when I say that there are two selves in (the concept) "I." The self that is common with all other human beings, and another singular self that is distinct from everyone; and these two selves sometimes oppose each other, and sometimes sympathetically conform to each other.

Note

Jibun is also used to refer to the partner or someone else. In this use it has an emphatic effect, because *jibun* adds not only a sense of the inner self, but also a sense of comparison with someone else's *jibun*. This effect is particularly evident in the following examples.

1. (Taken from *Long Love Letter Hyooryuu Kyooshitsu*, episode 6) The students cannot sleep because of the terrible incident of the night before. Asami refers to Yuka by *jibun*, comparing herself with students.

浅海： きのうの夜あんなことあったんだから当然か。
結花： 眠るの怖いんだよね。体は疲れてるのに。
浅海： **自分**もでしょ。

Asami: Kinoo no yoru anna koto atta n da kara toozen ka. (see E. 16 for *anna*)
Yuka: Nemuru no kowai n da yo ne. Karada wa tsukareteru noni. (see E. 11 for *kowai*)
Asami: **Jibun** mo desho.

Asami: Because last night such a terrible thing happened, so it may be natural (that they cannot sleep).
Yuka: They are scared of sleeping, although they are physically tired.
Asami: You, yourself, are also scared, right?

2. (Taken from *Ainori*) In this show, *Saigo no machi de gyooten koodoo onna* (Surprising female tour member's action at the final destination), Gachapin, one of the women on the show, criticizes another girl, Mikan, who simply cried instead of facing a problem. Note the mixture of *watashi* and *jibun*. *Jibun* is used in two ways, in self-reference (*jibunteki*) and in reference to someone else.

ガチャピン： みんなで行動しているときに、**自分**だけああいう行動とるってことは、仲間でいるってことを（うん）ある意味考えてないってことじゃん。それなのに泣くっていうことで、泣くっていう事がどういう表現か分かんないけど、**私**にはやっぱりそういう表現ができないから（うん）そういうのって**自分的**には、納得いかない。（うん）みかんの考え方と**私**の考え方があきらかに違うから、おなじ女の子としても、全然やっぱ考え方が違うってのがあるし。
ドボ： ガチャピン、分かろうとしなくてもいいんだよ。
ガチャピン： なんで？
ドボ： でガチャピンは、そうしてがまんしてきた。けど、出来ない子もいる。（うん）それだけでいいんじゃないん？

Gachapin: Minna de koodoo shiteiru toki ni, **jibun** dake aa yuu koodoo toru tte koto wa, nakama de iru tte koto o (un) aru imi kangaete-nai tte koto jan. Sorenanoni naku tte yuu koto de, naku tte yuu koto ga doo yuu hyoogen ka wakan-nai kedo, **watashi** ni wa yappari soo yuu hyoogen ga deki-nai kara (un) soo yuu no tte **jibunteki** ni wa, nattoku ika-nai. (un)

	Mikan no kangaekata to **watashi** no kangaekata ga akiraka ni chigau kara, onaji onna no ko to shitemo, zenzen yappa kangaekata ga chigau tte no ga aru shi. (see E. 66 for *wakara-nai*; E. 57 for *yappari* and *yappa*; E. 63 about the use of *shi*)
Dobo:	Gachapin, wakaroo to shi-nakutemo ii n da yo.
Gachapin:	Nande?
Dobo:	De Gachapin wa, soo shite gaman shite-kita. Kedo, deki-nai ko mo iru. (un) Sore dake de ii n ja-nai n?
Gachapin:	Doing such a thing apart from everyone when we all do things together (uh-huh) means, in a sense, that she doesn't think seriously about her being a part of the group. Despite that, she cries. I don't really understand what it means by crying, but I can't express myself like that. (uh-huh) So, I just can't personally approve of that. (uh-huh) You know Mikan's and my ways of thinking are clearly different. I'm a girl, too, but our ways of thinking are totally different after all, so.
Dobo:	Gachapin, you don't have to try so hard to understand her.
Gachapin:	Why is that?
Dobo:	Gachapin, you controlled your emotions and didn't cry. But there are others who can't quite do that. (uh-huh) That's all. Don't you think that's enough?

Additional Information

In *Santaku*, Sanma primarily uses *ore* to refer to himself, only changing to *boku* a few times. Kimura, however, mixes *ore* and *boku* according to the context. When Kimura addresses Sanma in a formal manner, *boku* is preferred as in example (3). But when he shows his inner self in casual situations, he says *ore,* as in example (4).

3. While throwing darts, Kimura realizes he may lose and becomes thoughtful. Given that they are in the middle of a serious game, Kimura chooses a more formal style, using *boku* instead of *ore*.

木村：	ごめんなさい、ごめんなさい。あの**ボク**ほんとに負けず嫌いなんですよ。#もうちょっとホントに、あの。
Kimura:	Gomennasai, gomennasai. Ano **boku** honto ni makezugirai na n desu yo. Moo chotto honto ni, ano. (see E. 25 for *chotto*)
Kimura:	Excuse me, excuse me. I really hate to lose. I mean, really, uh.

4. On the beach, Kimura is embarrassed by Sanma's comical behavior. Kimura's friends are watching.

木村：	**俺**ホント後ろ向けねえ、恥ずかしくて。#だめだ。
Kimura:	**Ore** honto ushiro muke-nee, hazukashikute. Dame da. (see Chapter 2 for *muke-nee* instead of *muke-nai*; E. 43 for *hazukashii*; E. 18 for *dame da*)
Kimura:	I really can't turn back, I'm too embarrassed. This is no good, I can't.

A number of pronouns and nouns are used for self-reference, including those below. People also refer to themselves by their given names, in which case there is an added sense of childishness or *amae*.

本人	*honnin*	the very person, himself or herself
こっち	*kotchi*	(lit.) this direction, I myself
おいら	*oira*	I (country-bumpkin-like, used by a male speaker)
当人	*toonin*	the person under discussion
我輩	*wagahai*	I (formal; archaic style)
我	*ware*	I, oneself (formal; archaic style)
わし	*washi*	I (archaic; used by mature male speakers)

43. Shyness

Key Expressions

恥ずかしい	*hazukashii*	shameful, embarrassing
(≈) 照れるよ	*Tereru yo.*	I'm embarrassed.

Explanation

Being shy is not necessarily a negative quality in Japanese interaction. In fact, a bit of shyness is favorably received. Being over-confident and too aggressive can put people off, not to mention putting them on their guard. Showing vulnerability and weakness can sometimes arouse sympathy and empathy. Expressions like *hazukashii* and *tereru* show that the speaker is self-conscious, and their use often solicits sympathy and understanding.

Hazukashii is used by a speaker who wants to convey shyness or embarrassment. Although the speaker's embarrassment may be related to any number of things, *hazukashii* sometimes has an implication of disgrace and shame because of wrongdoing. *Hazukashii* is also used as a descriptive term, as in *hazukashigariya* 'a shy person, who finds it difficult to be friendly with strangers'. Also, *hazukashisoo ni* is used meaning 'bashfully' and 'shyly', as in *Sono ko wa hazukashisoo ni shitsumon ni kotaeteita* 'The child bashfully answered the question'.

Tereru also refers to feeling embarrassed, bashful, and shy about something. *Tereru* is used particularly when you are being praised or admired and want to humbly express that you do not deserve such praise. One may also say *Tereru yo* to offset the shyness one feels. Partly because of this too-good-for-me feeling, *tereru* often occurs in the context of love relationships. For example, when someone's romance is announced, the person involved may say *tereru* because of his or her almost undeserved good fortune.

Example

a. (At a party, a woman is asked to sing)

(ma1a): じゃ、上野さんに一曲歌ってもらいましょう。
(≈fa1): やめてよ、**恥ずかしい**よ。
(ma1b): はい、皆さん、拍手をお願いします。

(ma1a): Ja, Ueno-san ni ikkyoku utatte-moraimashoo.
(≈fa1): Yamete yo, **hazukashii** yo.
(ma1b): Hai, minasan, hakushu o onegai shimasu.

(ma1a): Well then, let's have Ms. Ueno sing a song.
(≈fa1): Stop that. It's embarrassing.
(ma1b): O.K., everyone. Please give her a good hand (for her performance).

Authentic Examples

a. (Taken from *SMAP x SMAP*, New Year's special) Tsutsumi, a guest on the show, uses *hazukashii* to express his shyness.

堤：なんかさ食ってるとこ見られるの**恥ずかしい**ね。
中居：あ、そうなんですか。

Tsutsumi: Nanka sa kutteru toko mirareru no **hazukashii** ne. (see Chapter 2 for *kuu* instead of *taberu*)
Nakai: A, soo na n desu ka.

Tsutsumi: You know, I feel shy about being seen while I eat.
Nakai: Oh, is that so?

b. (Taken from *Ren'ai hakusho*, 14, p, 39) Kaho is surprised to find out that there is a hotel for sexual liaisons. *Dokidoki suru* is an onomatopoeic and mimetic word echoing the pounding sound of one's heart.

目の前には、ラブホテルの看板。
うわーっ。
やだ。
恥ずかしくって。
心臓がドキドキしてくる。
Me no mae ni wa, rabu hoteru no kanban.
Uwaa-tt. (see E. 21 for *Uwaa-tt*)
Ya da. (see E. 9 for *ya da*)
Hazukashikutte.
Shinzoo ga dokidoki shite-kuru.

In front of my eyes, I see a sign of a hotel for sexual liaisons.
Wow.
No.
I'm embarrassed.
My heart begins to pound fast.

c. (Taken from interview #79, with Nobuyuki Matsuhisa, owner and chef of Nobu Tokyo)

松久：　アメリカ人は、「グレート」とか言いますから、最初は**恥ずかしい**んですけど、言われて悪い気はしないですよね。

Matsuhisa: Amerikajin wa, "Gureeto" to ka iimasu kara, saisho wa **hazukashii** n desu kedo, iwarete warui ki wa shi-nai desu yo ne.

Matsuhisa: Americans say "This is great!" So at first it is a bit embarrassing, but it is true that I don't dislike hearing this praise.

d. (Taken from interview #78, with Naoki Ishikawa, adventurer) Ishikawa tells Hayashi that if Hayashi becomes a sponsor for his adventure, he will wear clothing items with an emblem that says "Mariko Hayashi, my life." Hayashi is a bit embarrassed by the offer.

石川：　「林真理子　命」とかワッペンつけて行きますよ。
林：　うーん、それはちょっと**恥ずかしい**な。(笑い)

Ishikawa: "Hayashi Mariko Inochi" toka wappen tsukete ikimasu yo.
Hayashi: Uun, sore wa chotto **hazukashii** na. (*warai*)

Ishikawa: I'll go to places wearing clothing items with an emblem that says "Mariko Hayashi, my life."
Hayashi: Uhh, that is a bit embarrassing, isn't it? (*laughs*)

e. (Taken from interview #155, with Yoshino Kimura, actress)

木村：	文章って難しいですよね。私、実は「WOWOW マガジン」で映画のコラムを書いてるんですけど。
林：	あ、そうそう。読んでますよ。
木村：	いやー、**恥ずかしい**。750 字なんですけど、死ぬ思いで。
Kimura:	Bunshoo tte muzukashii desu yo ne. Watashi, jitsu wa *WOWOW magajin* de eiga no koramu o kaiteru n desu kedo. (see E. 44 for *jitsu wa*; E. 63 for *kedo*)
Hayashi:	A, soo soo. Yondemasu yo.
Kimura:	Iyaa, **hazukashii**. Nanahyaku gojuu-ji nan desu kedo, shinu omoi de.
Kimura:	Writing is hard work, isn't it? To tell you the truth, I write a column about movies in *WOWOW Magazine*.
Hayashi:	Yes, that's right. I read it regularly.
Kimura:	Oh, no, I'm embarrassed. It's 750 characters long, but it is so difficult I could die.

f. (Taken from *Beautiful Life*, episode 11) Masao and Sachi are congratulated on their intimate love relationship.

杏子：	サチ、お兄ちゃん、おめでとう。
サチ：	なんか、**照れる**な。
杏子：	#みんなカンパイしようカンパイ！
Kyooko:	Sachi, oniichan, omedotoo.
Sachi:	Nanka, **tereru** na. (see E. 62 for *nanka*)
Kyooko:	Minna kanpai shiyoo kanpai! (see E. 24 about repetition)
Kyooko:	Sachi and brother, congratulations.
Sachi:	Uh, I'm a bit embarrassed.
Kyooko:	Everyone, let's drink to it, cheers!

g. (Taken from *Beautiful Life*, episode 11) Mayumi and Satoru tease Shuuji about setting up the special guest area for Kyooko. Satoru teases Shuuji, and Shuuji denies that he is embarrassed.

真弓：	柊二。
柊二：	はい。
真弓：	ねえ招待席は？この辺？
サトル：	花でもつけとくかぁ？**照れてる**。
柊二：	**照れてねえよ**、なんだよ。
Mayumi:	Shuuji.
Shuuji:	Hai.
Mayumi:	Nee, shootaiseki wa? Kono hen?

Satoru: Hana demo tsuketoku kaa? **Tereteru.** (see E. 62 for *demo*)
Shuuji: **Terete-nee yo,** nan da yo. (see Chapter 2 for *terete-nee* instead of *terete-nai*; E. 37 for *nan*)

Mayumi: Shuuji.
Shuuji: Yes.
Mayumi: Say, where should your guests be? Over here?
Satoru: Should we decorate it with flowers? Look, he's embarrassed.
Shuuji: What, I'm not embarrassed. What are you saying!

h. (Taken from *Strawberry on the Shortcake*, episode 4) Haruka visits Manato's home and prepares a dinner for him and Yui. Yui teases Manato and Haruka by saying that they talk like newlyweds. Manato's response prompts Yui to point out that he is bashful about it.

まなと： じゃできたら呼んで。
遥： はーい。
唯： 「じゃできたら呼んで」「はい」だって、ねえ、新婚さんみたいまなと。
まなと： キミうるさい！
唯： やだ何**照れてん**の。ねえ**照れてる**まなともかわいいね。

Manato: Ja dekitara yonde.
Haruka: Haai.
Yui: "Ja dekitara yonde" "Hai" da tte, nee, shinkon-san mitai Manato.
Manato: Kimi urusai! (see E. 39 for *urusai*)
Yui: Ya da nani **tereten** no. Nee **tereteru** Manato mo kawaii ne. (see E. 9 for *ya da*; E. 31 for *kawaii*)

Manato: Call me when it's ready.
Haruka: Sure.
Yui: "Call me when it's ready" and "Sure." This exchange is like that of newlyweds, Manato.
Manato: You be quiet!
Yui: What are you being bashful about? You know, bashful Manato is cute, too.

i. (Taken from *SMAP x SMAP,* special live show) Tsuyoshi, playing the role of the Bistro SMAP's owner, is a bit bashful. He first laughs and reveals that he feels shy about it.

剛： ワッハッハ。**照れる**な、これ。

Tsuyoshi: Wa-tt ha-tt ha. **Tereru** na, kore. (see E. 48 about inverted word order)

Tsuyoshi: Ha ha ha. I feel shy about this.

j. (Taken from *Chibi Maruko-chan*, 14: 67) Maruko's mother brings Japanese sweets to Maruko. Maruko was drawing a picture of her mother resembling the image of those sweets. In response to Maruko's praise, the mother comments that it is a bit embarrassing.

母：　＜はい食後の/おやつに/おまんじゅう/持ってきたわよ＞(...)
まる子：　＜まんじゅう/...... ＞
(...) ＜ ... さすが/だね .../ さすが/おかあさん＞ (...)
母：　＜あらやだ/そんなに感激/してもらうと/なんか**照れるね**＞

haha: Hai, shokugo no oyatsu ni omanjuu motte-kita wa yo.
Maruko: Manjuu......
(...) ...Sasuga da ne...Sasuga okaasan. (...) (see E. 57 for *sasuga*)
haha: Ara ya da. Sonna ni kangeki shite-morau to nanka **tereru** ne. (see E. 9 for *ya da*; E. 62 for *nanka*)

mother: Here you are. I brought some sweets as dessert.
Maruko: Sweets...
(...) As expected. Really you are great as always, Mother. (...)
mother: Oh, no. To see you that much moved, I'm a bit embarrassed.

44. Preamble to Frankness

Key Expressions

(≈) ていうか	*te yuu ka*	truthfully, to tell the truth
(≈) てか	*te ka*	to tell you the truth
実は	*jitsu wa*	in fact, to reveal the truth
実を言うと	*jitsu o yuu to*	to elaborate on the truth
正直言って	*shoojiki itte*	to be honest, honestly

Explanation

One frequently used preface to speech is *te yuu ka*, a preamble to being frank, particularly in anticipation of telling the truth. The truth here is not necessarily truth in the logical or moralistic sense. Rather, it is true in the sense of revealing honest thoughts and feelings. *Te yuu ka* appears in variations like *te ka, tsuu ka,* and *chu ka* and is used mostly in casual style. *Te yuu ka* is also used in utterance-final position (this use is discussed in Entry 63).

When a speaker is about to say something that might cause surprise or discomfort, he or she is particularly likely to begin the utterance with *te yuu ka*. This *te yuu ka* functions as a warning to the partner that something more revealing (closer to the honest, bottom-line, *honne* thoughts and feelings touched on in Chapter 3) is about to follow.

Jitsu wa '(lit.) in fact, as a matter of fact' is used in formal situations, particularly when the speaker senses that the time is right to reveal something. Overall, *jitsu wa* is used in broader contexts, both spoken and written. It is useful as a preface for discussing business or for announcing the main point or issue. When *jitsu wa* is used, the speaker is often expressing feelings related to the criticial issue by revealing something so far hidden. As a result, a sense of trust is instilled. *Jitsu wa* is also used as a preface to a request. *Jitsu o yuu to* 'to elaborate on the truth' is similar, but it is frequently followed by an elaborate discussion. After *jitsu o yuu to*, it is likely that the speaker will tell his or her secret in detail. Additionally, one may use such phrases as *hontoo no koto o yuu to* 'to tell the truth' or *hontoo no tokoro wa* 'in truth' as prefaces to being frank and perhaps to revealing one's *honne*.

Shoojiki itte 'to be honest' is often used before a speaker says something honestly, without altering its content. It is also useful when one is saying something contrary to what the partner is expecting.

Examples

a. (A man shares his frustration with a friend)

(≈ma1): 俺のこと誤解してんのかな。**てか**、全く分かってないんだ。
(≈ma2): そうかもな。

(≈ma1): Ore no koto gokai shiten no ka na. **Te ka,** mattaku wakatte-nai n da. (see E. 66 for *wakatte-nai*)
(≈ma2): Soo kamo na.

(≈ma1): It may be that they misunderstand me. To be truthful, they don't understand me at all.
(≈ma2): It may be so.

b. (Two friends chatting)

(my1a): どうしたんだい、なんか元気ないね。
(my2): **実は**、会社で大変なことが起きちゃってさ。
(my1b): えっ、おまえの課で？

(my1a): Doo shita n dai, nanka genki nai ne. (see E. 62 for *nanka*)
(my2): **Jitsu wa,** kaisha de taihenna koto ga okichatte sa. (see E. 17 for *okichatte*)
(my1b): E-tt, omae no ka de? (see E. 21 for *E-tt*; E. 30 for *omae*)

(my1a): What happened, you don't look too energetic.
(my2): To tell the truth, something terrible has happened at work.
(my1b): What? At your own section?

c. (Two men sharing doubts about what their friend is up to)

(my1a): だからさ、あいつはそう考えるかもしれないけど、俺はそうは思えないんだ。
(my2a): **正直言って**、あいつの考え方、絶対まちがってると思うよ。
(my1b): そうだろ。
(my2b): **実は**、あいつのことで変なうわさを聞いたんだ。

(my1a): Dakara sa, aitsu wa soo kangaeru kamo shirenai kedo, ore wa soo wa omoe-nai n da.
(my2a): **Shoojiki itte**, aitsu no kangaekata, zettai machigatteru to omou yo.
(my1b): Soo daro.
(my2b): **Jitsu wa**, aitsu no koto de henna uwasa o kiita n da. (see E. 30 about *aitsu no koto*)

(my1a): So, he may think that way, but I just can't (think so).
(my2a): To be honest, I think his way of thinking is absolutely wrong.
(my1b): Right.
(my2b): In fact, I heard some strange rumors about him.

Authentic Examples

a. (Taken from *Antiiku, seiyoo kottoo yoogashiten*, episode 6) Facing the possibility of the coffee shop's going into bankruptcy, Eiji expresses his frustration. Eiji reveals his true feelings by prefacing with *te yuu ka*.

エイジ： おやじは金持ちだからいいかもしれないけど、俺はここがなくなったら困るんだよ。# **ていうか**、ここにいたいんだよ、ずっと。

Eiji: Oyaji wa kanemochi da kara ii kamo shirenai kedo, ore wa koko ga naku nattara komaru n da yo. **Te yuu ka**, koko ni itai n da yo, zutto. (see E. 18 for *komaru*; E. 48 about inverted word order)

Eiji: You may think it fine because you are rich, but I will be in trouble if this place (shop) is closed. To tell you the truth, I want to stay here for a long time.

b. (Taken from *Beautiful Life*, episode 10) Shuuji and Kyooko are on the phone. Shuuji, after prefacing with *te yuu ka*, reveals his truer feelings, namely, that he feels lonely.

杏子： でもめずらしいね、こんな時間に電話。
柊二： や、ちょっと、眠れなくてさ。うん。**ていうか**、さみ、しい、っていうか。
杏子： ねえ、柊二。

柊二：　うん？
杏子：　あたし、いつも柊二のそばにいるよ。

Kyooko: Demo mezurashii ne, konna jikan ni denwa. (see E. 48 about inverted word order)
Shuuji: Ya, chotto, nemure-nakute sa. Un. **Te yuu ka**, sami, shii, tte yuu ka. (see E. 25 for *chotto*; E. 8 for *samishii*; E. 63 about utterance-final *tte yuu ka*)
Kyooko: Nee, Shuuji. (see E. 54 for *Nee*)
Shuuji: Un?
Kyooko: Atashi, itsumo Shuuji no soba ni iru yo.

Kyooko: But, it's unusual, isn't it, to call me at this late hour.
Shuuji: Yeah. Uh, I couldn't sleep. Uh. Truthfully, I feel lonely.
Kyooko: Shuuji.
Shuuji: Yes.
Kyooko: I'm always by your side, Shuuji.

c. (Taken from *Beautiful Life*, episode 5) Shuuji and Kyooko are upset after an unhappy evening out. Shuuji uses both *te ka* and *te yuu ka*, gradually coming closer to revealing his *honne*.

柊二：　ね、図書館司書ってさ、案外難しいんでしょ。俺あんたとつきあいだしてから、結構、まわりに聞いたんだけどさ。＃**てか**、案外プライド持ってやってんじゃないの？＃＃**ていうか**さ、逆にさ、美容師とかの方が、バカにしてんじゃないの？
杏子：　なんで？そんなわけないでしょう。

Shuuji: Ne, toshokan shisho tte sa, angai muzukashii n desho. Ore anta to tsukiai dashite kara, kekkoo, mawari ni kiita n da kedo sa. **Te ka**, angai puraido motte yatten ja-nai no? **Tte yuu ka** sa, gyaku ni sa, biyooshi toka no hoo ga, baka ni shiten ja-nai no? (see E. 47 for *tte*; E. 29 for *tsukiaidasu*)
Kyooko: Nande? Sonna wake nai deshoo.

Shuuji: You see, the job as a librarian is challenging, isn't it? After our relationship began, I asked around. Truthfully, you have pride in your job, don't you? More truthfully yet, you are the one despising a hair stylist's job, right?
Kyooko: How? How could I do that?

d. (Taken from *Long Love Letter Hyooryuu Kyooshitsu*, episode 1) Three female students are discussing their desire to graduate from high school. They were told by their teacher that they must retake the exam because they had cheated. Takagi tells them that she has a secret plan by prefacing with *te yuu ka*. (See Chapter 2 for the kind of youth language used here.)

東：	でもさあ、高校ぐらい卒業したくない？
川和：	あたししたい。でも今さらもうダメくねえ？
高木：	あたしもしたい。**ていうか**、する。＃で、いい考えがある。

Higashi:	Demo saa, kookoo gurai sotsugyoo shitaku-nai?
Kawa:	Atashi shitai. Demo ima sara moo dameku-nee? (see E. 42 for *atashi*)
Takagi:	Atashi mo shitai. **Te yuu ka**, suru. De, ii kangae ga aru.

Higashi:	But, don't you want to graduate from high school at least?
Kawa:	Yes, I want to. But now we can't do that, can we?
Takagi:	I, too, want to graduate. Or to tell you the truth, I am going to. I have a good idea.

e. (Taken from *Long Love Letter Hyooryuu Kyooshitsu*, episode 6) Asami is gravely ill, and Yuka encourages and supports him by saying that she won't let him die.

結花：	死なないっしょ。＃**ていうか**、死なせません。
Yuka:	Shina-nai ssho. **Te yuu ka**, shinasemasen.
Yuka:	You won't die. To tell you the truth, I won't let you die.

f. (Taken from *Dokkin paradaisu*, 3: 41) Ai tells what kind of person Akira is despite his nice-looking appearance.

１７歳の、とってもステキな高校生。
なのに**じつは**泥棒やってて、おまけに家事が大の得意。

Juunanasai no, tottemo sutekina kookoosei. (see E. 24 and E. 27 for *tottemo*; E. 13 for *sutekina*)
Nano ni **jitsu wa** doroboo yattete, omake ni kaji ga dai no tokui.

He is a very nice-looking seventeen-year-old high school student.
But, in truth, he is actually a thief, and in addition, he is an expert on house chores.

g. (Taken from *Dokkin paradaisu*, 3: 26) Ai explains the complicated relationship between her and the three boys with whom she lives. She prefaces her revelation with *jitsu o yuu to*.

神谷家の３人のおにいちゃんたちは、亜衣のママのお姉さんである、麻子おばちゃんの子供たち。
と、いうことは、亜衣にとってはイトコでしょ？
でもね。
じつを言うと、この３人のうちのひとりは、亜衣の本当のおにいちゃんなんだって。

Kamiyake no sannin no oniichantachi wa, Ai no mama no oneesan dearu, Asako obachan no kodomotachi.
To, yuu koto wa, Ai ni totte wa itoko desho?
Demo ne.
Jitsu o yuu to, kono sannin no uchi no hitori wa, Ai no hontoo no oniichan na n da tte.

The three brothers at the Kamiya family are the children of Aunt Asako, a sister of my mother.
That means, they are cousins for me (Ai).
But.
To elaborate, I was told that one out of the three is my real brother.

Additional Information

Te yuu ka occurs frequently in casual conversation. Its use is extensive, including cases in which it simply marks a shift in the topic of conversation (particularly when the speaker expresses views against the partner's expectation). In some use among youth, *te yuu ka* functions as a general preface to speech. In this case, *te yuu ka* simply marks upcoming speech and functions to get the partner's attention.

Because *te yuu ka* includes a quotation (the quotation marker *to* and *yuu* 'to say'), it gives the impression that the topic (or something related to the topic) has already been mentioned. Because of this, *te yuu ka* acts as a transitional phrase for introducing a new topic as if it had already been mentioned (and therefore accepted). (Additional discussion on topic marking using quotation appears in Entry 47.) For example, you may introduce a new topic by saying *Te yuu ka saa, ano shuukanshi no kiji yonda?* 'Say, did you read that magazine article?'. Or, *te ka* may preface the speaker's turn to present a view different from the partner's. When a partner suggests *soba* noodles for lunch, you may begin with *te ka* as in *Te ka, raamen tte no wa doo?* 'Uh, how about *raamen* noodles?'.

In the example that follows, *te yuu ka* is used as a general preface to speech.

1. (Taken from *Muko-dono*, episode 2) Both Ryoo and Yuuichiroo use *te yuu ka* as a general preface to speech. In both cases, however, one can recognize the shift to a new topic.

亮：	ノックぐらいしろよ。（祐一郎、ノックする）おせえよ。**ていうか**、何の用だよ。
祐一郎：	**ていうか**、ゴミある？
亮：	そこ。

Ryoo:	Nokku gurai shiro yo. (Yuuichiroo, nokku suru) Osee yo. **Te yuu ka,** nan no yoo da yo. (see Chapter 2 for *osee* instead of *osoi*)
Yuuichiroo:	**Te yuu ka,** gomi aru?
Ryoo:	Soko.
Ryoo:	Why don't you at least knock on the door (to my room)? (Yuuichiroo knocks on the door.) Too late. But, what do you want?
Yuuichiroo:	Uh, do you have trash?
Ryoo:	Over there.

45. Deflecting the Impact of a Remark

Key Expressions

(≈) なんて	*nan te*	such as I say
(≈) なんて言っちゃって	*nan te itchatte*	to say such and such
(≈) なんちゃって	*nan chatte*	to say such and such
冗談、冗談	*Joodan, joodan.*	It's a joke, I'm just joking.

Explanation

Sometimes one may reveal *honne* thoughts and feelings but regret having done so immediately. This is particularly so when the speaker realizes that what he or she has said is too revealing and is perhaps a bit difficult for the partner to take.

Expressions related to quotation such as *nan te*, *nan te itchatte* (and its casual version, *nan chatte*) can be appended to speech to make light of the situation when one realizes that the partner is concerned or uneasy. The *te* of *nan te* is a quotation marker. Accordingly, both *nan te* and *nan chatte* operate to quote your own speech even as you are speaking. Self-quotation offers an opportunity to qualify and to comment on your own speech by adding varied shades of feelings.

Joodan 'joke' is also used as an interjection. *Joodan, joodan!* may be used to add levity to an otherwise too serious or upsetting situation.

These phrases not only deflect the impact of a remark, but also contribute to filling awkward silences, which diminishes the sense of embarrassment. These expressions function along the lines of self-mocking English expressions like "He said seriously" or "She said jokingly" when a speaker playfully comments on his or her own speech.

Examples

a. (Kazuko and her friend talking about falling in love) Both speakers use utterance-final phrases to deflect the impact.

(≈fy1a): 彼のこと、愛してるんだ、**なんちゃって**。
(≈fy2a): 案外、それ本音じゃない。はっきり言って、最近、彼のことばっかりじゃん。
(≈fy1b): そう？
(≈fy2b): そうよ。いよいよ、和子の恋する季節、**なんてね**。

(≈fy1a): Kare no koto, aishiteru n da, **nan chatte**. (see E. 30 for *kare no koto*; E. 32 for *aishiteru*)
(≈fy2a): Angai, sore honne ja-nai. Hakkiri itte, saikin, kare no koto bakkari jan. (see Chapter 3 about *honne*; E. 69 for *hakkiri itte*)
(≈fy1b): Soo?
(≈fy2b): Soo yo. Iyoiyo, Kazuko no koisuru kisetsu, **nan te** ne. (see E. 32 for *koisuru*)

(≈fy1a): I love him, uh, I'm just kidding.
(≈fy2a): Actually, isn't that how you really feel? To be frank, recently, you are talking about him all the time.
(≈fy1b): Really?
(≈fy2b): That's right. Finally, Kazuko's season for love has arrived, I would say.

b. (Coworkers deciding to go out for the evening) After suggesting that it will be his senior partner's treat, the speaker takes it back by qualifying with *joodan*.

(≈ma1a): 今夜、仕事の成功を祝って、どこか行こうか。
(my1a): いいですねえ。
(≈ma1b): この間いい店見つけたんだ。そこ、行こう。
(my1b): じゃ、今夜は先輩のおごり、ってことで。いや、**冗談**ですよ。

(≈ma1a): Kon'ya, shigoto no seikoo o iwatte, dokoka ikoo ka.
(my1a): Ii desu nee.
(≈ma1b): Kono aida ii mise mitsuketa n da. Soko, ikoo.
(my1b): Ja, Kon'ya wa senpai no ogori, tte koto de. Iya, **joodan** desu yo.

(≈ma1a): Shall we go out for a celebration of a job well done this evening?
(my1a): That will be great.
(≈ma1b): I found a nice place the other day. Let's go there.
(my1b): Well then, it's your treat this evening, right? No, just kidding.

Authentic Examples

a. (Taken from *Beautiful Life*, episode 2) Kyooko, confined to a wheelchair, confesses her secret dream to Shuuji. Kyooko catches herself saying something that could be more revealing than she intends and perhaps misleading. Her romantic dream about *sukina hito* 'someone I love' is just a dream, and to bring the conversation back to reality, she adds *nan te*.

杏子： 好きな人と並んで歩くこと。いつもこうやって押してもらうじゃない、後ろで。そうじゃなくて、好きな人が横にいて、並んで歩くの。**＃なんて**。好きな人なんていないんだけどね。

Kyooko: Sukina hito to narande aruku koto. Itsumo koo yatte oshitemorau ja-nai, ushiro de. Soo ja-nakute, sukina hito ga yoko ni ite, narande aruku no. **Nan te.** Sukina hito nante i-nai n da kedo ne. (see E. 32 for *sukina*; E. 15 for *nante*)

Kyooko: My dream is to walk side by side with someone I love. You know I always have someone pushing (the wheelchair) behind me. Instead, someone I love is next to me, and we walk side by side. Oh, I shouldn't say that. I really don't have someone special that I love.

b. (Taken from *Long Love Letter Hyooryuu Kyooshitsu*, episode 1) Yuka and Asami chat at a coffee shop. Asami uses *nan te* to deflect the impact of his utterance. Yuka shares that feeling by repeating it .

浅海： ま、結局今って。
結花： うん。
浅海： 何が大切なのか分かりづらい時代なんだよ。
結花： ふーん。
浅海： **なんて**。
結花： **なんて**ね。

Asami: Ma, kekkyoku ima tte. (see E. 47 for *tte*)
Yuka: Un.
Asami: Nani ga taisetsuna no ka wakari zurai jidai na n da yo. (see E. 72 for *n da*)
Yuka: Fuun. (see E. 21 for *Fuun*)
Asami: **Nan te**.
Yuka: **Nan te** ne.

Asami: So, in conclusion, right now....
Yuka: Uh-huh.
Asami: It's an era when it is difficult to tell what is really important.
Yuka: I see.
Asami: Maybe I shouldn't say that. (Said he too seriously!)
Yuka: Maybe.

c. (Taken from *Buchoo Shima Koosaku*, 5: 75) At an exclusive club, a company president chats with the owner. When asked what kind of work the owner's family was engaged in, she answers, "We're the biggest thieves in

Japan." Immediately afterward, she adds an expression to deflect the impact, implying that what she said was meant as a joke.

社長：　＜おうちはどんな仕事を / してたんだ？＞
クラブのママ：　＜天下の大泥棒＞＜**なーんちゃってね**＞

shachoo: Ouchi wa donna shigoto o shiteta n da?
kurabu no mama: Tenka no oodoroboo. **Naan chatte ne.**

president: What kind of business did your family own?
club owner: We're the biggest thieves in Japan. I'm joking, of course.

d. (Taken from *Chibi Maruko-chan*, 13: 65) Tamae, always polite and kind, realizing that what she has just said may be a bit too offensive, expresses this with *naan chatte*. Note the pun used here between the name *Tamae* and the phrase *tamatama* (occasionally). See Entry 77 for further discussion of puns and jokes.

たまえ：　＜えっ/ 今の / うけた？＞　＜アハ ... アハハ　私も /「たまちゃん」ってなもんで / たまたまウケることも / あるもんだね　たまには / 面白いことも言わなきゃね / **なーんちゃって**＞

Tamae: E-tt, ima no uketa? Aha...aha ha. Watashi mo "Tama-chan" tte na mon de, tamatama ukeru koto mo aru mon da ne. Tama ni wa omoshiroi koto mo iwanakya ne, **naan chaatte.**

Tamae: Really, was it funny? Aha, aha ha. I'm Tama, so there are some occasions (*tamatama*) that I say funny things. Sometimes (*tama ni wa*) I must say something funny...I'm kidding.

46. Revealing One's Inner Psychological Process

Key Expressions

(≈) あ、そうだ	*A, soo da.*	Ah, I remembered something!'
(≈) そうか。もう八年になるのか	*Soo ka. Moo hachinen ni naru no ka.*	I see. It's been eight years since.
(≈) どうかな	*Doo ka na.*	I wonder about that.
(≈) そうなの？	*Soo na no?*	It is so, is it?
(≈) そうなんだ	*Soo na n da.*	I see, that's it.

Explanation

It is possible to reveal inner feelings without directly addressing the partner. For example, inner doubt may take the form of a self-addressed question. Even when one mumbles a question to her- or himself, the partner is likely to hear it. In fact, the speaker expects it, and the question becomes a tool for indirectly revealing one's inner psychological process. When revealing inner thoughts in words, because the utterance is not directly addressed to the partner, the speaker uses the [V/Adj informal] form.

A, soo da is said inadvertently when a speaker suddenly remembers something. Recognition of certain facts may call for *Soo ka* 'I see' first, then further thoughts, as in *Moo hachinen ni naru no ka* 'It's been eight years since.'

Doo ka na and *Soo ka na* express self-doubt. The speaker might ask *Soo na no?* when not completely convinced and seeking confirmation. In such a case, the speaker is already on the verge of accepting the information, so the phrase is not a question in the strict sense.

When the speaker has accepted information, he or she is likely to use *Soo na n da* (or *Soo na no*) with a falling tone. Because both *Soo na n da* and *Soo na no* are used to acknowledge information from the partner, they reveal the speaker's inner psychological process. Although *Soo na n da* and *Soo na no* are used by both males and females, *Soo na no* is considered more polite and is more frequently used in the less assertive "feminine" style.

Soo na no ka and *Soo na n desu ka* (both with *ka* and a falling tone) also reveal a speaker's psychological process when the speaker either discovers something new or is convinced of something.

Examples

a. (Two women discussing tomorrow's weather) Note that *Doo ka naa* appears in the [V/Adj informal] form (although [V/Adj formal] is maintained elsewhere). This phrase is not intentionally addressed to the partner; it is said almost as if the woman were talking to herself.

(fa1): 明日の天気予報、晴れだから、大丈夫ですよね。
(fa2): **どうかなあ。**あ、西の方から曇ってきてるんで、どうなんでしょうねえ。

(fa1): Ashita no tenki yohoo, hare da kara, daijoobu desu yo ne.
(fa2): **Doo ka naa.** A, nishi no hoo kara kumotte-kiteru n de, doo na n deshoo nee. (see Chapter 2 about style mixture)

(fa1): Tomorrow's weather, because the forecast is fair, it'll be fine, right?
(fa2): I wonder. Uh, it's getting cloudy to the west of here, so I'm not sure about that forecast.

b. (Two teenage boys chatting)

(≈mt1a): だから、負けた人のおごり。
(≈mt2a): えっ？**そうなの**？
(≈mt1b): 当たり前だろ。そういう決まりなんだから。
(≈mt2b): あ、**そうなんだ**。

(≈mt1a): Dakara, maketa hito no ogori.
(≈mt2a): E-tt? **Soo na no**? (see E. 21 for *E-tt?*)
(≈mt1b): Atarimae daro. Soo yuu kimari na n da kara.
(≈mt2b): **A, soo na n da.**

(≈mt1a): So, the loser pays.
(≈mt2a): What? That's so, is it?
(≈mt1b): Of course. That's the rule.
(≈mt2b): Oh, I see (I didn't know that).

c. (Two women talking about their teacher's marriage) In this conversation, both speakers mix styles when they reveal their thoughts.

(fy1a): あ、**そうだ**。あの、風間先生のこと聞きました？
(fy2a): いいえ。
(fy1b): 風間先生って、六月に結婚なさるんですって。
(fy2b): え。**そうなんですか**？
(fy1c): やっぱり知らなかったんですね。
(≈fy2c): えー。ふーん。**そうなんだ**。

(fy1a): A, **soo da**. Ano, Kazama-sensei no koto kikimashita?
(fy2a) Iie.
(fy1b): Kazama-sensei tte, rokugatsu ni kekkon nasaru n desu tte. (see E. 47 for *tte*)
(fy2b): E. **Soo na n desu ka**?
(fy1c): Yappari, shira-nakatta n desu ne. (see E. 57 for *yappari*)
(≈fy2c): Ee. Fuun. **Soo na n da.** (see E. 21 for *Fuun*)

(fy1a): I just remembered something! Hey, did you hear about Professor Kazama?
(fy2a): No.
(fy1b): Professor Kazama is getting married in June, I heard.
(fy2b): Ah, is that so?
(fy1c): As I thought, you didn't know about it.
(≈fy2c): No, I didn't. I see. It is so, I see.

Authentic Examples

a. (Taken from *Majo no jooken*, episode 1) Michi talks to Hikaru at school about an accident. Earlier that morning, while riding his motorcycle, Hikaru almost hit Michi, but he rolled over, avoiding her. Michi suddenly remembers about the cell phone.

未知：　ケガ、大丈夫？
光：　うん。
未知：　あ、**そうだ**。ケイタイ忘れたでしょ。後で渡す。

Michi: Kega, daijoobu? (see E. 60 for *daijoobu?*)
Hikaru: Un.
Michi: **A, soo da.** Keitai wasureta desho. Ato de watasu.

Michi: The injury. Are you all right?
Hikaru: I'm fine.
Michi: Oh, I remembered something. You left your cell phone (there). I'll give it back to you later.

b. (Taken from *Beautiful Life*, episode 11) Shuuji and Masao, Kyooko's brother, talk about a party celebrating Masao's possible marriage to Sachi. Note the transition between *Soo ka naa* (as an expression of self-doubt) and *Soo kamo na* addressed to Shuuji.

柊二：　ね、だってほら、サッちゃんがうれしいことは、あいつも、同じようにうれしいことだと思うし。あいつって、ね、そういうやつでしょ。
正夫：　**そうかなあ**。#そうかもな。

Shuuji: Ne, datte hora, Sat-chan ga ureshii koto wa, aitsu mo, onaji yoo ni ureshii koto da to omou shi. Aitsu tte, ne, soo yuu yatsu desho. (see E. 5 for *ureshii*; E. 30 for *aitsu* and *yatsu*; E. 63 about the use of *shi*)
Masao: **Soo ka naa**. Soo kamo na.

Shuuji: You see, what makes Sachi happy will make her happy as well. She is that kind of a person, don't you think?
Masaru: I wonder. Maybe so.

c. (Taken from *Chibi Maruko-chan*, 14: 82) Maruko's mother tells Maruko that a man (a roasted sweet potato vendor) was so kind that the sweet potato tasted especially good. The last line appears in the comic as Maruko's inner voice.

母：　<それはきっと / おじさんの心が / まる子達に伝わった / んだよ だから / 一番おいしいと / 思ったのよ>
まる子：　<ああ / **そうか** .../ そうだね ... >
そういえばやさしい味がしていたよ ...

haha: Sore wa kitto ojisan no kokoro ga Marukotachi ni tsutawatta n da yo. Dakara ichiban oishii to omotta no yo. (see E. 23 for *ichiban*)
Maruko: Aa **soo ka**...Soo da ne...
Soo ieba yasashii aji ga shiteita yo. (see E. 6 for *yasashii*)

mother: That is because the man's (kind) heart touched you and your friends. That's why it tasted best (of all the roasted sweet potatoes you have ever had).
Maruko: Ah, I guess...That's it, isn't it?
Come to think of it, it did have a warm, comforting taste.

d. (Taken from *Antiiku, seiyoo kottoo yoogashiten*, episode 4) Junko and Akane, Eiji's former girlfriends, visit the shop.

茜： エイジいます？
橘： エイジ？あ、神田でございましょうか。
茜： はい。あれ、いないの？
潤子： え、うそ。
橘： え、今、あいにく休憩中でございまして。
茜： あ、**そうなんだ**。

Akane: Eiji imasu?
Tachibana: Eiji? A, Kanda degozaimashoo ka.
Akane: Hai. Are, i-nai no?
Junko: E, uso. (see E. 21 for *uso*)
Tachibana: E, ima, ainiku kyuukeichuu degozaimashite. (see E. 63 about the [V/Adj-*te*] form)
Akane: A, **soo na n da**.

Akane: Is Eiji around?
Tachibana: Eiji? You mean Eiji Kanda?
Akane: Right. He isn't here?
Junko: Really? (It can't be.)
Tachibana: My apologies, but he is taking a break now.
Akane: Oh, I see.

12
Co-Experiencing Feelings

47. Sharing Topics

Key Expressions

(≈)って	*tte*	about
は	*wa*	as for
とは	*to wa*	speaking of
と言えば	*to ieba*	talking about
って言ったら	*tte ittara*	if you say it is
だったら	*dattara*	if it is
なら	*nara*	if it is
ことですが	*koto desu ga*	regarding (this), about (this)
じゃないですか	*ja-nai desu ka*	about (this), as you know

Explanation

Whenever we converse, we talk about something. In casual conversation, a topic develops as a result of the interaction between the speaker's presentation of a potential topic and the partner's response to it. The partner offers some comment, to which the speaker adds further comment, and so on. In this way, the topic is shared, and the participants both experience emerging empathy.

Topics are presented with markers like *tte* 'about', *wa* 'as for', *to wa* 'speaking of'. (*Tte* may appear as *te* following *n,* as in *Nihonjin te.*) *To wa* and *tte* can be preceded by the [V/Adj informal] structure or by nouns, but *wa* is usually preceded only by nouns. In spoken Japanese, particularly in casual speech, *tte* is the most common form, while in written text, *wa* is the most typical topic marker. *To wa* often presents a topic in an exclamatory manner, and it is not infrequently accompanied by *koto da* or *mono da.*

The conditional expressions associated with the verb *yuu* 'to say', such as *to* (or *tte*) *ieba*, *to* (or *tte*) *yuu to*, and *to* (or *tte*) *ittara* also introduce topics, as do other kinds of conditionals, for example, *dattara* and *nara*. All of these expressions contain a quotation, and/or an assumption that the topic has already been discussed. As a result, they occur primarily when the speaker presents topics drawn from the partner's prior speech, or, more generally, in association with current goings-on. They may pick up what is already being discussed, or they may be used to move to something new. They may even introduce a brand-new topic as if it had already come up.

Koto desu ga, usually appearing in the forms [N + *no koto desu ga*] and [V/Adj informal + *to yuu koto ni tsuite desu ga*], functions as a somewhat formal topic marker, although it is technically a prefacing strategy because of the connective *ga*. Its function as a preface often allows the presentation of a view indirectly, and therefore more politely.

Because an established topic is something that is already known and shared, it may not be explicitly stated. In such a situation, participants can usually identify the current topic with ease.

Ja-nai desu ka, preceded by [V/Adj informal], is an expression originally used by young speakers that has spread to the general public. Although *ja-nai desu ka* has a question marker, it is not really a question. When it is used without waiting for the partner's response, it functions as a topic-introducing strategy. (In this case, a falling intonation is used, unlike that of the *ja-nai desu ka* used in a question.) There is no need to respond yes or no to this *ja-nai desu ka*, because the speaker is encouraging the partner to recall the relevant information and is only soliciting empathy.

Because this *ja-nai desu ka* discourages the partner from speaking in turn, it sometimes gives the impression that the speaker is too pushy. For example, when a speaker says *Nattoo tte oishii ja-nai desu ka* 'You know, *nattoo* is delicious' (even though many people do not like it), it too enthusiastically assumes that the partner also likes *nattoo*. For this reason, some mature and senior speakers may object to this use of *ja-nai desu ka*. *Ja-nai desu ka* is related to its shortened and more colloquial version, *ja-nai*. In a way, *ja-nai desu ka* and *ja-nai* function like *ne*. They are used when the speaker assumes that the partner is already familiar with the information presented.

The use of *ja-nai desu ka* encourages a particular kind of interaction between speaker and partner. Although what precedes the phrase may be unexpected, the speaker's mere use of *ja-nai desu ka* solicits approval, understanding, or agreement. The partner, understanding the speaker's desire, accommodates accordingly. In this way the new information becomes familiar to both parties, and a topic is established and shared. *Ja-nai desu ka* engenders a sense of sharing and a feeling of empathy between participants.

Examples

a. (≈) 彼女**って**、東京出身？

Kanojo **tte**, Tookyoo shusshin?

Is she from Tokyo?

b. それで、この間の件**は**、どうなりました？

Sorede, kono aida no ken **wa**, doo narimashita?

So, what happened to the matter (we discussed) the other day?

c. (≈) 突然家出**とは**ひどいものだ。

Totsuzen iede **to wa** hidoi mono da.

Running away from home suddenly, that's horrible.

d. 京都**なら**、やっぱり秋がいいですね。

Kyooto **nara**, yappari aki ga ii desu ne. (see E. 57 for *yappari*)

If it is Kyoto, fall is the best time after all, isn't it?

e. 旅行の**ことですが**、イタリア**は**三日しかとれませんね。

Ryokoo no **koto desu ga**, Itaria **wa** mikka shika toremasen ne.

About the trip, we can spend only three days in Italy.

f. 海外旅行する**じゃないですか**。それ**って**特に若い女性の一人旅**なら**、リスクも大きいですよね。

Kaigai ryokoo suru **ja-nai desu ka**. Sore **tte** toku ni wakai josei no hitori tabi **nara**, risuku mo ookii desu yo ne.

You know people travel abroad. But if a young woman travels alone, there is a big risk, don't you think?

Authentic Examples

a. (Taken from *Long Vacation*, episode 5) Minami, although a new driver, gives Sena a ride. She can't even remember how to start the engine, but using *tte* makes it seem as if they've talked about this before.

南：　瀬名クン。
瀬名：　はい。
南：　発進**って**どうやるんだっけ？

Minami: Sena-kun.
Sena: Hai.
Minami: Hasshin **tte** doo yaru n dakke?

Minami: Sena.
Sena: Yes.
Minami: What (is it that) you do to start the engine?

b. (Taken from *Muko-dono*, episode 9) Yuuichiroo maintains the topic of traveling together as a family by using *tte* and *ja-nai desu ka*. He wants to go on talking about it, perhaps to say that he is looking forward to it. Kaede, who is upset that they will have to cancel it this year because of Yuuichiroo, takes over.

祐一郎： おれ、ほら、家族旅行とか**って**はじめて**じゃないですか**。
かえで： 今年**は**中止だね。
祐一郎： えっ？
かえで： えっじゃないわよ。さくら＃あんたのだんな**って**ほんとにバカだね。

Yuuichiroo: Ore, hora, kazoku ryokoo toka **tte** hajimete **ja-nai desu ka.**
Kaede: Kotoshi **wa** chuushi da ne.
Yuuichiroo: E-tt?
Kaede: E-tt ja-nai wa yo. Sakura, anta no danna **tte** honto ni baka da ne. (see E. 70 about echo responses)

Yuuichiroo: For me, it will be the first time to travel together as a family, so...
Kaede: We'll cancel it this year.
Yuuichiroo: What?
Kaede: Don't say "What?"! Sakura, your husband is a real fool, isn't he?

c. (Taken from *Shiretoko rausudake satsujin bojoo*, 115) Miyako and Shimon are talking on the phone about the weather.

「東京**は**雨よ」
「こっち**は**、まあまあの天気だった」

"Tookyoo **wa** ame yo."
"Kotchi **wa** maamaa no tenki datta."

"It's raining in Tokyo."
"Over here the weather was just so-so."

d. (Taken from *Shiretoko rausudake satsujin bojoo*, 95) Shimomura makes a comment about Taeko as he answers Shimon's questions.

「多恵子さんが自殺した場所へ花束を供える人**といったら**、彼女と親しかったとみていいですね」

"Taeko-san ga jisatsu shita basho e hanataba o sonaeru hito **to ittara,** kanojo to shitashikatta to mite ii desu ne."

"If it is a person who brings flowers to the place where Taeko committed suicide, we can think of this person to have been close to her, right?"

e. (Taken from interview #87, with Muneaki Masuda, company president)

増田： 例えば、結婚するとか、会社辞めるとか、どんな車買うとか、それを決める自分の生き方のスタイル**って**ある**じゃないですか**。それを提供することがいちばん大事だというのがTSUTAYAのミッション。

Masuda: Tatoeba, kekkon suru toka, kaisha yameru toka, donna kuruma kau toka, sore o kimeru jibun no ikikata no sutairu **tte** aru **ja-nai desu ka**. Sore o teikyoo suru koto ga ichiban daiji da to yuu no ga TSUTAYA no misshon. (see E. 32 for *kekkon suru*; E. 42 for *jibun*; E. 23 for *ichiban*)

Masuda: There is a personal lifestyle that determines how you do things, for example, getting married, quitting a job, purchasing a specific kind of car, right? The most important thing is to offer some suggestions about lifestyle, and this is TSUTAYA's mission.

f. (Taken from interview #75, with Tadanori Yokoo, artist)

横尾： 特に「ベルばら」**は**色がきれいですねえ。フィナーレでみんなダーッと並ぶ**じゃないですか**。あのときの色がすごくきれいだった。

Yokoo: Toku ni "Beru Bara" **wa** iro ga kirei desu nee. Finaare de minna daa-tt to narabu **ja-nai desu ka**. Ano toki no iro ga sugoku kirei datta. (see E. 24 for *sugoku*)

Yokoo: Especially in "Beru Bara" (*The rose of Versailles*), the color is beautiful. At the finale, everyone lines up altogether, you know. The color at that moment was extremely beautiful.

48. Putting Feelings First

Key Expressions

(≈) いやだなあ、あしたの試験	*Iya da naa, ashita no shiken.*	Disgusting it is, tomorrow's exam.
うれしいです、あなたに会えて	*Ureshii desu, anata ni aete.*	Very pleased I am, to see you.
(≈) なに、それ	*Nani, sore*	What (the heck) is that!

Explanation

Although the Japanese sentence is structured to present topic first, followed by comment, its order may be inverted, and certain elements may be postposed. As a basic rule, as Eguchi (2000) points out, any element of a sentence can be postposed as long as it is not the most important message. Inversion usually conveys a sense that the element now in initial position has become urgent. For example, when the speaker is moved, feelings come first, and then what the feelings are about follows. Inverted word order is most likely to happen when a speaker feels a high degree of surprise, excitement, enthusiasm, admiration, strong criticism, and so on. (The speaker may also delay the mention of certain information so that the partner may focus on the postposed element, but this use is rather limited.)

In some cases, inversion is the norm. One good example is *Nani, sore!* 'What (the heck) is that!' an expression used to show surprise, criticism, and often disgust. Although this expression results from the inversion of *Sore (wa) nani*, *nani* is the more immediate word. Consequently, inverted order has become the norm. Some of the examples show similar expressions with *nani* and inverted word order.

Examples

a. (A man comments on his girlfriend's dress) Both utterances use inverted word order; feelings come first.

(≈my1): **似合ってるね、そのドレス。**
(≈fy1): **やだなあ、そんなこと言って。**

(≈my1): **Niatteru ne, sono doresu.**
(≈fy1): **Ya da naa, sonna koto itte.** (see E. 9 for *ya da*)

(≈my1): Looks nice on you, that dress.
(≈fy1): Wow, it's embarrassing, that you would say such a thing.

b. (Two young women talking about the restaurant where they are having dinner) Note the three utterances with inversion.

(≈fy1a): **幸せ、お腹一杯食べて、おしゃべりして。**
(≈fy2a): ほんとね。結構**イケてるね、このレストラン。**
(≈fy1b): 雰囲気も文句なしよね。
(≈fy2b): **今度、来ようかな、彼と。**

(≈fy1a): **Shiawase, onaka ippai tabete, oshaberishite.** (see E. 5 for *shiawase*)
(≈fy2a): Honto ne. Kekkoo **iketeru ne, kono resutoran.** (see E. 25 for *kekkoo*; E. 13 for *iketeru*)

(≈fy1b): Fun'iki mo monku nashi yo ne.
(≈fy2b): **Kondo, koyoo ka na, kare to.** (see E. 30 for *kare*)

(≈fy1a): Happy I am, to have eaten until I'm full, and to have enjoyed chatting with you.
(≈fy2a): Really. Quite nice, this restaurant, isn't it?
(≈fy1b): The atmosphere is just perfect, you know.
(≈fy2b): Maybe I'll come again, with my boyfriend.

c. (A woman in a bad mood) Note the inverted expression in the man's response.

(≈fy1a): だから、手伝ってくれなくてよかったのに。
(≈my1a): ええっ？
(≈fy1b): 迷惑よ。
(≈my1b): **何だ、それ。**
(≈fy1c): ごめん。
(≈my1c): **どうかしてるよ、今日のお前。**
(≈fy1d): ごめん。

(≈fy1a): Dakara, tetsudatte-kure-nakute yokatta noni.
(≈my1a): Ee-tt? (see E. 21 for *Ee-tt?*)
(≈fy1b): Meiwaku yo.
(≈my1b): **Nan da, sore.**
(≈fy1c): Gomen.
(≈my1c): **Dooka shiteru yo, kyoo no omae.**
(≈fy1d): Gomen.

(≈fy1a): So, I'm saying that you didn't have to help me.
(≈my1a): What?
(≈fy1b): It's more of a bother to me.
(≈my1b): What (the heck) is that!
(≈fy1c): Sorry.
(≈my1c): Something is wrong with you today.
(≈fy1d): Sorry.

Authentic Examples

a. (Taken from *Long Love Letter Hyooryuu Kyooshitsu*, episode 3) Yuka's father eats sushi brought to him by Fujisawa, one of Yuka's former students. The father excitedly says *Umai, kore*, using inverted word order.

三崎： **うまいこれ。**
藤沢： ありがとうございます。

Misaki: **Umai, kore.**
Fujisawa: Arigatoo gozaimasu.

Misaki: Delicious, this is.
Fujisawa: Thank you.

b. (Taken from *Long Love Letter Hyooryuu Kyooshitsu*, episode 1) Ootomo complains about being ordered to come to school for remedial studies.

大友： 補習？#**マジかよこれ。**(...)
若原： マジだよ。

Ootomo: Hoshuu? **Maji ka yo kore.** (...) (see E. 67 for *maji*)
Wakahara: Maji da yo.

Ootomo: Remedial classes? Are they serious about this? (...)
Wakahara: We certainly are serious.

c. (Taken from *Long Vacation*, episode 4) Minami coached Sena on how to confess his love toward Ryooko, and Momoko is criticizing. Momoko's question is inverted, as is Minami's response to Sena.

瀬名： ちょっと何やってんの？
南： そっちこそ何やってんの。
「ここにいろよ。俺のそばにいろよ。どこへも行くなよ。」
桃子： **何なんですか、そのくさいセリフ。**
南： そんなくさい。超バッド？
瀬名： 話の流れ全然違うんで、そんなこと絶対言えません。
南： 流れって。**作りゃいいじゃん、自分で、流れを。**

Sena: Chotto nani yatten no? (see E. 25 for *chotto*)
Minami: Sotchi koso nani yatten no. (see E. 30 for *sotchi*)
"Koko ni iro yo. Ore no soba ni iro yo. Doko e mo iku-na yo."
Momoko: **Nan na n desu ka, sono kusai serifu.**
Minami: Sonna kusai. Choo baddo?
Sena: Hanashi no nagare zenzen chigau n de, sonna koto zettai iemasen.
Minami: Nagare tte. **Tsukurya ii jan, jibun de, nagare o.** (see E. 70 about echo responses; E. 42 for *jibun*)

Sena: What are you doing there?
Minami: What are YOU doing!
Remember? "Stay here. Stay beside me. Don't go anywhere else."
Momoko What are they? Those terribly unnatural made-up lines.
Minami: That terrible? Are they super bad?
Sena: The flow of talk is going in a completely different direction, so I can never say those lines.
Minami: What do you mean by the flow of talk! Why don't you make it, by yourself, I mean, the flow.

d. (Taken from *Strawberry on the Shortcake*, episode 1) Note the frequent use of the feeling-first expression in the following conversation. In casual conversation, inverted word order occurs frequently and may help the interaction flow smoothly.

遥：	ママは？
さとる：	**寝ちゃったよ、お酒飲んで。**
遥：	パパは？
さとる：	また出かけちゃった。
遥：	またけんかしたの？
さとる：	うん。
遥：	**だめねえ、さとるの前で。**
さとる：	**平気だよ、もう慣れちゃったから。**

Haruka:	Mama wa?
Satoru:	**Nechatta yo, osake nonde.** (see E. 17 for *nechatta*)
Haruka:	Papa wa?
Satoru:	Mata dekakechatta.
Haruka:	Mata kenka shita no?
Satoru:	Un.
Haruka:	**Dame nee, Satoru no mae de.** (see E. 18 for *dame*)
Satoru:	**Heiki da yo, moo narechatta kara.**

Haruka:	Where is Mom?
Satoru:	Went to bed, after drinking *sake*.
Haruka:	Where is Dad?
Satoru:	He went out again.
Haruka:	Did they fight again?
Satoru:	Yeah.
Haruka:	That's not good, is it, in front of you, Satoru.
Satoru:	It's O.K., I'm used to it.

49. Sharing the Target of Emotion

Key Expressions

星！	*Hoshi!*	Those stars!
きれいな月！	*Kireina tsuki!*	What a beautiful moon!
外は雪！	*Soto wa yuki!*	Snow outside!

Explanation

When a person is moved by something beautiful, the target of that emotion is presented in exclamatory phrases. These expressions provide targets of deep emotion that the speaker and partner can share. (See also the rhetoric of *futaku* discussed in Entry 52.) Grammatically, exclamatory nominal phrases take the form [N] or [Adj pre-nominal + noun]. (See Chapter 1 for this structure, a case of *kantai no ku* 'vocative-emotive phrase'.)

A similar effect may also be achieved by using a nominal phrase in the structure [N *wa* N]. Instead of creating a sentence like *Soto wa yuki da!* 'Outside is snow!' one may simply utter *Soto wa yuki!* 'Snow outside!'

Examples

a. (A young female friend bringing flowers to her friend)

(fy1a): **きれいな花！**
(fy2): でしょ。駅前の花屋で見かけて、あんまりきれいだったから。
(≈fy1b): どうもありがとう。

(fy1a): **Kireina hana!**
(fy2): Desho. Ekimae no hanaya de mikakete, anmari kirei datta kara.
(≈fy1b): Doomo arigatoo.

(fy1a): Beautiful flowers!
(fy2): Aren't they? I saw them at the florist in front of the station, and they were so beautiful, so.
(≈fy1b): Thank you very much.

b. **窓の外は雪！**

(≈) 今年も冬がやって来た。

Mado no soto wa yuki!
Kotoshi mo fuyu ga yatte-kita.

Outside the window is snow!
Winter is here again this year.

Authentic Examples

a. (Taken from *Beautiful Life*, episode 8) Kyooko admires the gift, using a nominal expression.

美山： これ、お見舞いです。
杏子： **きれいないちご。**
美山： でしょ。

Miyama: Kore, omimai desu.
Kyooko: **Kireina ichigo.**
Miyama: Desho.

Miyama: This is for you, wishing for a speedy recovery.
Kyooko: What beautiful strawberries!
Miyama: Aren't they?

b. (Taken from *Ren'ai hakusho*, 14: 194) Kaho is alone with her boyfriend, Tsubasa, during the school excursion to Kyoto. She uses exclamatory nominal phrases to show her feelings.

夜の闇の中。
白い桜の花。
あたしは、翼くんが大好き。

Yoru no yami no naka.
Shiroi sakura no hana.
Atashi wa, Tsubasa-kun ga daisuki. (see E. 42 for *atashi*; E. 32 for *daisuki*)

In the middle of the darkness of the night.
(Under) white cherry blossoms.
I love Tsubasa.

c. (Taken from *Dokkin paradaisu*, 3: 238) Having confessed to Akira that her dream is to marry him, Ai reveals her feelings by the [N *wa* N] structure.

この夢は亜衣の大事な宝物。
だから、暁兄にも知ってほしいの。

Kono yume wa Ai no daijina takaramono. (see E. 42 about the use of a personal name as a strategy for self-reference)
Dakara, Akira-nii ni mo shitte hoshii no.

This, a precious dream of mine.
So I want him to know about it.

d. (Taken from *Kitchin*, 49 [English translation, 31]) The narrator is overwhelmed by the preciousness of a glass given to her as a present.

「わー、うれしい。」
私は、泣きそうになりながら言った。
出ていく時、これを持ってゆくし、出てからも何度も何度も来て、おかゆをつくりますから。
口には出せずに、そう思った。
大切な大切なコップ。

"Waa, ureshii."
Watashi wa nakisoo ni narinagara itta. (see E. 2 for *nakisoo*)
Dete-iku toki, kore o motte-yuku shi, dete kara mo nando mo nando mo kite, okayu o tsukurimasu kara.
Kuchi ni wa dase-zu ni, soo omotta.
Taisetsuna taisetsuna koppu. (see E. 24 about repetition)

"Wow!" I said, on the verge of tears. "I'm so happy!"
When I move out I'll take this glass with me, and even after I move out I'll come back again and again to make soupy rice for you. I was thinking that but wasn't able to say it. What a special, special glass!

e. (Taken from *Iruka to Tsuiraku*, 219) Just before this passage, the author has been moved to discover that from his hotel he could actually see the old theater that he had heard about. He fondly looks over at the theater in the morning light. The nominal phrase presents the target of the writer's lingering emotion.

私はベッドから降りると、シャツを羽織ってベランダに出た。そして、そこから、昇る朝日を浴びて、白い壁が薄いピンクに染まるようになるまでアマゾナス劇場を見つづけた。**栄華の時代はとうに終わり、辛うじて生き延びているかに見えるその劇場を。**

Watashi wa beddo kara oriru to, shatsu o haotte beranda ni deta. Soshite, soko kara, noboru asahi o abite, shiroi kabe ga usui pinku ni somaru yoo ni naru made Amazonasu gekijoo o mitsuzuketa. **Eiga no jidai wa tooni owari, karoojite ikinobiteiru ka ni mieru sono gekijoo o.**

I got out of bed, and with just a shirt to cover my body I stepped out to the balcony. And from there I continued to gaze at the Amazonas Theater until its white walls turned pale pink from the rays of the rising sun. The theater whose era of fame and glory had long gone, a theater that now appeared to be barely surviving.

50. Meaning through Meaningless Words

Key Expressions

なになに	*nani nani*	let me see
(≈) なあんだ	*Naan da.*	Oh, that's what it is. That's it?
なんなら	*nan nara*	uh…
何ね	*nani ne*	say
なんの	*nan no*	no, not at all

Explanation

Nan(*i*) literally means 'what.' It appears as *nani*, except when preceding *da*, *de*, *no*, or *nara*, in which case *nan* usually is used. Although the word itself does not refer to a concrete object, it expresses a multitude of meanings. *Nan*(*i*) is used in exclamatory sentences, rhetorical questions, and interjections in varied ways.

I have already noted several uses of *nan(i)*. In Entry 21, its use as an expression of surprise was covered; in Entry 37, it appeared as a confrontational interjection; and in Entry 40, it took a part in framing rhetorical questions. This entry focuses on *nan(i)* as used to express anticipation or recognition, as well as its use as a conversation filler and a negative response. Although (or because) *nan(i)* has no specific referent, its use assumes mutual understanding, and it often engenders empathy.

In anticipation of something's happening, a speaker may say *nani nani*. For example, a speaker about to read a letter may mumble *Nani, nani*, as he or she opens the letter, wondering what it contains. *Nan da* and *naan da* are used to show that the speaker recognizes something that he or she was unaware of before. They are often used when revealing relief or disappointment; because they reveal inner psychological processes, these are likely to appear in the informal style (as explained in Entry 46).

The interjections *Nan nara* (or *Nan deshitara*) and *Nani ne* are used as fillers in conversation. The speaker inserts these phrases primarily to fill in a pause before starting to speak. *Nan nara*, because it contains the conditional *nara*, implies 'if that is the case'; as a result, it implies an alternative to what is being discussed.

Nan(i) is also used as a negative comment and response to what the partner has just said or asked. This use is more frequently observed among older speakers, where *nan(i)* also appears as *Nan no* and *Na(a)ni* 'No, not at all'.

Examples

a. (A woman opens an envelope in anticipation) *Nani nani* is used as an anticipatory expression; *Naan da*, as an expression of recognition.

(≈fy1a): **なになに**、何て書いてあるかな。
(≈fy2a): ひょっとしてラブレターだったりして。
(≈fy1b): 同窓会の知らせだ。
(≈fy2b): **なあんだ**。

(≈fy1a): **Nani nani**, nante kaite-aru ka na.
(≈fy2a): Hyotto shite raburetaa dattari shite. (see E. 63 for *dattari shite*)
(≈fy1b): Doosookai no shirase da.
(≈fy2b): **Naan da.**

(≈fy1a): Let's see, I wonder what it says.
(≈fy2a): Maybe it's a love letter.
(≈fy1b): Oh, it's an invitation for a class reunion.
(≈fy2b): That's it?

b. (Two coworkers talking about a meeting) When making a proposal, the speaker adds *Nan deshitara* to fill in the pause and to soften the impact of the statement.

(≈ma1a): どうしようかな、今日の会議。他の用事と重なっちゃってさ。
(my1a): 三時からの会議ですか。
(≈ma1b): ああ。
(my1b): **なんでしたら**私が行きましょうか。
(≈ma1c): そうしてくれると助かるよ。

(≈ma1a): Doo shiyoo ka na, kyoo no kaigi. Hoka no yooji to kasanatchatte sa. (see E. 17 for *kasanatchatte*)
(my1a): Sanji kara no kaigi desu ka.
(≈ma1b): Aa.
(my1b): **Nan deshitara** watashi ga ikimashoo ka.
(≈ma1c): Soo shite-kureru to tasukaru yo.

(≈ma1a): I wonder what I should do about today's meeting. I have to take care of something else then (and I can't make it).
(my1a): You mean the meeting from three o'clock on?
(≈ma1b): Yes.
(my1b): Uh, shall I attend the meeting?
(≈ma1c): It will be a big help if you can do so.

Authentic Examples

a. (Taken from *Chibi Maruko-chan*, 14: 5) Maruko opens a letter, mumbling *Nani nani*. The letter starts with *hajimemashite*.

＜**なになに**、/……はじめ/まして＞
＜突然ですが/「ちびまる子/ちゃん100回記念」/の巻で/ヒロシが/車を当てました/よね？＞

Nani nani, ……hajimemashite.
"Totsuzen desu ga, 'Chibi Maruko-chan hyakkai kinen' no maki de Hiroshi ga kuruma o atemashita yo ne." (see E. 69 for *totsuzen desu ga*)

Well, let's see……"How do you do."
"Excuse me for suddenly mentioning this but in the volume *The Hundredth Anniversary of Chibi Maruko-chan,* Hiroshi won a car as a prize, didn't he?"

b. (Taken from *Taiyoo wa shizuma-nai*, episode 2) Ami enthusiastically asks Nao a question.

亜美： 何ですか。あの、**なに、なに**？
直： ダサイよ、そのぬいぐるみ。

Ami: Nan desu ka. Ano, **nani, nani**? (see E. 24 for repetition)
Nao: Dasai yo, sono nuigurumi. (see E. 13 for *dasai*; E. 48 about inverted word order)

Ami: What is it? Say, what, what is it, please?
Nao: Out of fashion, that stuffed doll.

c. (Taken from *Suupaa Tokachi satsujin jiken*, 152) Aiko mentions that her friend wanted to go to a station called Koofukueki, which was something the senior detective Totsugawa had already guessed.

「何処って、聞いたら ……」
「幸福駅？」
「**なんだ**、刑事さん、知ってたんですか」

"Doko tte, kiitara……"
"Koofukueki?"
"**Nan da**, keiji-san, shitteta n desu ka." (see E. 72 for *n desu ka*)

"When I asked her where she wanted to go."
"Koofukueki (the Happiness Station)?"
"So you knew, Detective."

d. (Taken from *Furuete nemure*, 70) Yuriko has asked a clerk some questions by mentioning her father's name, and the clerk is responding. *Nan* is inserted as a filler without mentioning any specific piece of information.

「ああ、そんな名だったわね」
と、その女は肯いて、「立ち話も**なん**でしょ。その辺で話そうか」

"Aa, sonna na datta wa ne."
To, sono onna wa unazuite, "Tachi banashi mo **nan** desho. Sono hen de hanasoo ka."

"Yes, I recognize that name."
Said the woman, and as she nodded, she added "We can't have a talk standing like this. Shall we go over there?"

e. (Taken from *Beautiful Life*, episode 3) Kyooko apologizes to Sachi, but Sachi responds with *Nan no, nan no*, denying any inconvenience.

杏子： ごめんね、休みなのにつきあわせて。
サチ： ううんううん、**なんのなんの**。デートの約束があるわけじゃなし。

Kyooko: Gomen ne, yasumi na noni tsukiawasete. (see E. 48 about inverted word order)
Sachi: Uun uun, **nan no nan no**. Deeto no yakusoku ga aru wake janashi. (see E. 24 about repetition)

Kyooko: I'm sorry. I'm making you come along with me on a day off.
Sachi: No, no, don't worry about that. I don't have a date or anything like that anyway.

f. (Taken from *Shiretoko Rausudake satsujin bojoo*, 231–232) Shimon visits Sugano, the father of a murder victim's friend. Shimon apologizes that he is inconveniencing Sugano, and Sugano shrugs it off. He uses *Naani* as a denial.

(...) 紫門は恐縮し、「すみません」と頭を下げた。
「**なあに**、うちの者は馴れっこです」
菅野は、タバコをくわえると日本酒を注文した。

(...) Shimon wa kyooshuku shi, "Sumimasen" to atama o sageta.
"**Naani**, uchi no mono wa narekko desu."
Sugano wa, tabako o kuwaeru to nihonshu o chuumon shita.

(...) Shimon felt guiltily thankful and bowed his head, saying, "I'm sorry (to bother you)."
"Don't worry about it. My wife is used to it."
After putting a cigarette in his mouth, Sugano ordered sake.

51. Creating Phrases and Sentences Together

Key Expression

[共作] *kyoosaku* co-creation

Explanation

As intimacy increases, speaker and partner come to communicate as one, on the same wavelength, so to speak. The mutual understanding is so complete that one can almost predict what the other is about to say. In some cases, identical words may be spoken simultaneously. Jointly created phrases and sentences reflect and encourage intimacy and empathy between individuals.

Another strategy illustrating how alike speaker and partner think in interaction is completion of the sentence begun by the partner. When the speaker is hesitant and wonders what to say, the partner steps in. The hesitancy may be due more to reserve than to lack of knowledge, so the partner, realizing the speaker's feelings, finishes the sentence. This mutual creation of sentences dynamically enhances their shared sense of empathy.

It should be noted, however, that partners sometimes rudely and forcefully take over the speakers' turns. In this case, finishing someone's sentence is seen as a power play.

Examples

a. (Two coworkers agreeing on who should be in charge of the party) The two speakers point out in unison that Satoo is the best person to be in charge.

(≈fa1a): パーティーなら、幹事が必要ね。
(≈fa2a): あ、それなら。
(≈fa1b, fa2b): **佐藤さん。**
(≈fa2c): 彼女以外に適任なし、って感じ。
(≈fa1c): 確かに。

(≈fa1a): Paatii nara, kanji ga hitsuyoo ne. (see E. 47 for *nara*)
(≈fa2a): A, sore nara.
(≈fa1b, fa2b): **Satoo-san.**
(≈fa2c): Kanojo igai ni tekinin nashi, tte kanji. (see E. 64 for *tte kanji*)
(≈fa1c): Tashika ni.

(≈fa1a): We need someone to be in charge of the party.
(≈fa2a): In that case,
(≈fa1b, fa2b): Satoo.
(≈fa2c): There's nobody else for that role.
(≈fa1c): Indeed.

b. (A husband tells his wife that his colleague Professor Kawakami is returning from the United States) The wife wonders how soon the professor is coming back. The husband supplies the missing information and completes the sentence the wife started.

(≈ma1a): 川上さん、来月アメリカから帰ってくるって。
(≠fa1a): で、先生がお帰りになるのは、**来月の …**
(≈ma1b): **… 上旬。**
(fa1b): あ、そうなんですか。じゃ、卒業式に間に合うかもしれませんね。

(≈ma1a): Kawakami-san, raigetsu Amerika kara kaette-kuru tte.
(≠fa1a): De, sensei ga okaeri ni naru no wa, **raigetsu no…**
(≈ma1b): **…Joojun.**
(fa1b): A, soo na n desu ka. Ja, sotsugyooshiki ni maniau kamo shiremasen ne. (see E. 46 for *Soo na n desu ka*)

(≈ma1a): I heard that Kawakami is coming back from the United States next month.
(≠fa1a): I see, so she will be back in March…
(≈ma1b): …Early March, I think.
(fa1b): I see. Then, she may be back in time for the graduation ceremony.

Authentic Examples.

a. (Taken from *Beautiful Life*, episode 2) Kyooko and Sachi utter *Raamen!* simultaneously. This mutually created utterance illustrates how close they are.

サチ：	じゃあ、さあ、小腹すかない？
杏子：	それはちょっとすいたかも。
サチ：	ね、じゃ、行きますか。
杏子：	行きますか。飲んだ後と言えば、
サチと杏子：	**ラーメン！**
Sachi:	Jaa, saa, kobara suka-nai?
Kyooko:	Sore wa chotto suita kamo. (see E. 25 for *chotto*)
Sachi:	Ne, ja, ikimasu ka.
Kyooko:	Ikimasu ka. Nonda ato to ieba,
Sachi to Kyooko:	**Raamen.**
Sachi:	Say, aren't you a bit hungry?
Kyooko:	I guess, a little.
Sachi:	Right. So, shall we go?
Kyooko:	Shall we go? After having a few drinks,
Sachi and Kyooko:	Raamen noodles!

b. (Taken from *Muko-dono*, episode 7) Yuuichiroo and Sakura find out that they are astrologically a perfect match. They are excited and overjoyed, saying *yattaa* together.

さくらと祐一郎：	**やったー。**
祐一郎：	やったよさくら。やった、やった、やった。
Sakura to Yuuichiroo:	**Yattaa.** (see E. 5 for *yatta*)
Yuuichiroo:	Yatta yo Sakura. Yatta, yatta, yatta. (E. 55 about the use and non-use of *yo*; E. 24 about repetition)
Sakura and Yuuichiroo:	We did it!
Yuuichiroo:	We did it, Sakura! We did it! We did it! We did it!

c. (Taken from *SMAP x SMAP*, New Year's special) Tsutsumi, the guest on the show, is interviewed by Nakai. Nakai asks how Tsutsumi spent the New Year's holiday. In this segment, Nakai and Tsutsumi create sentences together. Nakai starts the sentence by *Datte ima dorama no satsueichuu*, and Tsutsumi continues with *Desu yo*.

中居：　堤さんは。
堤：　僕は、旅行。
中居：　旅行行かれましたか。
堤：　はい。
中居：　だって今ドラマの**撮影中 …**
堤：　**… ですよ。**
中居：　ですよね。そんな旅行行く時間なんかあったんですか。
堤：　三が日に、撮影はしないっしょ。
中居：　じゃその三日間の。
堤：　はい。
中居：　短い間に。
堤：　はい。

Nakai: Tsutsumi-san wa.
Tsutsumi: Boku wa, ryokoo.
Nakai: Ryokoo ikaremashita ka.
Tsutsumi: Hai.
Nakai: Datte ima dorama no **satsueichuu…**
Tsutsumi: **…Desu yo.**
Nakai: Desu yo ne. Sonna ryokoo iku jikan nanka atta n desu ka. (see E. 15 for *nanka*; E. 72 for *n desu ka*)
Tsutsumi: Sanganichi ni, satsuei wa shi-nai ssho.
Nakai: Ja sono mikkakan no.
Tsutsumi: Hai.
Nakai: Mijikai aida ni.
Tsutsumi: Hai.

Nakai: How about you, Mr. Tsutsumi?
Tsutsumi: I went for a trip.
Nakai: So you traveled.
Tsutsumi: Yes.
Nakai: But, in the middle of shooting the drama, you are…
Tsutsumi: Yes, I am.
Nakai: That's right, isn't it? Did you have time to go for a trip?
Tsutsumi: They don't shoot the drama during the New Year's holiday, so…
Nakai: So those three days.
Tsutsumi: Yes.
Nakai: During that short time.
Tsutsumi: Yes.

52. Sharing Visual Empathy

Key Expression

[付託] *futaku* the *futaku*-effect

Explanation

Futaku is a rhetorical figure in traditional Japanese poetics. *Futaku* (lit., commitment) is a method for expressing one's feelings by referring to something concrete. This method, which is particularly known in the world of Japanese *waka*, allows the poet to avoid directly stating what he or she feels. For example, instead of saying "I'm sad," the poet borrows something else and presents it to be seen by others. By describing a beautifully sad moon and sharing its beauty with the reader, the poet aims to express sadness indirectly and more movingly.

Futaku continues to survive in contemporary Japanese. Japanese speakers do express emotion directly, but there is also a sentiment that profound feelings can be better expressed indirectly. It is difficult to empathize deeply with a speaker who states feelings directly. But if the speaker presents an object or image as a target that reflects his or her emotion through *futaku*, the partner will see the target with the same eyes. This shared seeing of images from shared perspectives results in a particularly deep empathy. *Futaku* is an expressive rhetorical strategy. As visual targets, nature offers a wealth of resources (for example, the moon, the setting sun, the stars). A comprehensive understanding of expressive Japanese involves experiencing feelings that are not explicitly put into words.

Authentic Examples

a. (Taken from *Beautiful Life*, episode 10) Shuuji and Kyooko talk on the phone. By viewing the same moon, they share deep feelings.

杏子： もしもし。
柊二： あ、ごめん、もう寝てた？
杏子： ううん、起きてたよ。
柊二： ほんと。（ためいきをつく）
杏子： どうした？
柊二： いや、別に。
杏子： ねえ柊二。外見てみて。
柊二： なんで。
杏子： 月、きれえだよ。
柊二： うそ。(バルコニーに出て月を見上げて) # あ、ほんとだ。
杏子： ねえ。
柊二： うん。

Kyooko: Moshi moshi.

Shuuji: A, gomen, moo neteta?

Kyooko: Uun, okiteta yo.

Shuuji: Honto? (*tameiki o tsuku*)

Kyooko: Doo shita?

Shuuji: Iya betsu ni.

Kyooko: Nee Shuuji. Soto mite-mite. (see E. 54 for *Nee*)

Shuuji: Nande.

Kyooko: **Tsuki** kiree da yo.

Shuuji: Uso. (see E. 21 for *Uso*) (*barukonii ni dete tsuki o miagete*) A, honto da.

Kyooko: Nee.

Shuuji: Un.

Kyooko: Hello.

Shuuji: Ah, sorry, were you already in bed?

Kyooko: No, I was up.

Shuuji: Really? (*He sighs*)

Kyooko: Is something wrong?

Shuuji: No, not particularly.

Kyooko: Say, Shuuji. Look outside.

Shuuji: Why?

Kyooko: The moon is beautiful.

Shuuji: Really? (*after walking out to the balcony and looking up at the moon*) Ah, it really is.

Kyooko: Isn't it?

Shuuji: Sure is.

b. (Taken from *Long Vacation*, episode 6) Sena and Minami, standing on the roof of the building, look up at the stars together and share their thoughts and feelings.

瀬名： ねえ。

南： は？

瀬名： 空にさ。

南： 空？

瀬名： 空に**星**あるじゃん。

南： はい。

瀬名： あれってさ、**星**がキラキラ光って見えるのって、まわりに暗い部分があるからでしょ、闇っていうか。

南： うーん、確かに昼間**星**って見えないもんね。

瀬名： #**星**を輝かせるために存在する闇？俺ってそんな感じかな。

南： #詩人だね。

Sena: Nee. (see E. 54 for *Nee*)
Minami: Ha?
Sena: Sora ni sa.
Minami: Sora? (see E. 70 for echo questions)
Sena: Sora ni **hoshi** aru jan.
Minami: Hai.
Sena: Are tte sa, **hoshi** ga kirakira hikatte mieru no tte, mawari ni kurai bubun ga aru kara desho, yami tte yuu ka. (see E. 47 for *tte*; E. 63 for *tte yuu ka*)
Minami: Uun, tashika ni hiruma **hoshi** tte mie-nai mon ne.
Sena: **Hoshi** o kagayakaseru tame ni sonzai suru yami? Ore tte sonna kanji ka na.
Minami: Shijin da ne.

Sena: Say.
Minami: Huh?
Sena: In the sky.
Minami: Sky?
Sena: There are stars in the sky, right?
Minami: Yes.
Sena: We are able to see the stars twinkling because they are surrounded by a dark area, I mean, the darkness, right?
Minami: Uh, it is true that we cannot see stars during the daytime.
Sena: The darkness is there to make the stars shine. Am I like that (darkness)?
Minami: You are a poet, aren't you?

c. (Taken from *Majo no jooken*, episode 7) Hikaru and Michi sit together on the beach, looking at the stars. They share their deep feelings indirectly by focusing on the stars together.

光： 星ってさあ、今見えてる光ってさあ、確か、何年も前のものなんだよね。
未知： うん。
光： 俺達のことも、何年かたてば、笑い話になんのかな。##俺が大人になれば、みんな許してくれるのかなあ。##だったら、早く時間がたてばいいのに。

Hikaru: **Hoshi** tte saa, ima mieteru hikari tte sa, tashika, nannen mo mae no mono na n da yo ne. (see E. 47 for *tte*)
Michi: Un.
Hikaru: Oretachi no koto mo, nannen ka tateba, warai banashi ni nan no ka na. Ore ga otona ni nareba, minna yurushite-kureru no ka naa. Dattara, hayaku jikan ga tateba ii noni. (see E. 28 for *oretachi*)

Hikaru: You know the stars, the flickering light you see now is something that was produced many years before, right?
Michi: Yes.
Hikaru: Would our situation simply become a funny story after some years? When I become an adult, would people around us forgive us? If so, I wish time passed quickly.

d. (Taken from *Suna no ue no koibitotachi*, episode 11) Reiko and Akira, two lovers, are watching the sunset, which facilitates their sharing of their feelings. This is particularly so because Reiko and Akira both suffer from post-traumatic stress disorder, and they are temporarily color-blind. They are viewing the same scene in the same black-and-white images.

黎子： 地平線に沈む**夕日**、初めて見た。
朗： 海に沈む**夕日**だったら、うちのいなかでも見られた。
黎子： きれえ。
朗： 色分かるようになったんだ。
黎子： 記憶の中にある色を思い出してる。
朗： 俺も同じ。

Reiko: Chiheisen ni shizumu **yuuhi**, hajimete mita.
Akira: Umi ni shizumu **yuuhi** dattara, uchi no inaka demo mirareta. (see Chapter 3 for *uchi*)
Reiko: Kiree.
Akira: Iro wakaru yoo ni natta n da.
Reiko: Kioku no naka ni aru iro o omoidashiteru.
Akira: Ore mo onaji. (see E. 42 for *ore*)

Reiko: This is the first time I ever saw the sun set into the horizon.
Akira: You can see the sun set into the ocean from my home town.
Reiko: Beautiful.
Akira: So you can now see colors.
Reiko: I am recalling colors in my memory.
Akira: Me, too.

e. (Taken from *Strawberry on the Shortcake*, episode 5) Yui and Naoto stand together on the beach, looking at the sunset. Yui and Manato are not in love (they fall in love later in the series), but still they share some sweet moments by sharing the sunset.

唯： きれえ。
まなと： えっ？
唯： **夕日**。
まなと： #ああ。
唯： ##ねえ、まなと。聞こえる。

まなと： 何が。
唯： 太陽が海に沈んでいく音。じゅじゅじゅって。

Yui: Kiree.
Manato: E-tt? (see E. 21 for *E-tt?*)
Yui: **Yuuhi.**
Manato: Aa.
Yui: Nee, Manato. Kikoeru. (see E. 54 for *Nee*)
Manato: Nani ga.
Yui: Taiyoo ga umi ni shizunde-iku oto. Jujuju tte.

Yui: Beautiful.
Manato: What?
Yui: The evening sun.
Manato: Yes, it is.
Yui: Manato. I can hear it.
Minato: What do you mean?
Yui: The sound. The sound of the sun setting into the ocean.

53. Being at a Loss for Words

Key Expressions

言葉にならない	*kotoba ni nara-nai*	cannot put into words
表現できない	*hyoogen deki-nai*	cannot express in words
何とも言えない気持ち	*nan to mo ie-nai kimochi*	indescribable feelings

Explanation

Sometimes feelings are so overwhelming that it is impossible to find appropriate words for them. Japanese offers several expressions for this contingency. *Kotoba ni nara-nai* means that one's feelings cannot be put into words, and *hyoogen deki-nai* refers to the impossibility of expressing something in words. A feeling that one cannot quite describe is *nan to mo ie-nai kimochi*. All these phrases convey the sentiment that words are sometimes inadequate.

Several expressions similar to those above include *hyoogen no shiyoo ga nai* 'there is no way to describe it', *kotoba ni arawase-nai* 'cannot express in words', and *kotoba ni deki-nai* 'cannot put it into words'.

Examples

a. (≈) この気持ちはとうてい**言葉にならない**。

Kono kimochi wa tootei **kotoba ni nara-nai.**

This feeling is something that I cannot express in words.

b. あのドラマには心から感動しました。余りに感動して、何と言ったらいいのか、**言葉にできない**気持ちです。

Ano dorama ni wa kokoro kara kandoo shimashita. Amari ni kandoo shite, nan to ittara ii no ka, **kotoba ni deki-nai** kimochi desu. (see E. 1 for *kandoo*)

I was deeply moved by that drama. I was so moved, that my feelings cannot be expressed in words.

c. (Two women discussing a lost opportunity for a romantic relationship)

(≈fy1a): で、彼は、結局イギリスへ行ってしまったわけ？
(≈fy2a): そう。
(≈fy1b): 淋しいでしょ。
(≈fy2b): 淋しさもあるし。**何とも言えない気持ち**。
(≈fy1c): 好きだって言えばよかったのに。

(≈fy1a): De, kare wa, kekkyoku Igirisu e itte-shimatta wake? (see E. 17 for *itte-shimatta*)
(≈fy2a): Soo.
(≈fy1b): Sabishii desho. (see E. 8 for *sabishii*)
(≈fy2b): Sabishisa mo aru shi. **Nan to mo ie-nai kimochi.**
(≈fy1c): Suki da tte ieba yokatta noni. (see E. 32 for *suki*)

(≈fy1a): So, after all, he did leave for England?
(≈fy2a): Yes.
(≈fy1b): You must feel lonely.
(≈fy2b): Lonely and other feelings, too. I cannot quite put these feelings into words.
(≈fy1c): You should have told him that you love him.

d. (Two friends talking about an accident)

(ma1): あの事故から、もう一年になりますね。
(fa1): ほんとに。余りの惨事で、その恐ろしさは今でも**表現のしようがありません**。

(ma1): Ano jiko kara, moo ichinen ni narimasu ne.
(fa1): Honto ni. Amari no sanji de, sono osoroshisa wa ima demo **hyoogen no shiyoo ga arimasen.** (see E.11 for *osoroshisa*)

(ma1): Since that accident, it's been a year.
(fa1): Indeed. That incident was such a catastrophe that even now I cannot express that horror in words.

Authentic Examples

a. (Taken from BBS for *Beautiful Life*)

言葉にできないよ。

Kotoba ni deki-nai yo.

I cannot put it into words.

言葉に表せないよ、この感動。

Kotoba ni arawase-nai yo, kono kandoo. (see E. 1 for *kandoo*)

I cannot express in words, this deep feeling of being moved.

言葉にできないほどの感動をありがとう。

Kotoba ni deki-nai hodo no kandoo o aigatoo.

Thank you for the deep, moving emotion that I cannot quite express in words. (see E. 1 for *kandoo*)

胸がいっぱいで、**言葉が出てきません**。(see E. 3 for *mune ga ippai*)

Mune ga ippai de, **kotoba ga dete-kimasen.**

My heart is filled with emotion, and I cannot find words for it.

b. (Taken from *Beautiful Life*, episode 4) Kyooko's behavior is strange, and she is keeping her distance from Shuuji. Sachi, knowing that Kyooko is really in love with Shuuji, asks Shuuji to be more understanding.

サチ: 杏子のこと、好きなんでしょ。#だったら分かってあげてよ。杏子の**言葉にできない気持ち**。ていうか、言葉の向こうにある気持ち。

Sachi: Kyooko no koto suki na n desho. Dattara wakatte-agete yo. Kyooko no **kotoba ni deki-nai kimochi**. Tte yuu ka, kotoba no mukoo ni aru kimochi. (see E. 30 for *Kyooko no koto*; E. 32 for *suki*; E. 44 for *te yuu ka*)

Sachi: You love Kyooko, don't you? If so, will you please understand her? Her feelings that cannot be expressed in words. More accurately, her feelings beyond her words.

c. (Taken from *Taiga no itteki*, 241–242)

ぼくたちもできるだけ、言葉をもっと豊かに、そして自由に使いこなせるようにできたらいいな、と思うわけです。しかし、一方で、どんな言葉の名手でも、思いのたけをすべて表現しつくせるわけではない、必ず、**言葉にならない**思い、言葉にしたら色あせるものがあるのではないか、と考えるのです。

Bokutachi mo dekiru dake, kotoba o motto yutaka ni, soshite jiyuu ni tsukai konaseru yoo ni dekitara ii na, to omou wake desu. Shikashi, ippoo de, donna kotoba no meishu demo, omoi no take o subete hyoogen shitsukuseru wake de wa nai, kanarazu, **kotoba ni nara-nai** omoi, kotoba ni shitara iroaseru mono ga aru no de wa nai ka, to kangaeru no desu.

It is true that we too think it wonderful to be able to use language with rich meaning, and to make use of language freely. But, on the other hand, we also think that no matter how skillful a person is with language, it is impossible to fully express everything one feels. We think that certainly there are feelings that cannot be expressed in words, and there are also feelings that, if expressed in words, would fade.

d. (Taken from *Taiga no itteki*, 86)

そして高校三年生になると、約五十パーセント以上、つまり二人にひとりが自殺を頭のなかで考えたことがある、(…) というのです。これは**なんともいえない**重いニュースでした。

Soshite kookoo sannensei ni naru to, yaku goju-tt paasento ijoo, tsumari futari ni hitori ga jisatsu o atama no naka de kangaeta koto ga aru, (…) to yuu no desu. Kore wa **nan to mo ie-nai** omoi nyuusu deshita. (see E. 72 for *no desu*)

And I heard that when they become high school seniors, more than 50 percent, that is one out of two seniors, have thought about committing suicide (…). This is a piece of news so serious that it is indescribable.

e. (Taken from *Jisshuusen chinbotsu,* Feb. 21, 2001) The father of one of the students lost at sea comments on how angry he is about the tragic collision.

「単純ミスを平気で犯したことが事故につながった。**言葉では言い表せない**ほどの怒りを覚える」と語気を強めた。

"Tanjun misu o heiki de okashita koto ga jiko ni tsunagatta. **Kotoba de wa iiarawase-nai** hodo no ikari o oboeru" to goki o tsuyometa.

He firmly said, "Making careless mistakes has led to the incident. I am extremely angry, so much so that I cannot fully express my feelings in words."

13

Appealing to Empathy and *Amae*

54. Confirming Shared Feelings with the Particle *Ne*

Key Expressions

ね	*ne*	
残念ですねえ	*Zannen desu nee.*	Too bad, isn't it?
ねえ	*nee*	
(≈) 向こうに着いたら電話してね	*Mukoo ni tsuitara denwa shite ne.*	When you get there, please call me, will you?

Explanation

In spoken Japanese, interactional particles frequently appear, and they are important in making conversation go smoothly and comfortably. *Ne* is one of the most frequently used of these particles. It usually signals or solicits agreement or confirmation. *Ne* is chosen when the speaker assumes that the partner knows more than or at least as much as the speaker knows. When the speaker has exclusive information, *ne* cannot be used, as in **Atama ga itai desu ne* 'I have a headache'.

However, when *ne* accompanies information the partner does not know, because *ne* assumes the partner knows, it may add to the sense of empathy and intimacy. For example, when asked a question that requires some thought, the speaker answers *Soo desu nee. Yappari kodomo no koro ga ichiban natsukashii desu ne.* 'Let me think. After all, to me, childhood is the sweetest time of all'. Note, however, that obvious answers cannot take *ne*. For example, in answer to

Tanaka-san wa osumai wa dochira desu ka 'Ms. Tanaka, where do you live?' one cannot use *ne*; **Hachiooji desu ne* 'In Hachiooji' is not appropriate.

Ne is also used simply to add a tone of friendliness, at both phrase- and sentence-final positions. Some utterances may have multiple occurrences of *ne*, *de ne*, or *desu ne*, the last of which adds a tone of formality. The high frequency of *ne* is generally a sign of familiarity and friendliness. When the speaker is reserved or is talking impersonally (in a speech, for example), *ne* is seldom used.

A long *nee* uttered slowly at the end of a sentence emphasizes the speaker's commitment to the thoughts being expressed, including highest admiration, deepest sympathy, and heartfelt emotion. Utterance-initial *nee* is used to attract attention from someone in an empathy-soliciting way.

When conversation or written text is peppered with *ne*, the speaker or the writer is trying hard to seek agreement or confirmation. Overusing *ne* gives the impression that the user is too eager or too friendly and should be avoided. Limit the use of *ne* to those phrases and sentences necessary in which you want to directly and personally appeal to your partner.

In general, interactional particles should be used carefully. Because they convey a sense of familiarity and friendliness, they should be avoided when speaking to a person with whom a certain distance should be maintained. By the same token, in formal situations these particles are less frequently used.

Ne may be added when making a request, offering an invitation, and giving orders in the *nasai* form, for example, *Denwa shite ne* 'Please call me' and *Renraku shinasai ne* 'Make sure to contact me'. But it is especially important to avoid using *ne* when making a request from a person to whom one should be polite. **Kudasai ne* is not acceptable. Such an expression assumes that the person knows your request, but you are making sure of that knowledge unnecessarily (and perhaps too agressively).

Examples

a. 実は**ですね**、ちょっと**ですね**、お願いしたいことがありまして。

Jitsu wa **desu ne**, chotto **desu ne**, onegai shitai koto ga arimashite. (see E. 44 for *jitsu wa*; E. 25 for *chotto*)

Uhh, I'm afraid I have something that I must ask, a favor from you.

b. (Two women sharing friendly empathy by commenting on the weather)

(fs1): 寒くなりました**ねえ**。
(fs2): ほんとに**ねえ**。

(fs1): Samuku narimashita **nee**.
(fs2): Honto ni **nee**.

(fs1): It has gotten really cold, hasn't it?
(fs2): Indeed.

c. (Two friends chatting about what to do)

(≈fy1a): **ねえ**。
(≈fy2a): なに？
(≈fy1b): あした何時にする？
(≈fy2b): あ、図書館？
(≈fy1c): うん。

(≈fy1a): **Nee.**
(≈fy2a): Nani?
(≈fy1b): Ashita nanji ni suru?
(≈fy2b): A, toshokan?
(≈fy1c): Un.

(≈fy1a): Say.
(≈fy2a): What?
(≈fy1b): What time should we make it tomorrow?
(≈fy2b): Oh, you mean the library?
(≈fy1c): Yeah.

d. (A man gives his answer after a pause) The answer is given in a friendly way to solicit empathy.

(ms1): ここから原宿まで何分ぐらいですか。
(ma1): そうです**ね**。十五分ぐらいです**ね**。

(ms1): Koko kara Harajuku made nanpun gurai desu ka.
(ma1): Soo desu **ne**. Juugofun gurai desu **ne**.

(ms1): About how many minutes does it take from here to Harajuku?
(ma1): Let me see. About fifteen minutes, I think.

Authentic Examples

a. (Taken from *Long Vacation*, episode 5) Sena starts the talk by repeating *ne* and solicits Minami's attention.

瀬名： **ね、ねねねねね**。
南： あん？
瀬名： やいたりとかしちゃってんの？
南： #オーマイゴッド。バカじゃないのー。

Sena: **Ne, ne ne ne ne ne.**
Minami: An?
Sena: Yaitari toka shichatten no? (see E. 12 for *yaku*; E. 62 for *toka*; E. 63 for *yaitari [toka] shichatten*)
Minami: Oo mai goddo. Baka ja-nai noo. (see E. 58 about *Baka ja-nai no*)

Sena: Say.
Minami: Huh?
Sena: Are you being jealous (by chance)?
Minami: Oh my God. How silly!

b. (Taken from *Long Vacation*, episode 6) Minami and Sugisaki discuss the movie they saw that evening. Minami uses *ne* when she wants Sugisaki to confirm her views and feelings. The location of *ne* depends on where she wants support from Sugisaki or where she appeals for empathy. An independent *ne* appearing at the end of the conversation also expresses Minami's desire to be in empathetic relationship with Sugisaki.

南： いや笑っちゃいました**ね**。
杉崎： あ？
南： ビリヤードの試合でマイケルがポールの方見るところ。
杉崎： あったっけな。
南： ほらあったじゃないですか。マイケルがポールの方見ると**ね**、ポールが**ね**、こういうサインを送ってんですよ、こういう。だってふだんこんな渋くきめてるポールなのに、あん時、こんなんですよ、こんな。#たいしたシーンじゃなかったですから**ね**。
杉崎： ところでさ、どこでめし食おう。
南： #**ね**。

Minami: Iya waratchaimashita **ne.** (see E. 17 for *waratchaimashita*)
Sugisaki: A?
Minami: Biriyaado no shiai de Maikeru ga Pooru no hoo miru tokoro.
Sugisaki: Atta kke na.
Minami: Hora atta ja-nai desu ka. Maikeru ga Pooru no hoo miru to **ne,** Pooru ga **ne,** koo yuu sain o okutte n desu yo, koo yuu. Datte fudan konna shibuku kimeteru Pooru na noni, an toki, konna n desu yo, konna. Taishita shiin ja-nakatta desu kara **ne.** (see E. 72 for *n desu*; E. 16 for *konna*)
Sugisaki: Tokorode sa, doko de meshi kuoo. (see Chapter 2 about *kuoo* instead of *tabeyoo*)
Minami: **Ne.**

Minami: You know, I was laughing, and did you?
Sugisaki: Huh?

Minami: The situation where Michael looks toward Paul when playing pool.
Sugisaki: Was there such a scene?
Minami: There was, wasn't there? When Michael looks toward Paul, Paul is sending this sign, like this. You know, Paul, a cool guy who behaves seriously ordinarily, at that time, went like this, like this. Oh, well, that wasn't an important scene, so...
Sugisaki: By the way, where should we eat?
Minami: Right.

c. (Taken from *Suupaa Tokachi satsujin jiken*, 174–175) The senior detective Totsugawa asks Kosaka a question. When Kosaka offers new information, he uses *yo* instead of *ne*. Otherwise, both Totsugawa and Kosaka use *ne(e)*.

「安達社長の秘書兼、運転手だったそうです**ね**？」
と、十津川が、いうと、小坂は、また、ニヤッと笑って、
「正確にいえば、社長の彼女ですよ」
「彼女**ねえ**」
「若いし、美人だったですから**ねえ**。秘書ということで連れて歩いていましたが、誰が見たって、社長の彼女ですよ。本当の秘書の仕事なんか出来なかったんじゃありませんか**ねえ**。頭は、良かったんですが**ねえ**」

"Adachi shachoo no hisho ken, untenshu datta soo desu **ne**?"
to, Totsugawa ga, yuu to, Kosaka wa, mata, niya tto waratte,
"Seikaku ni ieba, shachoo no kanojo desu yo" (see E. 30 for *kanojo*)
"Kanojo **nee**"
"Wakai shi, bijin datta desu kara **nee**. Hisho to yuu koto de tsurete aruite-imashita ga, dare ga mitatte, shachoo no kanojo desu yo. Hontoo no hisho no shigoto nanka deki-nakatta n jaarimasen ka **nee**. Atama wa, yokatta n desu ga **nee**." (see E. 15 for *nanka*)

"I hear that she was a secretary and a chauffeur."
As Totsugawa said so, Kosaka smiled with a grin, and said,
"Accurately speaking, she is the president's lover."
"His lover, I see."
"She was young and beautiful. He was taking her around saying that she was his secretary, but she is his lover in anyone's eyes. I think she was unable to perform the secretarial job. She was smart, though."

d. (Taken from Shooji 2003a, 54) In *Hyaku-en no udon o tabe ni iku* (Going to eat a hundred-yen udon noodle dish), the writer emphasizes how extraordinary it is to order a hundred-yen noodle dish, and inserts *nee* repeatedly.

100円でこういうことができるわけです。
「フーン、そりゃよかった**ねー**」
あの**ねえ** ……。いまどき**ねえ**、たとえば**ねえ**、定食やのライスだって**ねえ**、200円なわけです。

Hyaku-en de koo yuu koto ga dekiru wake desu.
"Fuun, sorya yokatta **nee**."
Ano **nee**...... Ima doki **nee**, tatoeba **nee**, teishokuya no raisu datte **nee**, nihyaku-en na wake desu.

It's that you can do this for a hundred yen.
"I see, that's nice," (you say).
Listen, in this day and age, for example, rice at restaurants where they serve Japanese set entrees costs two hundred yen.

55. Soliciting the Partner's Emotional Response with the Particle *Yo*

Key Expressions

よ	*yo*	
(≈) 会いたい、会いたいよ	*Aitai, aitai yo.*	I want to, I really want to see you.
行きますよ、行けばいいんでしょ	*Ikimasu yo, ikeba ii n desho.*	I'm going, and that's what you want, right?

Explanation

The utterance-final particle *yo* is often used for emphatic appeal. In general, *yo* alerts the partner to focus on what is being said. For example, the speaker alerts a passerby who has accidentally dropped his ticket by saying *Kippu otoshimashita yo* 'You dropped your ticket'. *Yo* demands special attention.

Partly because of this request for attention, *yo* often appeals to the partner's emotions. Obviously, one can express feelings without *yo*. But an added *yo* conveys urgency and has the feeling of "I'm telling you, can't you understand?" or "I'm telling you, please understand me." For example, when a speaker responds to a request by saying *Ikimasu yo* 'I'm going', it can mean a strong understanding-seeking reply, bordering on a defiant attitude—I'm going, don't you get it? For this reason, *yo* may be used to pass judgment emphatically and to vent one's opinion strongly.

Yo may be used with a high or a low tone. The high tone, because it focuses on information, may imply overeagerness and admonition, as in *Ki o tsukete unten shite yo* (with high tone) 'Please drive carefully, O.K.?' Pronounced in a lower tone, as in *Kaigi wa jikan doori hajimemashoo yo* 'Let's start the meeting, as planned', *yo* does not carry as much admonition.

Yo also signals a strong desire to reach the partner's heart. It implies "Please understand me, please understand how I feel." This is particularly so when two similar utterances are repeated once with and once without *yo*. By saying *Aitai* 'I want to see you' first and repeating *Aitai yo* 'I really want to see you', the speaker's desperate desire to reach the partner emotionally is expressed. In this way *yo* solicits the partner's emotional response.

When the talk consists of multiple sentences, *yo* is added to the sentences containing the main points. *Yo*-sentences aim to appeal directly to the partner, and that intention is normally associated with more substantive sentences. Obviously one should not overuse *yo* by tacking it onto everything.

Because *yo* demands attention, you should avoid using it when it assumes lack of knowledge on the part of a person to whom you should show respect. It is important to remind your boss by saying *Kyoo gogo kara kaigi desu ne* 'There's a meeting today in the afternoon', instead of *Kyoo gogo kara kaigi desu yo* 'There's a meeting today in the afternoon, O.K.?'.

The difference between *yo* and *ne* can be generalized in the following way. *Ne* is a particle conveying your concern for your partner's thoughts and feelings. You want to focus on or confirm what your partner is thinking and feeling. In contrast, *yo* requests your partner's concern for your sentiments. You use *yo* to direct your partner to focus on what you are thinking or feeling.

The combination of *yo* and *ne* exists as *yo ne*, but not as **ne yo*. In Japanese, it is generally understood that the closer an expression is to the end of a sentence, the less it focuses on information. Since *yo* has more to do with information than *ne*, *yo* appears before *ne*. The meaning of *yo ne* is a combination of (1) focus on the content of what the speaker is saying (information), and (2) the speaker's overriding concern for the partner's thoughts and feelings.

Examples

a. (A man seeks another man's attention)

(ma1): あの、これ落としましたよ。
(ma2): えっ？あ、ほんとだ。すみません。

(ma1): Ano, kore otoshimashita **yo**.
(ma2): E-tt? A, honto da. Sumimasen. (see E. 21 for *E-tt?*)

(ma1): Excuse me, but you dropped this.
(ma2): What? Oh, right. Thank you.

b. (A wife is upset as her husband asks her to take out the garbage)

(≈my1): このゴミ出しておいてくれないか。
(fy1): はい、出しますよ！出せばいいんでしょ！

(≈my1): Kono gomi dashiteoite-kure-nai ka.
(fy1): Hai, dashimasu yo! Daseba ii n desho!

(≈my1): Will you take out this garbage?
(fy1): Yes, I certainly will! I will take it out, all right!

c. (A man is concerned about his female colleague's going out alone)

(≈ma1a): 心配だなあ、ひとりで行くなんて。
(fa1a): 大丈夫です。
(≈ma1b): そう？
(fa1b): 大丈夫ですよ。

(≈ma1a): Shinpai da naa, hitori de iku nante. (see E. 15 for *nante*; E. 48 about inverted word order)
(fa1a): Daijoobu desu.
(≈ma1b): Soo?
(fa1b): Daijoobu desu yo.

(≈ma1a): I'm worried to see you go alone.
(fa1a): I'll be fine.
(≈ma1b): Really?
(fa1b): I'll be fine, for sure.

Authentic Examples

a. (Taken from *Long Love Letter Hyooryuu Kyooshitsu*, episode 9) Maioka receives a piece of candy from Isehara. Isehara, though hurt, has kept a piece of candy for her. She tastes the candy and breaks into tears. The use of *yo* in the second utterance, in contrast with the first, signals her strong desire to appeal to him.

舞岡： おいしい。（泣きながら）おいしいよ。

Maioka: Oishii. (*naki nagara*) Oishii **yo**. (see E. 24 about repetition)

Maioka: Delicious. (*while crying*) It is delicious, indeed.

b. (Taken from *Long Love Letter Hyooryuu Kyooshitsu*, episode 11) Yuka attempts to convince students that there is meaning in life. Her desire to appeal to the students emotionally is expressed in part by the use of *yo* added to *aru* when it appears for the second time.

柳瀬：　やはり僕達も滅びる運命なんだ**よ**。生きる意味なんてもうないんだ**よ**。
結花：　生きる意味はある。＃＃ある**よ**！

Yanase: Yahari bokutachi mo horobiru unmei na n da **yo**. Ikiru imi nante moo nai n da **yo**. (see E. 57 for *yahari*; E. 15 for *nante*)
Yuka: Ikiru imi wa aru. Aru **yo**! (see E. 24 about repetition)

Yanase: After all, we are destined to perish. Our life doesn't have any meaning anymore.
Yuka: Our life has meaning. It has meaning, for sure.

c. (Taken from *Majo no jooken*, episode 5) Hikaru first expresses his desire to see Michi, but there is no answer. So he repeats what he just said, this time with *yo*, adding a strong sense of appeal.

光：　会いたい。＃会いたい**よ**。
未知：　もうちょっと、待って。

Hikaru: Aitai. Aitai **yo**. (see E. 24 about repetition)
Michi: Moo chotto, matte. (see E. 25 for *chotto*)

Hikaru: I want to see you. I really want to see you.
Michi: Just a bit more, please wait.

d. (Taken from *Majo no jooken*, episode 11) Hikaru talks to Michi (who is in a coma) lying on the hospital bed. Here, the three main points—today's hot weather, his determination to become a medical doctor, and his wish for her to sleep comfortably—are marked by *yo*.

光：　今日はやたら暑い**よ**。外に一歩も出たくないって感じ。俺、決めた**よ**。俺、医者になる。医者になって、未知を必ず、生き返らせてみせる。ひとりでも多くの人を、苦しみから救ってみせる。幸せにしてみせる。だから、安心して眠っていていい**よ**。俺のそばで、眠っていていい。

Hikaru: Kyoo wa yatara atsui **yo**. Soto ni ippo mo detaku-nai tte kanji. Ore, kimeta **yo**. Ore, isha ni naru. Isha ni natte, Michi o kanarazu, ikikaerasete-miseru. Hitori demo ooku no hito o, kurushimi kara sukutte-miseru. Shiawase ni shite-miseru. Dakara, anshin shite nemuttete ii **yo**. Ore no soba de, nemuttete ii. (see E. 64 for *tte kanji*; E. 71 for *ikikaerasete-miseru*)

Hikaru: It's really hot today. I feel like I don't want to step outside at all. I made up my mind. I will be a medical doctor. I will be a doctor and I will make you well again, Michi. And I will relieve as many people as possible from suffering. I will make them happy. So, don't worry, just continue sleeping. Be asleep by my side.

e. (Taken from *Muko-dono*, episode 10) In this scene, Ryoo answers the phone. His friend asks a question first without, then with *yo*: *Doo yuu koto yo*. The second question makes a stronger appeal to Ryoo than the first in part because of *yo*.

亮：	もしもし。やっぱりおまえか**よ**。
友達：	これ、亮の家だ**よ**ね。絶対そうだ**よ**ね。どういうこと？ねえ、これ、どういうこと**よ**。
亮：	(...)いろいろあってさあ。(...)いいか、ぜーったいに学校で騒ぐな**よ**。

Ryoo:	Moshi moshi. Yappari omae ka **yo.** (see E. 57 for *yappari*)
tomodachi:	Kore, Ryoo no uchi da **yo** ne. Zettai soo da **yo** ne. Doo yuu koto? Nee, kore, doo yuu koto **yo.** (see E. 54 for *nee*; E. 24 about repetition)
Ryoo:	(...) Iroiro atte saa. (...) Ii ka, zeettai ni gakkoo de sawagu-na **yo.** (see E. 27 for *zeettai ni* instead of *zettai ni*)

Ryoo:	Hello. I thought it was you.
friend:	This is Ryoo's home, isn't it? It is so, isn't it? What's happening? Really, what is happening?
Ryoo:	(...) Well, it's a bit complicated. (...) I'm telling you. Don't make a big fuss over this at school, got that?

f. (Taken from *Ren'ai hakusho*, 14: 121) Kaho talks with Sumire. Sumire is aggressive and orders Kaho around, saying things that Kaho doesn't know. Note the use of *nasai*, which shows Sumire's power over Kaho. Sumire is in a strong position and demands attention from Kaho. This is conveyed in part by the use of *yo*.

「どのヘン？」
「たしか、寺町通り**よ**」
すみれちゃんが口を挟んだ。
「ありがと」
「地図貸しなさい**よ**。ここ**よ**。ここ」
すみれちゃんが、あたしたちの間にぐっと割り込んでくる。
「今夜泊まる旅館から、すぐのとこ**よ**。ここの通りは、いいわ**よー**。一保堂っていうお茶のお店が、渋くていい感じなの**よ**。喫茶室もあってねー」

"Dono hen?"
"Tashika, Teramachi doori **yo**"
Sumire-chan ga kuchi o hasanda.
"Arigato"
"Chizu kashinasai **yo.** Koko **yo.** Koko"
Sumire-chan ga, atashitachi no aida ni gutto warikonde-kuru.

"Kon'ya tomaru ryokan kara, sugu no toko **yo**. Koko no toori wa, ii wa **yoo**. Ippoodoo tte yuu ocha no omise ga, shibukute ii kanji na no **yo**. Kissashitsu mo atte nee"

"Where is it?"

"I'm sure it is on Teramachi Street."

Sumire joined the conversation.

"Thank you."

"Give me the map. Here, you see. Right here."

Sumire approaches closer and comes between us.

"It is right close by the inn where we are staying tonight. This street is nice. The tea shop, Ippoodoo, is rustic and tasteful. They have a tea lounge, too."

56. Sharing Empathy through the Particle *Mo*

Key Expressions

も	*mo*	
(≈) あの子も高校に行く歳になったのね	*Ano ko mo kookoo ni iku toshi ni natta no ne.*	She has become the age to become a high school student (already).
(≈) 君も大変だったねえ	*Kimi mo taihen datta nee.*	It must have been very difficult for you (I know).

Explanation

The particle *mo* is often used as a topic marker to mean 'also' or 'too', as in *Watashi mo iku* 'I'm going, too'. *Mo* is also used to mean 'as many as' as in *Juunin mo kimashita* 'As many as ten people showed up' and 'even' as in *Sonna koto mo shira-nai n desu ka* 'You don't even know that?'

These and other meanings associated with *mo* originate in its basic meaning of 'also', which suggests and implies other related items. This entry focuses on a specific use of *mo*, namely, a situation in which the speaker realizes a change and compares it with how it used to be with a sense of surprise and admiration, as in *Ano ko mo kookoo ni iku toshi ni natta no ne* 'She has become the age to become a high school student (already)'. Here *mo* expresses varied feelings, including the sense of being moved, exclamation, sympathy, admiration, and support.

Examples

a. (Two women lamenting that the cherry blossoms are gone) Using *mo* here instead of *wa* adds to the exclamative effect. The speaker is that much moved, and the partner shares that feeling by making a similar comment.

(fs1): 今年の桜**も**もう終りですね。
(fs2): そうですね、もうほとんど散ってしまいましたね。

(fs1): Kotoshi no sakura **mo** moo owari desu ne.
(fs2): Soo desu ne, moo hotondo chitte-shimaimashita ne. (see E. 17 for *chitte-shimaimashita*)

(fs1): This year's cherry blossoms are over, aren't they?
(fs2): Indeed, most of them are gone.

b. (Two men expressing feelings of desperation after a bad meeting)

(≈ma1a): 世**も**末だ。
(≈ma2a): まったく。
(≈ma1b): あんなふざけた案が通ってしまうなんて、みんなどうかしてるよ。
(≈ma2b): ほんとだよ。議長**も**だらしないよな、全く。

(≈ma1a): Yo **mo** sue da.
(≈ma2a): Mattaku.
(≈ma1b): Anna fuzaketa an ga tootte-shimau nante, minna dooka shiteru yo. (see E. 15 for *nante*)
(≈ma2b): Honto da yo. Gichoo **mo** darashi-nai yo na, mattaku. (see E. 48 about inverted word order)

(≈ma1a): This is the end of the world.
(≈ma2a): Absolutely.
(≈ma1b): To approve such a silly proposal, everyone is crazy.
(≈ma2b): Really. The chairperson is hopeless, really.

c. (Two high school teachers talking about a problem student) The partner shows sympathy toward the teacher by using *mo*. Likewise, the teacher shows emotion toward the parents in part by using *mo*.

(≈ma1a): また、うちのクラスの生徒が事件を起こしちゃってね。
(fa1a): え、ほんとですか。
(≈ma1b): これで、もう三度目。
(fa1b): 先生**も**大変ですねえ。
(≈ma1c): ああいう子供を持つと親**も**苦労するよな。

(≈ma1a): Mata, uchi no kurasu no seito ga jiken o okoshichatte ne. (see Chapter 3 about *uchi*; E. 17 for *okoshichatte*)
(fa1a): E, honto desu ka. (see E. 21 for *E, honto desku ka*)
(≈ma1b): Kore de, moo sandome.
(fa1b): Sensei **mo** taihen desu nee. (see E. 61 for *taihen*)
(≈ma1c): Aa yuu kodomo o motsu to oya **mo** kuroo suru yo na.

(≈ma1a): Again, a student in my class has gotten involved in trouble.
(fa1a): Really?
(≈ma1b): This is the third time already.
(fa1b): It must be hard for you.
(≈ma1c): Having that kind of a child, the parents must have a very hard time.

Authentic Examples

a. (Taken from *Chibi Maruko-chan*, 14: 144-145) Maruko's grandfather talks to the father of Tamae, Maruko's best friend. The grandfather is overemotional and brings up the fact that Tamae will one day leave home to get married.

祖父： ＜たまちゃんも/いつか嫁に/行ってしまうん/ですね＞
たまえの父： ＜ハァ …＞
祖父： ＜おとうさんも / さみしいでしょう＞
たまえの父： ＜え…まだ/あんまり/考えたこと/ないですけど/……＞

sofu: Tama-chan **mo** itsuka yome ni itte-shimau n desu ne. (see E. 17 for *itte-shimau*)
Tamae no chichi: Haa…
sofu: Otoosan **mo** samishii deshoo. (see E. 8 for *samishii*)
Tamae no chichi: E,… mada anmari kangaeta koto nai desu kedo…… (see E. 63 for *kedo*)

grandfather: Tama-chan will one day marry and leave home, won't she?
Tamae's father: Yes, I suppose so.
grandfather: You must feel lonely as a father.
Tamae's father: Uh, I haven't thought about it much.

b. (Taken from *Kitchin*, 50 [English translation, 32]) The narrator emotionally realizes that time has passed and the man has grown old.

子供のころよく入った管理人室で、おじさんの入れたほうじ茶を飲んで話をした。彼も年を取ったなあ。と私はしみじみ思う。

Kodomo no koro yoku haitta kanrininshitsu de, ojisan no ireta hoojicha o nonde hanashi o shita. Kare **mo** toshi o totta naa. To watashi wa shimijimi omou. (see E. 1 for *shimijimi*)

Like we often did when I was a child, we drank tea and chatted in his office. I felt very keenly how old he had become.

c. (Taken from *Furuete nemure, sanshimai*, 72) Masako talks with Yuriko and offers an empathy-seeking comment by recognizing Yuriko's suffering.

夕里子は、自分の紅茶を一口飲んだが、苦くて、飲めたものではなかった。
「—でも、あんたも大変ね。一人っ子？」

Yuriko wa, jibun no koocha o hitokuchi nonda ga, nigakute, nometa mono de wa nakatta.
"—Demo, anta **mo** taihen ne. Hitorikko?" (see E. 30 for *anta*; E. 61 for *taihen*)

Yuriko had a sip of the tea, but it was too bitter to drink.
"—Anyway, you must have had a hard time. Are you an only child?"

57. Appealing to Social-Expectation-Based Empathy

Key Expressions

どうせ	*doose*	anyway
やっぱり	*yappari*	after all, as expected, as I thought
さすが	*sasuga*	indeed, as expected

Explanation

A number of Japanese adverbs express the speaker's attitude toward an event that is being described. Although the attitudes expressed by these adverbs are personal, they are closely associated with social expectations. Besides the attitudinal adverbs *semete*, *sekkaku*, and *masaka* introduced in Entry 14, this entry addresses three adverbs of attitude: *doose*, *yappari*, and *sasuga*.

Doose is used to express the speaker's attitude of resignation: "It can't happen anyway." The feeling is that no matter how one tackles the situation, a certain conclusion is predetermined and will inevitably ensue. This destined conclusion is partly based on how the speaker understands the way things happen in society. There is a sense of giving up in *doose*. When using *doose*, the speaker is abandoning the idea that he or she can make a difference. Things are going to happen anyway simply because this is how things are expected to happen in society, and there isn't much anyone can do to change it.

Yappari (formal *yahari*; very casual *yappa*) is used when an action turns out to be in accordance with the speaker's expectations. The expectation can be something personal, as, for example, when you see someone in the distance who looks like your friend. Then the person comes closer, and it turns out indeed to be the friend. You may say to yourself *Yappari Aoki-san da* 'It's Aoki, as I thought'. At the same time, one's expectation is often influenced by how society works. For example, the store always opens five minutes before the posted opening hour, and *yahari* it is open five minutes early this morning. *Yappari* is also used to point out that one's position is in agreement with the consensus. For example, everyone you know is against the strike, and you may join in with *Yappari watashi mo hantai desu* 'I'm also against it'.

Particularly interesting is the frequent use of *yappari* as conversation filler and preface. By inserting *yappari* during the pause, the speaker avoids a direct and straightforward presentation of his or her view while soliciting empathy. By prefacing with *yappari*, the speaker gives the impression that what follows is already relevant to the conversation, or that what follows is something the partner may also be thinking. *Yappari* implies that the topic has already been discussed and as a consequence adds to a sense of familiarity.

Yappari may also be used when the speaker insists on something on second thought or despite what is expected. For example, even when someone tells a man not to go, he may say *Ore yappari iku wa* 'I'm going after all'. In this case *yappari* corresponds with the speaker's earlier thought.

Sasuga is used to emphasize the truth held by most people in the society. For example, Mt. Fuji is known for its beauty. And when one sees it, one may say *Fujisan tte sasuga subarashii nee* 'Mt. Fuji is great, indeed (as understood in the society)'. Unlike *yappari,* which emphasizes the agreement between fact and convention, *sasuga* emphasizes the truth of the convention with a sense of admiration.

Authentic Examples

a. (Taken from *Majo no jooken*, episode 1) Hikaru shows resignation in part through *doose*. Hikaru has already left one high school, so he thinks this one isn't going to be fun either.

光：　なんか、中に入るのが気重くて。
未知：　どうして？
光：　**どうせ**この学校にいても、いいことなさそうだし。
未知：　あるわよ。
光：　えっ？

Hikaru: Nanka, naka ni hairu no ga ki omokute. (see E. 62 for *nanka*)
Michi: Doo shite?
Hikaru: **Doose** kono gakkoo ni itemo, ii koto nasasoo da shi. (see E. 63 about the use of *shi*)
Michi: Aru wa yo. (see E. 55 for *yo*)
Hikaru: E-tt? (see E. 21 for *E-tt?*)

Hikaru: Somehow I feel discouraged about going in.
Michi: Why?
Hikaru: It seems that good things won't happen at this school anyway.
Michi: Yes, they will.
Hikaru: What?

b. (Taken from *Chibi Maruko-chan*, 14: 111) Maruko's father is trying to quit smoking, and family members comment. Given past experiences, family members don't have much hope that the father will stick with his resolution. The grandmother expresses fatalism with *doose*, but Maruko expresses her admiration with *sasuga*.

姉： <おとうさん / けっこう我慢 / 強いね>
祖母： <ねえ　**どうせ** / 今日はもう / タバコ吸うと / 思って / いたのに>
まる子： <えらいね / **さすが** ..../ おとうさんだ>
父： <えっ / そうかい / アハハ>

ane: Otoosan kekkoo gamanzuyoi ne. (see E. 25 for *kekkoo*)
sobo: Nee. **Doose** kyoo wa moo tabako suu to omotteita noni.
Maruko: Erai ne. **Sasuga** ....otoosan da.
chichi: E-tt soo kai. Aha ha. (see E. 21 for *E-tt*)

sister: Father is quite persistent, isn't he?
grandmother: Isn't he? I thought he would start smoking today anyway.
Maruko: As expected, great, my father is great.
father: Really, you think so? Ha, ha.

c. (Taken from *Tsubasa o kudasai*, 191) Tsubaki accuses Kyooka of snitching to the teacher, implying that she is just such a person. Kyooka responds helplessly with *doose*.

「京歌。... あんたチクッたんでしょ」
「ちがうって言っても**どうせ**信じないんでしょう」

"Kyooka....Anta chikutta n desho." (see E. 30 for *anta*)
"Chigau tte ittemo **doose** shiji-nai n deshoo."

"Kyooka. You snitched to the teacher, didn't you?"
"Even if I deny it, you wouldn't believe me anyway."

d. (Taken from *Beautiful Life*, episode 5) Miyama brings Kyooko's old high school friend to the library. This friend, Tetsu, is also confined to a wheelchair.

美山：　なんかね、すっごいいい感じ。俺もうれしいなって思って。
杏子：　えっ？
美山：　**やっぱり**昔の仲間ってほっとできて安心するんですよね。

Miyama: Nanka ne, suggoi ii kanji. Ore mo ureshii na tte omotte. (see E. 62 for *nanka*; E. 24 and E. 27 for *suggoi*; E. 5 for *ureshii*)
Kyooko: E-tt? (see E. 21 for *E-tt?*)
Miyama: **Yappari** mukashi no nakama tte hotto dekite anshin suru n desu yo ne. (see E. 47 for *tte*; E. 22 for *hotto suru*; E. 72 for *n desu*)

Miyama: You know, you two together are really nice. I'm happy for you, too.
Kyooko: What?
Miyama: After all, friends from long ago are comforting, and you feel secure, I know.

e. (Taken from *Chibi Maruko-chan*, 14: 137) Maruko, disappointed, expresses her frustration with both *yappari* and *doose*.

まる子：　＜あーあ　**やっぱり** / ダメだったな＞ ＜おとーさんに / 言ったって / ムリなんだ / **どうせ** ... ＞

Maruko: Aaa **yappari** dame datta na. Otoosan ni ittatte muri na n da **doose**. (see E. 72 for *n da*; E. 48 about inverted word order)

Maruko: Oh well, it's no good after all. Asking my father won't do any good anyway.

f. (Taken from *SMAP x SMAP,* special live show) In this conversation, Shingo raises an issue with *yappari,* which Nakai has just used. Because *yappari* communicates the speaker's feelings, Shingo is concerned about Nakai's somewhat negative attitude.

中居：　難しいな。どこまでが冗談なのか、どこまでがまじめな話なのか、全然分かんないでしょ。
吾郎：　あ、ほんと。
中居：　何が。
吾郎：　や、本気、本気、本気。
中居：　あ、**やっぱり**かみあわない。
慎吾：　**やっぱり**ってどういうことよ。
中居：　**やっぱり**あわない、吾郎とは。
慎吾：　**やっぱり**とは。

Nakai: Muzukashii na. Doko made ga joodan na no ka, doko made ga majimena hanashi na no ka, zenzen wakan-nai desho. (see E. 67 for *majimena hanashi*; E. 66 for *wakan-nai*)
Goroo: A, honto.
Nakai: Nani ga.
Goroo: Ya, honki, honki, honki. (see E. 24 about repetition)
Nakai: A, **yappari** kamiawa-nai.
Shinko: **Yappari** tte doo yuu koto yo. (see E. 70 about echo questions)
Nakai: **Yappari** awa-nai, Goroo to wa. (see E. 48 about inverted word order)
Shingo: **Yappari** to wa. (see E. 70 about echo responses)

Nakai: I find it difficult. You never know how much of what he says is a joke and how much of it is serious, do you?
Goroo: Ah, it's true.
Nakai: What is true?
Goroo: So, I'm serious, serious, serious.
Nakai: Ah, as I thought (*yappari*), we don't quite understand each other.
Shingo: What do you mean by "*yappari*"?
Nakai: As I thought (*yappari*), I am not quite on the same wavelength with Goroo.
Shingo: What is this "*yappari*"?

g. (Taken from *Beautiful Life*, episode 5) Takumi, who works under Shuuji, is talking to a magazine editor. Takumi admiringly communicates to this editor that she is savvy, as a good editor is expected to be.

編集長：最近、柊二さんすごいわね、いろいろな雑誌でスタイリングしてて。
タクミ：あっ、**さすが**編集長。気づきました？
編集長：まあね。でもモデルつくってもらうのもいいんだけど、本人に出て欲しかったりして。彼カッコいいし。
タクミ：あ、そうですよね。

henshuuchoo: Saikin, Shuuji-san sugoi wa ne, iroirona zasshi de sutairingu shitete. (see E. 13 for *sugoi*; E. 48 about inverted word order)
Takumi: A-tt, **sasuga** henshuuchoo. Kizukimashita?
henshuuchoo: Maa ne. Demo moderu tsukutte-morau no mo ii n da kedo, honnin ni dete hoshikattari shite. Kare kakko ii shi. (see E. 42 for *honnin*; E. 63 for *hoshikattari shite*; E. 13 for *kakko ii*; E. 63 for *shi*)
Takumi: A, soo desu yo ne. (see E. 55 for *yo ne*)

editor:	Recently Shuuji is hot, isn't he? His hair styling is featured in many magazines.
Takumi:	Wow, as always, you (as an editor) notice those things, indeed!
editor:	I guess. You know, it's good to feature his styling, but I sort of want him, himself, to be featured. He is neat and nice-looking.
Takumi:	Yeah, he certainly is.

h. (Taken from *Long Love Letter Hyooryuu Kyooshitsu*, episode 1) Asami is talking to Wakahara about the students' behavior, particularly the fad of ear piercing.

浅海：	何て言うか#軽くなりたいんじゃないですかね。こう、風通しが良くなるっていうか。
若原：	**さすが**若者に理解が深いね、ミスター浅海。
Asami:	Nan te yuu ka, karuku naritai n ja-nai desu ka ne. Koo, kaze tooshi ga yoku naru tte yuu ka. (see E. 63 for *tte yuu ka*)
Wakahara:	**Sasuga** wakamono ni rikai ga fukai ne, misutaa Asami.
Asami:	How should I put it, isn't it that they want to feel light? In that way the wind goes through their (pierced) ears, should I say.
Wakahara:	As I thought, you understand how the young people feel, don't you, Mr. Asami.

58. Good-Natured Teasing

Key Expressons

(≈) ばかじゃない？	*Baka ja-nai?*	You foolish thing!
(≈) ばーか	*Baaka!*	You fool!
(≈) 憎いねえ、人気者！	*Nikui nee, ninki-mono!*	I could hate you (for it), Mr. Popular!

Explanation

Good-natured teasing is a sign of intimacy. Because teasing and the response to teasing involve seemingly derogatory terms, it is necessary to understand the context. Just as important are the accompanying cues, and particular facial expressions and tones of voice. They communicate that the speaker does not mean the words to be taken literally. He or she is simply enjoying some good-natured teasing.

When someone says *Baka!* 'Silly thing!' in a flirtatious way, it is an obvious expression of love. Even a phrase like *Nikurashii hito!* '(lit.) hateful person' can be used teasingly to show strong affection. Literal interpretation is hardly enough when interpreting expressive Japanese.

Examples

a. (A boy and a girl are teasing each other) *Baaka* and *baka ja-nee no* are used endearingly in a coy, flirtatious way.

(≈mt1a): 君のそういうとこ、かわいいよな。
(≈ft1a): **ばーか**。でも、茂樹ってやさしいよね。
(≈mt1b): そうかな。
(≈ft1b): そうだよ。だから好き。
(□mt1c): **ばかじゃねえの**、おまえ。

(≈mt1a): Kimi no soo yuu toko, kawaii yo na. (see E. 31 for *kawaii*)
(≈ft1a): **Baaka**. Demo, Shigeki tte yasashii yo ne. (see E. 47 for *tte*; E. 6 for *yasashii*)
(≈mt1b): Soo ka na. (see E. 46 for *Soo ka na*)
(≈ft1b): Soo da yo. Dakara suki. (see E. 32 for *suki*)
(□mt1c): **Baka ja-nee no**, omae. (see Chapter 2 for *ja-nee* instead of *ja-nai*; E. 30 for *omae*)

(≈mt1a): The way you do things is really cute.
(≈ft1a): Oh, dear, foolish you! But, Shigeki, you are a gentle person.
(≈mt1b): Am I really?
(≈ft1b): Yes. That's why I love you.
(□mt1c): You silly thing!

b. (A man teasingly congratulates his friend on his success)

(≈ma1a): なんか、また賞をもらったんだって？
(≈ma2a): うん、そうなんだ。
(≈ma1b): **憎いねえ**、人気者！
(≈ma2b): へへ、そういうわけでもないんだけどさ。

(≈ma1a): Nanka, mata shoo o moratta n datte? (see E. 62 for *nanka*)
(≈ma2a): Un, soo na n da.
(≈ma1b): **Nikui nee**, ninkimono!
(≈ma2b): He he, soo yuu wake de mo nai n da kedo sa. (see E. 63 for *kedo*)

(≈ma1a): I hear you received another award. Is that right?
(≈ma2a): Yeah, that's right.
(≈ma1b): Boy, I hate you, Mr. Popular!
(≈ma2b): Heh, heh. It's not that I'm really popular, you know.

Authentic Examples

a. (Taken from *Beautiful Life*, episode 11) Kyooko confesses it was wonderful to have known Shuuji. Kyooko is in the hospital, and she knows that she may not live long. Shuuji responds teasingly, partly to make light of things.

杏子：　でもさすが神様。最後にすごく素敵なことあった。
柊二：　何？
杏子：　柊二。私の人生のスペシャル。
柊二：　何言ってんの。**バカじゃねえの。**

Kyooko: Demo sasuga kamisama. Saigo ni sugoku sutekina koto atta. (see E. 57 for *sasuga*; E. 24 for *sugoku*; E. 13 for *sutekina*)
Shuuji: Nani?
Kyooko: Shuuji. Watashi no jinsei no supesharu.
Shuuji: Nani itten no? **Baka ja-nee no.** (see E. 40 for *Nani itten no?*)

Kyooko: But, God is really something. A wonderful thing happened to me at the end.
Shuuji: What is it?
Kyooko: You, Shuuji. A special event in my life.
Shuuji: What are you talking about? Silly thing, aren't you!

b. (Taken from *Beautiful Life*, episode 11) Masao teasingly talks about Shuuji, to which Kyooko responds with a teasing denial.

杏子：　そのチャパツ、髪くるくるぼうずって誰よ。
正夫：　おまえの、ダーリンだよ。
杏子：　何言ってんの？**バカじゃないの。**

Kyooko: Sono chapatsu, kami kurukuru boozu tte dare yo. (see E. 47 for *tte*)
Masao: Omae no, daarin da yo.
Kyooko: Nani itten no? **Baka ja-nai no.** (see E. 40 for *Nani itten no?*)

Kyooko: Who do you mean by a guy with curly brown hair?
Masao: I'm talking about him, your lover.
Kyooko: What are you talking about? You're being silly, aren't you?

c. (Taken from *Dokkin paradaisu*, 3: 103) Akira is a bit angry that his sister was wounded trying to save him. His use of *Baka da yo na* is not to be interpreted straightforwardly. It is an endearing expression, although on the surface it sounds like a criticism.

「**バカだよな**、お前」
やさしいけど、ちょっとだけ怒ったような声だった。
「ほんと**バカ**だぜ。なんだって、オレをかばって銃口の前に飛び出したりしたんだよ」

"**Baka da yo na,** omae." (see E. 30 for *omae*)
Yasashii kedo, chotto dake okotta yoona koe datta. (see E. 6 for *yasashii*; E. 10 for *okoru*)
"Honto **baka** da ze. Nan da tte, ore o kabatte juukoo no mae ni tobidashitari shita n da yo."

"You are a fool, really."
He said [this] in a tender but slightly angry voice.
"You are a fool. Why did you step in front of the muzzle of a gun to save me?"

59. Appealing to *Amae*

Key Expressions

(≈) だって…	*Datte.*	But…
(≈) だっておもしろくないんだもの	*Datte omoshiroku-nai n da mono.*	Because it isn't fun.
ねえ、いいでしょ	*Nee, ii desho.*	Please, please, can I?
お願い！	*Onegai!*	I beg you!
(≈) お願いだから	*Onegai da kara.*	Please, I beg you.

Explanation

As explained in Chapter 3, *amae* is based on a strong sense of intimacy. Once *amae* is established, the speaker may use expressions that appeal to this intimate relationship. Some representative phrases for this purpose are *datte*, *ii desho*, and *onegai*. Using these expressions confirms and enhances the *amae* relationship even more.

Datte is used when the speaker feels that he or she is being unjustly criticized and wants to correct it. Although the speaker may specify the desired correction, in an appeal for *amae*, *datte* often appears alone. By using *datte* only, the speaker hopes that there is no need to spell out reasons, which may simply be excuses or irrelevant points.

Sentence-final *mon(o)* is often used with *datte*. The nominalizer *mon(o)* (in this use) presents an explanation, not so much in the sense of cause and effect, but in the sense that it provides information unknown to the partner. When appealing to the *amae* relationship, the *datte* sentence often ends with *n(o) da mon(o)*.

Other frequent expressions related to *amae* are *Ii desho* '(lit.) It's O.K., isn't it?' and *Onegai* 'I beg you'. These are requests addressed to the *amae* partner and must be avoided toward a partner to whom one usually shows respect or from whom one maintains distance.

Examples

a. (A mother scolding her son) The son responds with *datte*(*e*) twice, only to provide an unconvincing excuse.

(≈fa1a): ご飯食べないで、アイスクリームなんか食べちゃだめでしょ。
(≈mc1a): **だってー。**
(≈fa1b): お腹こわすわよ。
(≈mc1b): **だって**、好きなんだ**もん**。

(≈fa1a): Gohan tabe-naide, aisukuriimu nanka tabecha dame desho. (see E. 15 for *nanka*)
(≈mc1a): **Dattee.** (see E. 27 for *dattee* instead of *datte*)
(≈fa1b): Onaka kowasu wa yo.
(≈mc1b): **Datte,** suki na n da **mon.**

(≈fa1a): You shouldn't have ice cream without eating a real meal, right?
(≈mc1a) But, you know...
(≈fa1b): You'll get an upset stomoch.
(≈mc1b): But, [it's] because I love ice cream.

b. (A child tries to convince her father to buy her a bicycle)

(≈fc1a): **お願い**！あの自転車買って。
(≈ma1a): ダメだ。
(≈fc1b): ねえ、**いいでしょ**。みんな自転車乗ってるよ。
(≈ma1b): ダメだよ。
(≈fc1c): **お願いだから**！

(≈fc1a): **Onegai!** Ano jitensha katte.
(≈ma1a): Dame da. (see E. 18 for *dame*)
(≈fc1b): Nee, **ii desho.** Minna jitensha notteru yo.
(≈ma1b): Dame da yo. (see E. 55 about the use and non-use of *yo*)
(≈fc1c): **Onegai da kara!**

(≈fc1a): Please, it's O.K., isn't it? Will you buy me that bicycle?
(≈ma1a): No.
(≈fc1b): Please, please, if you will. Everyone rides a bicycle.
(≈ma1b): No way.
(≈fc1c): Please, please (I beg you)!

Authentic Examples

a. (Taken from *Majo no jooken*, episode 3) Female students come to see Ms. Shimoda, who suggests that they should see Michi instead. A student uses *datte*, appealing to Shimoda's understanding.

下田：　これだったら広瀬先生に教えてもらいなさい。
女子生徒：　**だって**、ねえ。(笑う) 男ナンパする方法とかなら、教えてもらえそうだけどね。＃あ冗談ですよ。冗談。

Shimoda: Kore dattara Hirose-sensei ni oshiete-morainasai.
joshiseito: **Datte**, nee. (*warau*) Otoko nanpa suru hoohoo toka nara, oshiete-moraesoo da kedo ne. A joodan desu yo. Joodan. (see E. 29 for *nanpa suru*; E. 62 for *toka*; 47 for *nara*; E. 45 for *joodan*)

Shimoda: These questions, why don't you have Ms. Hirose tutor you?
female student: Because, you know...(*laugh*) Well, maybe she can give me instructions on how to seduce men, but...Oh, I'm just joking. It's a joke.

b. (Taken from *Muko-dono*, episode 8) Kaede appeals to her younger sister, Sakura, but Sakura senses the desire for *amae* and warns against it. Note that Sakura uses *amae* in her response.

かえで：　さくらちゃん。
さくら：　どうしてサイン会に行ったのよ。
かえで：　えへ。
さくら：　笑ってごまかさない。
かえで：　**だってー＝**
さくら：　＝甘えてもダメ。どうしてそう勝手なことするの？

Kaede: Sakura-chan.
Sakura: Dooshite sainkai ni itta no yo.
Kaede: Ehe.
Sakura: Waratte gomakasa-nai.
Kaede: **Dattee=**
Sakura: =Amaetemo dame. Doo shite soo kattena koto suru no? (see E. 18 for *dame*)

Kaede: Sakura.
Sakura: Why did you go to the book signing?
Kaede: Uh, heh.
Sakura: Don't think you can get away by laughing.
Kaede: Well, but =
Sakura: = No use sweetly trying to make me forgive you. Why do you do such selfish things?

c. (Taken from *Strawberry on the Shortcake*, episode 2) Yui, sleeping during her classical Japanese class in high school, is awakened by her teacher, who calls her last name. In response to Yui's *datte*, the teacher asks a question repeating the phrase.

先生： 入江。
唯： (眠りからさめて)はーい。
先生： 転校そうそういい度胸してるな。
唯： **だってー。**
先生： だって何だ。
唯： おもしろくないんだ**もん**。(他の生徒、笑う)

sensei: Irie.
Yui: (*nemuri kara asmete*) Haai.
sensei: Tenkoo soosoo ii dokyoo shiteru na.
Yui: **Dattee.**
sensei: Datte nan da. (see E. 70 about echo questions)
Yui: Omoshiroku-nai n da **mon**. (*hoka no seito, warau*)

teacher: Irie.
Yui: (*now awakened from her sleep*) Yes.
teacher: You are pretty bold to do this right after you were transferred to this school.
Yui: But...
teacher: But what?
Yui: It's not interesting. (*other students laugh*)

d. (Taken from *Antiiku, seiyoo kotto yoogashiten*, episode 7) Hideko asks her father, who is divorced, if she can stay with him. Hideko uses *amae*-seeking expressions, for example, *Nee ii desho*.

ヒデコ： **ねえ、いいでしょ**。#ね、いいよね。私パパといたい。パパと暮らしたい！#パパ。
父： ##それは困るな。

Hideko: **Nee, ii desho**. Ne, ii yo ne. Watashi papa to itai. Papa to kurashitai! Papa.
chichi: Sore wa komaru na. (see E. 18 for *komaru*)

Hideko: Please, it's O.K., isn't it? It's O.K., right? I want to be with you, Papa. I want to live with you, Papa.
father: That's a bit of a problem.

e. (Taken from *Muko-dono*, episode 7) Yuuichiroo, in a sweet *amae*-soliciting approach, begs Hakozaki to come along to help him.

祐一郎： あ#ハコさん一緒に来てくださいよ。
箱崎： 何で私が一緒に行かなきゃならないんだよ。

祐一郎：　**お願い**。
箱崎：　えー。
祐一郎：　**お願い**。
箱崎：　いやだよ。
祐一郎：　＃＃ねーもうハコさんしか頼れる人いないッスよ。
箱崎：　都合のいい時だけそんなこと言って。

Yuuichiroo: A, Hako-san issho ni kite-kudasai yo.
Hakozaki: Nande watashi ga issho ni ikanakya naranai n da yo. (see E. 40 about rhetorical questions)
Yuuichiroo: **Onegai.**
Hakozaki: Ee.
Yuuichiroo: **Onegai.**
Hakozaki: Iya da yo. (see E. 9 for *Iya da*)
Yuuichiroo: Nee moo Hako-san shika tayoreru hito i-nai ssu yo.
Hakozaki: Tsugoo no ii toki dake sonna koto itte. (see E. 63 about ending the utterance with the [V/Adj-*te*] form)

Yuuichiroo: Please, Hako, please come with me.
Hakozaki: Why do I have to go with you?
Yuuichiroo: Please.
Hakozaki: Now what.
Yuuichiroo: Please, please.
Hakozako: No, I won't.
Yuuichiroo Please, there is no one else but you, Hako, that I can depend on.
Hakozaki: You say so only when you need me, don't you.

Note

It should be noted that the combination of *datte* and *n da* or *mon*(*o*) is not used exclusively in *amae* relationships, but prefaces legitimate justifications or arguments as well. For example, observe (1), in which the clause following *datte* offers a relevant reason.

1. (Taken from *Kitchin*, 19 [English translation, 12])

「みかげさん、家の母親にビビった？」
彼は言った。
「うん、**だって**あんまりきれいなんだもの」

"Mikage-san, uchi no hahaoya ni bibitta?" (see E. 11 for *bibiru*)
Kare wa itta.
"Un, **datte** anmari kireina n da mono."

"Mikage," he said, "were you a little bit intimidated by my mother?"
"Yes," I told him frankly. "I've never seen a woman that beautiful."

60. Showing Concern

Key Expressions

(≈) 何かあった？	*Nan ka atta?*	Did something wrong happen? Is everything all right?
どうかしましたか？	*Doo ka shimashita ka?*	Is there something wrong?
どうしました？	*Doo shimashita?*	What happened (to you)?
大丈夫ですか？	*Daijoobu desu ka?*	Are you all right? Is everything O.K.?

Explanation

A number of expressions can be used to show concern. *Nan(i) ka atta?* 'Did something wrong happen?' is used in casual conversation to show concern for someone the speaker is familiar with. Answers vary. The partner may choose not to elaborate on the problem, but at least the speaker has conveyed his or her concern. A more polite way to show concern is to ask *Doo ka shimashita ka?* 'Is there something wrong?'. *Doo shimashita?* is slightly more direct because it assumes that something wrong did happen to the partner. The very polite forms of these expressions are *Doo nasaimashita ka* and *Doo ka nasaimashita?*.

Daijoobu desu ka? (or *Daijoobu?*) 'Are you all right?' usually occurs when the speaker knows something about the problem that seems to be bothering the partner. If the partner is all right, *Daijoobu desu* (or *Daijoobu*) is the most typical response.

Examples

a. (A young man is concerned about his friend)

(≈my1a): **何かあった？**
(≈my2a): どうして？
(≈my1b): だって、元気ないよ。
(≈my2b): うん。ちょっと困ってるんだ。

(≈my1a): **Nan ka atta?**
(≈my2a): Doo shite?
(≈my1b): Datte, genki nai yo.
(≈my2b): Un. Chotto komatteru n da. (see E. 18 for *komatteru*; E. 72 for *n da*)

(≈my1a): Did something wrong happen?
(≈my2a): Why?
(≈my1b): You look like you're down.
(≈my2b): Yeah. I'm having a bit of a problem.

b. (A woman politely asks a stranger who seems to be in trouble)

(≠fa1): **どうかなさいましたか。**
(fs1): いえ、**大丈夫です**。すみません。

(≠fa1): **Doo ka nasaimashita ka?**
(fs1): Ie, **daijoobu desu**. Sumimasen.

(≠fa1): Is there something wrong?
(fs1): No, I'm O.K. Thank you.

Authentic Examples

a. (Taken from *Majo no jooken*, episode 10) Michi senses that something is wrong.

未知： **何かあった？**
光： うちの病院、もう母さんのものじゃないんだ。
未知： えっ？
光： 乗っ取ろうとした奴がいて、そいつにだまされて。

Michi: **Nanka atta?**
Hikaru: Uchi no byooin, moo kaasan no mono ja-nai n da. (see Chapter 3 about the use of *uchi*; E. 72 for *n da*)
Michi: E-tt? (see E. 21 for *E-tt?*)
Hikaru: Nottoroo to shita yatsu ga ite, soitsu ni damasarete. (see E. 30 for *yatsu* and *soitsu*)

Michi: Did something wrong (bad) happen?
Hikaru: The hospital owned by my family, it is no longer owned by my mother.
Michi: What?
Hikaru: This guy tried to take it over, and she was deceived by him.

b. (Taken from *Ren'ai hakusho*, 14: 36–37) Maho shows concern for Kaho. Note how Kaho responds, pretending that there is nothing wrong.

「果歩？**どうかした**」(...)
「な …… なんでもないけど ……」
「なんでもないわけないでしょ？」
真保ちゃんが、突っ込む。
「ショックな顔してる」

「え？うそ、ほんと？」
「ほんとだってば」

"Kaho? **Doo ka shita**"
"Na......nan demo nai kedo......" (see E. 63 for *kedo*)
"Nan demo nai wake nai desho?"
Maho-chan ga, tsukkomu.
"Shokkuna kao shiteru" (see E. 21 for *shokku*)
"E? Uso, honto?" (see E. 21 for *E? Uso, honto?*)
"Honto da tte ba" (see E. 73 for *tte ba*)

"Kaho? What's wrong?"
"No, nothing..."
"It can't be nothing."
Maho insists.
"You look like you are in a state of shock."
"What? No kidding. Do I really?"
"It's true, I'm telling you."

c. (Taken from *Long Love Letter Hyooryuu Kyooshitsu*, episode 5) Asami has been injured fighting against intruders. First the students are concerned, and then Yuka shows concern. They all use the expression *daijoobu*. In this drama, high school students call their teacher by last name only.

安藤：　浅海、**大丈夫**？
浅海：　**大丈夫**。（学生が出ていってから）
結花：　**大丈夫**？
浅海：　だめかも。つうか、マジ痛い。

Andoo: Asami, **daijoobu?**
Asami: **Daijoobu.** (*gakusei ga dete-itte kara*)
Yuka: **Daijoobu?**
Asami: Dame kamo. Tsuu ka, maji itai. (see E. 44 for *tsuu ka*; E. 67 for *maji*)

Andoo: Are you all right?
Asami: Yes, I am all right. (*after students have left the room*)
Yuka: Are you all right?
Asami: Not really. To tell you the truth, seriously, it hurts.

d. (Taken from *Majo no jooken*, episode 1) Hikaru, riding a motorcycle, almost runs into Michi, and Michi speaks to him for the first time.

未知：　**大丈夫ですか**。今、救急車呼びますから。
光：　**大丈夫**だから。
未知：　でも。
光：　ほっといてくれよ。

Michi:	**Daijoobu desu ka.** Ima, kyuukyuusha yobimasu kara.
Hikaru:	**Daijoobu** da kara.
Michi:	Demo.
Hikaru:	Hottoite-kure yo.
Michi:	Are you all right? I'm calling the ambulance right away.
Hikaru:	I'm O.K.
Michi:	But...
Hikaru:	Leave me alone.

61. Expressing Sympathy and Compassion

Key Expressions

大変ですねえ	*Taihen desu nee.*	That must be difficult.
残念ですねえ	*Zannen desu nee.*	That is too bad.
(≈) 心配だね	*Shinpai da ne.*	You must be concerned. That is worrisome.
気の毒に	*Kinodoku ni.*	Sorry to hear that.
かわいそうに	*Kawaisoo ni.*	Poor thing.

Explanation

Showing sympathy and compassion becomes particularly important when someone is experiencing a hardship. Although it is important to show sympathy, one must also refrain from pitying. Sharing pain is important, but overdoing it comes across as patronizing. Nonetheless, tender and caring words are frequently used and appreciated among Japanese speakers. It is important to remember that these words are pronounced in compassionate tones and are accompanied by concerned facial expressions. In addition to the use of compassionate expressions as part of a sentence, they may preface one's speaking turn.

Even when there is no concrete reason to be sympathetic, *Taihen desu nee* expresses the speaker's respect for the partner's hard work and diligence. By using *Taihen desu nee*, the speaker conveys concern and admiration, which helps make the ensuing interaction more pleasant. *Taihen desu nee* may be used as a greeting as well.

Zannen desu nee is used when the speaker shows empathy with the partner for a misfortune. The speaker shares the disappointment with the partner. *Shinpai da ne* is intended to comfort the partner who is worried or in trouble by sharing the worried feeling. The speaker understands the partner's concern, and offers comfort.

Kinodoku ni (or *Okinodoku ni*) and *Kawaisoo ni* are often used to show sympathy and compassion for someone else. For example, you and your friend are discussing how unfortunate it was that your mutual friend has died. You may say *Kinodoku ni*, and your partner may respond with *Honto ni kawaisoo ni.*

It is possible to address *Kawaisoo* to the very person to whom the speaker wants to show sympathy and compassion. For example, when your partner is in trouble, you may say *Kawaisoo,* expressing sympathy. However, this use of *Kawaisoo* has a patronizing nuance, so it cannot be used when speaking to a person to whom one should show respect.

Examples

a. (Two women talking about a friend's father)

(fa1): **大変ですねえ**。山本さんのお父さんまた入院したんですって。
(fa2): そうなんですか。**心配ですねえ**。

(fa1): **Taihen desu nee.** Yamamoto-san no otoosan mata nyuuin shita n desu tte.
(fa2): Soo na n desu ka. **Shinpai desu nee.** (see E. 46 for *Soo na n desu ka*)

(fa1): It must be difficult. Yamamoto's father was hospitalized again.
(fa2): Is that so? That is worrisome, isn't it?

b. (A husband and wife talking about the death of a neighbor's wife)

(≈ma1a): **気の毒になあ**、あそこの奥さんまだ若いのに。
(≈fa1a): そうなのよ。まだ40代でしょ。
(≈ma1b): 亡くなってしまったなんて。
(≈fa1b): **かわいそうにねえ**。

(≈ma1a): **Kinodoku ni naa,** asoko no okusan mada wakai noni.
(≈fa1a): Soo na no yo. Mada yonjuudai desho.
(≈ma1b): Nakunatte-shimatta nante. (see E. 17 for *nakunatte-shimatta*; E. 15 for *nante*)
(≈fa1b): **Kawaisoo ni nee.** (see E. 54 for *nee*)

(≈ma1a): I'm sorry to hear about the wife. She's [was] still young.
(≈fa1a): Yes, indeed. She is [was] only in her forties.
(≈ma1b): To have passed away.
(≈fa1b): What a poor thing, indeed!

c. (Two women commenting on a disaster)

(fa1): 今回の大惨事、亡くなった方の家族の方達、**お気の毒ですよね**。
(fa2): ええ、ほんとに。さぞ**大変なことでしょう**。

(fa1): Konkai no daisanji, nakunatta kata no kazoku no katatachi, **oki-nodoku desu yo ne.**
(fa2): Ee, honto ni. Sazo **taihenna koto deshoo.**

(fa1): The recent disaster, I feel sorry for the surviving family.
(fa2): Yes, indeed. It must be very difficult.

Authentic Examples

a. (Taken from *Strawberry on the Shortcake*, episode 3) Haruka shows sympathy toward Yui's mother, who is in the hospital.

遥： お母さん**心配だね**。
唯： うん。でもねパパがついてるから。

Haruka: Okaasan **shinpai da ne.**
Yui: Un. Demo ne papa ga tsuiteru kara.

Haruka: You must be concerned about your mother.
Yui: Yes. But my father is with her, so.

b. (Taken from *Buchoo Shima Koosaku*, 5: 149) Masuda tells Shinko, a singer, that she failed to win an award by one vote. *Zannen datta* is used to show regret and sympathy.

増田： ＜新子／**残念だった**／一票差だった＞

Masuda: Shinko, **zannen datta**. Ippyoosa datta.

Masuda: Shinko, sorry for the result. It was by just one vote.

c. (Taken from *Jisshuusen chinbotsu*, Feb. 15, 2001) Upon returning to Japan from Honolulu, the crew members of the *Ehime Maru* were met by a Japanese government official, who made the following remark.

「このような事故が起きたことは非常に**残念です**」

"Kono yoona jiko ga okita koto wa hijoo ni **zannen desu.**"

"It is very regrettable that this kind of incident happened."

d. (Taken from *Antiiku, seiyoo kottoo yoogashiten*, episode 8) Eiji's past was revealed in a newspaper story recounting how Eiji had to give up being a boxer because of his eye problems. Eiji immediately responds when a passerby says *Kawaisoo*. In this usage, *Kawaisoo* is patronizing.

青年１： 神田エイジだろ。新聞読んだよ。
エイジ： えっ？
青年１： や、俺さ、けっこう好きだったんだよね、あんたのこと。**かわいそうに**なあ。

エイジ：　なんすか。**かわいそう**って。
青年2：　(...) いいんだよ。頑張ってよ。

seinen 1: Kanda Eiji daro. Shinbun yonda yo.
Eiji: E-tt? (see E. 21 for *E-tt?*)
seinen 1: Ya, ore sa, kekkoo suki datta n da yo ne, anta no koto. **Kawaisoo ni naa.** (see E. 25 for *kekkoo*; E. 32 for *suki*; E. 30 for *anta no koto*)
Eiji: Nan su ka. **Kawaisoo** tte. (see E. 70 about echo questions)
seinen 2: (...) Ii n da yo. Ganbatte yo.

young man 1: You are Eiji Kanda, right? I read about you in the newspaper.
Eiji: What?
young man 1: You know, I've been your fan. Poor thing, aren't you?
Eiji: What do you mean by "poor thing"?
young man 2: (...) Anyway. Best of luck to you.

e. (Taken from *Long Love Letter Hyooryuu Kyooshitsu*, episode 6) Faced with the realization that Asami's wound is seriously infected, the students discuss what to do. Ootomo expresses his emotion by the phrase *kawaisoo*.

大友：　殺そうか。
高松：　何言ってんだおまえまで。
大友：　だってあんなに苦しそうなんだぞ。#俺らに何ができるんだよ。あんな痛そうで苦しそうで、**かわいそう**だよ。だったらいっそ早く＝
高松：　＝ばかなこと言ってんじゃねえよ！

Ootomo: Korosoo ka.
Takamatsu: Nani itte n da omae made. (see E. 40 for *Nani itte n da*; E. 30 for *omae*)
Ootomo: Datte anna ni kurushisoo na n da zo. Orera ni nani ga dekiru n da yo. Anna itasoo de kurushisoo de, **kawaisoo** da yo. Dattara isso hayaku= (see E. 40 about rhetorical questions)
Takamatsu: =Bakana koto itte n ja-nee yo! (see E. 70 for *itte n ja-nee yo*)

Ootomo: Shall we kill him?
Takamatsu: What are you talking about!
Ootomo: But he is suffering so much. What can we do? He is undergoing so much pain and suffering. What a poor thing! So, quickly=
Takamatsu: =Don't say silly things!

f. (Taken from *SMAP x SMAP*, New Year's special) Osugi and Piiko, two guests on the show, join the SMAP members and play a game. As they are divided into two teams, Osugi says the following. *Kawaisoo* communicates that Osugi empathizes with Nakai, who turns out to be alone on a team.

おすぎ：　あら、中居くんひとり？**かわいそう**だから行ってあげるね。
中居：　おすぎの方がやさしい。

Osugi: Ara, Nakai-kun hitori? **Kawaisoo** da kara itte-ageru ne.
Nakai: Osugi no hoo ga yasashii. (see E. 6 for *yasashii*)

Osugi: Oh, Nakai, are you alone? Poor thing. I'll join you.
Nakai: Osugi is more kind and thoughtful.

14
Designing Utterances for the Partner

62. Being Artfully Vague

Key Expressions

の方	*no hoo*	(lit.) the direction of
でも	*demo*	or something
など	*nado*	and other things
なんか	*nanka*	somehow
とか	*toka*	or
らしい	*rashii*	it seems
ようだ	*yoo da*	it appears to me
と思います	*to omoimasu*	I think that

Explanation

Vagueness does not always mean insincerity. A certain vagueness helps people feel comfortable. For this reason, the speaker may want to speak vaguely even when matters are clear. Artful vagueness comes into play when, to avoid too direct and straightforward opinions or news, information is presented as if it were unclear. The speaker presents what must be said softly, avoiding unnecessarily shocking or offending the partner.

One example of artful vagueness is the use of the phrase *no hoo* '(lit.) the direction of' after a noun. Instead of simply saying *jimusho* 'office', for example, *jimusho no hoo* (lit., 'the direction of the office') adds vagueness to the utterance by broadening the referential territory.

Demo added to nouns is another device frequently used for vagueness. *Demo* offers extra choices to the partner by adding the meaning of 'or something', and it is frequently used when making suggestions or offers. *Demo* gives the impression that the speaker is presenting options; accordingly, the partner chooses what he or she likes from several possibilities. *No hoo* and *demo* are routinely added in Japanese conversation just to make interaction more pleasant.

Another phrase that offers options is *nado*. For example, instead of making a specific suggestion such as *Kono hon wa ikaga deshoo ka* 'How about this book?' the speaker chooses *Kono hon nado wa ikaga deshoo ka* 'How about this book or the like?' to make it less imposing. *Nado* is used in formal speech or written Japanese, while *nanka*, *nado*'s casual version, is used in ordinary conversation. This *nanka* is different from the adverbial *nanka* 'somehow' discussed immediately below.

When revealing inner feelings, one may feel a bit embarrassed. Here, vagueness, as indicated by such expressions as *nanka*, *toka*, and *rashii* helps. *Nanka* (or *nanika*) is an adverb used independently to add the meaning 'somehow,' 'somewhat', and is often used as a conversation filler as well. *Toka* is a particle added to indicate alternatives, and as a result, it softens the utterance.

Rashii, itself an adjective, expresses speculation based on secondhand information. *Rashii* conveys weak or no personal commitment to the statement it accompanies. The speaker's attitude may be best described in English by a variety of expressions including 'it seems', 'according to what I hear', and 'although I'm not going to bet on it.' Because *rashii* creates a gap between the speaker and the information, the speaker may use it deliberately to distance himself or herself even if in actual possession of the information. Information presented through *rashii* becomes indeterminate and free-flowing. Because it is not presented as hard fact, it becomes easier to accept.

Yoo da 'it seems, it appears to me' functions as a speculative modal conveying the speaker's assumptions. *Yoo da* is used when interjecting a personal judgment about the likelihood of a state or event. The addition of *yoo da* makes a statement become less direct, thus giving an impression of accommodation.

One frequently used method for making words less categorical is to add *to omou* 'I think' at the end. It is possible to say something without adding *to omou*, for example, *Sore ga ichiban ii desu* 'That is the best'. However, when *to omou* is added, the utterance is offered as an indication of one's thought processes, giving an impression of greater reserve. Placing the question marker *ka* in front of *to omou*, makes the utterance even less assertive. Either way, using *to omou* isolates the comment and renders the words almost as indirect quotation, if only in disguise.

Equally so, *to omou* may actually mean 'I think'. For example, when you say *Itta hoo ga ii to omou kedo* 'I think we should go, but...,' your partner may readily answer *Soo da ne. Soo shiyoo.* 'I guess so. Let's do that' or the like.

Three points should be noted about the use of *to omou*. First, it cannot be used for information to which only the speaker has access, as in, *Atama ga itai* 'I have a headache ' (not* *Atama ga itai to omou*). Second, *to omou* cannot be used in reference to someone else's thoughts. **Tanaka-san wa kore ga ii to omou* is not appropriate, although in English it is possible to use the verb *think* in reference to anyone. (The constraints explained in Chapter 1 apply here.) But it is possible to say something like *Tanaka-san wa kore ga ii to omou kamo* 'It may be that Tanaka thinks this is good'. As long as *to omou* is accompanied by modal expressions such as *kamo* (*shirenai*), *yoo da, rashii*, and so on, it can be used for someone other than the speaker. Third, in written text—unlike its use in spoken discourse—*to omou* makes a strong subjective statement. In part this is because the phrase is linked directly to the writer. For weak assertions, *to omowareru* 'it can be thought' or *to omowareteiru* 'it is thought' is used.

There is a clear difference between *omou* and *omotteiru*. *Omou* is used when the speaker just has an opinion; *omotteiru* suggests that the speaker thinks and has been thinking the same thing for some time. *Ano hito ga hannin da to omou* 'I think he is the culprit', simply states an opinion, whereas (*Ima no tokoro*) *ano hito ga hannin da to omotteru n da* '(At this point) I think he is the culprit' emphasizes that the speaker both thinks so now, and has been thinking so for a while. Unlike *omou*, *omotteiru* is not limited to the speaker's opinion. It is possible to state *Tanaka-san wa kore ga ii to omotteiru* 'Tanaka thinks (at this point, he is thinking) that this is good'.

In addition to the spoken phrases used for artful vagueness, speakers who want to be vague and hesitant must speak in an appropriate tone. A hesitant mumble is expected, not a clear, proud, enthusiastic voice.

Examples

a. (A businessman talking politely to a respresentative from another company) Note the use of *no hoo* and *yoo da*.

(≠ma1a): では、改めて、事務所**の方**におうかがいいたします。
(≠ma2a): あ、そうですか。すみませんねえ、わざわざ来ていただくことになってしまって。
(≠ma1b): いえ、お忙しい**ようです**し。
(ma1b): じゃ、そういうことで、よろしくお願いします。

(≠ma1a): Dewa aratamete, jimusho **no hoo** ni oukagai itashimasu.
(≠ma2a): A, soo desu ka. Sumimasen nee, wazawaza kite-itadaku koto ni natte-shimatte. (see E. 48 about inverted word order)
(≠ma1b): Ie, oisogashii **yoo desu** shi. (see E. 63 about the use of *shi*)
(ma2b): Ja, soo yuu koto de, yoroshiku onegai shimasu.

(≠ma1a): Well then, I will visit you at your office next time.
(≠ma2a): Please do. My apologies for making you come all the way.
(≠ma1b): No problem at all. Besides, you must be busy, so…
(ma2b): Well then, please take care of it that way.

b. (Two coworkers wondering about the unusual atmosphere at the office)

(≈fa1a): **なにか**、今日みんなの様子が変なんだけど。
(≈fa2a): ちょっとした問題**とか**、起きた**らしくて**。
(≈fa1b): えっそうなの？知ってるんだったら教えて。
(≈fa2b): 会計でミスがあったんだ。

(≈fa1a): **Nanika**, kyoo, minna no yoosu ga hen na n da kedo. (see E. 63 for *kedo*)
(≈fa2a): Chotto shita mondai **toka**, okita **rashikute**. (see E. 25 for *chotto*)
(≈fa1b): E-tt, soo na no? Shitteru n dattara oshiete. (see E. 21 for *E-tt*; E. 46 for *soo na no*)
(≈fa2b): Kaikei de misu ga atta n da. (see E. 72 for *n da*)

(≈fa1a): Somehow, everyone is behaving strangely today.
(≈fa2a): Some trouble seems to have occurred.
(≈fa1b): Really? If you know about it, tell me, will you?
(≈fa2b): Uh, there were some accounting errors, so…

c. まあそれが一番いい**と思います**。

Maa, sore ga ichiban ii **to omoimasu**. (see E. 23 for *ichiban*)

Well, I think that's the best.

d. この日がいい**かと思いますが**。

Kono hi ga ii **ka to omoimasu ga**.

I think perhaps this date is the best, but...

Authentic Examples

a. (Taken from *Muko-dono*, episode 1) An interviewer directs his guest toward a table. By avoiding plain references to *teeburu* and *shuzai*, the interviewer shows politeness.

では、あちらのテーブルの**方**で取材の**方**させていただけますか。

Dewa, achira no teeburu no **hoo** de shuzai no **hoo** sasete-itadakemasu ka.

Well then, would it be all right to interview you at the table over there?

b. (Taken from *Buchoo Shima Koosaku*, 5: 46) Shima uses *demo* when inviting someone for dinner.

島：　では / 食事**でも** / しましょうか＞

Shima:　Dewa shokuji **demo** shimashoo ka.

Shima:　Then shall we have the dinner?

c. (Taken from *Naku yo Uguisu*, 157) To comfort Sengoku, his friend Gotoo serves tea. In the frame, the tea is quite obvious, but Gotoo uses *demo*, nonetheless.

後藤：　これ**でも** / 飲んで元気 / だせよ ...... ＞

Gotoo:　Kore **demo** nonde genki dase yo.

Gotoo:　Drink this and get over with it.

d. (Taken from *Beautiful Life*, episode 2) Shuuji confesses his problem with his family to Kyooko. In this situation Shuuji "knows" that his family members do not like the idea that he is a hairstylist. Adding *nanka* and *rashii* makes the statement soft and therefore less shocking. Psychologically, Shuuji may not really want to admit the fact. At the same time, perhaps he is hoping that Kyooko will be compassionate and empathetic.

柊二：　**なんか**俺が美容師やってること、良く思ってない**らしい**からさ。

Shuuji:　**Nanka** ore ga biyooshi yatteru koto, yoku omotte-nai **rashii** kara sa.

Shuuji:　My family does not like my being a hairstylist (beautician), I'm afraid.

e. (Taken from *Beautiful Life*, episode 3) Kyooko confesses her worries about visiting Shuuji alone. Kyooko is raising a sensitive issue about Shuuji's former girlfriend, and she wants to be hesitantly indirect about it by adding *nanka* and *toka* and ending utterances with the [V-*te*] form.

杏子：　ひとりで会いに来るの、良くないと**思って**。
柊二：　うん？
杏子：　**なんか**、妙な誤解**とか**されたら悪いと**思って**。
柊二：　なに、誤解って。＃誰に誤解されるの？
杏子：　彼女**とか**に。

Kyooko:　Hitori de ai ni kuru no, yoku-nai to **omotte**.
Shuuji:　Un?
Kyooko:　**Nanka**, myoona gokai **toka** saretara warui to **omotte**.
Shuujii:　Nani, gokai tte. Dare ni gokaisareru no? (see E. 70 about echo questions)
Kyooko:　Kanojo **toka** ni. (see E. 30 for *kanojo*)

Kyooko: I thought it isn't good to come to see you alone.
Shuuji: What?
Kyooko: It won't be good if we are misunderstood, I thought.
Shuuji: What do you mean by misunderstanding? By whom are we misunderstood?
Kyooko: Well, your girlfriend, perhaps.

f. (Taken from *Majo no jooken*, episode 1) Michi shares her view with Hikaru by adding *to omou*. In this case *to omou* carries its literal meaning and a softening effect.

未知： だから、罪滅ぼしのつもりで、お金渡してるの？そんなの逃げてるだけだ**と思う**。
光： じゃあどうすりゃいいんだよ。

Michi: Dakara, tsumi horoboshi no tsumori de, okane watashiteru no? Sonna no nigeteru dake da **to omou**.
Hikaru: Jaa doo surya ii n da yo.

Michi: So, because you feel guilty you are giving him money? By doing that, I think you are only escaping from the real consequences.
Hikaru: Then what should I do?

g. (Taken from *Taiga no itteki*, 118–119) Here the author explicitly states what he thinks. In written text, *to omou* is a device for making an explicit personal statement. In this example, the specific mention of *boku wa* helps make the statement assertive.

事業に失敗したり、あるいは犯罪に走って仮に刑務所の塀のなかで一生を送るような人生であったとしても、それはそれで人間の価値というものには関係なく、やはり尊い一生であった、**と、ぼくは思います**。

Jigyoo ni shippai shitari, arui wa hanzai ni hashitte kari ni keimusho no hei no naka de isshoo o okuru yoona jinsei de atta to shitemo, sore wa sore de ningen no kachi to yuu mono ni wa kankei naku, yahari tootoi isshoo de atta, **to, boku wa omoimasu.** (see E. 57 for *yahari*)

I think (or, I believe) that even if one's life is such that a person has failed in business, or has committed a crime and must spend the entire life within prison walls, such a person's life is as valuable and precious as the lives of other people.

63. Ending the Sentence without a Tone of Finality

Key Expressions

が	*ga*	but
けれども	*keredomo*	but
けど	*kedo*	but
(≈)っていうか	*tte yuu ka*	I should say, should I say
(≈) 忙しくて	*Isogashikute.*	I'm busy, so...
(≈) 違ったりして	*Chigattari shite.*	Maybe it's wrong or something, so...
(≈) 時間かかるし	*Jikan kakaru shi.*	Besides it takes time, so...

Explanation

When expressing an opinion, it is advisable to add, at the end of one's thought, phrases that can potentially disarm a negative impact. One way to accomplish this is to add connectives. Adding connectives such as *ga* or *keredomo* (or its colloquial version, *kedo*) gives the impression that the utterance is unfinished, which adds to the sense that the speaker is open to other options. By avoiding finality, these dangling connectives render statements less offensive.

More concretely, *ga* (or *keredomo* or *kedo*) is used in conversation when (1) providing information that is not helpful enough and being apologetic about it, (2) making a statement that encourages the partner to continue with the topic, (3) responding with some doubt and uncertainty, and (4) giving information in anticipation of the partner's response. Ending the sentence with an apologetic attitude, as in case (1) above, overtly encourages empathy between speaker and partner.

Another strategy is to add phrases such as *tte yuu ka* (optionally *te yuu ka* after *n*). Utterance-final *tte yuu ka* has a nuance of young people's conversational style, but its use has spread among the general population. *Tte yuu ka* appears in varied colloquial forms, for example, *tchuuka* and *ttsuu ka*. *Tte yuu ka* avoids clear identification of a speaker's thoughts, and presents information with more options. (Contrast this utterance-final *tte yuu ka* with the utterance-initial *te yuu ka* discussed in Entry 44.)

The [V/Adj-*te*] form is sometimes used to leave the statement vague. Not completing a sentence leaves its meaning indirect. *Tari shite* 'maybe . . . or something' points out one action related to the verb, but with the implication that there are other options. Because of this possibility, *tari shite* is added to speech when the speaker avoids direct and clear statement. This is particularly common in young people's casual speech when the opinion expressed is unexpected or uncomfortable for the partner.

In conversation among youth, particularly among young women, the conjunction *shi* appears in final position to make an utterance sound soft. *Shi* is used grammatically to combine two or more clauses that have something in common, as in *Hito wa shinsetsu da shi, kikoo wa ondan da shi, honto ni sumiyasui tokoro desu* 'People are kind, and the weather is mild; this is a very comfortable place to live'. But even when it is used only once, the *shi*-marked phrase implies that some other information follows. This in turn gives the impression of a lingering, less final utterance that is more accommodating to the partner's feelings.

Examples

a. (≠) 申し訳ございません。課長は席をはずしておりますが。

Mooshiwake gozaimasen. Kachoo wa seki o hazushite orimasu **ga.**

I am very sorry. The section chief is not in now, but...

b. (Two men discussing what to do next) The second speaker adds *keredomo* to convey that his position differs from the first speaker's. He wants to present it hesitantly.

(ma1): 次のステップとして、顧問弁護士に相談してみましょうかねえ。
(≈ma2): どうかな。まだ、ちょっと時期的には早いと思う**けれども**。

(ma1): Tsugi no suteppu to shite, komon bengoshi ni soodan shitemimashoo ka nee.
(≈ma2): Doo ka na. Mada, chotto jikiteki ni wa hayai to omou **keredomo.** (see E. 25 for *chotto*)

(ma1): As the next step, should we consult our lawyer?
(≈ma2): I wonder. I think it may be a bit too early, but...

c. (A man answers apologetically) The second speaker adds *kedo* because he knows his answer is insufficient, showing a somewhat apologetic attitude.

(fa1): すみませんこの辺に交番ありませんか。
(ms1): さあちょっとわからないんです**けど**。

(fa1): Sumimasen. Kono hen ni kooban arimasen ka.
(ms1): Saa, chotto wakara-nai n desu **kedo.** (see E. 25 for *chotto*; E. 66 for *wakara-nai*; E. 72 for *n desu*)

(fa1): Excuse me. Is there a *kooban* (police box) around here?
(ms1): Well, uh, I'm not sure...

d. (Two men talking about a parked car) Note that the answer is given in such a way that the partner will continue with the topic.

(≈ma1a): あの車，おたくの？
(my1): ええ，そうです**けど**。
(≈ma1b): あそこ駐車違反なんだよね。

(≈ma1a): Ano kuruma, otaku no? (see E. 30 for *otaku*)
(my1): Ee, soo desu **kedo**.
(≈ma1b): Asoko chuusha ihan na n da yo ne. (see E. 72 for *n da*; E. 55 for *yo ne*)

(≈ma1a): Is that car yours?
(my1): Yes, it is…
(≈ma1b): It's no parking there, you know.

e. (An assistant reminds a professor about a meeting) *Kedo* is used in anticipation of the partner's response.

(fa1): 先生、ミーティング始まります**けど**。
(ma1): あ、すぐ行きます。

(fa1): Sensei, miitingu hajimarimasu **kedo**.
(ma1): A, sugu ikimasu.

(fa1): Professor, the meeting will start soon, but…
(ma1): Ah, I'll be right there.

f. (Two young men discussing whether or not a resolution is reasonable) *Tte yuu ka* and *kedo* are used to offer one speaker's view indirectly so as not to offend his partner.

(≈my1a): そんな結論じゃ、相手を説得できないんじゃないかな？
(≈my2): そんなことないだろ。
(≈my1b): だってそれじゃ、相手が全く損しちゃう**っていうか**かえって怒らせてしまうような気がする**けど**。

(≈my1a): Sonna ketsuron ja, aite o settoku deki-nai n ja-nai ka na?
(≈my2): Sonna koto nai daro.
(≈my1b): Datte sore ja, aite ga mattaku son shichau **tte yuu ka**. Kaette okorasete-shimau yoona ki ga suru **kedo**. (see E. 17 for *shichau*; E. 64 for *yoona ki ga suru*)

(≈my1a): Such a solution cannot persuade the other party, I wonder?
(≈my2): That's not so, is it?
(≈my1b): But, with that resolution, the other party will lose totally, I should say. It seems that we will make them even angrier…

g. (A mother asking her daughter why she doesn't study) The daughter ends her answer with *shi* for a lingering and therefore more indirect effect.

(≈fa1): どうして勉強しないの？
(≈ft1): だって、時間がかかるし。

(≈fa1): Dooshite benkyoo shi-nai no?
(≈ft1): Datte, jikan ga kakaru **shi**. (see E. 59 for *datte*)

(≈fa1): Why aren't you studying?
(≈ft1): 'Cause, it is time-consuming, and...

Authentic Examples

a. (Taken from *Long Vacation*, episode 1) Minami asks Sena what happened to Asakura, Minami's groom. Sena answers with *kedo*, knowing that his answer isn't something that Minami wants to hear.

瀬名： すいません。あの。朝倉さんだったら、荷物まとめて出ていきました**けど**。
南： 出て、出てったって？どこに？

Sena: Suimasen. Ano. Asakura-san dattara, nimotsu matomete dete-ikimashita **kedo**.
Minami: Dete, dete-tta tte? Doko ni? (see E. 70 about echo questions)

Sena: Sorry. Uh, Mr. Asakura packed up his things, took off, and is gone...
Minami: He's gone, but gone to where?

b. (Taken from *Beautiful Life*, episode 1) Shuuji apologizes to Kyooko on the phone. Here Shuuji must choose expressions that won't offend Kyooko. Shuuji combines several strategies to show hesitation: *nanka*, a half-question-like rising intonation, and utterance-final *ttsuu ka*. Speech is often a product of such expressive strategies.

柊二： え、ちょっと待てよ。なあ。#でも、あの雑誌見たら、なんかこっちまで↑やり切れなくなった**っつうか**。
杏子： 調子いい。

Shuuji: E, chotto mate yo. Naa. Demo, ano zasshi mitara, nanka kotchi made↑yarikire-naku natta **ttsuu ka**. (see E. 25 for *chotto*; E. 62 for *nanka*; E. 65 about question-like rising intonation)
Kyooko: Chooshi ii.

Shuuji: What, wait a minute. Say, when I saw that magazine, I began to feel painful; I couldn't stand it...
Kyooko: You're just saying that.

c. (Taken from *Tsubasa o kudasai*, 66) Kyooka's friend Hatano commits suicide because of being bullied by classmates. Takishita and Tsubaki comment on Hatano's death.

「しっかしばかだよな……秦野の奴。死ぬことなかったのによ」
(…)
「ほんとだよね。いい迷惑**っていうかぁ**」

"Shikkashi, baka da yo na……Hatano no yatsu. Shinu koto nakatta noni yo." (see E. 27 for *shikkashi* instead of *shikashi*; E. 30 for *yatsu*)
(…)
"Honto da yo ne. Ii meiwaku **tte yuu kaa.**"

"But, such a fool, Hatano is. He didn't have to die."
(…)
"Really. His death is more or less a nuisance to me…"

d. (Taken from *Beautiful Life*, episode 9) Kyooko gently suggests that people are intimidated by Shuuji, in part by using *tari suru*.

杏子：　でもさそれって、時々まわりにいる人たちは**まぶしすぎたりしちゃったりするんじゃない**かな。
柊二：　そんなまさか。何言ってんの？

Kyooko: Demo sa, sore tte tokidoki mawari ni iru hitotachi wa **mabushi-sugitari shichattari suru n ja-nai** ka na. (see E. 47 for *tte*)
Shuuji: Sonna masaka. Nani itte n no? (see E. 16 for *sonna*; E. 14 for *masaka*; E. 40 about rhetorical questions)

Kyooko: But, doesn't that make people around you feel intimidated because you are too brilliant?
Shuuji: Absolutely not, that can't be. What are you talking about?

e. (Taken from *Majo no jooken*, episode 2) A girl asks Hikaru if he has a girlfriend. Using *tari shi-nai no* makes the question more indirect and gentle.

クラスメート：　光くんおはよう。光くんて彼女**いたりしない**の？
光：　別に。

Kurasumeeto: Hikaru-kun, ohayoo. Hikaru-kun te kanojo **itari shi-nai** no? (see E. 47 for *te*; E. 30 for *kanojo*)
Hikaru: Betsu ni.

Classmate: Hikaru, good morning. Hikaru, do you have a girlfriend?
Hikaru: Not particularly.

Note

The expression *te yuu ka* is often used in casual conversation, but also appears in written text—sometimes in the form *to yuu no deshoo ka*—indicating the writer's hesitancy to show finality.

1. (Taken from *Taiga no itteki*, 129)

よくよく思い返してみると、ひとつの事実、ひとつの現実、などに対して、ぼくはいつも異なる二つの思い——アンビバレントな感情**というのでしょうか**、そんな感じを抱いていたという自覚があります。

Yokuyoku omoikaeshite-miru to, hitotsu no jijitsu, hitotsu no genjitsu, nado ni taishite, boku wa itsumo kotonaru futatsu no omoi—anbibarentona kanjoo **to yuu no deshoo ka**, sonna kanji o idaiteita to yuu jikaku ga arimasu. (see E. 1 for *kanjoo*)

As I think back carefully, I am aware that I have always harbored two different thoughts, should I say an ambivalent feeling, toward one fact or one reality.

64. Sharing Thoughts as Feelings

Key Expresssions

(≈)って感じ	*tte kanji*	have feelings like
(≈) みたいな	*mitaina*	like, seem
ような気がする	*yoona ki ga suru*	feel like, I get a feeling like
みたいな気がする	*mitaina ki ga suru*	I get a feeling like

Explanation

Kanji 'feeling' is used when presenting thoughts as feelings. In some cases *tte kanji* (optionally *te kanji* following *n*) means 'feeling' literally, but in many cases thoughts and feelings seem to merge, and distinguishing between them is difficult. By using *kanji*, the speaker creates a discourse that is suggestive of emotion. *Tte kanji* is usually preceded by [N] and [V/Adj informal].

Kanji may be used as a predicate as in *kanji da* 'it is a feeling like' or *kanji ga suru* 'I have a feeling like', but frequently it is used independently at the end of the utterance. Presenting thoughts as feelings has the effect of softening the statement, showing the speaker's desire to reach the partner's heart. In written text, *kanji ga suru* is used to explicitly state one's view as feelings.

Utterance-final *mitaina*, an [Adj-*na*], is often used in casual conversation among youth. *Mitaina* also adds a distancing and softening effect. By adding 'like', the speaker avoids a strong commitment to what is said. In the *mitaina* utterance, what precedes *mitaina* may take a rising intonation, adding to the noncommittal effect even further.

Both *tte kanji* and *mitaina* may be preceded by self-quotation, as in *Hayaku kaeritai naa tte kanji* 'I feel like I want to go home soon'. This *mitaina* is similar to the English interjection *like* used when approximately quoting one's own speech, as in "you know, like, what's the problem?" and "So I just went like yeah, yeah, yeah."

Because *mitaina* '(lit.) it appears' describes someone else's state, it gives the impression that the speaker is revealing his or her own thoughts and feelings as if they were observed as someone else's. This distancing effect is recognized as part of youth language (see Chapter 2).

Both *kanji* and *mitai(na)* may be pronounced with rising tone, as in *Akirameta tte kanji?* 'I feel like I've given up?' This question-like tone adds to the softening effect and gives the impression that the speaker is soliciting the partner's agreement, approval, or at least acknowledgment.

Yoona ki ga suru 'feel like, I get the feeling like' (or a casual version, *mitaina ki ga suru*) is another way to express thoughts as feelings. When the speaker uses *yoona ki ga suru* instead of *omou* there is less commitment to the thought and more appeal to shared feelings. *Yoona ki ga suru* is sometimes used in its literal sense, but even then, it seems to sustain a sense of indirect emotional appeal.

Examples

a. (Two teenage girls chatting)

(≈ft1): ミカって、彼のファン？
(≈ft2): そうなのよ。もう結婚して**って感じ**。カッコいいしね。

(≈ft1): Mika tte, kare no fan? (see E. 47 for *tte*)
(≈ft2): Soo na no yo. Moo kekkon shite **tte kanji**. Kakko ii shi ne. (see E. 13 for *kakko ii*)

(≈ft1): Mika, are you his fan?
(≈ft2): That's right. I feel like, please marry me. He's really nice-looking, you know.

b. (Two teenage girls talking about consecutive days off) The rising intonation (see Entry 65) is used before *mitaina*.

(≈ft1): ねえ、今度の連休どうする？
(≈ft2): 彼氏と思いっきり遊ぶ↑**みたいな**。

(≈ft1): Nee, kondo no renkyuu doo suru?
(≈ft2): Kareshi to omoikkiri asobu↑ **mitaina**. (see E. 30 for *kareshi*)

(≈ft1): Say, what are you going to do for the coming consecutive days off?
(≈ft2): Like, having a great time with my boyfriend?

c. (Two students discussing a report due the next day)

(≈ft1): どうしよう。あした提出するはずのレポート、すっかり忘れてた。今日中にできるかな。
(≈ft2): やだ。それって、不可能**みたいな**。

(≈ft1): Doo shiyoo. Ashita teishutsu suru hazu no repooto, sukkari wasureteta. Kyoojuu ni dekiru ka na.
(≈ft2): Ya da. Sore tte, fukanoo **mitaina**. (see E. 9 for *Ya da*; E. 47 for *tte*)

(≈ft1): What should I do? I've completely forgotten about the report due tomorrow. I'm not sure if I can finish it by the end of the day.
(≈ft2): Oh no. Like, that's almost impossible.

d. (Two mature men discussing a difficult project) The first speaker softens the assertions *muri da* and *zetsubooteki da* with *yoona ki ga suru* and *tte kanji*, respectively, expressing his thoughts as feelings.

(≈ma1a): でも、その計画、なんか、無理の**ような気がする**。
(≈ma2a): そうかなあ。
(≈ma1b): 絶望的**って感じ**。
(≈ma2b): そうでもないだろ。去年だって、やり遂げたんだから。

(≈ma1a): Demo, sono keikaku, nanka, muri no **yoona ki ga suru**. (see E. 62 for *nanka*)
(≈my2a): Soo ka naa. (see E. 46 for *soo ka naa*)
(≈my1b): Zetsubooteki **tte kanji**.
(≈ma2b): Soo demo nai daro. Kyonen datte, yaritogeta n da kara.

(≈ma1a): But that project, I feel like it is impossible.
(≈ma2a): I wonder about that.
(≈ma1b): It's like, there is no hope.
(≈ma2b): That isn't so, is it? Last year, we completed it, so…

Authentic Examples

a. (Taken from *Strawberry on the Shortcake*, episode 2) Manato tells Haruka that he is giving up on the college entrance exam.

まなと：　受験なら、今年はあきらめた**って感じ**。多分浪人すると思うよ。
遥：　だめだよ、そんな弱気なこと言っちゃ。

Manato: Juken nara, kotoshi wa akirameta **tte kanji**. Tabun roonin suru to omou yo. (see E. 47 for *nara*; E. 62 for *omou*)
Haruka: Dame da yo, sonna yowakina koto itcha. (see E. 18 for *dame*; E. 48 about inverted word order)

Manato: About the entrance exam, I've given up, I feel like. Perhaps I will prepare for the exam next year.
Haruka: You can't do that! Don't be so timid.

b. (Taken from *Antiiku, seiyoo kottoo yoogashiten*, episode 4) Junko, a woman in her early twenties, tells how she became intimate with Reiji. *Kanji* with rising intonation signals her desire to tell, while soliciting approval from her audience.

潤子：　それで、一緒に逃げながら、「俺の女になれよ」って言われて、「うん」てそのままなっちゃった**かんじ↑**。

Junko: Sorede, issho ni nigenagara, "Ore no onna ni nare yo" tte iwarete, "Un" te sono mama natchatta **kanji** ↑. (see E. 17 for *natchatta*)

Junko: So, while we were running away together, I was told "Why don't you be my woman," and I said "O.K.," and, like, I became his woman?

c. (Taken from *Kindaichi shoonen no jikenbo*, 5: 168) Hajime tastes tea and comments, using *kanji*? (*Chitto* is a very casual form of *chotto*).

はじめ：　＜砂糖なしで ちっと / 苦いけど大人の味 /**ってカンジ**？＞
けっこう / いけるぜ＞

Hajime: Satoo nashi de chitto nigai kedo otona no aji **tte kanji**?
Kekkoo ikeru ze. (see E. 25 for *kekkoo*; E. 13 for *ikeru*)

Hajime: Without sugar, it's a bit bitter, but it's like, a taste for grown-ups?
It's surprisingly good.

d. (Taken from *Ren'ai hakusho*, 14: 16) Kaho uses *tte kanji* when describing her parents. In this example, a quotation is used, which gives the impression that the parents' voice is integrated into Kaho's feelings.

パパもママも、勉強や受験のことは、なーんにも言わない。
果保が好きなようにしなさい。
って感じ。
放任主義なんだ。

Papa mo mama mo, benkyoo ya juken no koto wa, naan nimo iwa-nai. (see E. 27 for *naan nimo* instead of *nan nimo*)
Kaho ga sukina yoo ni shinasai.
Tte kanji.
Hoonin shugi na n da. (see E. 72 for *n da*)

Neither my mother nor father says anything about studying or the entrance examination.
Kaho, do as you like.
That's how they say, I feel like.
They go along with the let-it-be policy.

e. (Taken from *Taiga no itteki*, 85) The author expresses how he felt, in a quotation followed by *to yuu kanji*.

教育委員会のアンケートのなかに、「自殺を考えたことがあるか」という質問がはいっていたということが、ある意味ではぼくにはショックでした。うーん、すごいことだな、時代はそこまできたのかな、**という感じがしました。**

Kyooiku iinkai no ankeeto no naka ni, "Jisatsu o kangaeta koto ga aru ka" to yuu shitsumon ga haitteita to yuu koto ga, aru imi de wa boku ni wa shokku deshita. Uun, sugoi koto da na, jidai wa soko made kita no ka na, **to yuu kanji ga shimashita.** (see E. 21 for *shokku*; E. 13 for *sugoi*)

In a way, it was shocking to me that in the questionnaire administered by the Board of Education there was a question, "Have you ever thought of suicide?" And I felt, "Wow, what a serious situation, that such an era has arrived!"

f. (Taken from interview #88, with Shunji Iwai, music video producer and movie director) Although *mitaina* is used predominantly among youth, its use has spread among middle-aged speakers.

林：　今回の映画（…）深読みしようと思うと、それだけで本が一冊できちゃいそうですね。
岩井：　そうですね。でも、やってる当人はそんなに深く考えてないんで。ここまで深読みされても困るんだけどな、**みたいな。**

Hayashi: Konkai no eiga (...) fukayomi shiyoo to omou to, sore dake de hon ga issatsu dekichaisoo desu ne. (see E. 17 for *dekichau*)
Iwai: Soo desu ne. Demo, yatteru toonin wa sonna ni fukaku kangaetenai n de. Koko made fukayomisaretemo komaru n da kedo na, **mitaina.** (see E. 42 for *toonin*; E. 18 for *komaru*)

Hayashi: A whole book could be written about the movie you just directed, if you wanted to read (things) into it.
Iwai: It may be so. But, I who directed it haven't thought about it so deeply. Like, "I am a bit troubled by being read into so deeply."

g. (Taken from interview #157, with Hitomi Manaka, actress) Manaka recalls her experience of coming face-to-face with her adoring fans. Here she tells Hayashi that she prefers female fans to male fans because she is at a loss when a man tells her that he is her fan. Note that she uses both *to yuu kanji* and *mitaina* immediately following self-quotation.

林：　女の子に言われるほうがうれしい？
真中：　うれしいし、「ありがとう」って自然に返せるんです。男の人に言われると、えっと私、どうすればいいんだろう？**という感じ**で。
林：　「握手してください」とか言われると、引いちゃいます？
真中：　私、手を洗わなくていいのかな、**みたいな**。（笑い）

Hayashi: Onna no ko ni iwareru hoo ga ureshii? (see E. 5 for *ureshii*)
Manaka: Ureshii shi, "Arigatoo" tte shizen ni kaeseru n desu. Otoko no hito ni iwareru to, etto watashi, doo sureba ii n daroo? **to yuu kanji** de. (see E. 72 for *n desu*)
Hayashi: "Akushu shite-kudasai" toka iwareru to, hiichaimasu?
Manaka: Watashi, te o arawa-nakute ii no ka na, **mitaina**. (*warai*)

Hayashi: Are you happier when you are told so by girls?
Manaka: I'm happy, and I can naturally say thank you. When I am told so by men, I feel like, what, uh, what should I do?
Hayashi: Do you hesitate, when you are told, "Please shake hands with me"?
Manaka: It's like, shouldn't I wash my hands? (*laugh*)

h. (Taken from *Long Vacation*, episode 5) Minami uses *yoona ki ga suru* in a question as well as in a vague answer. Communicating information as feeling makes it possible for her to maintain her noncommittal attitude.

南：　なんかさ、ひまんなったら電話するってさ、もう一生かかってこない**ような気しない？**
瀬名：　そう言われればちょっと。
南：　でしょう？
瀬名：　そういうことあったんですか、今までに。
南：　うーんあった**ような気もする**かなあ。

Minami: Nanka sa, hima n nattara denwa suru tte sa, moo isshoo kakatte-ko-nai **yoona ki shi-nai?** (see E. 62 for *nanka*; E. 47 for *tte*)
Sena: Soo iwarereba chotto. (see E. 25 for *chotto*)
Minami: Deshoo?
Sena: Soo yuu koto atta n desu ka, ima made ni. (see E. 48 about inverted word order)
Minami: Uun atta **yoona ki mo suru** ka naa.

Minami: But, you know, when people say they will call you when they have time, don't you feel like they aren't going to call you during their entire lifetime?
Sena: When you say so, I begin to feel that way a bit.
Minami: Right?
Sena: Did such a thing happen to you before?
Minami: Maybe, I feel like, perhaps, there was such an occasion.

i. (Taken from *Shiretoko Rausudake satsujin bojoo*, 138) Shimon asks Reiko Kume, a reporter for a local newspaper, if she will come with him to the waterfall where he witnessed a mysterious woman. This *yoona ki ga suru* is used in its literal sense in that he is reporting how he feels, but it also adds to the indirect effect.

「久米さん。あしたの朝早く、フレペの滝へ行きませんか？」
「あすの朝……」
「けさと同じように、白菊の女性がくる**ような気がするんです**」
「さあ、どうでしょうか。お伴はしますけど」

"Kume-san. Ashita no asa hayaku, Furepe no taki e ikimasen ka?"
"Asu no asa......" (see E. 70 about echo responses)
"Kesa to onaji yoo ni, shiragiku no josei ga kuru **yoona ki ga suru n desu.**"
"Saa, doo deshoo ka. Otomo wa shimasu kedo." (see E. 63 for *kedo*)

"Ms. Kume. Early tomorrow morning, will you go to the waterfall of Furepe with me?"
"Tomorrow morning..."
"Just as this morning, I feel like, perhaps, that woman who brought those white chrysanthemums will come again."
"I wonder about that. But I will come along with you."

j. (Taken from *Majo no Jooken*, episode 1) Lying on the beach, Michi and Hikaru have a heart-to-heart talk.

未知： こうしてるとさあ、この世に存在するのは、青空と私達だけ**みたいな気がしてくる**ね。

Michi: Koo shiteru to saa, kono yo ni sonzai suru no wa, aozora to watashitachi dake **mitaina ki ga shite-kuru** ne.

Michi: Lying down on the beach like this, I begin to feel like all that exists in this world are this blue sky and us.

65. Using Question-like Intonation

Key Expressions

[半クエスチョン的上昇イントネーション]	*han kuesuchonteki jooshoo intoneeshon*	half-question-like rising intonation
(≈) 才能↑なんじゃない？	*Sainoo↑na n ja-nai?*	Isn't it the talent, perhaps?
(≈) 休んじゃうみたいな↑	*Yasunjau mitaina↑.*	Like being absent?

Explanation

Japanese questions usually have a rising intonation on the final syllable. In the sample questions that follow, the rising tone is on final *ka* and *ji*, respectively.

いつ出かけますか。

Itsu dekakemasu ka.

When will you go out?

(≈) 今、何時？

Ima, nanji?

What time is it?

The rising tone may also appear within a sentence at phrase-final position in either a statement or a question. This rising tone, which started being used frequently in the 1990s, signals a sense of hesitancy on the part of the speaker, even when the sentence is not really a question. It appears at the end of *bunsetsu*, that is, nouns, adverbs, adjectives, and verbs (followed by particles, if any).

In practice, the hesitancy producing question-like intonaton arises from (1) speaker's uncertainty about the choice of phrase, (2) talking while asking a self-addressed question, (3) wanting to avoid shocking the partner unnecessarily, and (4) using the phrase against social expectation, with the concomitant desire to have this flouting of convention sanctioned by the partner. The underlying motivation for the question-like rising intonation is self-defense. By generally softening the statement with a rising tone, the speaker hopes to avoid making the partner unnecessarily upset and creating a possibly uncomfortable situation.

Especially in youth language, affirmative and negative statements also end in question-like rising intonation, as if speakers, unable to make ordinary statements, turn everything into a question. This sentence-final rising tone is also linked to uncertainty, and, as discussed in Chapter 2, to a self-defensive and softening effect.

Examples

a. (A man and woman talking about a friend) The answer is given with notable hesitancy, marked by a rising tone.

(≈my1): あいつのすること、何でもすばらしいよな。
(≈fy1): それはやっぱり**才能**↑なんじゃない？

(≈my1): Aitsu no suru koto, nan demo subarashii yo na. (see E. 30 for *aitsu*)
(≈fy1): Sore wa yappari **sainoo**↑na n ja-nai? (see E. 57 for *yappari*)

(≈my1): Everything he does is simply great, isn't it?
(≈fy1): That's probably because he has, I guess, talent, don't you think?

b. (Two women chatting about their plans for the day) By using a rising tone aftere *deeto*, the speaker softens the potential impact of the shocking news.

(≈fy1) 今日は彼との**デート**↑って感じかな。
(≈fy2): へえ、そうなんだ。

(≈fy1): Kyoo wa kare to no **deeto**↑tte kanji kana. (see E. 64 for *tte kanji*)
(≈fy2): Hee, soo na n da. (see E. 46 for *soo na n da*)

(≈fy1): Maybe today I'm like, having a date with him.
(≈fy2): Wow, I see.

Authentic Examples

a. (Taken from *Beautiful Life*, episode 4) Kyooko is telling her parents that her "friend" (who is Shuuji, her boyfriend) is in the neighborhood. Kyooko is hesitant because she is describing her boyfriend as *tomodachi* 'friend', which doesn't quite characterize the true nature of their relationship. Her sense of uncertainty and perhaps guilt is expressed through the rising tone on the very word she hesitates to use.

杏子： なんか、**友達**↑近くまで来てんだって、用事あって。

Kyooko: Nanka, **tomodachi**↑chikaku made kite n datte, yooji atte. (see E. 62 for *nanka*; E. 48 about inverted word order)

Kyooko: Uh, my friend is near here, he has some business around here.

b. (Taken from *Long Love Letter Hyooryuu Kyooshitsu*, episode 1) Yuka shares her view of an ideal partner, at first with a bit of hesitation, marked by a rising tone. Then she repeats the phrase with more confidence.

浅海：　じゃあどういうのが理想？その一、広い海で、おぼれた時。

結花：　うん。手つないで、ともに、たくましく泳ぐみたいな。

浅海：　なんか彼が彼女命がけで救って死んじゃうとか、そういうんじゃないの？

結花：　それいやなの。**一緒に生きてく人↑**一緒に強く生きていく人、そういうのが理想。（浅海、うなずく）

Asami: Jaa doo yuu no ga risoo? Sonoo, hiroi umi de, oboreta toki.

Yuka: Uun. Te tsunaide, tomo ni, takumashiku oyogu mitaina. (see E. 64 for *mitaina*)

Asami: Nanka kare ga kanojo inochigake de sukutte shinjau toka, soo yuu n ja-nai no? (see E. 62 for *nanka*; E.30 for *kare* and *kanojo*; E. 62 for *toka*)

Yuka: Sore iya na no. **Issho ni ikiteku hito↑** issho ni tsuyoku ikite-iku hito, soo yuu no ga risoo. (see E. 9 for *iya*) (*Asami, unazuku*)

Asami: Then what is your ideal partner like? I mean when you are drowning in the wide ocean.

Yuka: Let me see. Like two people holding hands and courageously and strongly swimming together in the ocean.

Asami: Uhh, it isn't that a man dies saving his woman?

Yuka: No, I wouldn't like that. The person who goes on living with me, I guess, the person who determinedly goes on living with me. That is my ideal partner. (*Asami nods*)

15

Concerned with Conversational Empathy

66. Confirming Understanding

Key Expressions

(≈) 分かる？	*Wakaru?*	Do you understand it? Do you get it?
(≈) 分かんない	*Wakan-nai.*	I don't understand it. I don't get it.
(≈) 分かるよ、その気持ち	*Wakaru yo, sono kimochi.*	I understand your feelings.
分かりました	*Wakarimashita.*	I got it.

Explanation

Sometimes, to make sure your partner understands, you may use expressions such as *Wakaru?* 'Do you understand it?' If it gets annoying to hear someone repeating *Wakaru?* it might be a good idea to prevent the question with the counteraffirmative *Wakatteiru* (or *Wakatteimasu*). *Wakatteiru* tells your partner that you know about it already, with the clear implication that you would rather not hear about it anymore. It is not appropriate to use this expression to a person to whom you should show respect. For the same reason, it is rude to use *Wakatteiru* to someone who is explaining something as a favor or as an act of kindness.

Wakaru, in certain contexts, means more than just the fact that you understand something. It includes the meaning of personally understanding the other person's situation and feelings. Because of this, *wakaru* expresses empathy. For example, *Wakaru yo* 'I understand how you feel' is used to comfort someone who is in trouble.

Wakarimasu ka should be avoided in speaking to a person to whom one should show respect, because it comes across as too direct, and therefore, rude. The appropriate assumption here is that the person who is deserving of respect is more than capable of understanding; in fact, he or she fully understands. Under this circumstance, it is wise to use expressions such as *Yoroshii deshoo ka* 'Is it all right?' or *Tsugi e ittemo yoroshii deshoo ka* 'Is it all right to go ahead with the next item?'.

A very polite strategy for confirming understanding is to assume that the partner understands or knows already. For example, instead of **Gozonji desu ka* 'Do you know?', adding a preface like *gozonji no yoo ni* 'as you know', or *gozonji to omoimasu ga* 'as I think you already know', is a thoughtful way of confirming understanding.

Wakatta functions in two ways. First, it conveys an understanding of the explanation. Sometimes *Wakatta* may be repeated several times in rapid succession, as if to communicate "I know it already, I got it, so you don't need to explain any more." Second, *Wakatta* is used when accepting a request. In fact, *Wakarimashita* is frequently used as an acceptance of and willingness to meet the partner's request.

Examples

a. (Two young men chatting about a party)

(≈my1): いいかい？送別会は来週の土曜日。**分かった**？
(≈my2): **分かった**よ。

(≈my1): II kai? Soobetsukai wa raishuu no doyoobi. **Wakatta**?
(≈my2): **Wakatta** yo.

(≈my1): O.K.? The farewell party is next Saturday. Got it?
(≈my2): Got it.

b. (Two young men sharing the fact that they don't understand a mutual friend)

(□my1): **分かんねえ**。全然**分かんねえ**よ、あいつの言ってること。
(□my2): 俺も。だいたい彼女に謝るなんて、そんな気持ち**分かんねえ**な。

(□my1): **Wakan-nee.** Zenzen **wakan-nee** yo, aitsu no itteru koto. (see E. 48 about inverted word order)
(□my2): Ore mo. Daitai kanojo ni ayamaru nante, sonna kimochi **wakan-nee** na. (see E. 15 for *nante*)

(□my1): I can't understand. Not at all. I don't understand what he is saying.
(□my2): Me, either. To begin with, to apologize to her! I don't get that.

c. (A young woman complains to her boyfriend that he doesn't understand her)

(≈fy1a): 私の気持ちなんか全然**分かってくれない**んだから。
(≈my1a): そんなことないだろ。お前がつらい思いをしていることくらい**分かってる**よ。
(≈fy1b): あなたには、私の気持ちなんか**分からない**。
(□my1b): 勝手に決めつけるなよ。人の気持ちが**分からない**のはお前だろ。

(≈fy1a): Watashi no kimochi nanka zenzen **wakatte-kure-nai** n da kara. (see E. 15 for *nanka*)
(≈my1a): Sonna koto nai daro. Omae ga tsurai omoi o shiteiru koto kurai **wakatteru** yo. (see E. 30 for *omae*; E. 7 for *tsurai*)
(≈fy1b): Anata ni wa, watashi no kimochi nanka **wakara-nai**. (see E. 30 for *anata*)
(□my1b): Katte ni kimetsukeru-na yo. Hito no kimochi ga **wakara-nai** no wa omae daro.

(≈fy1a): You don't understand how I feel at all.
(≈my1a): That's not true. I understand that you are going through pain.
(≈fy1b): You don't understand my feelings.
(□my1b): Don't draw thoughtless conclusions. The one who doesn't understand the other's feelings is you, don't you see?

d. (Two mature coworkers planning for an event) *Wakarimashita* is used when willingly accepting the request.

(ma1): よろしいですか。来週は大切なお客さんがお見えになります。そのつもりで仕事を進めておいて下さい。
(fa1): **分かりました**。

(ma1): Yoroshii desu ka. Raishuu wa taisetsuna okyakusan ga omie ni narimasu. Sono tsumori de shigoto o susumete-oite-kudasai.
(fa1): **Wakarimashita.**

(ma1): Can I be absolutely clear about this? Next week we are expecting important visitors. Please proceed with that in mind.
(fa1): Certainly.

Authentic Examples

a. (Taken from *Beautiful Life*, episode 7) Masao challenges Shuuji about his relationship with Kyooko and asks Shuuji if he really understands her difficult situation.

柊二： はい。#ま、それは**分かっている**つもりです。
正夫： ちょっとやそっとつきあったくらいで、何が**分かる**って言うの？

Shuuji: Hai. Ma, sore wa **wakatteiru** tsumori desu.
Masao: Chotto ya sotto tsukiatta kurai de, nani ga **wakaru** tte yuu no? (see E. 29 for *tsukiau*; E. 40 for *nani ga wakaru tte yuu no?*)

Shuuji: Yes. I think I understand her situation.
Masao: You have been going steady with her only for a short time. How can you really understand her?

b. (Taken from *Strawberry on the Shortcake*, episode 4) Manato thinks he understands his friend Haruka, but Haruka is frustrated and screams that Manato (Irie) doesn't understand her.

まなと： **分かる**よ。
遥： **分からない**！＃入江君には、私の気持ちなんか**分かんない**！

Manato: **Wakaru** yo.
Haruka: **Wakara-nai!** Irie-kun ni wa, watashi no kimochi nanka **wakan-nai!** (see E. 15 for *nanka*)

Manato: I understand how you feel.
Haruka: No, you don't. Irie, you don't understand my feelings at all!

c. (Taken from *Santaku*) During a game of darts, Sanma scores more than Kimura and makes a big thing of it. Kimura repeats *wakatta*, assuring Sanma that he already knows, and there's no need to go on and on about it.

さんま： 49点ナハハハ。49点！＝
木村： ＝**分かった分かった分かった**＝
さんま： ＝カッコいい＝
木村： ＝**分かった**。
さんま： これも勝ってしまうんやろな＝
木村： ＝**分かった**。

Sanma: Yonjuukyuuten na ha ha ha ha. Yonjuukyuuten!=
Kimura: =**Wakatta wakatta wakatta=**
Sanma: =Kakko ii= (see E. 13 for *kakko ii*)
Kimura: =**Wakatta.**
Sanma: Kore mo katteshimau n yaro na=
Kimura: =**Wakatta.**

Sanma: 49 points, ha ha ha ha. I got 49 points!=
Kimura: =I got it, I got it, I got it=
Sanma: =How cool!=
Kimura: =I know it.
Sanma: Perhaps I'm going to win this game, too=
Kimura: =O.K., I got it.

d. (Taken from *Furuete nemure, sanshimai*, 15: 52) Negishi complains that people don't understand him.

「僕のことを、誰も**分かってないんです**」
と、根岸は続けて、「僕には、馬鹿な連中に頭を下げることなんかできないんです。そんなことをさせるべきじゃないんです。そう言っても、誰も**分からない**。(...)」
"Boku no koto o, dare mo **wakatte-nai n desu.**" (see E. 30 for *boku no koto*)
To, Negishi wa tsuzukete, "Boku ni wa, bakana renchuu ni atama o sageru koto nanka deki-nai n desu. Sonna koto o saseru beki ja-nai n desu. Soo it-temo, **dare mo wakara-nai.** (...)" (see E. 15 for *nanka*; E. 72 for *n desu*)

"Nobody understands me."
(So) said Negishi, and he continued, "I cannot bow my head to a bunch of fools. They should not make me do such a thing. Even when I insist, nobody understands me.(...)"

Note

When learning *wakaru* 'to understand', native speakers of English may easily confuse it with the verb *shiru* 'to know'. This is particularly likely when verbs are used in a negative response. *Wakara-nai* is used when you don't know the answer, although you think you should. *Shira-nai* is used when you haven't had the chance to get the information.

Using *Shirimasen* implies the attitude, "How should I know?" As a result, Japanese speakers in general prefer saying *Wakarimasen. Shirimasen yo* or *Shira-nai yo* functions as a warning and reprimand. For example, *Neboo shite densha ni okuretemo shirimasen yo* 'If you sleep late and are late for the train, that's not my fault (lit., I won't know the consequences)' may be given as a (presumably uncaring) warning. *Shira-nai!* (or the blunt *Shira-nee!*) 'Cut it out!' is also used to deny relevance in conflict situations.

67. Being Serious

Key Expressions

(≈) まじ	*Maji.*	I'm serious.
まじで	*maji de*	seriously, really
まじですか?	*Maji desu ka?*	Are you serious?
まじめな話	*majimena hanashi*	seriously speaking

Explanation

When getting involved in a serious discussion, using *maji* is a convenient way to question or confirm the level of seriousness. *Maji* is a shortened casual form of *majimena*, an [Adj-*na*], but it is extensively used even in formal style, as in *Maji desu ka* 'Are you serious?'. *Maji?* 'Are you serious?', and *maji de?* 'Seriously?' are used in casual conversation as devices to confirm the partner's seriousness and genuine intention. These phrases are also used as interjections to mean something like "Really?" when the speaker is surprised or is in a state of disbelief. *Maji* and *maji de* (with a falling tone) assure the seriousness of one's talk.

To indicate seriousness, the speaker prefaces his or her remarks by *majimena hanashi*, which literally (and immediately) establishes a serious tone.

Examples

a. (Two female coworkers chatting)

(≈fy1a): 啓子ちゃん、結婚するんだってよ、来月。
(≈fy2a): うそ。**まじで？**
(≈fy1b): うん、**まじで。**
(≈fy2b): 誰と？
(≈fy1c): うちの会社の人。社内結婚ってやつ。
(≈fy2c): **まじ？**

(≈fy1a): Keiko-chan, kekkon suru n datte yo, raigetsu. (see E. 32 for *kekkon*)
(≈fy2a): Uso. **Maji de?**
(≈fy1b): Un, **maji de.**
(≈fy2b): Dare to?
(≈fy1c): Uchi no kaisha no hito. Shanai kekkon tte yatsu.
(≈fy2c): **Maji?**

(≈fy1a): Keiko is getting married, next month.
(≈fy2a): No kidding. Seriously?
(≈fy1b): Yeah, seriously.
(≈fy2b): With whom?
(≈fy1c): A man in our company. The so-called office marriage.
(≈fy2c): Are you serious?

b. (Male coworkers talking about a colleague)

(≈ma1a): 山田さん、海外出張中に、病気になったらしいよ。
(ma2a): えっ、あいつそんなはずないっすよ。
(≈ma1b): いや、それがね、現地の病院に入院したって、聞いたよ。
(ma2b): **まじですか。**
(≈ma1c): ああ。

(≈ma1a): Yamada-san, kaigai shutchoochuu ni, byooki ni natta rashii yo.
(ma2a): E-tt, aitsu sonna hazu nai ssu yo. (see E. 30 for *aitsu*)
(≈ma1b): Iya, sore ga ne, genchi no byooin ni nyuuin shita tte, kiita yo.
(ma2b): **Maji desu ka.**
(≈ma1c): Aa.

(≈ma1a): I heard that Yamada got sick during his business trip abroad.
(ma2a): What? He can't be.
(≈ma1b): But, I heard that he is now staying at the local hospital.
(ma2b): Are you serious?
(≈ma1c): Yes.

c. (Two female friends chatting)

(fa1): 田中さん、また、離婚するらしいですよ。
(fa2): **まじめな話**、あの人の考え方は全く分かりませんよね。

(fa1): Tanaka-san, mata, rikon suru rashii desu yo.
(fa2): **Majimena hanashi**, ano hito no kangaekata wa mattaku wakarimasen yo ne. (see E. 66 for *wakarimasen*; E. 55 for *yo ne*)

(fa1): It seems that Mr. Tanaka is going to go through a divorce once again.
(fa2): Seriously, I can't understand the way he thinks. Can you?

Authentic Examples

a. (Taken from *Muko-dono*, episode 10) Yuuichiroo and other family members find themselves unable to leave their home. A lot of reporters with cameras are stationed in front of the house because they have found out that Yuuichiroo and Sakura are married. Family members use *maji* in disbelief.

祐一郎： いくらマスコミだってそこまではしませんって。
亮： するみたい。
父： えっ？
亮： 外、出らんねえよ。
祐一郎： うっそー。（レポーターが家に押し寄せ、玄関の呼び鈴を鳴らし続ける）
祐一郎とさつきとあずさ：
まじ？（呼び鈴が鳴り続ける）
祐一郎： **まじー？**

Yuuichiroo: Ikura masukomi datte soko made wa shimasen tte. (see E. 73 for *tte*)
Ryoo: Suru mitai.
chichi: E-tt? (see E. 21 for *E-tt?*)

Ryoo: Soto deran-nee yo. (see Chapter 2 for *deran-nee* instead of *derare-nai*)
Yuuichiroo: Ussoo. (see E. 21 and E. 27 for *Ussoo*) (*repootaa ga uchi ni oshiyose, genkan no yobirin o narashitsuzukeru*)
Yuuichiroo to Satsuki to Azusa:
Maji? (see E. 51 about making utterances together) (*yobirin ga naritsuzukeru*)
Yuuichiroo: **Majii?** (see E. 27 for *majii* instead of *maji*)

Yuuichiroo: Even media people won't dare do such a thing.
Ryoo: They do, I'm afraid.
father: What?
Ryoo: I can't go outside.
Yuuichiroo: You must be kidding. (*Reporters are in front of the house, ringing the door bell*)
Yuuichiroo, Satsuki, and Azusa together:
Is this real? (*The doorbell goes on ringing*)
Yuuichiroo: Is this really real?

b. (Taken from *Long Love Letter Hyooryuu Kyooshitsu*, episode 2) The students are now facing a big earthquake.

大友： ね、ゆれてる。
高松： うそ！
大友： **マジマジ。**

Ootomo: Ne, yureteru.
Takamatsu: Uso! (see E. 21 for *Uso!*)
Ootomo: **Maji maji.** (see E. 24 about repetition)

Ootomo: Wait, it's shaking.
Takamatsu: Don't say that!
Ootomo: Serious, seriously.

c. (Taken from *SMAP x SMAP*, special live show) Kimura comments on a dish Nakai made during the earlier Bistro SMAP show. He particularly praises the cooked vegetables, which have a nice glaze.

木村： 野菜の照りがねえ、すごいんだよ。(煮物を食べて) うまいよ、**マジで。**

Kimura: Yasai no teri ga nee, sugoi n da yo. (see E. 13 for *sugoi*; E. 72 for *n da*) (*nimono o tabete*) Umai yo, **maji de.**

Kimura: The (cooked) vegetables are glazed nicely. (*eating a piece of cooked vegetable*) This is delicious, seriously.

d. (Taken from *Iruka to tsuiraku*, 143–144) The writer recollects how he felt when he finally realized that the airplane he was in was about to crash. Note the use of two different *kanji* for *ochiru*, emphasizing the meaning of crashing versus falling.

どうやら、飛行機が墜ちるらしいということになって、思わず私の口をついて出てきそうになった言葉はこれだった。
—— **マジかよ。**
マジで落ちるつもりなのかよ、と。

Dooyara, hikooki ga ochiru rashii to yuu koto ni natte, omowazu watashi no kuchi o tsuite dete-kisoo ni natta kotoba wa kore datta.
—**Maji ka yo.**
Maji de ochiru tsumori na no ka yo, to.

When I realized that the airplane was going to crash, without thinking, the words almost coming out of my mouth were these.
—It is serious, is it?
Is this seriously going to fall down?

68. Seeking Permission to Ask a Personal Question

Key Expressions

(≈) 言っていい？	*Itte ii?*	Can I say this?
聞いていいですか？	*Kiite ii desu ka?*	May I ask you a question?
ちょっとお聞きしたいことがあるんですけど	*Chotto okiki shitai koto ga aru n desu kedo.*	I have something I would like to ask you (and may I?)
(≈) つかぬことを聞くけど	*tsukanu koto o kiku kedo*	excuse me for asking something unrelated (out of nowhere), but

Explanation

When you find it necessary to ask permission to say something that may intrude on your partner's privacy or be upsetting, *Itte ii?* 'Can I say this?' is a useful expression. In reality, you are not so much asking a question or expecting a negative answer as you are giving warning that what you are about to ask may be a bit touchy.

Asking permission to ask a question, as in *Kiite ii desu ka* 'May I ask you a question?' is a way of showing concern for your partner's feelings. This is similar to English prefacing such as "Can I ask you a personal question?". When you ask for permission for privacy, your partner may say yes and then will be psychologically prepared for something private and/or unpleasant.

A rather indirect strategy for asking a question is to state *Chotto okiki shitai koto ga aru n desu kedo* 'I have something I'd like to ask you (and may I?)', After receiving permission, for example, *Nan deshoo* 'What would that be?', you continue. If the question is out of context, or if you want to treat the question as if it were out of context (potentially for the purpose of excusing youself for being rude), *tsukanu koto o kiku kedo* is useful. *Tsukanu koto* refers to something unexpected or unrelated to the current situation, or irrelevant to the current topic.

There are other variations that serve to preface one's commentary, one example of which is given in the authentic example (c). Overall, prefacing a question is an explicit way of showing respect toward one's partner.

Examples

a. (≠f) **お聞きしてもよろしいかしら。**

Okiki shitemo yoroshii kashira.

Could I ask you a question?

b. (Two friends chatting)

(≈my1a): **聞いていい？**
(≈fy1a): うん。
(≈my1b): その傷、事故？
(≈fy1b) うん、そう。小さい時ね、転んで大ケガしたんだって。覚えてないけど。

(≈my1a): **Kiite ii?**
(≈fy1a): Un.
(≈my1b): Sono kizu, jiko?
(≈fy1b): Un, soo. Chiisai toki ne, koronde ookega shita n datte. Oboetenai kedo.

(≈my1a): Is it O.K. if I ask you (a question)?
(≈fy1a): Sure.
(≈my1b): Is that scar, is it because of an accident?
(≈fy1b): Yeah. I fell and got seriously injured when I was a child. I don't remember it, though.

c. (Two women talking)

(≠fa1a): **お聞きしてもよろしいかしら。**
(fa2a): ええ。何？
(≠fa1b): お宅のご主人、銀行にお勤めでいらっしゃるわね。
(fa2b): ええ。
(≠fa1c): それで、ちょっと、**つかぬことをお聞きするんだけど。**
(fa2c): えっ、何？

(≠fa1a): **Okiki shitemo yoroshii kashira.**
(fa2a): Ee. Nani?
(≠fa1b): Otaku no goshujin, ginkoo ni otsutome de irassharu wa ne.
(fa2b): Ee.
(≠fa1c): Sore de, chotto, **tsukanu koto o okiki suru n da kedo.**
(fa2c): E-tt, nani? (see E. 21 for *E-tt*)

(≠fa1a): Could I ask you a question?
(fa2a): Sure. What is it?
(≠fa1b): Your husband works for a bank, right?
(fa2b): Yes.
(≠fa1c): So, excuse me for asking something out of nowhere, but...
(fa2c): What! What is it?

d. (Two men talking about Sendai, a city in northern Japan)

(≈ma1a): **ちょっと聞きたいことがあるんだけど**さ。
(ma2a): はい。
(≈ma1b): 君の郷里は仙台だったよね。
(ma2b): そうですけど。
(≈ma1c): 仙台市内でいいホテル知らないか。

(≈ma1a): **Chotto kikitai koto ga aru n da kedo** sa.
(ma2a): Hai.
(≈ma1b): Kimi no kyoori wa Sendai datta yo ne. (see E. 55 for *yo ne*)
(ma2b): Soo desu kedo. (see E. 63 for *kedo*)
(≈ma1c): Sendai shinai de ii hoteru shira-nai ka.

(≈ma1a): Say, I've got something I wanted to ask you.
(ma2a): What is it?
(≈ma1b): You are from Sendai, aren't you?
(ma2b): Yes, I am.
(≈ma1c): Do you know some nice hotel in (the city of) Sendai?

e. (A man asks about his female colleague's daughter) The question is out of context, and because of the potential surprise, the speaker prefaces it with *tsukanu koto o kiku kedo*.

(≈ma1): **つかぬことを聞くけど**、お宅のお嬢さん、北中学校の二年生？
(fy1): ええ、そうですけど。

(≈ma1): **Tsukanu koto o kiku kedo**, otaku no ojoosan, kitachuugakkoo no ninensei?
(fy1): Ee, soo desu kedo. (see E. 63 for *kedo*)

(≈ma1): By the way (this question may come out of nowhere, but), is your daughter a second-year student in the North Junior High?
(fy1): Yes, she is.

Authentic Examples

a. (Taken from *Beautiful Life*, episode 1) Shuuji prefaces a sensitive question with *Kiite ii?*

柊二： **聞いていい**？
杏子： うん。
柊二： それ事故？
杏子： ううん、病気。十七ん時までは歩けてたんだ。けっこうイケてたんだ。
柊二： 今もイケてんじゃん。

Shuuji: **Kiite ii?**
Kyooko: Un.
Shuuji: Sore jiko?
Kyooko: Uun, byooki. Juushichi n toki made wa aruketeta n da. Kekkoo iketeta n da. (see E. 25 for *kekkoo*; E. 13 for *iketeta*)
Shuuji: Ima mo iketen jan.

Shuuji: Can I ask you about something?
Kyooko: Sure.
Shuuji: Is it because of an accident?
Kyooko: No, I've been sick. I was able to walk until I was seventeen. Actually, I was quite attractive.
Shuuji: You are attractive now, too.

b. (Taken from *Beautiful Life*, episode 1) Sachi comments on Kyooko's hair style.

サチ： ねえ。
杏子： うーん？
サチ： ずっと思ってたんだけど、**言っていい**？
杏子： いいよ。
サチ： その髪型変だよ。
杏子： 分かってるよ。

Sachi: Nee.
Kyooko: Uun?
Sachi: Zutto omotteta n da kedo, **itte ii?**
Kyooko: Ii yo.
Sachi: Sono kamigata hen da yo.
Kyooko: Wakatteru yo. (see E. 66 for *wakatteru*)

Sachi: Say.
Kyooko: Uh?
Sachi: I've been thinking about this, but can I say it?
Kyooko: Sure.
Sachi: Your hairstyle, it's weird.
Kyooko: I know.

c. (Taken from *Doomoto Tsuyoshi no shoojiki shindoi*, with Ryooko Kuninaka as the guest) In this segment, Doomoto introduces a new topic unexpectedly.

堂本： ああの**全く関係ない話していいかなあ**。
国仲： うん。
堂本： あのさあ、お茶の宣伝やってるやんか。あれ何て言ってんの？

Doomoto: A ano **mattaku kankei-nai hanashi shite ii ka naa.**
Kuninaka: Un.
Doomoto: Ano saa, ocha no senden yatteru yan ka. Are nante itten no?

Doomoto: Uh, can I say something totally unrelated?
Kuninaka: Sure.
Doomoto: You know, you are in that tea commercial. What are you saying in that commercial?

69. Leading Up to Negative or Sudden News

Key Expressions

言いたくないけど	*iitaku-nai kedo*	I don't want to say this, but
こう言っちゃ何だけど	*koo itcha nan da kedo*	perhaps I shouldn't say this, but
(≠) はっきり申し上げて	*hakkiri mooshiagete*	frankly speaking, to put it bluntly
突然なんですけど	*totsuzen na n desu kedo*	sorry to talk about something suddenly, but
いきなりなんだけど	*ikinari na n da kedo*	it's rather sudden, but

Explanation

There are a number of formulaic expressions for alerting your partner to forthcoming bad news. *Iitaku-nai kedo* '(lit.) I don't want to say, but' is used to reveal hesitancy to speak, as in *Konna koto iitaku-nai kedo*, 'I don't want to say this, but'. This expression is ritualized, however, and consequently the speaker's intention may be to reveal bad news with only a semblance of hesitation. *Koo itcha nan da kedo* (or *koo itcha nan na n da kedo*) 'perhaps I shouldn't say this, but' prefaces words that are likely to be upsetting. This expression, with *nan*, is used to delay and soften the potential blow to your partner's feelings.

Sometimes it is best to reveal the bad news with *hakkiri yuu to* or *hakkiri itte*, which is similar to English "frankly (speaking)." When a very polite expression is required, *hakkiri mooshiagete* is preferred. By prefacing the directness of the communication, one's partner senses that what follows will not be pleasant. Psychologically, alerting is motivated by a need to bridge the gulf between *tatemae* and *honne* (discussed in Chapter 3).

Another strategy for communicating an out-of-context comment is to begin with phrases like *totsuzen na n desu kedo* 'sorry to talk about something suddenly' and *ikinari na n da kedo* 'it's rather sudden, but'. These expressions mark a departure from the topic under discussion to one that may be a bit sensitive.

Authentic Examples

a. (Taken from *Beautiful Life*, episode 6) Mayumi tells Kyooko that Kyooko isn't suitable for Shuuji.

真弓： こないだのライブだってあんたのせいでめちゃくちゃになったし、店ん中でなんかあいつ浮いてるし。**こんなこと言いたくないけど**、もっとお似合いの人、いるんじゃないのかな。

Mayumi: Konaida no raibu datte anta no sei de mechakucha ni natta shi, mise n naka de nanka aitsu uiteru shi. **Konna koto iitaku-nai kedo**, motto oniai no hito, iru n ja-nai no ka na. (see E. 30 for *anta*; E. 62 for *nanka*; E. 30 for *aitsu*)

Mayumi: The live show we held the other day, that was a total disaster because of you, and he has become isolated among us at the (beauty) salon. I don't want to say this to you, but isn't there someone else more suited for Shuuji?

b. (Taken from *Beautiful Life*, episode 6) Kosugi, who is confined to a wheelchair, shares his feelings with Kyooko, who is also confined to a wheelchair.

小杉： 杏子ちゃんさ、俺と一緒にこの仕事やらないか。
杏子： えっ？
小杉： (…) **こう言っちゃあ何だけど**、車いすの人の都合って、やっぱりそうじゃないと分かんないんだよ。
杏子： うん。

Kosugi: Kyooko-chan sa, ore to issho ni kono shigoto yara-nai ka.
Kyooko: E-tt? (see E. 21 for *E-tt?*)
Kosugi: (…) **Koo itchaa nan da kedo**, kurumaisu no hito no tsugoo tte, yappari soo ja-nai to wakan-nai n da yo. (see E. 57 for *yappari*)
Kyooko: Un.

Kosugi: Kyooko, will you do this kind of work with me?
Kyooko: What?
Kosugi: (…) I perhaps shouldn't say this, but how people in wheelchairs feel cannot be understood unless they also are.
Kyooko: Yes.

c. (Taken from *Santaku*) Kimura is driving an SUV, with Sanma in the passenger seat. They are on their way to the ocean in Chiba. Kimura mentions that as a child he used to watch Sanma's television programs, prefacing it with *ima yuu no wa nan desu kedo* 'it is a bit awkward to mention this now'.

木村： あの、さんざんぱらいろんな仕事とかさせてもらって、**今言うのはなんなんですけど**。俺スゲー見てましたよ、ひょうきん族。(さんま、笑う)スゲー見てましたよ。(さんま、笑う)マジで。

Kimura: Ano, sanzanpara ironna shigoto toka sasete-moratte, **ima yuu no wa nan na n desu kedo**. Ore sugee mitemashita yo, *Hyookinzoku*. (see E. 24 and Chapter 2 for *sugee*; E. 48 about inverted word order) (*Sanma, warau*) Sugee mitemashita yo. (*Sanma, warau*) Maji de. (see E. 67 for *maji*)

Kimura: Uh, (thanks to you) I've had opportunities to work with you so many times, and it is a bit awkward to mention this now. But I used to watch (your television variety show) *Hyookinzoku* a lot. (*Sanma laughs*) I used to watch it all the time. (*Sanma laughs*) Honestly.

d. (Taken from *Long Love Letter Hyooryuu Kyooshitsu*, episode 1) Yuka is upset and starts to criticize Asami, but only by prefacing her comment.

結花： じゃ、**言わしてもらいますけど**、私が思うに、生徒と教師においては常にどんな関係であれ、教師の方により大きな責任があると思うんです。向こうが向こうがってそれおかしいですよ。

Yuka: Ja, **iwashite-moraimasu kedo**, watashi ga omou ni, seito to kyooshi ni oite wa tsune ni donna kankei deare, kyooshi no hoo ni yori ookina sekinin ga aru to omou n desu. Mukoo ga mukoo ga tte sore okashii desu yo. (see E. 62 for *to omou*; E. 72 for *n desu*; E. 47 for *tte*)

Yuka: Then, let me say this. As far as I'm concerned, whatever relationship it may be, if it is between a teacher and his or her student, more responsibility lies with the teacher. It is wrong to say *she* did this and *she* did that.

e. (Taken from *Buchoo Shima Koosaku*, 5: 25) Shima mildly suggests that the guest should leave the party, with a preface apologizing for the rudeness. *Iinikui* means 'difficult to say'.

島： < **大変言いにくい / ことなんですが** / 周りの招待客が / あなた方の存在を / 気にされています >

Shima: **Taihen ii nikui koto na n desu ga** mawari no shootaikyaku ga anatagata no sonzai o ki ni sareteimasu.

Shima: It is difficult to say this, but other guests are being upset by your presence.

f. (Taken from *Buchoo Shima Koosaku*, 5: 44) Facing the corporate restructuring of the company, Shima reveals some bad news to his colleague.

島： < **はっきり申しあげて** / あなた方 2 人を除いて / ほとんど全員 / リストラの対象となっています >

Shima: **Hakkiri mooshiagete** anatagata futari o nozoite hotondo zen'in risutora no taishoo to natteimasu.

Shima: To put it bluntly, except you two, almost everyone is being considered as a target for the corporate restructuring (and is likely to be fired).

g. (Taken from *Shiretoko Rausudake satsujin bojoo*, p. 69) Shimon prefaces a sensitive question to Tomoko.

「お辛いところへ、**こんなことを伺うのは失礼と思いますが**、妹さんの自殺の原因には思い当たるところがありますか？」
紫門はきいた。

"Otsurai tokoro e, **konna koto o ukagau no wa shitsurei to omoimasu ga,** imootosan no jisatsu no gen'in ni wa omoiataru tokoro ga arimasu ka?" (see E. 7 for *tsurai*; E. 16 for *konna*)
Shimon wa kiita.

"I realize it is impolite to ask such a question, particularly at this painful time, but can you think of something significant about the cause of your sister's suicide?"
Shimon asked.

h. (Taken from *Long Love Letter Hyooryuu Kyooshitsu*, episode 7) Asami prefaces his suggestion that he and Yuka have a date.

浅海： あのー。（結花、振り向く）**突然なんですけど**、#今日とか、明日とか、あさってとか週末とかいつか暇ですか。

Asami: Anoo. (*Yuka, furimuku*) **Totsuzen na n desu kedo,** kyoo toka, ashita toka, asatte toka shuumatsu toka itsuka hima desu ka.

Asami: Uhh, excuse me. (*Yuka turns her head [toward Asami].*) It's sudden, but are you free today, tomorrow, the day after tomorrow, the weekend, or some other time?

i. (Taken from *Long Love letter Hyooryuu Kyooshitsu*, episode 1) Asami visits Yuka at her father's flower shop and begins to say something out of context, prefacing it with *ikinari na n desu kedo*. The viewer suspects that Asami wants to say he likes her. But another shopper comes in, and Yuka attends to her.

浅海： **いきなりなんですけど。**
（ここで話がとぎれる）
結花： ごめん、何だっけ。
浅海： いいや。

Asami: **Ikinari na n desu kedo.**
(*Koko de hanashi ga togireru*)
Yuka: Gomen, nan dakke.
Asami: Ii ya. (see E. 13 for *ii*)

Asami: Uh, this is rather sudden, but…
(*The talk is interrupted here*)
Yuka: Sorry, what was it?
Asami: Oh, it's O.K.

70. Echo Questions and Responses

Key Expressions

(子供が走ってる) (≈) 子供が走ってる？	*(Kodomo ga hashit-teru.) Kodomo ga hashitteru?*	(A child is running.) Did you say "A child is running"?
(なんで？) (≈) なんでって	*(Nan de?) Nande tte.*	(Why?) You say why, but...
(あきらめろよ) (□) あきらめろだと？!	*(Akiramero yo.) Akiramero da to?!*	(Give it up.) What!? To give up?!
(えっ？) (≈) えっじゃないわよ	*(E-tt?) E-tt ja-nai wa yo.*	(What?) Don't say "What." Stop that nonsense!
(□) 勝手に言ってろ	*Katte ni ittero.*	Go ahead and go on saying silly things.
(□) そんなこと言うなよ	*Sonna koto yuu na yo.*	Don't say such a thing.
(≈)って言われてもねえ	*tte iwaretemo nee*	You say so, but...

Explanation

Commenting on your partner's speech becomes necessary for a variety of reasons. Simply repeating what is said (usually without politeness expressions) with a rising tone is used to request clarification or confirmation from the partner. This is called the "echo question" and is often used to confirm a question or to convey surprise.

Echo questions may also accompany the quotation marker *to* or (*t*)*te*. Quotation plays an important role here. By saying *Nande tte* 'You say *nande*, but', for example, you highlight the fact that your partner asked *Nande* 'Why'. This *tte*-marked phrase often initiates the next topic of conversation, as discussed in Entry 47. In some cases, the quoted portion is followed by *da*. This *da* adds to the emphatic effect, as, for example, in cases of surprise or disbelief.

In addition to echo questions, when your partner comments on your speech, the comment may be no more than an echo response. For example, your partner may reiterate something you said as he or she digests the information, or may echo the phrase as a potential topic, to which you may add further comment. Echo response is accompanied with a falling tone, and I present it without a question mark.

Ja-nai is used to indicate disapproval of what your partner says or does by denying it. For example, in response to *E-tt*, you may yell "*E-tt,*" *ja-nai* (*wa*) *yo*. *Ja-nai* indicates strong disapproval and is used in angry response to a nonsensical utterance or action.

Katte ni ittero (or *Katte ni ieba*) 'Go ahead and go on saying silly things' is another angry response. One can also tell the partner directly not to say what has been just said, as in *Sonna koto iwa-naide yo* 'Please don't say such a thing' or *Sonna koto yuu-na yo* 'Don't say such a thing'. Of course, what has been said cannot be unsaid, but by telling a partner not to say such a thing, the speaker successfully conveys both awareness and criticism. Other similar expressions include *te yuu n desu ka* 'are you saying so and so' used as a criticism, and *tte iwaretemo* 'even if you say so'.

Examples

a. (Two college students talking about an acquaintance) An echo question is used to clarify uncertain information.

(≈my1a): きのう、マークに会ったんだ。
(≈my2a): **マーク？**
(≈my1b): ほら、この間の飲み会であった留学生。
(≈my2b): あ、あいつね。

(≈my1a): Kinoo, Maaku ni atta n da.
(≈my2a): **Maaku?**
(≈my1b): Hora, kono aida no nomikai de atta ryuugakusei.
(≈my2b): A, aitsu ne. (see E. 30 for *aitsu*)

(≈my1a): I saw Mark yesterday.
(≈my2a): **Mark?**
(≈my1b): You know, the foreign student we met at the drinking party the other day.
(≈my2b): Ah, that guy.

b. (Two women talking about joining an organization)

(fa1a): それが、二万円だったんですよ。
(fa2a): **二万円って？**
(fa1b): 入会金。
(fa2b): そんなにするんですか、入会金だけで。

(fa1a): Sore ga, niman'en datta n desu yo.
(fa1a): **Niman'en tte?**
(fa2b): Nyuukaikin.
(fa2b): Sonna ni suru n desu ka, nyuukaikin dake de. (see E. 16 for *sonna ni*; E. 48 about inverted word order)

(fa1a): It was 20,000 yen.
(fa2a): 20,000 yen?
(fa1b): The new membership fee.
(fa2b): It costs that much just to join the organization!

Authentic Examples

a. (Taken from *Kookaku kidootai*, 246 [English translation, 248]) Aramaki uses *da* in the echo question to show his total disbelief.

ロボット： ＜壱生命体として / 政治的亡命を / 希望する …. ＞
荒巻： **＜生命体 / だと !? ＞**

robotto: Ichi seimeitai to shite seijiteki boomei o kiboo suru….
Aramaki: **Seimeitai da to!?**

robotto: <As a self-/ aware/ life-form…/ a spirit…I/ formally/ request/ political/ asylum.>
Aramaki: <What?!/ a/ ghost?!>

b. (Taken from *Long Love Letter Hyooryuu Kyooshitsu*, episode 1) Takamatsu and Kaoru are in love. Kaoru gets upset because Takamatsu doesn't seem to understand her. Takamatsu's utterance is an example of the echo response (with falling tone) as he comments by repeating Kaoru's utterance *waraeru*.

高松： え。なに。怒ってるの？
かおる： 怒ってない。笑える。(その場を去る)
高松： **笑えるって。**おまえ、ちょ、かおる待て。#おい、待ってろよ、おまえ。

Takamatsu: E. Nani. Okotteru no? (see E. 10 for *okoru*)
Kaoru: Okotte-nai. Waraeru. (*sono ba o saru*)
Takamatsu: **Waraeru tte.** Omae, cho, Kaoru mate. Oi, mattero yo, omae. (see E. 30 for *omae*; E. 55 about the use and non-use of *yo*)

Takamatsu: Huh? What? Are you mad?
Kaoru: No, I'm not. This is something I get to laugh about. (*she leaves Takamatsu behind*)
Takamatsu: Something to laugh about, you say. Hey, you, wait, Kaoru. Wait, you wait for me.

c. (Taken from *Long Vacation*, episode 7) Minami has lost Sugisaki's undeveloped film. Sena comments by quoting Minami's phrase *inochi* and continues with *inochi* as a topic.

南：　首でしょ、もちろん。撮ること仕事としてる人にとって撮ったものって、命なんだから。

瀬名：　**命なんだからって**。命があればまた撮れるじゃん。

南：　同じものは撮れない。

Minami: Kubi desho, mochiron. Toru koto shigoto to shiteru hito ni totte totta mono tte, inochi na n da kara.

Sena: **Inochi na n da kara tte**. Inochi ga areba mata toreru jan.

Minami: Onaji mono wa tore-nai.

Minami: Of course, I will be fired. For the person whose job is to take photographs, photographs are his life.

Sena: His life, you say. But, if he is alive, he can take photographs again.

Minami: But the same photographs he won't be able to take.

d. (Taken from *Kindaichi shoonen no jikenbo*, 5: 8) Hajime doesn't understand why Saki (a junior high school boy) is visiting Hajime's high school. Saki answers by repeating Hajime's phrase *nande* in his echo response.

佐木：　＜どうも～～～♡ / お久しぶりです＞

はじめ：　＜さっ…佐木いい～～～！！！＞＜なっ…なっ…/ なんで中坊の / お前がここに / ！？＞

佐木：　＜**なんでって** / 校内見学ですよ～♡ / ボクも一応 / 受験生ですから！＞

Saki: Doomo. Ohisashiburi desu.

Hajime: Sa, ...Saki-ii!!! Na-tt,... na-tt,... nande chuuboo no omae ga koko ni!?

Saki: **Nande tte** koonai kengaku desu yo. Boku mo ichioo jukensei desu kara! (see Chapter 2 about the use of *ichioo*)

Saki: Hi. Haven't seen you for a long time, but how are you?

Hajime: Sa, Saki!! Wh, wh, why are you, the junior high school student, here!?

Saki: You ask me why, but I'm just visiting the open house. I am also a senior who will be taking the high school entrance examination, (don't you know?).

e. (Taken from *Beautiful Life*, episode 10) Shuuji strongly disapproves of what Kyooko says and uses *ja-nai* to say so.

杏子：　ほんと？

柊二：　うん。外泊扱いにしてもらったからさ。

杏子：　あ、よかった。ほっとした。

柊二：　**ほっとしたじゃねえだろ**。

杏子：　ごめん。

Kyooko: Honto?
Shuuji: Un. Gaihaku atsukai ni shite-moratta kara sa.
Kyooko: A, yokatta. Hotto shita. (see E. 22 for *yokatta* and *hotto shita*)
Shuuji: **Hotto shita ja-nee daro.**
Kyooko: Gomen.

Kyooko: Really?
Shuuji: Yeah. They will treat this as an overnight stay.
Kyooko: Ah, that's good. I'm relieved.
Shuuji: Relieved? You shouldn't be saying that.
Kyooko: Sorry.

f. (Taken from *Muko-dono*, episode 10) In this scene, Yuuichiroo's marriage is going to be made public. Hakozaki, Yuuichiroo's manager, strongly denies Yuuichiroo's comment by using *ja-nai*.

祐一郎： えっ、あーっ。
(…)
祐一郎： どうしてー、ハコさん。
箱崎： **どうしてじゃない**よ。あれだけ注意しろって言っただろ。おまえこれ、今日発売だぞ！

Yuuichiroo: E-tt, Aa-tt. (see E. 21 for *E-tt*)
(…)
Yuuichiroo: Dooshitee, Hako-san.
Hakozaki: **Dooshite ja-nai** yo. Are dake chuui shiro tte itta daro. Omae kore, kyoo hatsubai da zo! (see E. 73 for *itta daro*)

Yuuichiroo: What? Oh no.
(…)
Yuuichiroo: Why is this, Hako?
Hakozaki: Don't say "Why is this?". So many times I told you to be careful. This is going to be on sale at the store today!

g. (Taken from *Santaku*) Sanma tries to change the topic to surfing by mentioning something related to it. He asks a question about Kimura's prior speech, in which he mentions that salt water comes out of his nose after surfing. Note that in response to Kimura's surprise, Sanma responds with *E-tt ja-nashi ni*. Through this expression, Sanma shows his disapproval of Kimura's reaction. This example illustrates that topics are sometimes overtly negotiated.

さんま： あ、そうか、塩水でる？
木村： えっ？
さんま： ちゃう。もう、うまいことつないでもらうねん、もう。**えっじゃなしに。**
木村： はい、ごめんなさい。

Sanma: A, soo ka, shiomizu deru?
Kimura: E-tt? (see E. 21 for *E-tt?*)
Sanma: Chau. Moo, umai koto tsunaide-morau nen, moo. **E-tt ja-nashi ni.**
Kimura: Hai, gomennasai.

Sanma: I see, so the salt water comes out?
Kimura: What?
Sanma: Wait. Won't you make this connected to what we are talking about? Come on, don't say "What?".
Kimura: Right, sorry about that.

h. (Taken from *SMAP x SMAP,* New Year's special) During the Bistro SMAP section of the show, Tsutsumi comments on the dish Tsuyoshi made for him. Kimura and Nakai also comment. *Nanja, koryaa* is a stylized version of *Nani, kore*. Note that this style is out of place, in that it is an imagined (obsolete and fictitious) style. Tsutsumi plays with this style (called *roojingo* 'old man style') to express his surprise in a borrowed voice (more about this in Entry 76).

堤： なんじゃ、こりゃあ。
木村： **#なんじゃこりゃあって。**
中居： あんま人にメシつくってもらって**なんじゃこりゃってあんまり言わないですよね**

Tsutsumi: Nan ja, koryaa. (see E. 21 for *nani kore*)
Kimura: **Nan ja koryaa tte.**
Nakai: Anma hito ni meshi tsukutte-moratte **nan ja koryaa tte anmari iwa-nai desu yo ne.**

Tsutsumi: What (in the world) is this?
Kimura: You say, "What is this," but...
Nakai: It's not too often that people say, "What is this?" when you have someone prepare dishes for you, you know.

i. (Taken from *Beautiful Life*, episode 7) At Hotlip, Takumi challenges Shuuji, and Shuuji in the end ignores Takumi.

タクミ： 柊二さん、俺に自分の客取られるの怖いんじゃないですか。店長に俺が見込まれて自分がぬいていかれるのが怖いんじゃないすか。
柊二： 何言ってんの、おまえ。
タクミ： 関係ないかもしれませんよね。柊二さんここ出ていくんだし。(...)
柊二： **勝手に言ってろ**、おまえ。

Takumi: Shuuji-san, ore ni jibun no kyaku torareru no kowai n ja-nai desu ka. Tenchoo ni ore ga mikomarete jibun ga nuite-ikareru no ga kowai n ja-nai su ka. (see E. 11 for *kowai*)
Shuuji: Nani itten no, omae. (see E. 40 for *nani itten no*; E. 30 for *omae*)
Takumi: Kankei nai kamo shiremasen yo ne. Shuuji-san koko dete-iku n da shi. (...) (see E. 63 about the use of *shi*)
Shuuji: **Katte ni ittero,** omae.

Takumi: Shuuji, you are probably afraid that your clients will be mine. You are afraid that the manager thinks highly of me and I will surpass you, right?
Shuuji: What are you talking about! (What nonsense!)
Takumi: Maybe you don't have much to do with us. Shuuji, you are going to leave us, so.
Shuuji: Go ahead and just go on talking nonsense!

j. (Taken from *SMAP x SMAP,* New Year's special) During the Bistro SMAP section, Tsutsumi shows little interest in the dish prepared for him. Nakai comments accordingly.

中居： 堤さん、オムライス。
堤： 別にどうでもいい。
中居： **そんなこと言わないでくださいよ**。これから出るんですから。

Nakai: Tsutsumi-san, omuraisu.
Tsutsumi: Betsu ni doo demo ii.
Nakai: **Sonna koto iwa-naide-kudasai yo**. Kore kara deru n desu kara.

Nakai: Mr. Tsutsumi, an omelet (with fried rice inside), how about it?
Tsutsumi: Whatever.
Nakai: Don't say that, please. It will be served to you later.

k. (Taken from *SMAP x SMAP,* special live show) Kimura comments on what Shingo says. By telling Shingo not to say what he has already said, Kimura expresses a critical attitude.

慎吾： 別にどっちでもいいんだよ。
(...)
木村： ちょっと待て。**どっちでもいいなんて言うなよ**。俺はあれに一番てこずってんだ。（中居、膝をたたいて笑いころげる）な。
慎吾： はい。

Shingo: Betsu ni dotchi demo ii n da yo.
(...)

Kimura: Chotto mate. **Dotchi demo ii nan te yuu na yo.** Ore wa are ni ichiban tekozutte n da. (see E. 25 for *chotto*; E. 23 for *ichiban*) (*Nakai, hiza o tataite waraikorogeru*) Na.

Shingo: Hai.

Shingo: It really doesn't matter, either way is fine.
(…)

Kimura: Wait a minute. Don't say that either way is fine. I've been bothered by that and made an extra effort for that. (*Nakai taps on his thigh and laughs a big laugh*) You got that?

Shingo: Right. (I'm sorry.)

l. (Taken from *Long Vacation*, episode 4) Sena reveals his inner feelings, to which Minami responds mildly, commenting on Sena's phrases. Minami's feeling here is something like "I sympathize with you, but isn't it something that you must deal with yourself?".

瀬名： 僕の胸を、#マシンガンみたいに撃ち抜いたんですよ。
南： **撃ち抜いたって言われてもねえ。**

Sena: Boku no mune o mashingan mitai ni uchinuita n desu yo.
Minami: **Uchinuita tte iwaretemo nee.**

Sena: (Those words) shot through my chest like machine gun bullets.
Minami: Well, you tell me that they shot like machine gun bullets, but…

16
Asserting Oneself Expressively and Being Creative

71. Showing Conviction and Determination

Key Expressions

(≈) 絶対勝つ！	*Zettai katsu!*	I'm definitely going to win!
(≈) 勝ってみせる	*Katte-miseru.*	I'll win; you wait and see.
(≈) 勝ってやる	*Katte-yaru.*	I will win for sure.

Explanation

The simplest way to show conviction and determination is to use the dictionary form (V basic) of the verb with an emphatic tone. The *desu/masu* form may also be used in formal situations, as in *Ikimasu!* '(No matter what) I am going!'.

[V-*te* + *miseru*] is used for showing strong will and determination, especially when addressed to a specific person. The verb *miseru* 'to show' indicates your hope that your determination will bring about some result you want the person to whom you are talking to see. For example, when a young man pledges that he will make something of himself to his parents, [V-*te* + *miseru*] is appropriate. The implication is that the achievement may require time, but that the positive results will be clear to the person addressed.

[V-*te* + *yaru*] is another structure used to show strong determination. It has the additional connotation of a desire that goes against expectations. So, for example, when a less experienced player is determined to win in a tennis tournament despite other people's predictions, *Katte-yaru!* (with a tinge of defiance) is appropriate.

Examples

a. 行きます！

Ikimasu!

I'm determined to go!

b. (≈) 今日中にこの仕事、**仕上げてみせる**。

Kyoojuu ni kono shigoto, **shiagete-miseru.**

I will complete this task by the end of the day, for sure.

c. (A man is determined to fight and win)

(≈my1a): 今度の試合に負けたら、それで終りだな。
(≈my2): ああ。
(≈my1b): いや、諦めるのはまだ早い。**勝つぞ**！絶対**勝ってやる**。

(≈my1a): Kondo no shiai ni maketara, sore de owari da na.
(≈my2): Aa.
(≈my1b): Iya, akirameru no wa mada hayai. **Katsu zo!** Zettai **katte-yaru.** (see E. 20 for *akirameru*; E. 24 about repetition)

(≈my1a): If we lose this match, that will be the end of it, won't it?
(≈my2): I'm afraid so.
(≈my1b): No, it's too early to give up. We will win! (Even against all odds) we're going to win!

Authentic Examples

a. (Taken from *SMAP x SMAP,* New Year's special) At the end of the Bistro SMAP section of the show, Shingo insists that he's going to complete the cooking.

慎吾： **できる！**
木村： #できてねーじゃん。
中居： あ、できてないですか。
木村： できてねーじゃんよ。

Shingo: **Dekiru!**
Kimura: Dekite-nee jan. (see Chapter 2 for *nee* instead of *nai*)
Nakai: A, dekite-nai desu ka.
Kimura: Dekite-nee jan yo. (see E. 24 about repetition; E. 55 about the use and non-use of *yo*)

Shingo: I can do it!
Kimura: It's not done yet, right?
Nakai: Ah, it's not done yet?
Kimura: It's not done yet.

b. (Taken from *Kindaichi shoonen no jikenbo*, 5: 181) Hajime is challenged by his rival, Takatoo, to solve a mystery case. He declares his determination.

高遠：　＜つまり今のところ / 君は私に遅れを / とってるわけだ / ——それでも / 私に勝つ / 自信があると ....？＞

はじめ：　＜.... ああ !/ 必ず**勝って / みせる**..！！＞

Takatoo: Tsumari ima no tokoro kimi wa watashi ni okure o totteru wake da.—Sore demo watashi ni katsu jishin ga aru to....? (see E. 30 for *kimi*)

Hajime: ....Aa! Kanarazu **katte-miseru**..!!

Takatoo: In other words, right now, you are way behind me. Even then you are confident to beat me?

Hajime: Yes, absolutely. I will beat you without fail!!

c. (Taken from *Majo no jooken*, episode 11) Hikaru shows Michi his strong determination to be a doctor.

光：　俺、**医者になる**。医者になって、未知を必ず、**生き返らせてみせる**。ひとりでも多くの人を、苦しみから**救ってみせる**。幸せ**にしてみせる**。

Hikaru: Ore, **isha ni naru**. Isha ni natte, Michi o kanarazu, **ikikaerasete-miseru**. Hitori demo ooku no hito o, kurushimi kara **sukutte-miseru**. Shiawase ni **shite-miseru**. (see E. 5 for *shiawase*)

Hikaru: I will be a medical doctor. I will make you well again, Michi. And I will relieve as many people as possible from suffering. I will make them happy.

d. (Taken from *Muko-dono*, episode 7) Satsuki begs her boss to let her be the director of the radio program. Satsuki is hoping that she will be able to show impressive results to the manager.

さつき：　部長！＃部長！＃私にディレクターをやらせてください。絶対**成功させてみせます**。

Satsuki: Buchoo! Buchoo! Watashi ni direkutaa o yarasete-kudasai. Zettai **seikoo sasete-misemasu**.

Satsuki: Mr. Manager! Mr. Manager! Let me be the director. I will make it a success without fail.

e. (Taken from *Long Love Letter Hyooryuu Kyooshitsu*, episode 7) Yuka is determined to find the medicine Asami needs.

結花：　横浜じゅう、ううん、東京だろうが、千葉だろうが、全部**捜してやる！**
大友：　超前向き。
高木：　だな。

Yuka: Yokohama juu, uun, Tookyoo daroo ga, Chiba daroo ga, zenbu **sagashite-yaru.**
Ootomo: Choo maemuki. (see E. 24 for *choo*)
Takagi: Da na.

Yuka: All over Yokohama, no, whether it takes us to Tokyo, Chiba, or wherever, I'm going to look for it.
Ootomo: Super positive.
Takagi: Right.

f. (Taken from *Furuete nemure, sanshimai*, 15: 96) Yuriko talks to the murderer on the phone.

向こうはしばらく沈黙していた。そして、
「—— 運が強いな」
と言った。「必ず**始末してやる**」

Mukoo wa shibaraku chinmoku shiteita. Soshite, (see E. 75 about silence)
"—Un ga tsuyoi na"
to itta. "Kanarazu **shimatsu shite-yaru.**"

The other party stayed silent for a while. And,
"You are fortunate (so far),"
said he. "I'll kill you for sure."

g. (Taken from interview #85, with Eiji Okuda, movie actor and director) Okuda expresses his determination in no uncertain terms.

奥田：　30 代で (...) キャーキャー言われて 40 代で映画で主演男優賞を九つもらった。50 代では監督で頂点を**きわめてやろう**と思って。
林：　カッコイイ！

Okuda: Sanjuudai de (...) kyaa kyaa iwarete yonjuudai de eiga de shuen dan'yuushoo o kokonotsu moratta. Gojuudai de wa kantoku de chooten o **kiwamete-yaroo** to omotte.
Hayashi: Kakko ii! (see E. 13 for *kakko ii*)

Okuda: In my thirties (...) I was popular among young women, and in my forties I received nine awards as a leading actor. In my fifties, I am thinking that I will reach the top as a director.
Hayashi: Cool!

72. Expressing Assertiveness through *N(o) da*

Key Expressions

だから行ったんです	*Dakara itta n desu.*	That's why I went.
(≈) 俺行く。どうしても行くんだ！	*Ore iku. Dooshitemo iku n da!*	I'm going. No matter what, I'm going!
(≈) どこへ行けばいい？どこへ行けばいいの？	*Doko e ikeba ii? Doko e ikeba ii no?*	Where should I go? Really, where should I go?

Explanation

N(o) *da* is a common clause- and sentence-final form that often marks words that provide explanation. For example, when *Ginkoo e itte-kita n desu* 'It's that I went to the bank' is chosen instead of *Ginkoo e itte-kimashita* 'I went to the bank', the speaker points out that going to the bank provides relevant explanation.

Explanation is only one of the many functions of *n*(o) *da*, however. The structure is very versatile. Here I concentrate on the use of *n*(o) *da* for expressing an assertive attitude. For example, to emphasize that you went, *Dakara itta n desu* 'That's why I went' may be used. The *n desu* expression adds some explanation as well as emphasizing the fact that you did indeed go. You may demonstrate firm determination by using *n da* or *no*, as in *Dooshitemo iku n da!* or *Dooshitemo iku no!* 'No matter what, I'm going!'.

This and other functions of *n*(o) *da* are related to the fact that the structure contains a nominalized clause. The content of the nominalized clause (the *n*[o] clause) is already presumed and presupposed, so the speaker is not offering its content as a new piece of information. Instead of the information, the person using the expression comes to the fore; consequently it adds assertiveness.

This characterization holds true for questions with *n*(o) as well. When a question is asked using *n*(o) or *n*(o) *desu ka*, the speaker is focusing on the addressee's will and feelings, as associated with the content of the *no*-clause. When a speaker asks *Doko e ikeba ii no?* instead of *Doko e ikeba ii?*, an intense desire to appeal to the partner is made apparent.

However, because *n*(o) *desu ka* both assumes and asserts, it may imply criticism. When one says *Yasunda n desu ka?* 'So you were absent, were you?' in a context where one's partner should have been present, it reconfirms the truancy and sounds critical.

Examples

a. (A mother and son in conflict) The son expresses his determination by *n da*.

(≈fa1): もうやめたら。そんなにたくさん食べるとお腹痛くなるわよ。
(≈mc1): やだ。せっかく注文したんだから絶対全部食べる**んだ**！

(≈fa1): Moo yametara. Sonna ni takusan taberu to onaka itaku naru wa yo. (see E. 16 for *sonna ni*)
(≈mc1): Ya da. Sekkaku chuumon shita n da kara zettai zenbu taberu **n da!** (see E. 9 for *ya da*; E. 14 for *sekkaku*)

(≈fa1): Why don't you stop? If you eat that much, you'll have a stomachache.
(≈mc1): No way. We ordered the food, so I'm definitely going to eat everything.

b. (Two adult friends talking about drinking sake) The second speaker is interested in confirming what the first has said.

(≈fa1): お酒は全然飲めなくて。
(≈fa2): だめ**なの**？一滴も？

(≈fa1): Osake wa zenzen nome-nakute..
(≈fa2): Dame **na no**? Itteki mo?

(≈fa1): I can't drink sake at all…
(≈fa2): You can't drink sake? Not even a drop?

Authentic Examples

a. (Taken from *Muko-dono*, episode 9) The father repeats *n da* for an assertive effect; Yuuichiroo acknowledges this.

父： あいつは、さくらと母親に一言もあやまらなかった**んだ**よ。そればかりかあいつは、母親に、自分を生んだのが間違いな**んだ**って言った**んだ**よ。#自分を生んでくれた母親に、そんな言葉を投げ捨てて、家を出ていった**んだ**よ、あいつは。#だから#私は#あいつを許さない！
祐一郎： そうだった**んですか**。

chichi: Aitsu wa, Sakura to hahaoya ni hitokoto mo ayamara-nakatta **n da** yo. Sore bakari ka aitsu wa, hahaoya ni, jibun o unda no ga machigai na **n da** tte itta **n da** yo. Jibun o unde-kureta hahaoya ni, sonna kotoba o nagesutete, uchi o dete-itta **n da** yo, aitsu wa. Dakara watashi wa aitsu o yurusa-nai! (see E. 42 for *jibun*; E. 48 about inverted word order)
Yuuichiroo: Soo datta **n desu ka**.

father: He never apologized to Sakura and his mother. Not only that, he said to his mother that it was a mistake to give birth to him. He left home after shouting those words to his mother, who gave him life. So I can never forgive him.

Yuuichiroo: I see, I understand the situation.

b. (Taken from *Taiyoo wa shizuma-nai*, episode 7) Nao reports to Kirino that he won the *kendoo* match. Note the use of *uchi no kookoo* that enhances a sense of belongingness, as discussed in Chapter 3.

直： 桐野さん、#今日の試合、負けてませんよ。団体戦だから、3、2でうちの高校の負けだったけど#けど僕は、##勝ちました。#勝った**んです**！

Nao: Kirino-san, kyoo no shiai, maketemasen yo. Dantaisen da kara, san, ni de uchi no kookoo no make datta kedo, kedo boku wa, kachimashita. Katta **n desu**!

Nao: Ms. Kirino, today's match, I didn't lose. Because it was a group match between schools, our school lost. But I won (my match). I did win!

c. (Taken from *Chibi Maruko-chan*, 14: 153) Kosugi's determination is expressed in part by *n da*.

小杉： ＜ボクは/ただのデブちんから/卒業したい**んだ**＞
＜だから/明日の体力テストで/がんばってみんなを/驚かせてやる**んだ**＞

Kosugi: Boku wa tada no debuchin kara sotsugyoo shitai **n da**.
Dakara ashita no tairyoku tesuto de ganbatte minna o odorokasete-yaru **n da**. (see E. 71 for *odorokasete-yaru*)

Kosugi: I want to graduate from being just an ordinary fat boy.
So, I will definitely do my best in tomorrow's physical fitness test and will surprise everyone.

d. (Taken from *Chibi Maruko-chan*, 13: 158) Maruko and her classmates go to the mountain to look for fireflies. Although they haven't found any so far, Yamada refuses to go back home, insisting that he'll find some. His *n da* illustrates his determination.

山田： ＜いやだっ/探すもんねっ/帰らないぞっ＞
まる子： ＜山田っ＞
(...)
山田： ＜いやだっ/探す**んだっ**＞＜オイラ/ひとりでも/探す**んだっ**＞

Yamada: Iya da-tt. Sagasu mon ne-tt. Kaera-nai zo-tt. (see E. 9 for *iya da*)
Maruko: Yamada-tt.
(...)
Yamada: Iya da-tt. Sagasu **n da-tt.** Oira hitori demo sagasu **n da-tt.** (see E. 42 for *oira*)

Yamada: No way. I'm going to look for them. I'm not going home.
Maruko: Yamada.
(...)
Yamada: No way. I'm going to look for them. Even if I am the only one, I'm still going to look for them.

e. (Taken from *Majo no jooken*, episode 3) This example contrasts two ways of asking a question, one with and the other without *no*. The second question does not focus so much on information as on feeling. When Michi repeats her question, she means "I'm asking you, please answer. Where is it that I should go?"

未知： 会いたい！
光： えっ？
未知： どこ行けばいい？どこ行けばいいの？

Michi: Aitai!
Hikaru: E-tt? (see E. 21 for *E-tt?*)
Michi: Doko ikeba ii? Doko ikeba ii **no**?

Michi: I want to see you.
Hikaru: What?
Michi: Where should I come to see you? Where is it that I can come to see you?

Additional Information

N(*o*) *da* is also used for the following effects.

1. When what precedes *n*(*o*) *da* offers a reason or cause related to the issue at hand.
2. To offer recognition of information, as in *Sorede itta n da* 'I see, that's why she went'. *Soo na n da* is used interjectionally when the speaker realizes that he or she understands something (see Entry 46).
3. To communicate a discovery. For example, when you find a book you had misplaced, you may say *Konna tokoro ni atta n da* 'It was here, I see'.
4. When prefacing a request or making a request in a mild tone, as in *Okiki shitai koto ga aru n desu ga* 'I have something I would like to ask you' and *Kyoo chotto hayaku kaeritai n desu ga* 'I would like to go home early today, if I may'.

5. When insistently ordering the partner to do something, as in *Sugu iku n da!* 'Go right away!'.
6. When persuading oneself, as in *Isshookenmei benkyoo shita n da. Dakara daijoobu* 'I studied hard, indeed. So I should do fine'.

73. Commenting on One's Own Speech

Key Expressions

(□)って言ってるだろ	*tte itteru daro*	I'm saying so
(≠) 申し上げております	*mooshiagete-orimasu*	that is what I am saying
(≈)って	*tte*	I'm telling you
(≈)っつうの	*ttsuu no*	I'm telling you, can't you get it?
(≈)ってば	*tte ba*	I'm telling you, don't you get it?

Explanation

Commenting on speech reflects concern you have about what is being said. Such qualification may be in reference to your own or your partner's speech. By calling attention to your own words, you are claiming that your speech is special, extraordinary, and deserving of attention. The effect may be either emphasis or hesitation. (See the note at the end of this entry for the effect of hesitation.) The emphatic effect occurs in English as well in such similar expressions as "I'm telling you!" and "That's what I'm saying!".

Tte itteru daro (or *tte itten daro*) 'I'm saying so' is a blunt expression, but similar expressions appear at various politeness levels, for example, *tte itteru n desu*, *to mooshiageteiru n desu*, and *to mooshiagete-orimasu*. These phrases, because they tell your partner unequivocally that you have already made your point, add emphasis to your words. *Itta daro* or *Itta desho* reminds the partner that what is said has already been said before.

In casual situations, young people in particular use the quotation marker *tte* (optionally *te* following *n*) or a quotation phrase, *ttsuu no,* at the end of speech. The conditional *ba* may also be attached, as in *tte ba*. To mark their emphatic effect, these phrases are usually pronounced clearly and strongly.

Examples

a. (A man angrily reassures his friend)

(□ma1): だから、明日持ってくる**って言ってんだろ。**
(≈ma2): 分かったよ。

(□ma1): Dakara, ashita motte-kuru **tte itte n daro.**
(≈ma2): Wakatta yo. (see E. 66 for *wakatta*)

(□ma1): So, I'm telling you that I'll bring it tomorrow.
(≈ma2): O.K., I got it.

b. (≈) うるさいなあ、分かってる**って。**

Urusai naa, wakatteru **tte.** (see E. 39 for *urusai*; E. 66 for *wakatteru*)

You are getting on my nerves. I know that, I'm telling you.

c. (A man emphasizes his point)

(□my1): あいつに頼んだって、ダメだ**っつうの！**
(my2): そんな。

(□my1): Aitsu ni tanondatte, dame da **ttsuu no!**
(my2): Sonna. (see E. 16 for *sonna*)

(□my1): Even if you ask him, it won't work, I'm telling you!
(my2): You say so, but...

d. (Two young men talking about a camera)

(≈my1a): あいつ、俺のデジカメ、こわしちゃったんじゃないだろうな。
(≈my2a): そんなことないよ。ただ、忘れてんだ**ってば。**
(≈my1b): でも、もう二週間になるってのに返してくれないんだ。きっと、こわしちゃたんだよ。
(≈my2b): 絶対そんなことない、って**言ってんのに。**

(≈my1a): Aitsu, ore no dejikame, kowashichatta n ja-nai daroo na. (see E. 17 for *kowashichatta*)
(≈my2a): Sonna koto nai yo. Tada, wasurete n da **tte ba.** (see E. 16 for *sonna*; E. 72 for *n da*)
(≈my1b): Demo, moo nishuukan ni naru tte noni kaeshite-kure-nai n da. Kitto, kowashichatta n da yo.
(≈my2b): Zettai sonna koto nai, tte **itte n noni.**

(≈my1a): He hasn't returned my digital camera. I hope he didn't break it.
(≈my2a): I don't think so. He just forgot.
(≈my1b): But, it's been two weeks, and he hasn't returned it to me. I swear he broke it.
(≈my2b): That can't be, I'm telling you, don't you see?

Authentic Examples

a. (Taken from *Beautiful Life*, episode 2) Tsuchiya, Hotlip's manager, reprimands Takumi, who is late for the morning meeting. The manager reminds Takumi that he had already told him the time of their regular meetings. This meaning is enhanced by the use of [V-*te-aru*], which describes an action performed for a specific purpose. Note that, as explained in Chapter 2, *nere-nakute* (instead of *nerare-nakute*) shows *ra*-deletion.

タクミ：　遅くなりました。
土屋：　定例会議は始業時間の三時間前**って言ってあるだろ**。
タクミ：　すみません。きのう寝れなくて。

Takumi: Osoku narimashita.
Tsuchiya: Teirei kaigi wa shigyoo jikan no sanjikan mae **tte itte-aru daro.**
Takumi: Sumimasen. Kinoo nere-nakute.

Takumi: Sorry for being late.
Tsuchiya: Didn't I tell you that our regular meeting starts three hours before the shop opens?
Takumi: Sorry. I couldn't sleep last night.

b. (Taken from *Majo no jooken*, episode 7) Kiriko visits Masaru's apartment. Masaru doesn't want to see her.

大：　帰ってくれないか。
桐子：　大さん。
大：　帰れ**って言ってんだろ**！

Masaru: Kaette-kure-nai ka.
Kiriko: Masaru-san.
Masaru: Kaere **tte itten daro**!

Masaru: Will you leave?
Kiriko: Masaru.
Masaru: Leave, I'm telling you!

c. (Taken from *Doomoto Tsuyoshi no shoojiki shindoi*, with Ryooko Kuninaka as the guest) At the end of the show, Doomoto comments on Kuninaka, explaining their relationship. Note that he comments on his speech first in the Kansai dialect (*itteru yan ka*) and then in Tokyo speech (*itta desho*). Doomoto uses both the Kansai dialect and Tokyo speech in his television shows, but because he is from the Kansai area, when he breaks into this dialect, his true feelings seem to be revealed more directly.

堂本：　だからあんまり仲よくない**って言ってるやんか**。そこまで仲よくないよってこと**言ったでしょ**。

Doomoto: Dakara anmari nakayoku-nai **tte itteru yan ka**. Soko made nakayoku-nai yo tte koto **itta desho**.

Doomoto: So, I'm telling you we really aren't that tight, as good friends. I told you, didn't I? We aren't that close.

d. (Taken from *Muko-dono*, episode 6) Kaede, Tsutomu's mother, argues with Tsutomu's friend and the friend's mother. (When the friend's mother says *To yuu n desu ka*, it does not qualify her own speech, but challenges Kaede's in an accusatory tone.)

かえで：　だからうちの努はやってない**って言ってるんです**。いじめてたのはその子でしょ。
努：　うん。
友達：　うそつくな！
かえで：　うそついてるのはあなたでしょう！
友達の母：　家の息子がうそをついてると言うんですか！
かえで：　だから何度も**言ってますように**、息子は間違っても子犬をいじめたりするような子じゃありません。

Kaede: Dakara uchi no Tsutomu wa yatte-nai **tte itteru n desu**. Ijimeteta no wa sono ko desho. (see Chapter 3 about *uchi*)
Tsutomu: Un.
tomodachi: Uso tsuku-na!
Kaede: Uso tsuiteru no wa anata deshoo! (see E. 30 for *anata*)
tomodachi no haha: Uchi no musuko ga uso o tsuiteru to yuu n desu ka!
Kaede: Dakara nando mo **ittemasu yoo ni**, musuko wa machigattemo koinu o ijimetari suru yoona ko jaarimasen.

Kaede: So, I'm telling you that my son Tsutomu hasn't done that. The one that was taunting the puppy is him, right?
Tsutomu: Yes.
friend: Don't lie to me!
Kaede: You are the one telling a lie!
friend's mother: Are you saying my son is a liar?
Kaede: So, as I've already said many times, my son isn't the type who would abuse a puppy, no matter what.

e. (Taken from *SMAP x SMAP*, New Year's special) Nakai teases Shingo, who is preparing an omelet with fried rice inside during the Bistro SMAP section. Shingo insists that his cooking is going just fine, in part by using *ttsuu no*.

中居：　慎吾頑張ってね。
慎吾：　はい。
中居：　あ、失敗しましたね、これ。
慎吾：　してねえっ**つうの**。
中居：　ああ。
慎吾：　大成功だよ。

Nakai: Shingo ganbatte ne.
Shingo: Hai.
Nakai: A, shippai shimashita ne, kore. (see E. 18 for *shippai shita*; E. 48 about inverted word order)
Shingo: Shite-nee **ttsuu no.** (see Chapter 2 for *shite-nee* instead of *shite-nai*)
Nakai: Aa.
Shingo: Daiseikoo da yo.

Nakai: Shingo, do your best.
Shingo: O.K.
Nakai: Ah, you messed this up.
Shingo: No, not at all, I'm telling you.
Nakai: Oh.
Shingo: This is a big success.

f. (Taken from *Strawberry on the Shortcake*, episode 5) Yui and Saeki are going for a drive. Yui is excited and bothers Saeki by making unreasonable requests. Saeki's answers contain comments about his own speech, which causes an emphatic effect.

唯：　ねえ、あとで唯にもちょっと運転させて。
佐伯：　だめー。免許ない人はだめー。
唯：　（ハンドルに触る）いいじゃん、ちょっとぐらい。
佐伯：　あっ、あぶねえっ**てば**。
唯：　へへ。先輩のびっくりした顔はじめて見た。（ワイパーを作動させようとする）これはこれは？
佐伯：　だめ。あぶねえっ**つうの**！め！
唯：　ごめんなさい。

Yui: Nee, ato de Yui ni mo chotto unten sasete. (see E. 54 for *Nee*; 25 for *chotto*)
Saeki: Damee. Menkyo nai hito wa damee. (see E. 18 for *dame*; E. 27 for *damee* instead of *dame*)
Yui: (*handoru ni sawaru*) Ii jan, chotto gurai.
Saeki: A-tt, abunee **tte ba.** (see Chapter 2 for *abunee* instead of *abunai*)

Yui: He he. Senpai no bikkuri shita kao hajimete mita. (see E. 21 for *bikkuri shita*) (*waipaa o sadoo saseyoo to suru*) Kore wa kore wa?
Saeki: Dame. Abunee **ttsuu no**! Me!
Yui: Gomennasai.

Yui: Say, later will you let me drive the car a bit?
Saeki: No way. Those who don't have a license cannot.
Yui: (*touching the steering wheel*) Isn't it O.K., just a little?
Saeki: Hey, that's dangerous. Can't you get it?
Yui: Heh heh. This is the first time I've seen your surprised face. (*trying to turn on the windshield wiper*) This, how about this?
Saeko: Stop that. It's dangerous. Don't you get it? Stop it.
Yui: Sorry.

g. (Taken from Konishi, 2003a, 16) In this essay, which accompanies a photograph of a French politician, Konishi, a fashion commentator, makes the following remark. Although *ttsuu no* is primarily used in casual speech, the writer uses it in his essay to express his intense emotion.

そんな彼が世界の舞台で発言するんだから、フランスもオーダーのスーツくらい税金で買ってやれ**っつうの**。

Sonna kare ga sekai no butai de hatsugen suru n da kara, Furansu mo oodaa no suutsu kurai zeikin de katte-yare **ttsuu no**. (see E. 16 for *sonna*)

Because a guy like him has the world as a stage to make his statement, I'm telling you, the French government should buy him a made-to-order suit.

Note

Another effect associated with commenting on one's own speech is a hesitation that weakens the impact. This kind of qualification has the question marker *ka* and a hesitant tone of voice; it usually occurs with the quotation marker *to*/(*t*)*te* only, or, less frequently, with [*to*/(*t*)*te* + *omou*]. In either case, it is spoken hesitantly and often trails off. For example, one may express hesitancy by saying *Ano hito, moo atashi no koto suki ja-nai no ka naa tte* 'I'm thinking that maybe he doesn't love me anymore'.

74. Sarcasm and Tautology

Key Expressions

(≈) 俺の顔に泥を塗ってくれて、ありがとうよ	*Ore no kao ni doro o nutte-kurete, arigatoo yo.*	(lit., Thanks for painting my face with mud.) Thanks for dishonoring me!
(≈) 勝ちは勝ち	*Kachi wa kachi.*	Victory is victory.

Explanation

Sarcasm and irony are universal. In every language, certain expressions and strategies signal irony, which often encourages sarcastic interpretation.

In order to convey sarcasm, the speaker must send signs that contradict the literal meaning of what is being said. For example, although on the surface one may be saying *Arigatoo* 'Thanks', the tone of voice and facial expression are anything but grateful when one is being sarcastic. As important is the context in which *Arigatoo* is uttered. If the situation does not call for it, and in fact, the situation calls for a reaction that is the opposite of gratitude, most likely *Arigatoo* is intended as sarcasm. It is also possible to construct a sentence that makes no sense when taken literally. For example, you may refer to some harm caused by your partner by thanking him or her for it, expressing your deep anger sarcastically. A well-known Japanese sarcastic expression is *Kao ni doro o nutte-kurete, arigatoo yo* '(lit.) Thanks (a lot) for painting my face with mud'.

Devices that signal irony include exaggeration and alienation. In exaggeration the speaker uses hyperbole, exaggerated intonation, vowel lengthening, and repetition—all normally unnecessary. Excessively polite style is also a signal of irony. In alienation, the speaker does not really agree with what she or he is saying and conveys this by using phrases that dissociate the speaker from the statement. One clear device is to frame the utterance by adding phrases related to saying, for example, *nan te* '(to say) so, (to say) such as'. This phrase qualifies the preceding speech in such a way as to deflect the impact of a remark (as explained in Entry 45) and consequently signals it as sarcastic.

Sarcasm or irony is creative speech intended to subvert literal meaning. By using sarcasm or irony, the speaker confirms empathy with the partner by the assumption that they are on the same wavelength.

Tautology is another universal rhetorical strategy. The sentence structure [A is A] points to something so obvious that it demands a special interpretation. [A is A] is obvious, so why is the speaker bothering to say so? Tautology emphasizes that, no matter what, the fact remains that [A is A]. This kind of emphatic statement denies any possibility that A could be something other than what it is. For example, *Kachi wa kachi* 'Victory is victory' denies that a victory may be considered anything else and declares that no matter what people think, and no matter what the situation has been, the fact of victory cannot be denied. In interaction, because tautology is used to emphasize the fact that A is nothing but A with a strong tone of finality, the partner is often shut off from continuing the same topic or, especially, from repeating points already made. Tautology often brings discussion to a halt through its undeniable assertive force.

Examples

a. (Two young workers complaining about a colleague) Exaggeration, communicated through *mattaku* and the repetition of *kanpeki*, signals irony and encourages a sarcastic interpretation.

(≈my1): ほんと、佐川のやることって**まったく完璧。完璧。**
(≈my2): あいつ、また失敗やらかしたの？

(≈my1): Honto, Sagawa no yaru koto tte **mattaku kanpeki. Kanpeki.** (see E. 47 for *tte*)
(≈my2): Aitsu, mata shippai yarakashita no? (see E. 30 for *aitsu*)

(≈my1): Really, what Sagawa does is perfect. Simply perfect.
(≈my2): Did he make a goof again?

b. (Two high school students talking about their teacher) Given the first speaker's bad news, the second speaker's sarcastic attitude is clear. Note the use of *nan te*, which deflects the impact of what precedes it.

(≈ft1a): 山田先生って、自分のクラスでいじめがあること、全然気づいていない。
(≈ft2): そう、そりゃ、**すばらしい、なんて。**
(≈ft1b): まったく、絶望的なのよ、あの先生。

(≈ft1a): Yamada-sensei tte, jibun no kurasu de ijime ga aru koto, zenzen kizuitei-nai. (see E. 42 for *jibun*)
(≈ft2): Soo, sorya, **subarashii, nan te.** (see E. 45 for *nan te*)
(≈ft1b): Mattaku, zetsubooteki na no yo, ano sensei. (see E. 48 about inverted word order)

(≈ft1a): Ms. Yamada has no idea at all that some bullying is going on in her own class.
(≈ft2): Is that right? That's just wonderful, I'd say.
(≈ft1b): Absolutely hopeless, that teacher.

c. (Two researchers lamenting that visitors are coming to the lab)

(≈my1): また、**お偉いさん**が何人か見学に来るらしいよ。
(≈my2): いやになっちゃうね。難しい実験の最中なのにさ。

(≈my1): Mata, **oeraisan** ga nannin ka kengaku ni kuru rashii yo. (see E. 62 for *rashii*)
(≈my2): Iya ni natchau ne. Muzukashii jikken no saichuu na noni sa. (see E. 9 for *iya*; E. 17 for *natchau*)

(≈my1): Again, those great and respected ones are coming to observe us.
(≈my2): Oh, boy, that's too bad. We are in the middle of difficult experiments, you know.

d. (Two men commenting on a woman)

(≈my1a): まったく広瀬の言葉づかいにはあきれるよ。あんなの女じゃない。
(≈my2a): 言葉づかいがひどくたって**女は女だ**よ。彼女、けっこう気持ちはやさしいよ。
(≈my1b): そうかなあ。
(≈my2b): そりゃ、そうだよ。何て言ったって、**女は女なんだ**から。

(≈my1a): Mattaku Hirose no kotoba zukai ni wa akireru yo. Anna no onna ja-nai.
(≈my2a): Kotoba zukai ga hidokutatte **onna wa onna da** yo. Kanojo, kekkoo kimochi wa yasashii yo. (see E. 25 for *kekkoo*; E. 6 for *yasashii*)
(≈my1b): Soo ka naa. (see E. 46 for *Soo ka naa*)
(≈my2b): Sorya, soo da yo. Nan te ittatte, **onna wa onna na n da** kara.

(≈my1a): I'm really taken aback by the way Hirose talks. She is not (like) a woman.
(≈my2a): Even with a terrible way of speaking, a woman is a woman. She is tenderhearted, you know.
(≈my1b): I doubt it.
(≈my2b): She is (tenderhearted), for sure. No matter what, a woman is a woman.

Authentic Examples

a. (Taken from *Antiiku, seiyoo kottoo yoogashiten*, episode 3) In the following scene, although Kage apologizes, his face shows defiance, and he does not bow for the apology as is expected. This mismatch signals that Kage's apology is sarcastic.

かげ： ま、あえて説明する程、おもしろいことじゃないですけどね (…) 私が隠密のかげ、わかが、若侍の役で。まあ、それ以来。
エイジ： ふーん。ほんと説明する程のことじゃねえなあ。
かげ： **すいません。**

Kage: Ma, aete setsumei suru hodo, omoshiroi koto ja-nai desu kedo ne (…) watashi ga onmitsu no kage, waka ga, wakazamurai no yaku de. Maa, sore irai.
Eiji: Fuun. Honto setsumei suru hodo no koto ja-nee naa. (see E. 21 for *Fuun*; Chapter 2 for *ja-nee* instead of *ja-nai*)
Kage: **Suimasen.**

Kage: Well, it's not really interesting enough to bother you with an explanation, but (in our childhood plays) I was Kage, the shadow, and Waka played the young (*waka*) samurai. Since that time (we call each other Kage and Waka).
Eiji: I see. It's true, not quite worthy of explanation.
Kage: (sarcastically) Excuse me.

b. (Taken from *Beautiful Life*, episode 1) At the library, Shuuji wants to use a copying machine for which a long line has already formed. Kyooko insists that he get in line, or copy the content by hand. Shuuji, clapping his hands, yells *Omoshirooi*, but he is not happy at all, as is evident from the context. The sarcastic reading is encouraged by his over-exaggerated pronunciation of the word, accompanied with an almost theatrical clapping of his hands.

杏子： 何よ。とにかくあなたも並んで。
柊二： 時間ないんですよ。
杏子： だったらこれ貸してあげるから、書き写したら。
柊二： **おもしろーい！**

Kyooko: Nani yo. Tonikaku anata mo narande. (see E. 37 for *Nani*)
Shuuji: Jikan nai n desu yo. (see E. 72 for *n desu*)
Kyooko: Dattara kore kashite-ageru kara, kakiutsushitara.
Shuuji: **Omoshirooi!** (see E. 27 for *omoshirooi* instead of *omoshiroi*)

Kyooko: What do you want? At any rate, you, too, get in the line.
Shuuji: I don't have time.
Kyooko: Then I'll let you use this, so why don't you hand copy (the book)?
Shuuji: (sarcastically) Wow, what fun!

c. (Taken from *Long Love Letter Hyooryuu Kyooshitsu*, episode 4) Yuka and Asami, in the middle of their supposedly romantic first date, find evidence that they may have been transported into the future. They end up searching for additional evidence all night. Asami's comment is sarcastic.

結花：	すごーく印象的な初デートだったね。
浅海：	**超ロマンチックでした！**

Yuka:	Sugooku inshootekina hatsu deeto datta ne. (see E. 24 and E. 27 for *sugooku*; E. 29 for *deeto*)
Asami:	**Choo romanchikku deshita!** (see E. 24 for *choo*)

Yuka:	It was an extremely impressive first date.
Asami:	Yes, it was super romantic!

d. (Taken from *Strawberry on the Shortcake*, episode 5) Manato's father is secretive about his new wife's health. He refuses to elaborate on it, in part through tautology. Manato gets the message that he must drop the topic.

まなと：	病院？
父：	ああ。
まなと：	退院できるって聞いたけど。
父：	まあ、いろいろあってな。
まなと：	いろいろって？
父：	**いろいろはいろいろだ。**
まなと：	うん、そう。

Manato:	Byooin?
chichi:	Aa.
Manato:	Taiin dekiru tte kiita kedo. (see E. 63 for *kedo*)
chichi:	Maa, iroiro atte na.
Manato:	Iroiro tte? (see E. 70 about echo questions)
chichi:	**Iroiro wa iroiro da.**
Manato:	Un, soo.

Manato:	Hospital?
father:	Yeah.
Manato:	I've heard that she is being released from the hospital.
father:	Well, there are some circumstances.
Manato:	What do you mean by some circumstances?
father:	Some circumstances are some circumstances.
Manato:	Uh, I see.

e. (Taken from *Antiiku, seiyoo kottoo yoogashiten*, episode 6) When Tachibana answers with tautology, Eiji challenges it, but only with *Nan da yo, sore*. The topic is then dropped.

エイジ：	なあ。
橘：	あっ？
エイジ：	先生、帰ってくるよな。##帰ってくるよな。
橘：	#うー、それは帰ってくんだろ。

エイジ：	帰ってこないと困るよ。店つぶれちゃうよ。
橘：	**その時はその時だ。**
エイジ：	何だよ、それ。

Eiji:	Naa.
Tachibana:	A-tt?
Eiji:	Sensei, kaette-kuru yo na. Kaette-kuru yo na. (see E. 24 about repetition)
Tachibana:	Uu, sore wa kaette-kun daro.
Eiji:	Kaette-ko-nai to komaru yo. Mise tsuburechau yo. (see E. 18 for *komaru*; E. 17 for *tsuburechau*)
Tachibana:	**Sono toki wa sono toki da.**
Eiji:	Nan da yo, sore. (see E. 48 for *Nan da yo, sore*)

Eiji:	Say.
Tachibana:	What?
Eiji:	My teacher, he will be back. He will be back, won't he?
Tachibana:	Uh, I think he will.
Eiji:	We'll be in trouble if he doesn't come back. The shop will go belly up.
Tachibana:	Then is then. (If that happens, that happens.)
Eiji:	What (the heck) is that!

f. (Taken from *Strawberry on the Shortcake*, episode 10) Saeki's lover leaves him, and he is now in a position to be nice to Yui. Yui has long been in love with Saeki; she had insisted earlier that she would eventually become Saeki's number one lover. The tautological expression emphatically asserts this, and its effect is to override all possible doubts.

唯：	二番から一番に昇格だね。
佐伯：	うん。
唯：	不戦勝だけど。
佐伯：	まあそう言わずに。
唯：	**勝ちは勝ちだね。**
佐伯：	そうそう。

Yui:	Niban kara ichiban ni shookaku da ne. (see E. 23 for *ichiban*)
Saeki:	Un.
Yui:	Fusenshoo da kedo.
Saeki:	Maa soo iwa-zu ni.
Yui:	**Kachi wa kachi da ne.**
Saeki:	Soo soo.

Yui:	So I've risen to the status of number one (the first in line) from number two.

Saeki: Yes.
Yui: Although I didn't really fight for it.
Saeki: Well, don't say so.
Yui: Victory is victory, isn't it?
Saeki: It sure is.

g. (Taken from *Taiyoo wa shizuma-nai*, episode 1) By using tautology, Nao emphasizes that, after all, he lost in the *kendo* match.

亜美： あの試合、一緒に見てた友達みんな言ってました。すごいいい試合だったって。あたし、真崎さんの名前と顔それでおぼえたんです。
直： **負けは負けだ。**
亜美： でも私は真崎さんの方が勝ってたと思います。

Ami: Ano shiai, issho ni miteta tomodachi minna ittemashita. Sugoi ii shiai datta tte. Atashi, Masaki-san no namae to kao sore de oboeta n desu. (see E. 24 for *sugoi*; E. 72 for *n desu*)
Nao: **Make wa make da.**
Ami: Demo watashi wa Masaki-san no hoo ga katteta to omoimasu.

Ami: That match, everyone was talking about it. It was a really great match. I got to know your name and face because of that.
Nao: Losing is losing.
Ami: I think you are the one who won.

h. (Taken from *Santaku*) Sanma comments on Fukatsu (an actress) who went to see the SMAP concert. He talks especially about her outfit. In the tautological expression *Ano onna mo ano onna ya dee* 'That woman is that woman', Sanma expresses amazement.

さんま： 深津さんはかわいそうに、半袖で来たんや、ライブだから。ワーと叫ぶから、あつくなるだろうと思って＝
木村： ＝うん。
さんま： 半袖で行ったんや。**あのー女もあの女やわ。**
木村： いや、あの女じゃないですよ。
さんま： **あの女もあの女やでえ。**

Sanma: Fukatsu-san wa kawaisoo ni, hansode de kita n ya, raibu da kara. Waa to sakebu kara, atsuku naru daroo to omotte= (see E. 61 for *kawaisoo ni*)
Kimura: =Un.
Sanma: Hansode de itta n ya. **Anoo onna mo ano onna ya wa.**
Kimura: Iya, ano onna ja-nai desu yo. (see E. 70 for *ja-nai desu yo*)
Sanma: **Ano onna mo ano onna ya dee.**

Sanma: Poor Fukatsu, she came in short sleeves. Because it was a live concert. Because she thought she would scream, and get hot=
Kimura: =Right.
Sanma: She went (to the concert) in short sleeves. That woman is that woman.
Kimura: Don't say "that woman."
Sanma: That woman is that woman, for sure.

75. Asserting in Silence

Key Expression

[沈黙] chinmoku silence

Explanation

Silence or refusal to communicate can have dire consequences for a relationship. The ultimate breakup among friends, for example, results in a sustained and complete absence of communication.

Silence or a pause during conversation, however, can mean many things. It is known that Japanese speakers may keep silent in conversation defensively (1) to avoid telling a lie, (2) to avoid social rejection, (3) to avoid embarrassment, and offensively (4) to show hostility or defiance.

A prolonged silence or lack of response in conversation, because not normally expected, is interpreted as meaningful. What the silence means exactly depends on the context.

Authentic Examples

a. (Taken from *Beautiful Life*, episode 4) Satoru refuses to answer Tsuchiya, Hotlip's manager. Satoru is jealous of Shuuji, and finds it less than exciting to see Shuuji being promoted. But in the end he reluctantly gives in. His less-than-enthusiastic (and mildly hostile) attitude is expressed by his silence in conversation.

土屋： サトル。どうだ。
サトル： えっ？
土屋： おまえはこの店の看板だ。柊二がトップスタイリストの仲間入りしてもいいと思うか。(サトルは答えない)どうした。このヘアスタイル見てどう思うかってことだよ。(まだサトルからの反応なし。土屋、今度は真弓に)真弓、おまえはどうだ。

真弓：　いいと思います。(...)
土屋：　俺もそう思うよ。あとはサトルの意見だ。サトル、どうだ。
サトル：いいと思います。

Tsuchiya: Satoru. Doo da.
Satoru: E-tt?
Tsuchiya: Omae wa kono mise no kanban da. Shuuji ga toppu sutairisuto no nakamairi shitemo ii to omou ka. (*Satoru wa kotae-nai*) Doo shita. Kono heasutairu mite doo omou ka tte koto da yo. (*Mada Satoru kara no hannoo nashi. Tsuchiya, kondo wa Mayumi ni*) Mayumi, omae wa doo da.
Mayumi: Ii to omoimasu. (...)
Tsuchiya: Ore mo soo omou yo. Ato wa Satoru no iken da. Satoru, doo da.
Satoru: Ii to omoimasu.

Tsuchiya: Satoru. What do you think?
Satoru: What?
Tsuchiya: You are the star hairstylist of this shop. Do you think it is O.K. for Shuuji to join the ranks of the "top stylists"? (*Satoru does not respond*) What's the matter? I'm asking you your thoughts on this hairstyle. (*Satoru still remains silent; Tsuchiya talks to Mayumi*) Mayumi, what do you think?
Mayumi: I think it is fine.
Tsuchiya: I think so, too. So, it depends on Satoru's opinion. Satoru, what will you say?
Satoru: I think it is fine.

b. (Taken from *Beautiful Life*, episode 10) Masao, who does not like Shuuji, makes nasty remarks, to which Shuuji remains silent. That silence is itself a denial. Masao realizes this and apologizes.

正夫：　さっきの話の続きだけどさ、もしかして、どうせあとちょっとなら、あいつでもいいって。その後、別の女と、つきあえばいいとかって、あんた思ってんじゃないの？（柊二は何も言わない。それを見て正夫が続ける）ごめんな。
柊二：　俺今そっちが運転中じゃなかったらなぐってましたよ。
正夫：　ごめんな。あんたもつらいよな。

Masao: Sakki no hanashi no tsuzuki da kedo sa, moshika shite, doose ato chotto nara, aitsu demo ii tte. Sono ato, betsu no onna to, tsukiaeba ii toka tte, anta omotte n ja-nai no? (see E. 57 for *doose*; E. 29 for *tsukiau*) (*Shuuji wa nani mo iwa-nai. Sore o mite Masao ga tsuzukeru*) Gomen na.
Shuuji: Ore ima sotchi ga untenchuu ja-nakattara naguttemashita yo. (see E. 30 for *sotchi*)
Masao: Gomen na. Anta mo tsurai yo na. (see E. 30 for *anta*; E. 7 for *tsurai*)

Masao: About what we were discussing a while ago, you are perhaps thinking "If she is going to be with us for only a short while anyway, I will be with her. After that (after she is gone), I will find some other woman." (*Shuuji does not say anything; observing that, Masao continues*) I'm sorry.

Shuuji: If you were not driving, I would have beaten you up.

Masao: Sorry. It is painful for you, too, isn't it?

c. (Taken from *Majo no jooken*, episode 3) Michi's mother asks Michi if she really loves Hikaru. Michi keeps silent but does not deny her mother's assumption, avoiding a lie by maintaining silence. The silence signals an indirect positive answer in this case.

未知の母： あんたその生徒のこと本気で？（未知からの反応なし）そうなの？（やはり答えなし）

Michi no haha: Anta sono seito no koto honki de? (*Michi kara no hannoo nashi*) Soo na no? (*Yahari kotae nashi*)

Michi's mother: Are you serious about that student? (*there is no answer from Michi*) Is it so? (*no answer is given*)

Additional Information

Different cultures value talkativeness and silence in different ways. In the continuum from silence to talkativeness, traditional Japanese culture is skewed toward silence. Discretion, which often means remaining silent when one would rather speak, is an important skill in all cultures. What is significant here is to realize that words are not the sole conveyers of meaning. The ways language is not used also have meaning. One must be vigilant of nonverbal clues, including facial expression, gaze, posture, and so on.

76. Being Playful and Creative by Mixing Styles

Key Expression

［スタイル混用］ *sutairu kon'yoo* style mixture

Explanation

Although stylistic choice, especially *da* and *desu/masu* verb endings, is often based on particular genres and social situations, styles are not chosen only for external reasons. For a variety of reasons, style mixture may occur within a discourse segment created by a single person addressed to the same partner (see Chapter 2 and Entry 33).

In this entry I focus on a variety of style mixtures, including those that go beyond verb endings. For the sake of convenience, I discuss style mixture first in spoken discourse and then in written discourse. Within the spoken language, I introduce two kinds of style mixture: (1) that used for mixing different genres, and (2) that used for playing different roles. Then I discuss style mixture in written discourse, as used (3) for expressing intense emotion, (4) for borrowing someone else's voice, and (5) for creative purposes.

Style Mixture in Spoken Discourse

1. For presenting different genres

a. (Taken from *Suna no ue no koibitotachi*, episode 1) Hitomi and Akira are lovers, and they speak in casual style. But when Hitomi mixes formal style, it catches the attention. Sentences ending with formal endings give the impression that they are a part of a story Hitomi is telling. The style mixture foregrounds the genre mixture, between narration and conversation.

ひとみ： 私は今、ファミレスで**働いています**。でもそれは、ほんとにやりたい**仕事ではありませんでした**。ほんとにやりたいことは何かも、**分かっていませんでした**。#でもねえ、#朗に会って、#ちょっとずつ見えてきた。
朗： ほんとにやりたいこと？（ひとみ、うなずく）何？
ひとみ： まだ秘密だなあ。

Hitomi: Watashi wa ima, famiresu de **hataraiteimasu**. Demo sore wa, honto ni yaritai **shigoto dewa arimasen deshita**. Honto ni yaritai koto wa nani ka mo, **wakatteimasen deshita**. Demo nee, Roo ni atte, chotto zutu miete-kita.
Akira: Honto ni yaritai koto? (*Hitomi, unazuku*) Nani?
Hitomi: Mada himitsu da naa.

Hitomi: Currently, I am working at a chain restaurant. But, it was not the kind of job I truly wanted to take. I didn't know what I truly wanted to do, either. But, you know, after I met you, Roo, I am beginning to gradually see things more clearly.
Akira: The thing you truly want to do? (*Hitomi nods*) What is it?
Hitomi: That's a secret for now.

2. For playing different roles

b. (Taken from *Long Vacation*, episode 9) At this point in the drama, Sena demonstrates how to play the piano, to which Minami responds as a student. In this drama, Minami mostly speaks in casual style toward Sena. The formal style contrasts with her usual style. The style mixture reflects her changing role from friend to student. Minami's role-playing adds to the sense of empathy.

瀬名：　だめだ、そんな指ねかして弾いてちゃ。
南：　**すみません。**
瀬名：　お手本をやるからさ。
南：　**はい。**

Sena: Dame da, sonna yubi nekashite hiitecha. (see E. 18 for *dame da*; E. 16 for *sonna*; E. 48 about inverted word order)
Minami: **Sumimasen.**
Sena: Otehon o yaru kara sa.
Minami: **Hai.**

Sena: Playing (the piano) with your fingers laying so flat (on the piano), that's not right.
Minami: I'm sorry.
Sena: I'm going to demonstrate how it should be.
Minami: Yes.

Style Mixture in Written Discourse

3. For expressing intense emotion

c. (Taken from Konishi 2003a, 16) The writer is critiquing the fashion of celebrities. In this particular essay a French politician is the subject. The essay is written in casual style, but extremely casual blunt style is mixed in as a device through which the writer expresses raw emotion.

しかし、そんな主張と顔立ちとは裏腹に、スーツ姿はかなりイケてない。まずスーツのサイズがだぼだぼ。肩のラインといい襟の形といい、古くささも満点。こりゃあ、何年か前に買った吊るしだよ、きっと。

長身でハンサムだから、一見知的でストイックに見えてるが、まるでファッションはとんちんかんと見た。そんな彼が世界の舞台で発言するんだから、フランスもオーダーのスーツくらい税金で買ってやれ**っつうの**。おまけにシャツの襟は内側に巻き込んでるわ、ネクタイはひん曲がってるわ。色づかいもフランス人らしからぬ地味さで、てんでダメ**じゃん**。

Shikashi, sonna shuchoo to kaodachi to wa urahara ni, suutsu sugata wa kanari ikete-nai. Mazu suutsu no saizu ga dabodabo. Kata no rain to ii eri no katachi to ii, furukusasa mo manten. Koryaa, nannen ka mae ni katta tsurushi da yo, kitto. (see E. 25 for *kanari*; E. 13 for *ikete-nai*)

Chooshin de hansamu da kara, ikken chiteki de sutoikku ni mieteru ga, marude fasshon wa tonchinkan to mita. Sonna kare ga sekai no butai de hatsugen suru n da kara, Furansu mo oodaa no suutsu kurai zeikin de katte-yare **ttsuu no**. Omake ni shatsu no eri wa uchigawa ni makikonderu wa, nekutai wa hinmagatteru wa. Irozukai mo Furansujin rashikara-nu jimisa de, tende dame **jan**.

But, unlike those opinions and his face, his suit is rather shabby. First, the size is too big. The shoulder line and the shape of the collar, completely outdated. This is a ready-made suit he bought several years ago, for sure.

Because he is tall and handsome, at first glance he looks intellectual and stoic, but his sense of fashion is completely off. Because a guy like him has the world as a stage to make his statement, I'm telling you, the French government should buy him a made-to-order suit. On top of that, the shirt collars are bent inward, and his tie is crooked. The color combination is, unlike Frenchmen, too sedate, and it's a total disaster.

Ttsuu no 'I'm telling you' is used only in very casual style (as mentioned in Entry 73), and mixing this in with the essay adds an element of surprise. The use of *jan* is also restricted to very casual speech. *Jan* is a colloquial (and somewhat vulgar) version of *ja-nai ka*, which is used when the speaker is seeking agreement and/or confirmation. Both *ttsuu no* and *jan* are typically associated with the speech of young males. By mixing in this extremely casual style, the writer communicates a flippant spontaneity and an irreverence strongly associated with youth. This style expresses the writer's emotion in a straightforward and revealing way.

d. (Taken from Saitoo, 13) In this essay, *Kangoshi to Josanshi* 'Nursing staff and maternity staff', the writer discusses how the traditional female nursing position should be open to males as well; accordingly, the phrases referring to nurses are being changed. The essay is in casual style, but it mixes in a blunt expression, *ja-nee no?* 'isn't it?'.

あ、そうそう。法改正で名称こそ変わったものの、まだ男性に門戸が開かれていない職種に「助産師」がある。「男性助産師、いいじゃないの。男の産婦人科医もいるんだし」といったら、反対論者に一蹴された。「スケベ心で助産師を志す不逞のヤカラがいたら、どーするのよ」。

またもう、すぐそういう妄想を働かせる。それって、「看護婦さん」のコスプレに性的妄想をかきたてられてんのと同じレベル**じゃねーの**?あ、違いますか。

A, soo soo. Hookaisei de meishoo koso kawatta monono, mada dansei ni monko ga hirakaretei-nai shokushu ni "josanshi" ga aru. "Dansei josanshi ii ja-nai no. Otoko no sanfujinkai mo iru n da shi" to ittara, hantaironsha ni isshuu sareta. "Sukebe gokoro de josanshi o kokorozasu futei no yakara ga itara, doo suru no yo."

Mata moo, sugu soo yuu moosoo o hatarakaseru. Sore tte "kangofusan" no kosupure ni seiteki moosoo o kakitaterareten no to onaji reberu **ja-nee no?** A, chigaimasu ka. (see E. 47 for *tte*)

Oh, I remembered. The name itself has changed due to the change in the law, but an occupation from which men are excluded is "maternity nursing specialist." When I said, "There are male gynecologists, so male maternity nursing specialists are fine, right?" those who oppose this attacked me by saying, "What are you going to do if there were men who want to be male maternity nursing specialists who are perverts?"

You are imagining those peculiar things again, you know. Isn't it on the same level as being aroused by a sexual fantasy of being dressed like a nurse? Ah, I see, that's wrong, is it?

Ja-nee no? 'isn't it?' is in extremely casual style, and it demonstrates a stark bluntness. Although the writer's strong assertive attitude is present elsewhere in this piece, *ja-nee no?* catches the attention because of its naked force. The writer's intense emotion shows through. Curiously, *ja-nee no?* is stereotypically associated with more assertive "masculine" style than it is with "feminine" style. In this essay traces of the feminine voice are largely absent. Instead, the essay foregrounds an unconstrained, bold, and somewhat controversial character, rendering the author's actual character beside the point. The character presented through the writing, however, is frank and opinionated. By purposefully making use of the ideology of "gendered" speech and by evoking the typicality of "masculine" voice, the writer most effectively expresses her views.

It is also interesting to observe the stylistic gap between the blunt *ja-nee no* and the formal *chigaimasu ka*. It appears that the writer compensates for the blunt expression by choosing a style that formally addresses the reader. This juxtaposition makes the writing curious, exciting, and humorous.

4. For borrowing someone else's voice

Style mixture is used when the writer mixes someone else's voice for expressive purposes. Here we study two cases: (1) where the writer borrows a "feminine" voice, as in (e), and (2) where the writer borrows a middle-aged male's voice, as in (f).

e. (Taken from Shiga, 4) The writer comments about fashion in this short essay article, *Feikumono de okanemochi o yosootte-mimasu?* (Would you enjoy being like a rich person with fake jewelry?). It is written in casual style.

本物以上に光り輝くフェイクのダイヤや真珠、金メッキのアクセサリーが、ここんとこ流行ってるけど、キモはその"なんちゃって感"だ。本物だったらいったい**お幾ら万円するのかしら**、なデカさと輝きのアクセは、バカバカしいものほどベター。

Honmono ijoo ni hikari kagayaku feiku no daiya ya shinju, kinmekki no akusesarii ga kokon toko hayatteru kedo, kimo wa sono "nanchatte kan" da. Honmono dattara ittai **oikuraman-en suru no kashira** na dekasa to kagayaki no akuse wa, babakashii mono hodo betaa.

Recently accessories made of fake diamonds, pearls, and gold plate are in fashion, but the main attraction is the sense of "feeling like." Regarding gemstones that are large and shiny, the kind of gemstones that someone might comment on, "I wonder how many tens of thousand yen this would cost if it were genuine," the sillier the better, I think.

The expression *oikuraman-en suru no kashira* 'I wonder how many tens of thousand yen this would cost' is a mock-stereotypical "feminine" voice (note the use of *oikura*, a combination of the polite prefix *o-* and the noun *ikura* 'how much', and *kashira*). The choice of supra-polite "feminine" style is in part motivated by the fact that jewelry is typically something women wear, and the shopping scene often involves presumably rich, affected, pretentious women.

Although traditional "feminine" and "masculine" styles are no longer viable, here the writer effectively mimics the stereotypical "feminine" voice to capture an attitude associated with a snobbish, prudish, and coy woman. By exploiting the stereotype to the level of caricature, and by mixing in this style, the writer brings out another voice, the borrowed voice of a "feminine" fetish for jewelry. By borrowing voices associated with certain social groups, the writer creates a very expressive discourse.

f. (Taken from BBS for *Taiyoo no kisetsu*) This example illustrates a case where the writer borrows a speech style stereotypical of someone else to create a distancing effect. The entry is written in the formal style. (NG stands for "No Good." Note the smiling face icon at the end of the first sentence.)

２シーン見ました。正直、ちーちゃんのＮＧが見られるなんて思いもせずなんかうれしかった（* ＾ ＾ *)

高岡さんのリアクションも良かったし、由紀のパパのＮＧ後の笑い顔も最終回後ならではでなんかホッとしてしまいました。

タッキーは２シーンともＮＧに笑うだけで、タッキー自身のＮＧは見られずちょっと残念。

でもこのまだ余韻に浸っている時に見なくて良かったのかな。

民代さんや耕平なんかも見たかったなぁ。

ファンとしてはたくさん見たかったという事ですな。ハハハ

でも放送が終わったあと寂しさをみなさん感じているようですし、もちろんこの私も同様なので、率直にうれしかったです。

2 shiin mimashita. Shoojiki, Chii-chan no NG ga mirareru nante omoi mo se-zu nanka ureshikatta. (see E. 5 for *ureshii*)

Takaoka-san no riakushon mo yokatta shi, Yuki no papa no NG go no waraigao mo saishuukai naradewa de nanka hotto shite-shimaimashita. (see E. 22 for *hotto suru*)

Takkii wa 2 shiin tomo NG ni warau dake de, Takkii jishin no NG wa mirare-zu chotto zannen. (see E. 61 for *zannen*)

Demo kono mada yoin ni hitatteiru toki ni mi-nakute yokatta no ka na.

Tamiyo-san ya Koohei nanka mo mitakatta naa.

Fan to shite wa takusan mitakatta to yuu koto desu na. Ha ha ha.

Demo hoosoo ga owatta ato sabishisa o minasan kanjiteiru yoo desu shi, mochiron kono watashi mo dooyoo na node, sotchoku ni ureshikatta desu. (see E. 8 for *sabishisa*)

I saw those two scenes. Honestly speaking, I didn't think I could see some Chii's "NG," so I was pleased.

Takaoka's reaction was great, and the smiling face of Yuki's father after his "NG" was something expected for the final episode, and it was comforting to see that.

All Takkii did was to laugh at those two scenes, and it was a bit disappointing not to be able to see Takkii's "NG."

But maybe it was a good thing that I didn't see it while I was still in the middle of the lingering effect.

I wanted to see Tamiyo's and Koohei's "NG" as well.

I guess it is that as a fan, I wanted to see as many as possible. Heh heh heh.

But after the broadcast was over, it seemed that everyone was feeling a bit lonesome, and of course I was like that, so honestly I was pleased (to see them).

Fan to shite wa takusan mitakatta to yuu koto desu na 'I guess it is that as a fan, I wanted to see as many as possible' is a style used primarily by middle-aged males (Ozaki 2001). As mentioned in Chapter 2, Ozaki (2001) refers to this particular style, ending in *desu na(a)* and *masu na(a)*, as a style connected with a subgroup of male speakers in their forties and older. Ozaki, reporting on the survey of the Kokuritsu Kokugo Kenkyuujo (2000), states that 18.4 percent of men in their sixties and 7.5 percent of men in their forties use the *desu/masu na(a)* form, although almost none of them had used it in their twenties. In other words, this is a generational style used by a group of speakers at a certain stage in their lives.

The writer borrows a speech style typically connected to a social subgroup. Because this style deviates from that of the other sentences, it reminds us that something else is going on. At the point of *Fan to shite wa takusan mitakatta to yuu koto desu na*, the writer's perspective becomes that of an observer in the distance, causing a distancing effect. This is partly because the middle-aged male style carries with it a reflective attitude, and partly because a different self (speaking in a borrowed voice) comes to the fore.

I should add that although it is impossible to know who the actual (or pretended) writer is when it comes to Internet write-ins, there is evidence that this was not written by a middle-aged male. First, these BBS entries are mostly written by young people and housewives. Second, the writer refers to the main actor as *Takkii* (the intimate vocative for the main actor), and it is difficult, to the point of impossibility, to assume that the writer is a middle-aged man.

5. For creative purposes

Style mixture is also useful for creative purposes. Here two types are introduced. The first is irony, often associated with the supra-polite style, and the second is the use of imagined (obsolete) style for creating colorful discourse.

g. (Taken from Uchidate 2003a, 66) In this essay, *Daigakuin no nyuugakushiki* (The Graduate School Entrance Ceremony), the writer comments on how her mother responded when she asked her to come along.

すぐに母につき添いを頼んだところ、
「仙台には行きたいけど入学式に出席なんてやーよ。このトシになって、このトシの娘の入学式なんて」
と鼻で笑う。だが、私が弟の言葉を伝えると、
「そりゃそうね。でも、保護者だって牧子より若いわよ。牧子のトシだと、普通は子供も大学卒業してるわ」
と、実母とは思えない**シビアなお言葉**。そして、
「いいわ、行く。でも一人は恥ずかしいから節子も誘うわ」
と言う。節子とは母の妹で仙台にいる。姉妹で恥ずかしさを分けあえばいいと思ったらしい。

Sugu ni haha ni tsukisoi o tanonda tokoro, "Sendai ni wa ikitai kedo nyuugakushiki ni shusseki nante yaa yo. Kono toshi ni natte, kono toshi no musume no nyuugakushiki nante." (see E. 15 for *nante*)

To hana de warau. Daga, watashi ga otooto no kotoba o tsutaeru to, "Sorya soo ne. Demo, hogosha datte Makiko yori wakai wa yo. Makiko no toshi da to, futsuu wa kodomo mo daigaku sotsugyoo shiteru wa" to, jitsubo to wa omoe-nai **shibiana okotoba**. Soshite, "Ii wa, iku. Demo hitori wa hazukashii kara Setsuko mo sasou wa" (see E. 43 for *hazukashii*) to yuu. Setsuko to wa haha no imooto de Sendai ni iru. Shimai de hazukashisa o wakeaeba ii to omotta rashii.

Right away I asked my mother to come with me, and then, (she said,) "I do want to visit Sendai, but I don't want to attend your entrance ceremony. An entrance ceremony for this old daughter when I've become this old."

She chuckles it away. But when I told her what my younger brother said (she said), "That makes sense. But, I don't want to be your guardian, because their (guardian) parents are younger than you are. At your age, ordinarily your children would have graduated from college."

Like this, her words are so harsh that it is difficult to think that they are coming from my own mother's mouth. Then, "O.K., I'm going. But I am embarrassed to go alone, so I'll invite Setsuko to come along."

She says. Setsuko is my mother's sister, who lives in Sendai. My mother seems to have thought that having two sisters share the embarrassment would be better.

As explained in Entry 74, irony is basically the rejection of a literal reading of an expression. To let us know that an expression is meant to be sarcastic, a signal is necessary. Given that the writer almost always maintains the casual style, *okotoba* (a combination of the polite prefix *o-* and the noun *kotoba* 'word') is obviously excessive. The supra-polite expression used in association with her mother is out of place, cluing us that something is wrong. The use of *okotoba* demands a sarcastic reading, namely, the writer's unhappiness (and disbelief) that her own mother would say such things.

The creativity associated with style mixture takes an interesting turn when the style chosen is imagined and/or obsolete. Imagined, "virtual" language (Kinsui 2003) is deliberately used for rhetorical effect. The imagined style observed in the examples reflects the kind of speech associated with certain characters in certain fictional worlds.

The first style is called *roojingo*, 'old man style', and characteristically uses *ja* and the negative *n*. *Ja* (instead of *da*) was used as a (modal) verb primarily in the western provinces in pre-modern Japan. The negative morpheme *n* (instead of *nai*) is also used mainly in western Japan. According to Kinsui (2003), these features are often used in a virtual language stereotypically connected to old men and/or old scientists, who are knowledgeable, respected, authoritative, and sometimes forgetful.

h. (Taken from Nobumoto, 124) This particular essay, written in casual style, discusses the movie *Thelma and Louise*.

ブラピちゃんはとても良かった。彼には何の罪もない。だが、あの女ドモはなんだ？ジーナ・テイヴィスは、好きなタイプの女優だ。スーザン・サランドンも、役者としては凄いと思う。しかし、ストーリー上の女ドモは、むかついてしゃーない。アレをかっこいい女とか言ってる奴も居るが、**どこがじゃ**！ウザイ馬鹿女にしか私には**見えん**！ああ、ああ、勝手にしたらいいさ。車ごとどこにでも突っ込んでくれ。

Burapi-chan wa totemo yokatta. Kare ni wa nan no tsumi mo nai. Daga, ano onnadomo wa nan da? Jiina Deivisu wa, sukina taipu no joyuu da. Suuzan Sarandon mo, yakusha to shite wa, sugoi to omou. Shikashi, sutoorii joo no onnadomo wa, mukatsuite shaa nai. Are o kakko ii onna toka itteru yatsu mo iru ga, **doko ga ja!** Uzai baka onna ni shika watashi ni wa **mie-n!** Aa, aa, katte ni shitara ii sa. Kuruma goto doko ni demo tsukkonde-kure. (see E. 10 for *mukatsuku*; E. 26 for *shaa nai* which is a casual version of *shikata* [*ga*] *nai*; E. 13 for *kakko ii*; E. 39 for *katte ni suru*)

Brad Pitt was really nice. He has nothing to be blamed for. But, what are those women? Geena Davis is the kind of actress I like. I think Susan Sarandon is great as an actress, too. But I am totally angry about the women in the story. There are some people who think those women are cool, but how in the world! To me they look like nothing but bothersome, stupid women! Ah, well, do whatever they want to do. Go ahead and crash into somewhere together in a car.

The expressions *doko ga ja* 'how in the world' and *mie-n* 'they look like nothing but' echo the voice of the old-man style, although they appear here in a female writer's discourse. Mixing this imagined style helps make the writing more interesting, humorous, and entertaining. The writer, by using *doko ga ja* and *mie-n*, introduces the authoritative, adamant voice associated with the imagined old-man style. For a moment she speaks in his voice.

Virtual Japanese is used not only by professional writers but in ordinary writings as well. The second example is an imagined "princess" speech.

i. (Taken from BBS for *Taiyoo no kisetsu*) The writer of this BBS entry refers to herself (or himself) as "princess," and addresses the commentary to another frequent contributor, *Tsubone-sama*. This BBS is written generally in formal style, but many different styles are mixed. Of particular interest is the use of supra-polite forms and the expression *de gozaru*.

局さま、やはり、外国の空気を知ってらっしゃる方でしたのですね。

あなた様の一言で、11月 o r 1月に、ベルリンののりちゃんとロンドンの友人の所へゆくこと悩んでいたのですが、(仕事の調整がむずかしくて)・・やはり、ふたたび・・ゆくことにしました。

ありがとうです。

希望の光のメッセージに、同感、同意いたしますのよ〜〜〜。

又、書き込みくださいね。

局さんのファンだから・・・ひめくんのあたまのなか、滝、滝、タッキー、滝、滝の洪水**でござる**。

Tsubone-sama, yahari, gaikoku no kuuki o shitterassharu kata deshita no desu ne. (see E. 57 for *yahari*)

Anata-sama no hitokoto de, juuichigatsu or ichigatsu ni Berurin no Nori-chan to Rondon no yuujin no tokoro e yuku koto nayandeita no desu ga, (shigoto no choosei ga muzukashikute)..yahari, futatabi..yuku koto ni shimashita.

Arigotoo desu.

Kiboo no hikari no messeeji ni, dookan, dooi itashimasu no yooo.

Mata, kakikomi kudasai ne.

Tsubone-san no fan da kara...hime-kun no atama no naka, Taki, Taki, Takkii, Taki, Taki no koozui **de gozaru.**

Tsubone (Lady of the Court), you are someone who knows things about overseas, I understand.

With your one word, I made up my mind. I was wondering about it (because of scheduling problems with my work) but I decided again to go and visit my friend in London in November or in January, with Nori-chan, who is in Berlin.

Thank you.

I agree and sympathize with your message that casts a ray of hope.

Please write again for me.

I'm Tsubone's fan...and the heart of this princess is flooded with Taki.

In this BBS, the writer uses supra-polite forms as in *shitterassharu kata deshita no desu ne* 'you are someone who knows' and *dookan, dooi itashimasu no yoo* 'I agree and sympathize with'. The respectful form *irassharu* (instead of *desu*), the noun *kata* (instead of *hito*), and the *desu/masu* form before *no* all contribute to an extraordinary level of politeness. The supra-polite expressions are used as the writer addresses *Tsubone-sama. Tsubone* itself is a term referring to a lady of the court during the feudal age and this writer behaves as if the addressee were such a person. By addressing this imaginary BBS contributor in an excessively supra-polite style, the writer creates a fictional world.

The term *de gozaru* (polite and/or respectful form of *da*) is obsolete today, but using this imagined style recalls a world where such a style was (presumably) used. The writer refers to herself (or himself) as "princess," and *de gozaru* is something that a princess might say. This role-playing adds to the creation of a fictional world. Through this interaction between the "princess" and the "lady of the court," the scene is set in a palace somewhere in pre-modern Japan. In this way, the use of imagined style "creates" a world of its own.

77. Showing Intimacy through Banter, Puns, and Jokes

Key Expressions

[からかい]	*karakai*	banter
[だじゃれ]	*dajare*	puns
[ジョーク]	*jooku*	jokes

Explanation

As in many other cultures, to show intimacy and friendliness, banter, puns, and jokes are used among acquaintances and friends. In addition to the good-natured teasing discussed in Entry 58, this entry illustrates how speakers use humor to enhance the feeling of intimacy. My examples are drawn from articles and television variety shows that are the work of professional writers and entertainers, although these expressive strategies occur in ordinary communication to convey goodwill, interest, and a fun-loving attitude.

Authentic Examples

a. (Taken from Tatekawa, 76) In this series of articles, the writer comments about television programs.

感心だらけ。感心の大安売り。この感心好きめ。
ひいきのチームは**感心タイガース**って、われながらまずい洒落。

Kanshin darake. Kanshin no ooyasuuri. Kono kanshin zuki me.
Hiiki no chiimu wa **Kanshin Taigaasu** tte, ware nagara mazui share. (see E. 42 for *ware*)

We overuse this sense of *kanshin* (amazement). It's like a big sale on the idea of *kanshin*. You, the *kanshin* lover.
My favorite team is the "Kanshin Tigers," but this is a silly joke even for me.

Kanshin Taigaasu is a pun associated with *Hanshin Taigaasu* 'the Hanshin Tigers', a baseball team. The writer uses similar phrases to create puns, then immediately makes self-conscious comments like *ware nagara mazui share* 'a silly joke even for me'. This comment functions to let readers know—if they hadn't noticed already—that *Kanshin Taigaasu* is meant as a pun.

b. (Taken from Tatekawa, 76) In the same essay, the writer continues with another pun.

コメント考えながらの食事だから、うわの空、目はうつろ、いくらびっくり目して「おいしい」なんて言っても、結局、目はうつろ、**うつろの正面だーあれ**。まだ言っている。

Komento kangae nagara no shokuji da kara, uwa no sora, me wa utsuro, ikura bikkurime shite "Oishii" nan te ittemo, kekkyoku, me wa utsuro, **Utsuro no shoomen daare**. Mada itteiru. (see E. 21 for *bikkuri*)

Because I'm eating this dish thinking about what kind of comment I can make, I'm absent-minded, and my eyes are not focusing on anything. Even if I say with a surprised expression "This is delicious," in the end, my eyes are still *utsuro* 'hollow'. Who is in *utsuro* (instead of *ushiro* 'behind')? Whoops, I'm still saying (a silly joke).

Utsuro no shoomen daare is a pun associated with a well-known children's folk song, *Ushiro no shoomen daare* 'Who is right behind you?'. The writer plays on the word *utsuro* that appears repeatedly, connecting it to the song. Immediately after this pun, the writer self-consciously comments *Are, mada itteiru* 'Whoops, I'm still saying (a silly joke)', another signal that the preceding statement is a pun. Banter, puns, and jokes are also used in conversation, as the two examples to follow illustrate. In *Santaku*, Sanma and Kimura exchange jokes in good-natured camaraderie.

c. (Taken from *Santaku*) After going surfing, Sanma is chatting with a group of people on the beach. When Kimura comes back to the beach, Sanma invites him to have some fish.

さんま：　い，いわ、いわし食べる？
木村：　いわしじゃなくて。
さんま：　おいしいのよ。
木村：　**さんまがいわしすすめてどうすんのよ。**

Sanma: I, iwa, iwashi taberu?
Kimura: Iwashi ja-nakute. (see E. 70 for *ja-nakute*)
Sanma: Oishii no yo.
Kimura: **Sanma ga iwashi susumete doo sun no yo**. (see E. 19 for *doo sun no yo*)

Sanma: Would you like some sardines?
Kimura: Don't say "sardines," forget about it.
Sanma: It's delicious.
Kimura: How is it that you, Sanma (a Pacific fish) recommend sardines?

Kimura's joke is on the literal meaning of the name "Sanma." Because *sanma* is a kind of fish, and because he is saying that a small grilled sardine is delicious, Kimura associates these two. The sentence he chooses here, *doo sun no yo* '(lit.) what do you do,' is a rhetorical question, further indicating that this is meant as a joke.

d. (Taken from *Santaku*) Sanma admits that he is interested in going surfing with Kimura. Note Sanma's use of a pun on the basis of the phrase *noru* 'to ride'.

木村：	今、この時期でやるってことですか。
さんま：	そうや、そうや。あ冬の、#波が一番ええ。#だからちょっとねえ、生まれて初めて、あのう、波に乗ろうと。ずーっとねえ、30 年近くは**調子には乗っとったけど**。(笑いながら) あの、#今の＝
木村：	＝その、その、#その階級だったらプロですよ。(さんま、笑う) プロサーファーですよ。
さんま：	(笑いながら) 30 年も、調子、調子に乗ってたら。
木村：	レジェンドですよ、レジェンド。

Kimura:	Ima, kono jiki de yaru tte koto desu ka.
Sanma:	Soo ya, soo ya. A fuyu no, nami ga ichiban ee. Dakara chotto nee, umarete hajimete, anoo, nami ni noroo to. Zuutto nee, sanjuunen chikaku wa **chooshi ni wa nottotta kedo**. (see E. 23 for *ichiban*; E. 25 for *chotto*) (*warainagara*) Ano, ima no=
Kimura:	=Sono, sono, sono kaikyuu dattara puro desu yo. (*Sanma, warau*) Puro saafaa desu yo.
Sanma:	(*warai nagara*) Sanjuunen mo, chooshi, chooshi ni nottetara.
Kimura:	Rejendo desu yo, rejendo. (see E. 24 about repetition)

Kimura:	You mean you are going surfing now, at this time (of the year)?
Sanma:	That's right, that's right. Ah, the winter waves are the best. So, just a little bit, I was thinking that I would ride the waves for the first time. For a long time, nearly thirty years, I've been "riding" the fun-loving, easy-going waves. (*laughing*) So, now=
Kimura	=That, that rank would make you a professional surfer. (*Sanma laughs*) A professional surfer, really.
Sanma:	(*laughing*) If you've been "riding" fun-loving, easy-going waves for thirty years, then...
Kimura:	Legend, you are legend.

Sanma uses the Japanese idiomatic expression *chooshi ni noru* 'to go about fun-loving and easy-going ways' and associates it with the phrase *nami ni noru* 'to ride the surf'. In this interaction, Kimura responds to Sanma's pun with banter, saying that he is really a legend. They joke and laugh together, acting out their friendship.

Appendix

Information about Authentic Sources

What follows presents brief descriptions of each data source. Characters whose speech samples are used in this book are also introduced.

Television Dramas

***Antiiku, seiyoo kottoo yoogashiten*. 2001. Fuji Television. Original story by Fumi Yoshinaga.**

『アンティーク　西洋骨董洋菓子店』(2001) フジテレビ、原作：よしながふみ

A story about four men who work at Antique, a fancy pastry shop and cafe in Tokyo. The story revolves around Eiji Kanda (male, 20), an ex-boxer, who joins the pastry shop as an apprentice. A reporter, Momoko Iizuka (female, 25), follows Eiji to his new job and becomes involved with the events and incidents that happen at Antique.

Other characters include: Tachibana (owner of Antique, male, 35); Chikage "Kage" (cousin of the owner, male, 35); Kage's daugher, Hideko or Deko (female, 14); Akane (Eiji's former girlfriend, female, 24); Junko (another of Eiji's former girlfriends, female, early 20s). Also appearing in the drama are a number of Antique's customers, including Tamami (female, early 20s), and Kayoko (female, 8).

***Beautiful Life*. 2000. TBS. Screenplay by Eriko Kitagawa.**

『ビューティフルライフ』(2000) TBS、脚本：北川悦吏子

A love story between Shuuji and Kyooko. Shuuji Okishima (male, 27) is a hairstylist at a fashionable hair salon, Hotlip, in Tokyo, and Kyooko Machida (female, 27) is a librarian who has been confined to a wheelchair for the past ten years. Also regularly appearing are Sachie (Sachi) Tamura (female, 27) who is Kyooko's best friend and a coworker at the library, and Masao Machida (male, early 30s), Kyooko's brother, who falls in love with Sachi. After some happy and difficult events, Shuuji and Kyooko realize they are deeply in love, but Kyooko dies of a serious illness.

Other characters include Miyama, a volunteer who has a crush on Kyooko (male, late 20s); Kosugi, Kyooko's high school friend (male, 27); Mayumi, Shuuji's colleague at Hotlip and former lover (female, late 20s); Satsuki, Shuuji's former girlfriend (female, 27); Tsuchiya, Hotlip's manager and Shuuji's boss (male, late 30s); Satoru, Shuuji's colleage and competitor at Hotlip (male, late 20s); and Takumi,Shuuji's assistant at Hotlip (male, early 20s).

Long Love Letter Hyooryuu Kyooshitsu. **(2002). Fuji Television. Screenplay by Mika Oomori.**

『ロングラブレター　漂流教室』(2002) フジテレビ、脚本：大森美香

A story about a group of high school students and teachers who find themselves transported into the future. Students and teachers endure hardships while trying to survive in their high school, which is the only building left on the devastated and deserted planet. A love relationship develops between Yuka and Asami. Yuka Misaki (female, 28) was once a high school teacher, and Akio Asami (male, 23) is the math teacher at the high school.

Other teachers at the high school are Mr. Wakahara (male, late 40s), and Ms. Sekiya (female, 32). Students include: Aikawa (female, 17), Andoo (female, 17), Fukasawa (female, 16), Gamoo (female, 16), Hata (male, 17), Higashi (female, 17), Ichinose (referred to as Kaoru, female, 17), Ikegaki (male, 17), Isehara (male, 17), Kanazawa (female, 17), Kawa (female, 17), Kawada (female, 17), Maioka (female, 17), Nishi (female, 16), Ootomo (male, 17), Takagai (female, 17), Takamatsu (male, 17), and Yanase (male, 17). In addition, Yuka's father, Shigeo Misaki (male, 50s) and Fujisawa (Yuka's former student, male, 20) appear in the drama.

Long Vacation. **1996. Fuji Television. Screenplay by Eriko Kitagawa.**

『ロングバケーション』(1996) フジテレビ、脚本：北川悦吏子

A love story between Minami and Sena. Hidetoshi Sena (male, 24) is a shy pianist-in-training, and Minami Hayama (female, 31) is an ex-model who becomes a photographer's assistant. Minami's groom, who failed to show up at their wedding, used to share the same apartment with Sena. Minami forces her way into Sena's apartment, where they live together as friends. Also appearing are Ryooko Okusawa (female, 21), a woman whom Sena admires, but who falls in love with Minami's brother, Shinji; Tetsuya Sugisaki (male, mid-30s), who has a relationship with Minami; and Momoko Koishikawa (female, 23), a model and Minami's friend. After many ups and downs, Minami and Sena realize that they are in love. At the conclusion of the series they marry.

Majo no jooken. **1999. TBS. Screenplay by Kazuhiko Yukawa.**

『魔女の条件』(1999) TBS、脚本：遊川和彦

A love story between Michi and Hikaru. Michi Hirose (female, 26) is a high school teacher who falls in love with Hikaru, one of her students. Hikaru Kurosawa (male, 17), after his father dies, is in rebellion against his mother, who runs a hospital. Also appearing are Masaru Kitai (male, 31), to whom Michi is engaged (Michi eventually breaks up with him), and Kiriko Uda (female, late 20s), Michi's friend. Michi and Hikaru, after eloping and breaking up once, finally find happiness after their relationship has been approved by the people around them.

Other characters include Ms. Shimoda, a colleague of Michi's at the high school (female, 50s); Dr. Godai, a physician who works for the Kurosawa Hospital (male, 40s); and Kinoshita (Hikaru's classmate, female, 17).

Muko-dono. 2001. Fuji Television. Screenplay by Yoshihiro Izumi.

『ムコ殿』(2001) フジテレビ、脚本：いずみ吉紘

A love comedy between Sakura and Yuuichiroo. Yuuichiroo Sakuraba (male, 23) is a popular singer and songwriter who marries into Sakura's family. Sakura Arai (female, 21) is the youngest daughter in the Arai family. Other family members include Kaede Takeyama (female, 40), the eldest (married) daughter of the Arai family; Azusa Arai (female, 33), the second daughter, an unmarried mother with a seven-year-old boy (Tsutomu); and Satsuki Arai (female, 29), the third daughter, a producer at a radio station. In addition, Ryoo Takeyama (male, 17) is Kaede's son and a high school student, and Masaki Arai (male, 30s) is a son of the Arai family who ran away from home. Another important character is Hakozaki, "Hako-san," Yuuichiroo's manager (male, 39).

Strawberry on the Shortcake. 2001. TBS. Screenplay by Shinji Nojima.

『ストロベリー・オンザ・ショートケーキ』(2001) TBS、脚本：野島伸司

Love stories of the high school students Manato, Yui, Tetsuya, and Haruka. Manato Irie (male, 17) is a high school student whose mother abandoned him and his family, and whose father is about to marry his own high school sweetheart. Yui Irie (female, 16) is the daughter of the woman who marries Manato's father. Tetsuya Saeki (male, 20) is a high school student who is in love with a female teacher and is refusing to graduate. Haruka Sawamura (female, 17) is Manato's next-door neighbor and classmate; she is in love with Manato. In the end, Manato and Yui fall in love, and Haruka joins Saeki, who goes to New York.

Suna no ue no koibitotachi. 1999. Fuji Television. Screenplay by Kazuhiko Ban.

『砂の上の恋人たち』(1999) フジテレビ、脚本：伴一彦

A love story between Akira and Rei. Akira (Roo) Takano (male, 23) is an architect who works in a small firm in Tokyo. Reiko (Rei) Tsujitani (female, 23) is studying abroad in Australia. While Akira and his friends are traveling in Australia, Akira's lover (Hitomi, female, 23) dies in an accident in which Reiko was involved. Akira and Reiko return to Japan, and after many hardships, travel to Australia again. At that point they realize that they are in love.

Also appearing are Erika Sawai, Akira's colleague (female, 23); Igarashi, Reiko's fiancé and lawyer (male, early 30s); and Noguchi, Akira's boss (male, mid-40s).

Taiyoo wa shizuma-nai. 2000. Fuji Television. Screenplay by Fumie Mizuhashi.

『太陽は沈まない』(2000) フジテレビ、脚本：水橋文美江

Nao Masaki (male, 17) is a high school student who is trying to find the real cause for his mother's sudden death. Setsu Kirino (female, 27) is a lawyer who helps Nao find the truth about his mother's death. Ami Isetani (female, 16) likes Nao, but turns out to be the daughter of the doctor responsible for Nao's mother's death. In spite of this, Nao and Ami maintain a friendly—and romantic—relationship.

Television Variety Shows

Variety shows with studio audience

***SMAP x SMAP*. 2002. Fuji Television. "Shinshun supesharu nama hoosoo (New Year's special, January 7, 2002); and Kinkyuu nama hoosoo, go-nin sorotte sumappu ga shutsuen (Five members of SMAP on the show [special live show], January 14, 2002).**

SMAP x SMAP (2002) フジテレビ、新春スペシャル生放送 (2002 年 1 月 7 日).
SMAP x SMAP (2002) フジテレビ、緊急生放送、五人そろってスマップが出演 (2002 年 1 月 14 日)

The show aired on January 7, 2002, features three different segments. First is the "Bistro SMAP" segment, during which SMAP members prepare dishes to the guests' orders. The two guests invited were Shin'ichi Tsutsumi (actor, b. 1964) and Eri Fukatsu (actress, b. 1973). Second is a debate game called "Mausu Tenisu" (mouse tennis), where the SMAP members and two guests, Osugi and Piiko (twin brothers, mid-50s), debated a topic. The topic for this show was which is more enjoyable—professional baseball or soccer. Third was a game of *karuta*, where SMAP members and the guests ran to grab specific cards called out by Nakai.

The January 14, 2002, show featured an incident in which Goroo Inagaki was involved, and his return to the entertainment world. Inagaki was involved in a traffic accident in August 2001 and was unable to work until January 14, 2002. The show consists of clips from SMAP members's activities while Goroo was away, members' comment on Goroo's comeback, and a formal apology by Goroo.

The five members of SMAP are: Masahiro Nakai (male, b. 1972) who is the leader, Takuya Kimura (male, b. 1972), Goroo Inagaki (male, b. 1973), Tsuyoshi Kusanagi (male, b. 1974), and Shingo Katori (male, b. 1977). Among them, the older members have higher status; normally Nakai's and Kimura's blunt speech style is accepted by Goroo, Tsuyoshi, and Shingo, but not vice versa.

Reality-variety shows

***Ainori*. 2003. Fuji Television. "Saigo no machi de gyooten koodoo onna" (May 12, 2003) and "Chikyuu isshuu daigookyuu ketsumatsu" (May 19, 2003).**

「あいのり」(2003) 最後の街で仰天行動女 (2003 年 5 月 12 日)
「あいのり」(2003) 地球一周大号泣結末 (2003 年 5 月 19 日)

Ainori is a documentary-variety show where, as seven young men and women tour the world in a van, their developing relationships are reported. It calls itself *sabaibaru ren'ai tsua* 'survival love tour' and takes the form of a reality show. In the particular two shows from which examples have been drawn, Saki, one of the women on the tour, confesses her love for Dabo, one of the men. The rule was that whoever confessed love would offer the other a return ticket to Japan. If the person accepts the ticket, showing that the love is reciprocated, the couple returns to Japan. The remaining members, with new added members, continue with the tour.

Celebrity-and-guest variety shows

***Doomoto Tsuyoshi no shoojiki shindoi*. 2003 Terebi Asahi. Ryooko Kuninaka, guest (May 28, 2003); Sakura Uehara, guest (June 4, 2003).**

「堂本剛の正直しんどい」(2003) テレビ朝日、ゲスト国仲涼子 (2003 年 5 月 28 日)
「堂本剛の正直しんどい」(2003) テレビ朝日、ゲスト上原さくら (2003 年 6 月 4 日)

Doomoto Tsuyoshi no shoojiki shindoi is a show featuring a popular talent, Tsuyoshi Doomoto (male, b. 1979), a member of the signer/dancer duo KinKi Kids. In each show, Doomoto interacts with guest(s) who are actors, actresses, comedians, and other kinds of entertainers. Doomoto goes along on some events with the guest(s) and later comments on what happened. In the two shows from which examples have been taken, a young actress/entertainer friend is the guest. Doomoto was born in Nara and sometimes speaks in the Kansai dialect.

Television Talk Show

***Santaku*. 2003. Fuji Television. January 3, 2003.**

「さんタク」(2003) フジテレビ (2003 年 1 月 3 日)

Santaku is a television talk variety show with a title that combines *San* and *Taku,* parts of the given names of the comedian Sanma Akashiya (male, b. 1955) and the SMAP member/actor Takuya Kimura (male, b. 1972). They are known to be good friends, and in this two-hour program, they not only talk but also play games of darts and pool. In addition, they go surfing at the beach in Chiba. Sanma often speaks in the Osaka dialect and is known for his puns, quips, and jokes.

Comics

***Buchoo Shima Koosaku*. Vol. 5. 2003. Kenshi Hirokane. Tokyo: Koodansha.**

『部長島耕作』Vol. 5.(2000) 弘兼憲史 東京：講談社

A comic series about the businessman Koosaku Shima (male, 40s). In this volume, Shima is involved in promoting a female singer, Shinko Yatsuhashi (female, 50) who is represented by the talent agent, Masuda (male, 50s). Yatsuhashi dies of cancer soon after a successful grand performance. (A Japanese-English bilingual versions of *Buchoo Shima Koosaku* is available as *Buchoo Shima Koosaku*, *Bairingaru-ban*, translated by Ralph McCarthy and published by Kodansha.)

***Chibi Maruko-chan*. Vol. 13. 1995. Momoko Sakura. Tokyo: Shuueisha.**
***Chibi Maruko-chan*. Vol. 14. 1996. Momoko Sakura. Tokyo: Shuueisha.**

『ちびまる子ちゃん』Vol. 13 (1995) さくらももこ 東京：集英社
『ちびまる子ちゃん』Vol. 14 (1996) さくらももこ 東京：集英社

A series of stories about Maruko, a third-grader. Other characters include her mother, father (Hiroshi), elder sister, grandfather (Tomozoo), and her classmates. Maruko's best friend is Tamae. Other classmates include the boys Fujiki, Kosugi, Nagasawa, Yamada, and Yamane.

***Kindaichi shoonen no jikenbo*. Vol. 5. 2000. Seimaru Amagi, Fumiya Satoo. Tokyo: Koodansha.**

『金田一少年の事件簿』Vol. 5 (2000) 天城征丸、さとうふみや 東京：講談社

Hajime Kindaichi (male, a high school student) is a part-time detective. He is a grandson of a famous detective, and shows unusual talent in solving complicated cases. Miyuki Nanase (female, a high school student), Hajime's friend, assists him. Hajime and Miyuki maintain a lover-like relationship. In this episode, guests are invited to a mansion, but they are murdered one by one. The butler of the mansion is Tashiro (male, 62), and the guests include Kaoru Umezono (female, 28), Raimu Yuzuki (female, 32), Sukaaretto Roozesu (male, 30s, alias Takatoo).

***Kookaku kidootai*. Vol. 1. 1991. Masamune Shiroo. Tokyo: Koodansha. Translated as *Ghost in the Shell* by Frederik Schodt and Toren Smith (Milwaukie, Ore.: Dark Horse Comics, 1995).**

『攻殻機動隊』Vol. 1 (1991) 士郎正宗 東京：講談社

A science fiction series set in the year 2029 about a government agency that defends Japan from domestic and international terrorism. Key members of the agency are Major Motoko Kusanagi, a cyborg (female, late 20s), her boss Aramaki (male, 60s), and her subordinates Batou (male, 40s) and Togusa (male, 30s).

***Naku yo Uguisu*. Vol. 3. 2000. Yasuaki Kida. Tokyo: Koodansha.**

『泣くよ うぐいす』Vol. 3 (2000) 木多康昭 東京：講談社

A story about high school baseball players and their competition. The main character is Uguisu Sengoku (male, 15) who is an ace batter for the Makuhari First High School baseball team. His rival is Soga of Haramaku (Harajuku Makuhari) High School.

Romance Novels

***Dokkin paradaisu*. Vol. 3. 2000. Mito Orihara. Tokyo: Koodansha.**

『Dokkin パラダイス』Vol. 3 (2000) 折原みと 東京：講談社

A love story between Ai and Akira. Ai Kamiya (female, 16), adopted by the Kamiya family, is a high school student in love with Akira. Akira Kamiya (male, 17), is a high school student who is smart and attractive. He gradually realizes that he loves Ai as well. In the story, Akira is called Akira-nii 'brother Akira'. Other characters include Sootaroo Kamiya, or Soo-nii (male, 19), Akira's half-brother, who is a college student, and Ryuunosuke Kamiya, or Ryuu-nii (male, 18), Akira's other half-brother, who is a high school student. Ai's friends include Tokutake (male, 16) and Shinomiya (male, 17).

Himawari nikki. 1992. Yuu Asagiri. Tokyo: Koodansha.

『ひまわり日記』(1992) あさぎり夕 東京：講談社

A love story between Konomi and Satoo. Konomi Satoo (female, 14) is a junior high school student, and Naoyuki Satoo (male, 16) is a student at the same junior high school (he happens to have the same family name). Konomi secretly loves Satoo, but it turns out that Satoo was always interested in Konomi. They find each other and fall in love.

***Ren'ai hakusho*. Vol. 14. 2000. Miyuki Kobayashi. Tokyo: Koodansha.**

『恋愛白書』Vol. 14. (2000) 小林深雪 東京：講談社

A love story between Kaho and Tsubasa. Kaho Hirooka (female, 14) is a junior high school student, one of whose classmates is Tsubasa Ooishi (male, 14), captain of the soccer team. Despite some misunderstandings, Kaho and Tsubasa reaffirm that they are in love during a school excursion to Kyoto. Another important character is Sumire Itoo (female, 14), another classmate.

***Tsubasa o kudasai*. 2000. Momo Tachibana. Tokyo: Koodansha.**

『翼をください』(2000) 橘もも 東京：講談社

A story about bullying (*ijime*) that happens in Kyooka Tateyama's class at junior high school. Kyooka (female, 15) herself suffers from classmates' bullying, although her situation is less desperate than that of one of her classmates, Taketo Hatano (male, 15), who has been bullied so badly that he commits suicide. Kyooka survives through her friendship with Tsubasa Suzumoto (male, 14), a boy Kyooka had met a long time ago. Other classmates include Takeshita (male, 15) and Ishimura (male, 15).

Novel

***Kitchin*. 1991. Banana Yoshimoto. Tokyo: Fukutake Shoten. Translated as *Kitchen* by Megan Backus. (New York: Grove Press, 1993)**

『キッチン』(1991) 吉本ばなな 東京：福武書店

A novel by Banana Yoshimoto (female, b. 1964) that is narrated by the character Mikage Sakurai. Her warm feelings toward a kitchen are described in the context of events following her grandmother's death. After her grandmother's death, Mikage lives with the Tanabe family.

Mystery Novels

Furuete nemure, sanshimai. Vol. 15. 2001. Jiroo Akagawa. Tokyo: Koodansha.

『ふるえて眠れ、三姉妹』三姉妹探偵団 Vol. 15 (2001) 赤川次郎 東京：講談社

This book by the popular mystery novel writer Jiroo Akagawa (male, b. 1948), is about three sisters who become involved in many mysterious incidents. The three sisters are Ayako Sasaki (20), a college student, Yuriko Sasaki (17), a high school student, and

Tamami Sasaki (15), a junior high school student. Detective Kunitomo (male, late 20s) is Yuriko's lover and is like an elder brother to the three sisters. In this volume, the three sisters are the targets of murder plots, but they find the guilty party, who turns out to be one of their father's business rivals.

Shiretoko Rausudake satsujin bojoo. 1999. Rintaroo Azusa. Tokyo: Koobunsha.

『知床・羅臼岳殺人慕情 』(1999) 梓林太郎 東京：光文社

This murder mystery by Rintaroo Azusa (male, b. 1933) features a mountain rescue officer, Ikki Shimon (male, 30s), and his lover, Miyako Katagiri (female, late 20s). It is set in the Rausudake mountain area of Hokkaidoo. A young woman, Taeko (female, 21), has committed suicide. Taeko's mother, Tomoko (female, 37), after murdering the character Kusama (male, 32) and Masuda (male, 46), who betrayed Taeko, herself commits suicide. Another important character is Furuo (male, 30s), an old friend of Shimon's.

Suupaa Tokachi satsujin jiken. 2000. Kyootaroo Nishimura. Tokyo: Koobunsha.

『スーパーとかち殺人事件』(2000) 西村京太郎 東京：光文社

This mystery by the popular author Kyootaroo Nishimura (male, b. 1930), has two detectives, Senior Detective Totsugawa (male, early 60s) and Detective Kamei (male, 40s), his sidekick. They investigate a murder in a night club in Tokyo that turns out to be connected to another murder that took place in an express train, Super Tokachi, in Hokkaidoo. (One of the customers at the club is the murderer.)

Interviews

***Mariko no koko made kiite ii no ka na*. 2001, 2003 (issues as listed below). Mariko Hayashi. In *Shuukan asahi*.**

「マリコのここまで聞いていいのかな」(2001, 2003) 林真理子 『週刊朝日』

Interviews between Mariko Hayashi and a guest appearing in the weekly magazine, *Shuukan asahi*. Mariko Hayashi (female, b. 1954) is a novelist, essayist, critic, and celebrity. The interviews from which I have taken examples are with:

- #75, Tadanori Yokoo (male, b. 1936), artist (July 6, 2001)
- #76, Teruhiko Kuze (male, b. 1935), writer and producer (July 13, 2001)
- #78, Naoki Ishikawa (male, b. 1977), adventurer (July 27, 2001)
- #79, Nobuyuki Matsuhisa (male, b. 1949), owner and chef of Nobu Tokyo (August 3, 2001)
- #80, Ukon Ichikawa (male, b. 1963), kabuki actor (August 10, 2001)
- #82, Masashi Sada (male, b. 1952), musician (August 31, 2001)
- #83, Rei Asami (female, b. 1950), actress (September 7, 2001)
- #85, Eiji Okuda (male, b. 1950), movie actor and director (September 21, 2001)
- #86, Mayumi Narita (female, b. 1970), winner of Special Olympics gold medal in swimming (September 28, 2001)
- #87, Muneaki Masuda (male, b. 1951), company president (October 5, 2001)
- #88, Shunji Iwai (male, b. 1963), music video producer and movie director (October 12, 2001)

#89, Baku Yumemakura (male, b. 1951), writer (October 19, 2001)
#154, Masahiro Takashima (male, b. 1965), actor (February 14, 2003)
#155, Yoshino Kimura (female, b. 1976), actress (February 21, 2003)
157, Hitomi Manaka (female, b. 1979), actress (March 7, 2003)

Essay Articles in Magazines

Ebisu, Yoshikazu (male, b. 1947). 2003. *Eiga to watashi*. In *Kinema junpoo*, 2nd issue in May: 118–119.

蛭子能収 (2003) 映画と私『キネマ旬報』5 月下旬号 118-119.

Iijima, Ai (female, b. 1972). 2003a. *Yokan*. In the series *Iijima Ai no kinshichoo inzei seikatsu. Shuukan asahi*, February 14: 132.

飯島愛 (2003)「予感」「飯島愛の錦糸町印税生活」『週刊朝日』2 月 14 日号 132.

———. 2003b. *Shanhai*. In the series *Iijima Ai no kinshichoo inzei seikatsu. Shuukan asahi*, June 13: 124.

飯島愛 (2003)「上海」「飯島愛の錦糸町印税生活」『週刊朝日』6 月 13 日号 124.

Konishi, Don (male, b. 1950). 2003a. *Chooshin to hansamu buri ga haeru oodaa no suutsu, katte-agete-kuremasen ka ne, Furansu seifu-san*. In the series *Don Konishi no iketeru fasshon chekku. Shuukan asahi*, April 4: 16.

ドン小西 (2003a)「長身とハンサムぶりが映えるオーダーのスーツ、買ってあげてくれませんかね、フランス政府さん」「ドン小西のイケてるファッションチェック」『週刊朝日』4 月 14 日号 16.

———. 2003b. *Naimen no takumashisa mo fukumete fasshon. Sonna jidai, shushoo fujin no suutsu wa, otokomono?* In the series *Don Konishi no iketeru fasshon chekku. Shuukan asahi*, August 8: 16.

ドン小西 (2003b)「内面のたくましさも含めてファッション。そんな時代、首相夫人のスーツは、男物？」「ドン小西のイケてるファッションチェック」『週刊朝日』8 月 8 日号 16.

Nobumoto, Keiko (female, b. 1964). 2002. *Eiga to watashi*. In *Kinema junpoo*, 2nd issue in March: 124–125.

信本敬子 (2002)「映画と私」『キネマ旬報』3 月下旬号 124-135

Oomori, Sumio (male, b. 1967). 2003. *Eiga to watashi*. In *Kinema junpoo*, 2nd issue in November: 118–119.

大森寿美男 (2003) 映画と私『キネマ旬報』11 月下旬号 118-119.

Saitoo, Minako (female, b. 1956). 2003. *Kangoshi to josanshi*. In the series *Pinpon dasshu. Gengo*, May: 12–13.

斎藤美奈子 (2003)「看護師と助産師」「ピンポンダッシュ」『言語』5 月号 12-13.

Shiga, Akio (male, b. 1973). 2002. *Feiku mono de okanemochi o yosootte-mimasu? Popeye*, September 9: 6.

志賀アキオ (2002)「フェイクものでオカネモチを装ってみます？」『Popeye』9 月 9 日号 6.

Shooji, Sadao (male, b. 1937). 2003a. *Hyaku-en no udon o tabe ni iku*. In the series *Are mo kuitai kore mo kuitai*. *Shuukan asahi*, February 14: 54–55.

東海林さだお (2003a) 「100 円のうどんを食べに行く」「あれも食いたいこれも食いたい」『週刊朝日』2 月 14 日号, 54–55.

———. 2003b. *Moriawase no shisoo to wa*. In the series *Are mo kuitai kore mo kuitai*. *Shuukan asahi*, February 21: 56–57.

東海林さだお (2003b) 「『盛り合わせ』の思想とは」「あれも食いたいこれも食いたい」『週刊朝日』2 月 21 日号, 56–57.

Tatekawa, Sadanji (male, b. 1950). 2003. *Sadanji no terebi shadanki*. *Shuukan asahi*, June 13: 76.

立川左談次 (2003)「左談次のテレビ斜断鬼」『週刊朝日』6 月 13 日号, 76.

Uchidate, Makiko (female, b. 1949). 2003a. *Daigakuin no nyuugakushiki*. In the series *Noren ni hijitetsu*. *Shuukan asahi*, May 2–9: 66–67.

内館牧子 (2003a)「大学院の入学式」「暖簾にひじ鉄」『週刊朝日』5 月 2–9 日号, 66–67.

———. 2003b. *Nee, moratte yo*. In the series *Noren ni hijitetsu*. *Shuukan asahi*, May 30: 58–59.

内館牧子 (2003)「ねえ、もらってよ」「暖簾にひじ鉄」『週刊朝日』5 月 30 日号, 58–59.

Essay

***Taiga no itteki*. 1999. Hiroyuki Itsuki. Tokyo: Gentoosha.**

『大河の一滴』(1999) 五木寛之 東京：幻冬舎

A collection of essays written by the writer, essayist, and producer Hiroyuki Itsuki (male, b. 1932). (*Tariki*, which contains essays of a similar nature is available in English translation as Hiroshiki Itsuki, *Tariki*, translated by Joseph Robert. 2001. Tokyo: Kodansha.)

Nonfiction

***Iruka to tsuiraku*. 2002. Kootaroo Sawaki. Tokyo: Bungei Shunjuu.**

『イルカと墜落』(2002) 沢木耕太郎 東京：文藝春秋

A story about a trip to Brazil by the nonfiction writer Kootaroo Sawaki (male, b. 1947). Sawaki, along with a camera crew, visited Brazil to document native people. The book contains a mixture of adventure and reflection. The title comes from the pink dolphins Sawaki saw in the Amazon and the plane crash he experienced.

Newspaper Articles

***Jisshuusen chinbotsu*. 2001.**

「実習船沈没」

Articles collected from Mainichi shinbun on-line (http://www.mainichi.co.jp) reporting the collision between the *Ehime Maru*, a Japanese high school training vessel for fisheries, and the USS *Greeneville*, a U. S. Navy fast-attack nuclear submarine. The articles were collected from the special section titled *Jisshuusen chinbotsu* (The sinking of the training ship) reported from February 10 and March 23.

I have drawn some examples from the tragic incident for pedagogical reasons. I sincerely hope that these examples do not cause distress or anguish for those involved. My thoughts and prayers are with those men and boys who were lost at sea.

Internet Bulletin Boards (BBS)

BBS for *Beautiful Life*. TBS 2000.

『ビューティフルライフ』の公式サイトの 2000 年 3 月 26 日から 6 月 30 日までのカキコミ

Examples were collected between March 26 and June 30 from the bulletin board accessible from the *Beautiful Life* home page at http://www.tbs.co.jp/. Comments on this bulletin board came from the general viewing public.

BBS for *Taiyoo no kisetsu*. TBS 2002.

『太陽の季節』の公式サイトの 2002 年 9 月 21 日から 10 月 10 日までのカキコミ

Examples were collected between September 21 and October 10 from the bulletin board accessible from the *Taiyoo no kisetsu* home page at http://www.tbs.co.jp/. Comments were written by the general viewing public.

Suggested Reading

References in English for Learning the Japanese Language

Chino, Naoko. 1991. *All about Particles.* Tokyo: Kodansha International.

———. 1996. *Japanese Verbs at a Glance.* Translated by Tom Gally. Tokyo: Kodansha International.

Cipris, Zeljko, and Shoko Hamano. 2002. *Making Sense of Japanese Grammar: A Clear Guide through Common Problems.* Honolulu: University of Hawai'i Press.

A Handbook of Common Japanese Phrases. 2002. Compiled by Sanseido; translated and adapted by John Brennan. Tokyo: Kodansha International.

Horvat, Andrew. 2000. *Japanese beyond Words: How to Walk and Talk like a Native Speaker.* Berkeley: Stone Bridge Press.

Kamiya, Taeko. 1998. *Japanese Particle Workbook.* New York: Weatherhill.

Makino, Seiichi, and Michio Tsutsui. 1986. *A Dictionary of Basic Japanese Grammar.* Tokyo: Japan Times.

———. 1996. *A Dictionary of Intermediate Japanese Grammar.* Tokyo: Japan Times.

Maynard, Michael L., and Senko K. Maynard. 1993. *101 Japanese Idioms: Understanding Japanese Language and Culture through Popular Phrases.* Lincolnwood, Ill.: NTC.

Maynard, Senko K. 1990. *An Introduction to Japanese Grammar and Communication Strategies.* Tokyo: Japan Times.

———. 1997a. *Japanese Communication: Language and Thought in Context.* Honolulu: University of Hawai'i Press.

———. 1998a. *Principles of Japanese Discourse: A Handbook.* Cambridge: Cambridge University Press.

McGloin, Naomi Hanaoka. 1989. *A Students' Guide to Japanese Grammar.* Tokyo: Taishukan.

Mizutani, Osamu, and Nobuko Mizutani. 1977. *Nihongo Notes.* Vol. 1. Tokyo: Japan Times.

———. 1979. *Nihongo Notes.* Vol. 2. Tokyo: Japan Times.

———. 1980. *Nihongo Notes.* Vol. 3. Tokyo: Japan Times.

———. 1981. *Nihongo Notes.* Vol. 4. Tokyo: Japan Times.

———. 1983. *Nihongo Notes.* Vol. 5. Tokyo: Japan Times.

———. 1984. *Nihongo Notes.* Vol. 6. *Situational Japanese,* vol. 1. Tokyo: Japan Times.

———. 1986. *Nihongo Notes.* Vol. 7. *Situational Japanese,* vol. 2. Tokyo: Japan Times.

———. 1987. *How to Be Polite in Japanese.* Tokyo: Japan Times.

Murakami, Mamiko. 1997. *Love, Hate and Everything In Between: Expressing Emotions in Japanese*. Tokyo: Kodansha International.

Shooji, Kakuko. 1997. *Basic Connections: Making Your Japanese Flow*. Tokyo: Kodansha International.

———. 1999. *Core Words and Phrases: Things You Can't Find in a Dictionary*. Tokyo: Kodansha International.

Suleski, Ronald, and Hiroko Masada. 1982. *Effective Expressions in Japanese: A Handbook of Value-Laden Words in Everyday Japanese*. Tokyo: Hokuseido Press.

Suzuki, Takao. 1978. *Japanese and the Japanese: Words in Culture*. Translated by Akira Miura. Tokyo: Kodansha International.

Tanahashi, Akemi, and Yayoi Oshima. 1998. *Sounding Natural in Japanese: 70 Phrases to Enhance Your Daily Conversation*. Tokyo: Japan Times.

Watt, Yasuko Ito, and Richard Rubinger. 1998. *Reader's Guide to Intermediate Japanese: A Quick Reference to Written Expressions*. Honolulu: University of Hawai'i Press.

References

Eguchi, Takumi. 2000. Nihongo no toochibun. *Gengo bunka kenkyuu*, 2: 81–93.

Endoo, Orie. 1998. Tookyoo no josei no kotoba no ima. *Gengo* 27 (January): 76–81.

Fukao, Madoka. 1998. Daigakusei no keigo ishiki: Teineisa to shitashisa no choosetsu ni tsuite. *Nihongogaku ronsetsu shiryoo* 35/5: 110–122.

Ikegami, Akira. 2000. *Nihongo no daigimon*. Tokyo: Koodansha.

Ikegami, Yoshihiko. 1981. *Suru to naru no gengogaku*. Tokyo: Taishuukan.

———. 1991. Do-language and become-language: Two contrasting types of linguistic representation. In *The Empire of Signs*, edited by Yoshihiko Ikegami, 258–326. Amsterdam: John Benjamins.

Jinnai, Masataka. 1998. *Nihongo no ima*. Tokyo: Aruku.

Joomoo shinbun. 2000. Kotoba zukai ni seisa nashi, josei ga kaiwa o riido, "Byuutifuru raifu" ninki dorama de kenshoo. November 11.

Kinsui, Satoshi. 2003. *Vaacharu nihongo yakuwarigo no nazo*. Tokyo: Iwanami.

Kokuritsu Kokugo Kenkyuujo (ed.). 2000. *Shin "kotoba" shiriizu*. Vol. 12. *Kotoba ni kansuru mondooshuu: Kotoba no tsukaiwake*. Tokyo: Ookurashoo.

Koyano, Tetsuo. 1996. Terebi kotoba to wakamono kotoba. *Nihongogaku* 15 (September): 36–45.

Kudo, Tsutomu, and David Matsumoto. 1996. *Nihonjin no kanjoo sekai: Misuteriasuna bunka no nazo o toku*. Tokyo: Seishin Shoboo.

Kumagai, Tomoko. 2003. Shinario no aru kaiwa, dorama no nihongo no tokuchoo. *Nihongogaku* 22 (February): 6–14.

Maynard, Michael L. 2003. From global to glocal: How Gillette's SensorExcel accommodates to Japan. *Keio Communication Review* 25: 57–75.

Maynard, Senko K. 1991a. Buntai no imi, da-tai to desu/masu-tai no kon'yoo ni tsuite. *Gengo* 20 (February): 75–80.

———. 1991b. Pragmatics of discourse modality: A case of *da* and *desu/masu* forms in Japanese. *Journal of Pragmatics* 15: 551–582.

———. 1993. *Discourse modality: Subjectivity, Emotion and Voice in the Japanese Language*. Amsterdam: John Benjamins.

———. 1997b. Manipulating speech styles in Japanese: Context, genre, and ideology. *Proceedings of the Fifth Princeton Japanese Pedagogy Workshop*, 1: 24.

———. 1998b. Patosu toshite no gengo. *Gengo* 27 (June): 34–41.

———. 1999. A poetics of grammar: Playing with narrative perspectives and voices in Japanese translation texts. *Poetics* 26: 115–141.

———. 2000. *Jooi no gengogaku: "Bakooshooron" to nihongo hyoogen no patosu.* Tokyo: Kuroshio.
———. 2001a. *Koisuru futari no "kanjoo kotoba": Dorama hyoogen no bunseki to nihongoron.* Tokyo: Kuroshio.
———. 2001b. Falling in love with style: Expressive functions of stylistic shifts in a Japanese television drama series. *Functions of Language* 8: 1–39.
———. 2002. *Linguistic Emotivity: Centrality of Place, the Topic-Comment Dynamic, and an Ideology of Pathos in Japanese Discourse.* Amsterdam: John Benjamins.
Mizuhara, Akito. 1999. Tsukuru danwa: Kyakuhon seisaku no genba. *Nihongogaku* 18 (October): 28–39.
Moriya, Yuuji. 1999. *Kirikaeshi wajutsu no umai hito ga seikoo suru.* Tokyo: Seibidoo.
Nakamura, Akira. 1979. *Kanjoo hyoogen jiten.* Tokyo: Rokkoo Shuppan.
Ozaki, Yoshimitsu. 2001. Nihongo no sedaisa wa nakunaru ka. *Gengo* 30 (January): 66–72.
Sakai, Miiko. 1996. *Kaiwa no oshare.* Tokyo: Mikasa Shoboo.
Satake, Hideo. 1995. Wakamono kotoba to retorikku. *Nihongogaku* 14 (November): 53–60.
———. 1997. Wakamono kotoba to bunka. *Nihongogaku* 16 (April): 55–64.
Shiina, Makoto. 1984. *Ka.* Tokyo: Shinchoosha.
Suzuki, Akira. 1824 [1979]. *Gengyo shishuron.* Tokyo: Benseisha.
Takasaki, Midori. 2002. "Onna kotoba" o tsukurikaeru josei no tayoona gengo koodoo. *Gengo* 31 (February): 40–47.
Yamada, Yoshio. 1936. *Nihon bunpoogaku gairon.* Tokyo: Hoobunkan.
Yonekawa, Akihiko. 1999. Omoshiroi gendaigo goi. *Nihongogaku* 18 (January): 41–50.

For information about other significant works in the field of Japanese linguistics, see references in Maynard (2002).

Index of English Cues and Subject Index

The following index includes English cues for key expressions, English cues for the terms appearing in Additional Information, and subjects treated in Chapters 1 through 3. Entry numbers are given first, in parentheses, followed by page numbers.

Index of Japanese Expressions

The following index includes key expressions, listed terms appearing in Entries, and those expressions introduced in Additional Information. Entry numbers are given first, in parentheses, followed by page numbers.

CPSIA information can be obtained at www.ICGtesting.com
Printed in the USA
BVOW08s1353030816

457592BV00019B/19/P